Raindrops and Sawdust

By

Afton W. Minga

ISBN: 1-4033-6726-4 (e-book)
ISBN: 1-4033-6727-2 (Paperback)

This book is printed on acid free paper.

1stBooks - rev. 01/14/03

Dedication

To God
who created me with a longing to write,
And
To my parents, William and Ada Todd Weaver,
who sacrificed so much to help me achieve an
education,
And
To my beloved husband, Thomas E. Minga, Sr.,
whose faith in me would not let me give up,
I humbly dedicate my novel
Raindrops and Sawdust

PROLOGUE

Raindrops and Sawdust

The idea for my novel *Raindrops and Sawdust* was developed from an actual event that happened to my widowed great-grandmother Todd during the Civil War.

According to my mother's father, Jonathan Criswell Todd, General Sherman (an officer in the Union Army), camped with his troops on my grandmother Todd's farm one night as they were making their famous "March to the Sea" through the state of Georgia. Also, according to my grandfather, General Sherman slept in their home that night. My grandfather was ten years of age at the time. (This event is recorded in the genealogy records of the Todd family.)

There was always bitterness evident when my mother would retell the story that she had heard so often from her father when he was alive. How the Northern troops confiscated practically everything edible that they owned, and even tore down the smokehouse and rail fences to be used for fuel. However, the story always ended on a positive note. When the soldiers discovered some wheat that my great-grandmother had tried to hide in the attic, General Sherman ordered the men to leave the wheat alone with these words: "We will leave this widow woman some bread."

With the exception of the above episode and the historical facts relating to the time frame of the Civil

War and the Reconstruction Period, the plot for my novel has been drawn strictly from my imagination. Any resemblance to any other persons, living or dead, is purely coincidental.

All scripture references have been taken from the King James Version of the Bible.

CHAPTER 1

"One of these days I'm going to marry someone rich, and I'm NEVER going to chop cotton or hoe corn again!" Liza, a disgruntled young lady in her late teens, flopped down on the bench by the dining table in the large kitchen, and propping her elbows on the planks with a thud, sat with her head in her hands while glaring at nothing in particular.

This often-repeated statement of Liza's brought a fleeting smile to her mother Elvina's face, momentarily relieving the tired lines so evident most of the time. Without comment, Elvina continued to stir the contents of the large black pot hanging over the fire in the oversized fireplace. Melinda, Liza's older sister by less than two years, continued placing silverware by each plate on the table, her placid expression concealing the pain caused by her aching muscles.

All three of the women reflected extreme weariness, not only by their expressions, but in their physical movements as well. Signs of perspiration showed dark around their hairlines, the dampness causing the hair to stick close to their scalps.

Robinson, the only living male member of the family and the youngest, appeared in the doorway silhouetted by the fading sunset. Silently he moved into the room, placing the bucket of milk he had brought from the barn on a small table near the stove. Turning to the water shelf near the door, he dipped some water into the wash pan, and reaching for the lye soap, began to scrub his face and hands vigorously.

1

After splashing water on his face several times to remove all traces of the harsh soap, he reached for the homespun towel hanging on a peg nearby. After rubbing his stubble of a beard dry, he crossed the dimly lit room to sit down at the far end of the table, his movements also reflecting weariness. This was Elvina's signal to start dishing up the food.

To the casual passer-by there was nothing out of the ordinary about the log cabin protected from the main roadway by a grove of large trees. There was nothing to make one think that wealth had ever been a part of the household. But the well cared for appearance of the place in general proclaimed that it was loved and protected by a meticulous overseer.

The weeds and tall grass were cropped back well away from the house, and the section of the yard immediately surrounding the dwelling house was scraped clean of every blade of grass, leaving it as hard and white as a sun baked bone. Outlining the entire yard, both front and back, was a rough rail fence dark and weather-beaten that had been constructed from logs painstakingly split with a wedge and sledgehammer. The outbuildings located a hundred yards or so behind the cabin were also enclosed by a rail fence. The barnyard was clear of all debris except for the fresh droppings from the animals.

A sweet shrub and a holly tree decorated the yard near the front of the cabin. To the east of the dwelling, a large wisteria vine, untamed for an unknown number of years, stretched upward to the massive limbs of a giant oak. Its long tendrils entwined in and out among the branches, decorating the tree in the springtime with large clusters of blossoms that hung in profusion like fragile bunches of concord grapes. Each spring bumblebees hummed busily as they flew in and out of the foliage, their bodies and legs heavy and swollen with the yellow pollen they had greedily collected.

It was late spring, the time of year that boasts warm days and cool nights. Every tree and bush had swelled forth with bright green foliage, and an atmosphere of freshness prevailed over the entire outdoors. The farmland had been ploughed and some of it planted weeks earlier. On the slopes, small lines of green could be discerned down the middle of each row. The field of winter wheat was well on its way toward maturity, and the apple blossoms were all gone from the knotty old tree on the hillside. In their place, small green apples, not much larger than a small grain of corn, decried the signs of old age and gave youth to the gnarled old tree.

Not too far from the back of the house at the foot of a hill a spring bubbled forth cold water from a bed of colorful stones. It was here by the spring that the family wash was done. The spring water was free of harsh minerals and when combined with homemade lye soap, left linens and wearing apparel as fresh and clean as the air of a Georgia spring day.

Nighttime was rapidly approaching and near the hen house, a few stragglers lingered just outside the door. A big black rooster flaunting a massive red comb and a yellow bill was searching with a couple of female companions for some last morsel of food. As the twilight deepened, the stragglers joined the rest of the flock on the roosting poles inside the chicken house.

In the barnyard the cow lay contentedly chewing her cud. She had been fed and milked and turned out to graze by Robinson. Inside the barn in one of the stalls, the mule stood quietly, its head drooping in half-sleep. On its neck and back were the outlines of the harness that had been strapped during work hours, the hair still moist and sticky, matted close to the skin.

A whippoorwill lit in one of the nearby trees and started its frantic call for its mate. A bat darted over the barn after some small flying insect, and the call of a field lark rang out clear and unruffled, the melodious strain fading as the bird sailed away toward its own place of shelter for the night.

The Stuart family had just finished eating their evening meal, and it was that brief moment of time, when for a short while, all of the pressing chores that had filled their day were pushed aside. Here, too, twilight was bringing changes in the large kitchen, and shadows were beginning to fill in the corners of the room. The kitchen seemed to shrink in size as darkness approached, the figures of the mother, her two daughters in their late teens, and her son, Robinson, the youngest, creating a shadowy scene of peace and tranquility in the soft candlelight. A bed of coals in the broad stone fireplace glowed a fiery red; their usefulness no longer needed as far as the preparation of the evening meal was concerned.

The dining table had been constructed by hand many years back by John Stuart, Elvina's deceased husband. He had painstakingly hewed its thick planks from a large pine log the first year of his and Elvina's marriage. Years of use had worn the top smooth, its color now a rich dark brown. The underside of the table had never been hand finished, evidenced by the grooves and rough spots left untouched, the color not as dark as the topside. On either side of the oblong table was a bench, the same length as the table. The benches had also been constructed by hand. Their design was simple, consisting of a large flat slab of pine, smoothed on top, with legs constructed from two pieces of short sturdy pine slabs crisscrossed like the letter X and spliced with wooden pegs. At each end of the table there was a high backed dining chair, two of the few pieces of store bought furniture in the room. Elvina's place at the table was the end nearest the fireplace, to make serving the food more convenient.

Moving in slow motion, Elvina stood up and walked over to the fireplace where the family Bible rested in its lofty position on the mantle. Returning to her chair, she opened the book to the page where they had left off reading the night before.

Robinson sat leaning forward slightly in his chair, his left elbow resting on the table, his strong young chin cupped in the palm of his hand, expression pensive. As long as he could remember, reading from the Scriptures had been a nightly ritual with his family. Without changing position, his gaze shifted to Liza and then to Melinda. Melinda's profile was serene, her manner attentive, even though her large gray eyes were half-closed from weariness and fatigue.

A slight expression of amusement lighted Robinson's eyes as his gaze shifted back to Liza. Sitting slumped down on the bench with her legs tucked up beside her, light brown hair now straggling loose around her shoulders, she appeared oblivious to all else around her as she toyed absent-mindedly with the silverware placed neatly across her plate. Robinson's gaze lingered on the silverware momentarily, a crooked smile tugging at the corners of his mouth. As far back as he could remember, in good times and bad, with food plenteous or scanty, his mother always insisted on proper table setting and manners.

"How different our lives are now as compared to hers when she was our age," he mused. As Elvina began to read, Robinson's thoughts were not on the words from the Scriptures but flashed back instead to a city named Boston in the state of Massachusetts; a place that he had never visited nor seen except through the verbal descriptions of his pa and ma.

CHAPTER 2

Robinson's mother, Elvina Melinda Robinson, was born to immigrant parents in 1824, the oldest child in a family of three girls and two boys. Her father, struggling to provide for his family against ethnic and educational barriers, found it almost impossible to furnish them with even the bare necessities of life. In order to survive, the proud Robinson family found it necessary at times to accept, what was often disdainfully referred to as charity, from Christian workers in the area. It was through the efforts of Mrs. Althea Brown, a member of a local church, that Elvina was accepted as a live-in nursemaid and part-time housemaid in the home of Mr. and Mrs. Oren Lowell, one of Boston's well-to-do upper middle class families.

The Lowell's had three young daughters: Rebecca Sue, Amy Yvonne, and Oren Gail, all under ten years of age. The terms of the arranged agreement between Elvina and the Lowell's were simply defined and quite acceptable by both parties; for assisting with the cleaning, cooking, and helping look after the children, Elvina would receive food and quarters, plus a small monthly salary.

The day that Mrs. Brown had taken Elvina to meet the Lowell family, Elvina had been captivated immediately by Mrs. Lowell's quick smile and gracious manner. Her small bone structure and slender waist had made her appear much taller than her five feet six inches, and with her mass of black hair coiled upon her head, she radiated an air of feminine helplessness which Elvina would soon discover was entirely misleading. Beneath that willowy frame was a willpower and determination equal to the strength of steel. However, this characteristic did not lessen Elvina's admiration for her. Rather, Mrs. Lowell's ability to cope with the multiple problems of running her household and managing three children with next to no help from Mr. Lowell, was to enhance Elvina's youthful respect for the older woman in the years ahead.

Mrs. Lowell met them at the door, and after greeting them most cordially, invited them inside and on into the drawing room. Mrs. Brown and Mrs. Lowell had been acquaintances for many years; therefore, the first few minutes of their visit was confined to their reminiscing and engaging in small talk.

Elvina sat stiffly upright in a plush wing back chair, feeling extremely uncomfortable and out of place. This was her first time to be inside of a house so grandiose.

Sensing the young girl's discomfort, Mrs. Lowell graciously included Elvina in the conversation by tactfully asking questions regarding her educational background and experience with children.

"I... I don't have too much schooling, Ma'am," Elvina stammered, eyes dark with anxiety. Then, fearing Mrs. Lowell would think her stupid and not capable of performing her expected duties, hastened to add, "But I love to learn, and I've had a lot of experience with taking care of little ones. I... I have

two younger sisters and two brothers, and I help my
Ma with taking care of them."

"Will your coming to work here create a hardship
on your mother?" Mrs. Lowell inquired gently.

Blushing, Elvina dropped her head for a moment,
recalling her mother leaving the house each day to go
to work as a part-time domestic servant, seeing her
come home weary and exhausted; her own desperate
longing to help relieve some of the burden on her
mother. With renewed courage, Elvina lifted her head
and in a tone that bordered on gentle defiance,
answered softly, "I hope to help out with my earnings,
Ma'am."

"I see," Mrs. Lowell answered thoughtfully,
expression kind. Then, changing the subject abruptly
inquired brightly, her smile including both Elvina and
Mrs. Brown, "Would you like to meet my girls?"

Extremely apprehensive and somewhat shaken,
Elvina smiled a weak assent as she arose somewhat
awkwardly to follow the older ladies out of the room
into the entrance hall that boasted an enormous
winding stairway to the second floor.

"The girls are in the playroom," Mrs. Lowell
informed them at the top of the stairs as she turned to
walk down the hallway to a door just past the stair
landing.

With squeals of delight the children ran forward to
meet their mother. Picking up the youngest, a pink-
faced cherub with long yellow curls, Mrs. Lowell
kissed her soundly on the cheek and announced to her
visitors who had followed her into the room, "This is
Oren Gail." Then nodding in the direction of the other
two, "And this is Rebecca Sue, and everyone seems to

9

think she looks like me!" Mrs. Brown nodded pleasantly, turning toward Elvina to see if she agreed. Elvina nodded vigorously, secretly admiring the slender dark-skinned little girl who was an exact replica of her mother.

Turning to the child on her left, Mrs. Lowell lovingly placed an arm around the other little girl's shoulder. "And this is Amy Yvonne!" Then, with a slight movement of her hand that included all three of her children, announced, "Girls, you already know Mrs. Brown. And this is Elvina Robinson."

Amy slipped from under her mother's arm, and the auburn curls that framed her oval face seemed to come alive as she began to bounce up and down. "Is this our new nursemaid that you were telling us about, Mother?"

"Possibly," Mrs. Lowell said cheerfully while setting Gail down with an affectionate spank on her broadside. "But we must find out if she likes us first?"

Speechless, Elvina stood staring at Mrs. Lowell. It had never occurred to her that accepting or rejecting the job would be left up to her. All of her fears had been associated with the possibility that she wouldn't be offered the position.

"Let's show Mrs. Brown and Elvina the room that we have ready for Elvina, if she comes to work for us," Mrs. Lowell suggested, and the three girls bounded for the door, skirting around Elvina and the other two women.

"Girls! Girls! You are forgetting your manners," Mrs. Lowell cautioned, only slightly raising her voice above normal. To Elvina's amazement, the girl's response was immediate as they quickly, but more sedately, led the way to the room next door, standing aside politely for their mother to open the door and lead the way into the room.

To someone who had not been used to sharing three crowded rooms with a family of seven, the room might have appeared to be small. But to Elvina, it was like stepping into a dream. The walls were painted an off-white, which reflected the light from the window. The furniture had been painted a soft yellow, and there were yellow ruffled curtains on the window. A multi-floral bedspread blended with the room beautifully, and there were small ruffled cushions piled on a lounge chair near the window. A dressing table with an oval, yellow-framed mirror and a skirt made from the same material as the bedspread brought a gasp of delight from Elvina.

"It's ... it's beautiful!" she whispered, eyes incredulous. She had expected a small dark room in the back of the house.

As they started toward the stairs, Amy and Gail rushed forward, one on either side of Elvina, eagerly claiming one of her hands with their own.

In the months that followed, Elvina could never remember being so happy, even though she missed her family's togetherness. Even the menial tasks that were part of her job were pleasant for she loved every room of the Lowell's large, two-story house, especially the library. But she was careful not to linger too long with the books for she remembered with painful embarrassment that she was chastised once by her mistress for taking so long to dust the volumes that seemed to draw her like magic.

Before coming to live at the Lowell's, Elvina's schooling had been extremely limited. She knew the ABC's and could read simple words. But she possessed an insatiable appetite for learning and was quick to take advantage of the opportunity to learn from the girls' lessons. Many times after the children were tucked away for the night, Elvina would read and study the lesson assignments left in her keeping by the tutor of her young protégés, oftentimes pouring over them until weariness and fatigue would force her to blow out the light and go to sleep. And as time passed, she was able to acquire a small collection of books of her own. Occasionally, the children would accompany Mrs. Lowell shopping. This meant that Elvina would be needed to go along to help look after them. Sometimes the opportunity would present itself for Elvina to browse in a little bookshop where used books could be purchased for a nominal amount of their original cost. It mattered not that the books had been used and the covers soiled a bit. This didn't change the beauty and wonder of the words, nor the joy of ownership. And, occasionally, Mrs. Lowell would surprise her with a brand new one for her growing collection.

Sunday was Elvina's day off, and she usually attended church in the mornings. She tried to visit her family at least once a month during the summer, but in the winter, it was hard for her to make the trip and return before dark and have any time to spend with the family. To fill the lonely hours, she spent more and more time with her books.

The Lowell household was a house of plenty. Many things that Elvina considered useful and even luxurious were thrown out with the trash. If Elvina could retrieve such items without being detected, she would hide them away to take to her family. Then, quite frequently Mrs. Lowell would give Elvina items of food and clothing to take home, and occasionally, toys the girls no longer enjoyed. However, Elvina was extremely cautious about letting anyone from the household know that she ever salvaged discards, and particularly mindful to never hint for anything. According to her mother's teaching, begging was degrading and destroyed a person's self-respect.

Many changes came about in the Lowell household those first two years, and Elvina's physical appearance was one of the most noticeable. Proper diet and regular sleeping habits transformed her once thin and bony figure into lovely feminine proportions, complimented by a complexion that glowed with robust good health. Her dark auburn hair, thick and shining with golden highlights, hung below her waist when she removed the pins and let it hang loose for brushing. She had grown much taller, too, which would have been a personal disaster for her before coming to live at the Lowell's. Inadvertently and without knowledge of the fact, Mrs. Lowell was responsible for Elvina's new image regarding tall women. Not only was she proud of her height but dreamed of being as elegant someday as her beloved employer. It had its financial advantages, also. With only minor alterations, Elvina could wear discarded items from Mrs. Lowell's wardrobe that fortunately came about with the arrival of each new season's fashions. Not that Mrs. Lowell's vanity demanded following the fashion trends particularly, but she felt that she owed it to her husband since high fashion was his cherished enterprise.

If someone had asked Elvina what her plans for the future were, or what her goals in life were, it is doubtful that she could have identified anything specifically. But there were times when she felt restless and even the constant demands of helping with the house and children didn't seem to completely make the gnawing feelings of discontent go away. Only when the chores were done for the day and she was alone in the quiet recess of her room, buried in the make believe world found in books, did her restlessness find relief. But, then, this didn't always help, either, for there was a yearning to actually participate in the exciting experiences and travel to far away places.

Sometimes she tried to imagine what her ideal man for a husband would be like and invariably her thoughts would center on Mr. Lowell. It wasn't that she didn't admire her father, for she could think of no one who had worked harder or who had a more sterling character. But there was something about Mr. Lowell's poise, the way he was always impeccably dressed and the aura of self-confidence he seemed to emit, that captivated her romantic imagination. And from all accounts, he was unquestionably faithful to Mrs. Lowell. Without a doubt, he was her dream of a dashing prince.

Elvina had just turned eighteen when she met John Stuart for the first time. John was twenty-four, tall, robust, with a face far too rugged to be considered handsome by most critics. He was employed as an overseer on one of the largest truck and dairy farms just outside the city limits of Boston. John's employer sold dairy products and fresh produce (when in season) to the grocery stores in town and to private customers, delivering the goods to their doors. Ordinarily, John did not make the deliveries himself, but on this particular day one of the deliverymen was sick and John was covering his route.

Since it was the regular delivery day, Elvina answered a knock at the back door expecting to see a familiar face. Opening the door she found herself staring into the eyes of a total stranger, a man whose gaze was as steady and unwavering as steel.

"Good morning, Ma'am, I have your order from Mr. Mueller's."

"Oh, yes, … yes, of course," Elvina stammered, extremely agitated with herself for feeling so flustered. "Just bring the things in here, please," she directed, stepping backward into the small hallway that led to the large kitchen.

It had been necessary for John to return to the wagon for part of the order. Peeking from behind the window curtain, Elvina watched admiringly as he made his way to and from the wagon.

"My, he certainly doesn't act and look like a delivery man," she mused, excitement making her pulse quicken and her face flush ever so slightly. She noted that even though his steps were swift, he didn't seem to give the impression of being in a hurry. The way he moved with dignity, even while carrying the laden basket, impressed her immensely.

Elvina quickly moved away from the window before he came back through the door. Silently, without looking in her direction, he unloaded the items from the basket onto the kitchen table.

"Have you been working for Mr. Mueller long?" she asked, embarrassed somewhat by her own boldness.

"Yes, quite a while," he answered, glancing momentarily in her direction. "But this isn't one of my regular duties. I'm just helping out because we're short handed today."

Cradling the empty basket under his arm, he said matter-of-factly, "My name is John Stuart."

"How do you do, Mr. Stuart," she responded in her best imitation of Mrs. Lowell's manners. "My name is Elvina Robinson."

"Then, you aren't a member of the Lowell family?"

"No, I work here," she answered, wondering if he hadn't noticed her uniform. "I came to work here as a nursemaid several years ago." Then hesitating somewhat added quietly, "I also help with the household chores."

"You must have been quite young to assume such heavy responsibilities?"

"Not if you are used to it and you need the money badly enough! And my family and I did," Elvina retorted, lifting her chin, eyes defiant.

"Oh?" he responded kindly. "I... I can understand that," his tone now somewhat apologetic.

The silence was suddenly heavy and strained, and thinking that possibly he had offended her, John nodded politely. "Well, I have some more deliveries to make. The route is new to me and it takes me longer than the regular man. I'm sure some of the customers have all but given me out."

A slight nod from Elvina was the only indication that she had heard him. Without another word, John turned and left the room.

In the days that followed, her thoughts kept returning to John Stuart. Remembering his dark blue eyes that seemed to be fathomless, made her shiver. His relaxed manner, coupled with profound dignity, excited her. Repeatedly her mental image of his broad shoulders and the way the muscles flexed beneath his jacket kept returning, sending her emotions into a whirl. And tall, too! So tall that it had been necessary for her to look up at him during their conversation. There had been an air of mystery about him that tantalized her, and the question kept repeating itself over and over in her mind, "Will I ever see him again?" Then, an anxious thought sent her dreams plummeting, "What if he is married?" The possibility left her devastated. Funny that she hadn't thought of that before? That would certainly account for his apparent aloofness. She recalled, now, that his extremely polite manner had puzzled her at the time. Most of the delivery men that came to the house seemed to take it for granted that they could attempt advances, if it suited them, since she was one of the hired help. "Maybe that is why I was so drawn to him," she mused sadly. "I didn't have to fight him off."

But he had returned the next delivery day, and the next, and the next. And Elvina wasn't to know for weeks to come that John had left the regular delivery boy sitting on the curb two streets over, while he personally took care of the Lowell's order.

And John's strategy paid off. He felt quite smug about his maneuvering since Elvina had finally agreed for him to come calling, after he had convinced her that he wasn't a married man. And just in time, too, for Mr. Mueller had begun to question the necessity of John's occasional personal supervision of their delivery service.

Common to most normal young women, Elvina often dreamed of meeting someone special, falling in love, and someday becoming a bride. However, living in another part of the country had never been a part of that dream - especially in the Deep South. Her dreams for the future, however meager, had always centered on her family and the city that had always been her home.

But her involvement with John had changed all that, frighteningly so at first, into a vision of sorts, for John had a dream, too. His was a fresh start, a new beginning on a farm of his very own - down South where the growing seasons were long, where the land was fertile for raising money crops, and where there was plenty of timber for building. As time passed and she spent more and more time with John, listening to his plans, making plans of her own, the idea became more and more enticing. It wasn't many months until she, too, looked forward with great anticipation to the time when they would actually be married and leaving on this great adventure. And John's only explanation for why they couldn't get married was that he wanted to have a certain amount saved "after he met his obligations."

As time went by, however, and John never seemed to have saved any appreciable amount, Elvina's questions began to turn to anxious doubt, and then John was forced to tell her that he was indebted to Mr.

Mueller; something about a bond - a particular type of indebtedness.

John's reluctance to discuss the matter with her hurt her deeply at first. Didn't he know that he could trust her to understand? Finally, she realized that if she were going to have any peace of mind, she had to settle it once and for all. Was she going to accept the John she knew and loved on faith, or was she going to let the ugly doubts and suspicions destroy their future together? Therefore, exercising more determination than she thought possible considering her impatient nature, she put the matter behind her, promising herself that she wouldn't dwell on it anymore. And from that day forward, John and his dream were more important to her than any other human being had ever been before, and her love for him made him great in her eyes! A conquering hero! Even though he had evidently made a grave mistake somewhere back in his past, he could still make anything happen.

John believed in her love and in her willingness to wait for him. They worked, and planned, and dreamed of owning vast acres of land someday on which their home would be a great white antebellum house with huge columns extending from a large sweeping veranda to the very roof of the two-story mansion. Many Sunday afternoons, they poured over the books in the Lowell library, studying the pictures of homes like theirs was going to be, and making their own plans.

When John and Elvina first announced their intentions to be married, the opposition from Elvina's family and from the Lowell's was not surprising. Not that either family had any real objections to her marrying John. He had gained their respect, and actually, all of them were quite fond of him. But it was the condition of their marriage; that they would be moving down South.

Mrs. Lowell had been dismally apprehensive as she tried to discourage Elvina by relating disparaging stories she had been told regarding the aristocracy of the large plantation owners. How the small planters were looked down upon by most of them as white trash. Why, didn't Elvina know that even her manner of speaking would be offensive to most Southern folk? It was beyond her comprehension how John and Elvina could possible be happy in that kind of situation.

Elvina listened to her logic with quiet patience, heart pounding. She loved and respected Mrs. Lowell, who, in many respects, was as dear to her as a mother. Therefore, she could not bring herself to argue with her - even about something as important as her love for John. But she couldn't help but wonder why Mrs. Lowell thought her social status could be much lower in the South or anywhere else, than it was in Boston. Household servants just didn't make the social register.

The Lowell girls' reaction had been understandably emotional with many tearful objections, and for weeks the subject could not be mentioned without remonstrations because their "Vi" was moving so far away. To them, it was a threat in the very immediate future, but when Elvina didn't "up and get married" and leave right away, and time faded into weeks, then months, their objections all but ceased as they realized her leaving wasn't something that would happen any time soon. Even Elvina's parents displeasure softened with time. After all, they reasoned, wasn't it a dream that brought them to America? And in the days and weeks to come the objections from all sources calmed, and all but ceased entirely, before Elvina and John became man and wife.

John stubbornly held to his conviction that there must be enough money saved to guarantee their railroad fares and other transportation cost plus enough left over to pay for farm tools and work animals. They would need a cow, and there must be adequate funds for food and supplies until their first crop could be planted and harvested, to say nothing of a substantial down payment on their land. Mr. Lowell had tactfully tried to persuade John to look into Federal land grants that were available for purchasing homesteads, but John would not even discuss it with him at any length, dogmatically clinging to his desire to buy and pay for his land independent of what he termed as "governmental control."

So it was that for over six years John's dream remained in the embryonic state, dormant, yet, very much alive, like the larvae in a cocoon, just waiting for the right time to burst forth.

And, Elvina? Elvina waited patiently and made plans with John. But as the years slipped quickly by, she no longer dreamed of the great white antebellum house with its huge white columns reaching to the roof of the second story. Not as an immediate reality, anyway. And when their marriage day finally arrived, it went by almost unnoticed by the Lowell household, due to the excitement created by a party being planned by Mr. and Mrs. Lowell to announce the forthcoming engagement and marriage of their eldest daughter, Rebecca Sue.

CHAPTER 3

Locating the amount of land that John wanted to buy, at the price he could afford and in the right location, had not been an easy accomplishment. John had placed an ad in the Southern Miscellany and Upper Georgia Whig, and as a result, a land agent named Enoch Rawlings had contacted him.

It had required several hundred dollars to close the deal. The terms of the mortgage had been set up on a three-year basis, with a note coming due each fall after the crops had been harvested and sold. In their small hotel room, John filled Elvina in on the final details.

"We have one hundred and twenty acres, forty that is rich bottom land," he explained, eyes shining. "According to my calculations, we have enough good farm land to raise all the cotton we will need to make our mortgage payments, enough corn and hay for our livestock, if and when we get any, and plenty of rolling pasture land. There's timber, too, growing mostly on the crest of the hills. The trees aren't real large because most of the older ones have been cut, but there's more than enough to supply our building needs and plenty for cooking and heating."

"When will I get to see it, John?" Elvina demanded, her eyes shining from excitement.

"We'll leave early in the morning," he answered jubilantly, picking her up and swinging her around the small room.

The next morning the sun was just appearing above the treetops as their wagon creaked past the outskirts of town. Since Elvina had not made the long trip with John and Mr. Rawlings to inspect the property, this would be her first time to see their new home. But John had described it to her so many times she felt as if she had actually been there. She glanced sideways at her husband. Sensing her gaze, he turned to smile down at her. Elvina snuggled close and ran her arm through his.

"Tell me about the place, again, John."

"It has only one room Vi," he began, a slight frown replacing his happy smile, "but the roof is high pitched with a half-ceiling across part of the inside that can be used for a loft or additional sleeping and storage space." His tone was optimistic, but his quizzical expression as his eyes searched hers, was full of doubt. "It's not much to look at now, Vi," he kept repeating doggedly, almost defiantly, "but the land is good and we'll build a better house just as soon as we can."

Not many miles from town the road wound by a large antebellum house with slave quarters and outbuildings scattered over many acres. "That's the Templeton plantation," John advised quietly, somewhat subdued from his former exuberance.

Elvina stared wonderingly, as she had many times during their long journey south. There were so many marked contrasts in standards of living in this part of the country, as it was in Boston. And the vastness of acreage owned by some was mind-boggling! At least, that was the way it appeared, evidenced by the skeletal remains in the fields of cotton, corn, and other crops.

Elvina sighed. Then, it came without warning; a gnawing feeling in the pit of her stomach that spread upward, settling in her throat, creating a sensation of choking. Despair, dark and smothering, caused tears to burn behind her lids begging for release. She stared off across the fields, keeping her head averted so that John could not glimpse her face. "I must not cry!" she told herself furiously, panic stricken and fearful that John would notice her prolonged silence. "It must have been the slave quarters at the Templeton plantation that caused my despair", she argued silently for what John had told her about their new home, it wouldn't be much larger, or better, than any one of those crude buildings. Then, in the wake of the acute moment of despair, an onslaught of guilt swept over her as she remembered that the Bible plainly states that coveting someone else's possessions is a grave sin. "Besides," she reasoned silently, enjoying a brief moment of self-righteousness, "wasn't it slave owners like the Templeton's who were causing all the war talk between the North and the South?"

"Only a few more miles," John explained, pointing off to the right of the wagon. "That's the boundary of the Templeton place."

The boundary of the Templeton's farmland was clearly distinguishable from that of the small landowners. Even the Templeton's ditch banks were cut back, leaving no threat of encroaching weeds and bushes along the edges of the fields.

Occasionally they passed a farmhouse, small but comfortable, usually boasting a barn, a corncrib, and possibly one or two other farm buildings scattered in the background. Oftentimes small children could be seen playing in the yards, their activity forgotten as they stood staring, sometimes waving, at the man and woman in the creaking wagon that was piled high with household furnishings, trunks, and farm tools. Her mood of melancholia became less painful as she realized that a vast majority of their neighbors-to-be was no better off financially than they were.

A gesture from John brought Elvina's attention back to the man beside her. "That's the Wheeler place," he explained knowingly, pointing out a two-story house barely visible a half-mile or so off to the left of the main road. "They will be our nearest neighbors. Mr. Rawlings said they are fine folk."

John leaned forward slightly to tap the mules to a faster pace, his profile blocking Elvina's view of the Wheeler house. She noted the flush of his cheeks, the aura of subdued excitement that seemed to radiate from him. It was catching, and her heart began to beat a little faster.

There were no more farms buildings after they passed the Wheeler farm. Most of the fields were overgrown with blackberry vines and small bushes, and an occasional small forest of towering pines bordered the roadway. Hardwood trees that had already shed their leaves for the winter stood bare and silent beneath a sky that was overcast with gray clouds.

"There it is, Vi! See! Over there through the trees?"

Following the direction of John's finger, Elvina glimpsed through the leafless limbs the top of a high-pitched roof. Further on, he pointed to a tree that had a bright splash of paint on its side. "That's where our land begins," he exclaimed jubilantly, pulling Elvina close to him and squeezing her waist until she gasped. Laughing boyishly, he removed his arm and once again, urged the mules to a faster gait.

Soon he was turning the team from the main road onto another one that was barely distinguishable because of the tall weeds and small bushes. To prevent the limbs of the bushes from scratching her face, Elvina turned her face toward John's shoulder, her arm thrown up for protection.

"Whoa!" John called loudly to the mules, and when all motion had ceased, Elvina cautiously lowered her arm and opened her eyes.

John dropped the lines, not even bothering to tie them, and jumping quickly to the ground, hurried around to Elvina's side of the wagon. But something about her rigid posture and solemn expression caused him to stop just behind her, a terrible feeling of misgiving keeping him from breaking the silence.

Elvina sat staring at the small building that was to be her home. It had been constructed from logs and the spaces between logs filled in with some form of red clay that, in many places, had fallen out. The roof was steep, much taller than most of the cabins they had seen on their way out from town. A large stone fireplace dominated one end, the rocks jutting in and out unevenly, displaying their natural formation.

She stared fixedly, her mind whirling. Was this what she had left her home and friends for? Suddenly, she was aware of John standing quietly; his face upturned expectantly, a mixture of anxiety and happiness creating an expression that could not have been identified as a smile or a frown. Elvina swallowed hard, forcing a bright smile.

Jubilantly, John lifted her down, hugging her hard against him. With one arm around her waist and holding her close, he guided her toward the cabin, his free hand pushing the head-high weeds, now brown and brittle from the first frost, out of their way. John's heart was beating wildly. Suddenly, he was terribly afraid! Had he made a mistake? Would this place and its raw beauty, its potential, not appeal to Elvina as it had to him?

The interior of the cabin was in far better condition than the outside. The floor had been constructed from wide hardwood planks that were tight fitting, with no wide cracks between. The walls were in good condition, too, smooth, and dry, the clay chinking not loose and falling out like the exterior.

They made their way through the back door and down to the spring. Elvina was glad that she had followed John's advice and had worn suitable boots for walking. The spring was located approximately fifty yards down a slight incline where a large rock formation protruded from the side of the hill. From the shelter of this overhang, clear cold water rushed forth, its force temporarily quieted as it became a part of a large pool of water that accumulated in a rock basin just below the mouth of the spring, overflowing at the opposite end to push its way down the hill and on through sections of pasture land. The moving water seemed to add a mystical note to the scene, and Elvina found her spirits lifting as she and John followed its path through beds of carpet-soft, moss-covered rocks, which formed the sides of the narrow creek. In the valley below, the water wound in and out among the trees, creating wide shallow pools where rock beds existed.

The log barn with honeysuckle vines climbing all the way to its roof and beyond, weaving back and forth in the wind, was the site of their next exploration. Evidently from the remains of what was once a split-rail fence, the barn and lot had been situated where the water from the spring could be piped through hollowed out logs into a watering trough for the farm animals. The barn had four stalls, two on each side of an open hallway, and a loft which had a permanent opening at the front for pitching hay in or out. To the left of the barn, a small corncrib, built high off the ground and resting on large rock pillars was almost hidden by vines also.

Later, as they dipped cold water from the spring with their cupped hands to quench their thirsts, they stood quietly lost in thought, gazing about them, each lost in their own private world of appraisal; the cabin with its stately oak tree in the front yard, the mules still hitched to the wagon, waiting patiently; the rich farmland down in the valley, covered now with blackberry vines and other small plant life; the foliage dry and dead except for a bright brier leaf here and there that had defied the season's first killing frost, seemingly determined to use the last moments of life to paint the fields with vivid splashes of color.

John stood silently watching for Elvina's reaction. He was much more encouraged now by her actions than when they first arrived. Yet, he hesitated, afraid to ask her what she was thinking.

It was getting on into the afternoon and a sudden rush of cold wind whipped their coats about them, causing Elvina to shiver violently. John moved close to her, wrapping his great coat around her, holding her close within the confines of his big arms, feeling the warmth and closeness of her.

"The first thing I must do is get a large fire going in the fireplace," John stated emphatically, concern drawing his eyebrows close together as he stood shielding her from the wind and looking down into her beloved face. He let go of his coat and reached up to cup her face in his large hands. Across his memory flashed a play back of all the years that he had planned for this moment, and all the years Elvina had uncomplainingly waited and planned with him, helping him arrive at this time and place. It seemed that the gratitude and love that he felt for her would make his chest explode.

"It seems almost a sin to be so happy," he whispered gruffly, dropping his arms to embrace her once again, lowering his head to press his face against her hair.

Elvina stood quietly in his arms, her gaze traveling across their land. Off in the distance a crow cawed, and nearby, she could hear the rippling of the water. She thought about Boston and the security she had given up, where comfort was a way of life and there was never a real lack of anything as far as material needs. "But I was lonely there," she mused, "because John wasn't an integral part of it." Then, a profound truth came to rest in her heart; that even in this backwoods place, she would never really feel entirely alone as long as she had John. That somehow, everything would work out all right.

"It's good to be home," she said softly, shifting her gaze upward to meet his, tilting her head so that their lips could meet.

CHAPTER 4

They slept rolled up in blankets on the floor before the fire that first night in their new home, having mutually agreed that the cabin must be thoroughly cleaned before they unloaded the wagon. As a precaution against the possibility of rain, John had moved the wagon into the hallway of the barn.

After breakfast the next morning they decided that scrubbing the smoke stained ceiling and smudged walls, cleaning out the loft, and removing grease splatters from the floor would be their first challenges. However, gallons of hot water would be needed, and to have hot water, wood was needed for the fire. That was John's first major undertaking.

Cobwebs and dust were everywhere, especially in the loft. Rats and mice had been frequent inhabitants, as evidenced by the signs they left behind. The lower floor required the most effort, for over the years the greasy spots had become engrained in the wood and seemed to defy the cutting power of hot water and soap. Finally, they resorted to scrubbing the floor with sand before all traces of the stains were gone.

Nightfall found them once again exhaustedly eating a sparse meal near the fire, with the necessity of sleeping on the floor facing them again. The weather had not cooperated at all, and a low cloud cover, accompanied by dense fog mixed with light rain, had completely blocked any penetration of the sun's rays. Unloading their belongings in the rain was out of the question, and, too, they felt it best to let the cabin walls and floors completely dry before bringing in furnishings and clothing. Thankfully, the floor near the fireplace had dried, and the repugnant foulness of mildew and mustiness that had permeated the cabin the day before had been replaced by the pungent odor of strong soap.

Even though Elvina's employment at the Lowell's had oftentimes demanded long arduous hours and almost Herculean strength to meet the constant needs of the family, it had not fully prepared her for the stress of coping daily with the lack of conveniences and the limited space of the cabin. To someone who had always lived in a large city, and who had spent almost half of their lifetime in comfortable, spacious surroundings, Elvina's new lifestyle appeared as formidable sometimes as a raw wilderness.

There was always the problem of water, a precious commodity that she quickly learned to use sparingly. Bringing buckets of water up the hill from the spring made her arms sore and her back ache, and she dismally questioned the wisdom of the builder who constructed the house so far from the water source. Washday was something she quickly came to dread, and to eliminate the need of carrying water from the spring, she set up her wash pot and wooden tubs down by the spring. "Without a doubt this has to be the coldest, most miserable job in the world," she would sigh as she bent over the rub board, the cold wind twisting her long skirt around her ankles.

Keeping the fire going in the fireplace was another constant vigil, for if she let it die down, the temperature dropped quickly in the cabin, the cold creeping through small cracks and crevices, bringing

31

with it an encroaching chill that seemed to penetrate the very marrow of her bones. Meal preparation had not been one of her regularly assigned duties at the Lowell's, and her inexperience, coupled with the struggle of cooking over the fire, resulted in many mealtime disasters. She often murmured a prayer of gratitude for the swinging iron bars that someone in time past had installed in the fireplace, making it possible for her to heat water and cook food without getting her face and hands seared.

After much deliberation, they decided that it would not be to their advantage financially to buy a cow until later. Hay and grain would have to be purchased and that would be costly. Grass would be plentiful in the spring, eliminating that added expense.

But despite the hardships, there were many new aspects of beauty in her life, particularly, the long walks she and John took through the woods, usually on Sunday afternoons, weather permitting. Sunday, the Lord's Day was their day of rest, and they restricted themselves to doing only the necessary chores of preparing their food and feeding the animals.

John never tired of walking over his land. Besides his intense pride of ownership, he, like Elvina, enjoyed the beauty that was evident in any direction. There were moss-covered rocks protected in a valley or on a hillside from the wintry blasts, emerald green and velvety to the touch. Lichens growing on dead limbs created miniature bouquets of gray and red flowers, and there was no end to the varied sizes, shapes and kinds of colorful rocks exposed on the hillsides by the absence of foliage on the bushes and trees. The wind moving through the trees, especially the tall pines, seemed to be relaying a message, and Elvina came to understand what the poet was trying to express when he wrote of the "singing pines." Red birds and robins came to investigate their premises, and some stayed. And when the rains came down in torrents, the water pelting the roof, Elvina experienced a keener awareness of the rawness of nature, and she often laid in bed at night listening to the pounding rain and the moaning wind, giving thanks for having a warm, dry place to escape such onslaughts.

But as time progressed, Elvina began to experience strange moods of sadness, which oftentimes culminated into a deluge of tears. "Maybe I feel this way because Christmas is only a few weeks away and we are so far away from everybody," she sniffed one morning as she stirred a pot of beans simmering over the fire. "Home," she whispered brokenly, the word lingering longingly on her lips. Impatiently she shrugged her shoulders as if to toss the thoughts way. "I must never, never, let John know how miserable I feel sometimes," she cautioned herself sternly.

Working outside seemed to help more than anything else to overcome her depression. On days when the weather permitted, she cleared away dead weeds and brush from around the cabin. And when there was no more of that to be done, she began to seek out John, helping him whatever way she could. And his work was endless! From the time it became light enough for him to see in the mornings, he was cutting wood for the fireplace, preparing a spot for their vegetable garden, repairing the barn, building some other needed shed, or splitting rails for fencing. Only when encroaching darkness made it necessary for him to put aside his saw, axe, grubbing hoe, or whatever tool the job at hand had required, did he quit, and then with tired reluctance.

John welcomed Elvina's company even though at times she was more hindrance than help. And he was not oblivious to her needs, either, for he had noticed how quiet she had become some days not having much to say; hardly ever laughing. And that disturbed him. Her laughter always lifted his spirits. But he was reluctant, almost afraid, to ask her what was wrong for fear of hearing her say that she was sorry she had come south with him. Without actually acknowledging her problem, he would talk about his own pressing needs. Holding her close and talking low as if he were sharing a confidence, he would plead his cause. "Vi, if I don't get the repair work and construction completed before plowing time, then it will just have to go undone until the crop is laid by." He kissed her tenderly, and then pushed her away from him so that he could look into her eyes. Not trusting herself to speak, Elvina nodded silently, struggling with the self-pity that threatened to play havoc with her emotions. After a few moments of silence, she was able to respond cheerfully, "Well, let's get on with it!"

She made it all right for a few days, then the loneliness returned, crowding in upon her at the most unexpected moments. And if she were alone, she let the tears flow unchecked. The longing to see her loved ones was almost unbearable at times. She had written after they were settled, but she had not received a reply. This was to be expected since her parents could neither read nor write the English language.

Then, one afternoon Elvina had just finished washing the dishes used for their noonday meal when she heard the sounds of wheels grinding on the rocks in their drive and a masculine voice called out loudly, "Whoa!"

Elvina peeked out the small window, but could see no one from that angle, making it necessary for her to go open the door. A tall man wearing a wide-brimmed hat was assisting a woman from the buggy. When the woman was safely standing on the ground, she and the man looked toward the cabin, and seeing Elvina standing in the doorway, waved enthusiastically, the man touching the brim of his hat in a jaunty manner. They started toward the house, but suddenly the woman turned around and hurried back to the buggy to pick up a dish. In a few moments she had joined the man again who had paused to wait patiently.

"Good afternoon, neighbor," the man's voice boomed cheerfully as the two approached. "James Wheeler, here, and this is my missus, Rosemary. We're neighbors just over the way," he explained, turning to gesture in the direction of their home. "Heard in town you two had moved in."

Elvina hurried down the steps holding out her hands in welcome. "Welcome, neighbors," she smiled, a lilt in her voice. "John pointed your house out to me as we came out from town the day we arrived. I'm so glad you have come... please come in," she encouraged, hurrying to open the door for them. She stepped aside, holding the door, and caught a glimpse of John hurrying up the path. "Oh, here comes John! He's been repairing the barn roof. He must have seen you." As he approached, she called to him happily,

"John, we have company! It's James and Rosemary Wheeler, our neighbors!"

The two men shook hands and then all of them went inside.

Elvina knew immediately that she was going to like these new friends, especially Rosemary. There was no mistaking the warmth of her easy smile, the quick way she had of laughing that made her blue eyes, framed by a mass of auburn hair speckled with gray, dance mischievously.

"Please sit down," Elvina urged their guests, pushing the coffeepot closer to the coals. "It's so nice of you to come," she assured them again, a warm smile making her eyes sparkle with pleasure.

"I brought you some fried apple pies," Rosemary announced, placing the dish she was carrying on the table.

"Oh, thank you! I... I'm afraid John has gone somewhat lacking for pies and cakes since... since we've moved in."

"How lovely she is," Rosemary thought, her admiring gaze following Elvina as she hurried to remove cups and saucers from a shelf. She had wondered what her new neighbor, and hopefully friend, would be like, but certainly had not expected to find this refined, seemingly cultured person with an accent so markedly different from Georgia natives.

Unobtrusively Rosemary's glance took in the room. A large poster bed with a colorful hand braided rug by its side dominated one corner. Two large trunks and some large packing crates filled in the other corner. To one side of the fireplace, a high-backed, dark mahogany rocking chair with delicate hand carvings and a bright patchwork cushion gave an unprecedented elegance to the rustic interior of the cabin. Over near the door, above the small table which served as a shelf for the water bucket and dipper, a large oval mirror with a wide wooden frame added depth and light to that section of the room. From her seated position on one of the benches by the table, Rosemary quietly admired Elvina's graceful movements as she placed the cups on the table.

But it was Elvina's hands that puzzled Rosemary. Her movements were graceful, her manner unaffected, portraying breeding and good taste. However, her hands, large and big-knuckled, resembled those of a woman who had spent years at hard labor of some kind.

Elvina poured the coffee, apologizing for not being able to offer them cream, explaining that they had not, as yet, bought a cow.

"You don't have a cow!" James' deep southern drawl seemed to vibrate off the walls of the cabin. "Well, we'll fix you folks up right away. One of our cows found a new calf a couple of weeks ago, and we're been feeding milk to the hogs to get rid of it. You all just come on over! You'll be doing us a favor to take it off our hands."

"That's certainly generous of you, James," John smiled, "but we couldn't take it without paying."

"Shucks, no!" James retorted. "Wouldn't be the neighborly thing to do. And if you don't come get it, I'll just bring it over myself. By the way! What part of the country do you folks hail from?"

"Boston," John answered. "Boston, Massachusetts."

"Well, that explains the strange way you talk!" he laughed, slapping his knees.

Elvina glanced at Rosemary. Rosemary laughed lightly, shrugging her shoulders. "Guess you could say the same thing about us, huh?" The women stared at each other for a brief second, then burst out laughing.

Too soon it was time for the Wheelers to go. "Do you have to go?" Elvina pleaded, disappointment clouding her eyes. "You're our first visitors since moving in."

But the Wheelers couldn't stay longer, explaining that they had two boys at home; Doug ten years old, and Wray, age nine.

John and Elvina walked out to the buggy with them and sent them off with much waving and a warm invitation to come back soon. Elvina felt as if a touch of spring had moved into her world for just a little while. And the most important thing, she thought happily, the Wheeler's had invited them to visit Big Spring Church the coming Sunday, and home for dinner with them afterwards.

They stood watching until the Wheeler's buggy was out of sight. "We have a lot in common with those folks," John commented. "They're small land owners same as we are, who don't own slaves and wouldn't own one under any circumstances."

"I don't think I can wait until Sunday gets here!" Elvina exclaimed, happiness creating a lilt to her voice. Impulsively, she turned and hugged John hard.

John's arms encircled her - holding her tight. "It's so good to hear you laugh again," he said, his eyes solemn as they searched her face.

Sunday morning dawned clear and balmy, one of those rare winter days when the temperature climbs into the sixties. Elvina had hurriedly prepared their breakfast, hardly giving John time to eat once it was ready, before she started clearing the table. She had carefully selected the dress she would wear the day before and it lay neatly folded across the back of her rocker.

Selection of what to wear had not been a simple matter. One by one she had laid the velvets, silks, and taffetas aside that had been discards of Mrs. Lowell. The dress she finally decided upon was one that Mrs. Lowell had called a "day dress," soberly cut and opening in the front. There was also a matching bonnet. She would wear a shawl for warmth.

When she was ready to go, she turned to John for his approval. "What do you think, John?" she asked as she turned slowly for his appraisal. When he didn't answer right away, she explained haltingly, "I don't want to appear to be something I'm not."

"What do you mean 'something you're not,' young lady?" he demanded.

"I think it would be in bad taste for me to dress so... so flamboyantly," she explained, her eyes pleading for understanding.

John stood gazing down at her for a long moment. Slowly the dark frown of displeasure disappeared and a twisted smile softened his stern expression. "You're right, of course," he agreed amiably, removing his arms from around her waist and walking over to stand staring into the fire. Why had Elvina's words disturbed him that way? Especially since her sense of decorum in all matters was one of the special qualities he had always admired about her. Turning to face her, he haltingly tried to explain how he felt. "In my mindset, Vi, I don't see this little one-room cabin and our sparse belongings as our real life style, but what it will be someday."

"I know, John," she agreed patiently, "but we must deal with life as it is now."

Shrugging impatiently, as if to throw off the troublesome thoughts, he walked to the back of the room and started changing into his Sunday clothes.

Their first attendance at Big Spring Church had been full of surprises. First of all, the church had been filled to overflowing with men, women, and children, many of whom had traveled for miles in wagons and buggies. And the warmth of their acceptance of Elvina and John as total strangers had created a beautiful lasting memory in two lonely people's hearts.

"What a marvelous, simply glorious day!" Elvina exclaimed joyously on their way home that afternoon. "The people were so friendly! And James and Rosemary inviting us to their home was even better. I don't feel isolated and alone anymore. And the hens Rosemary gave us! We'll have fresh eggs, now!" Happily she turned to look over her shoulder at the chicken coop tied securely in the back of the wagon containing the five black and white speckled hens that occasionally emitted loud squawks of displeasure.

Relaxed and smiling, John's eyes devoured Elvina's flushed face, her eyes warm with excitement. How good it was to see her so happy! "How beautiful she is," he thought, as he had hundreds of times past. He tied the reins to the side of the wagon seat and folded her in his arms, kissing her long and hungrily.

They drove the remainder of the way home with her head snuggled against his shoulder.

The sun was beginning to slip down behind the trees when they drove into their yard. While John unhitched the mules and led them to the barn, Elvina hurried inside the cabin. After removing her cape, she walked over to the fireplace to uncover the coals John had buried in ashes that morning. She stood a long moment gazing about her. How plain and crude it seemed when compared to the Wheeler's nice home. The dark despair that had been engulfing her at times recently reared its ugly head and she stood rigidly fighting back the tears. "This is wrong!" she silently chastised herself, shaking her head as if to throw off such thoughts. Almost frantically she uncovered the coals and added logs. From the wood box she selected a small piece of rich pine to put beneath the logs to hurry the blaze. Upon impulse, she pulled the braided rug up close to the hearth. "Tonight, we're going to have our supper by the fire," she determined, her previous dark mood slowly dissipating.

Elvina had their light supper ready when John came in from the barn. "I fed and watered the mules," he announced. "Also, I placed the hens inside the barn in their coop for the night just in case some varmint decided to make a meal out of them."

They sat on the rug in front of the fire, basking in its warmth and enjoying their simple meal of biscuits and fried meat left from breakfast, made festive by the cold, cream-rich milk that Rosemary had insisted on giving them.

"This reminds me of another job I have to get finished by spring," John commented lazily, holding up his glass of milk for emphasis.

"Oh?" Elvina questioned, eyebrows raised quizzically. "And what is that?"

"A springhouse for our milk and butter and other perishables. We'll have to have one when the weather turns warm."

"And we get a cow!" Elvina laughed teasingly. "And don't forget the hen house," she reminded him happily. "Oh, John," she breathed, her voice warm and husky with emotion. "Hasn't this been a wonderful day?" She sat staring into the fire, a soft smile caressing her full lips. "I... I was beginning to get a little lonely," she confessed wistfully, and then afraid he would misunderstand, hurried on to explain. "For friends. You know what I mean, don't you, John?"

When John didn't respond she turned anxiously to look at him, afraid that she had offended him someway. Instead, she met his gaze focused upon her, not in hurt, or anger, but dark and fathomless, as they always were when he was deeply touched. Without a word, he placed his plate and glass on the floor. Then, very carefully, so as not to pull her hair, he removed the pins that held it in place. It tumbled down around her shoulders, not stopping until it touched the floor, framing her face in a dark mass that seemed to come alive as the flickering flames picked up its highlights.

"I've never seen you look more beautiful," he whispered hoarsely, as he reached for her, pulling her down beside him on the rug.

As his lips found hers, he could feel the warmth of the fire upon her face and slender body.

CHAPTER 5

In a mystical sense, time had passed swiftly those first months in Georgia, more so for John than for Elvina. For her, the days seemed to meld into a day in, day out existence, the monotony of which made room for nostalgic thoughts of her former life in Boston and the friends and family she had left behind. Back then, each day had been earmarked for some particular activity, creating a sense of urgency, a tension that was often exhausting but at the same time exhilarating and challenging. Now, her days consisted of preparing meals with very limited resources, bringing water from the spring, scrubbing clothes on the rub board, and hardest of all, struggling against the drastic change of being almost isolated from the outside world.

The Wheeler's cheerful neighborliness had been the ray of sunshine needed to cope with the isolation of their new surroundings. The visits in each other's homes had been a sustaining force even though time, distance, and respective workloads, had limited the occasions. Too, the fellowship compensated somewhat for the loss of former friends and family. Also, James and Rosemary's friendship had made their acceptance into the community easier. John and Elvina's articulate and seemingly abrupt manner of speaking was strange to many. This resulted in the misconception at times that "the Stuart's were uppity." But Southern hospitality and the Stuart's friendliness overcame these minor obstacles and in time, Elvina was invited to join the ladies' quilting bee. She was soon instructing the ladies in the art of braiding rugs from discarded clothing and other materials (an art she had been taught by her mother). In turn, they shared many of their handed-down methods of utilizing the natural resources available. One was the making of lye soap, an operation that would inevitably involve John. On the farm where he had worked in Massachusetts, John had often seen soap being made but never actually participated in the process. Now, he found himself meticulously following instructions given to him by James for building what was called an ash hopper. When the hopper was finished, it had to be carefully lined with straw and a layer of unslacked lime applied. Hardwood ashes from the fireplace were stockpiled in the hopper until it was filled within a few inches of the top. Then, a basin was formed in the top of the ashes, allowing space for the water that was to be added. It took many gallons of water and numerous trips to the spring before a dark gray liquid began to drip from the opening in the bottom of the hopper. When the bucket underneath the hopper was full, the liquid was transferred to the wash pot. When the wash pot was filled with the amount needed, John built a fire around it and the last stages of the soap-making project began. Rosemary, who had come over to supervise Elvina's trial run, brought old cooking grease, another necessary ingredient. The mixture was kept cooking until Rosemary's test with a hen's feather told her it was "just right."

Washday was the proving ground for the product. It far exceeded Elvina's expectations for it removed the ground-in dirt from John's work clothes with half the effort needed heretofore. But Elvina was to learn painfully that her miracle worker had its disadvantages, too. The cleaning power that left her clothes clean and fresh and cut grease magically from dishes and cooking utensils, also caused her fingertips to crack open and bleed, especially when the weather was cold.

John had kept his promise to build a springhouse before warm weather arrived. The location he chose was several feet below the mouth of the spring. Elvina's chore was helping remove the rocks and dirt so that the ground would be level for the foundation. The first few feet of the walls were built out of stone. The rest of the wall was constructed logs and the space between chinked with clay. Wooden shingles were used for the roof and an air vent for circulation crowned the two miniature gables. When the project was completed inside and out, the cold water from the spring entered the building from a holding trough made from white oak. Inside the springhouse there was another large open trough built at different levels so that the water could flow unimpeded through the springhouse, down the trough and out the other side. The trough would be the container for keeping their milk cold and fresh. Around the inside of the springhouse, above water level, were shelves for storing vegetables and other perishables during the blistering heat of summer.

There was a welcome break in the weather in February - the sun radiant as only it can be after the earth has been shrouded in winter rain. The bluebirds began to build their nests - making innumerable trips from the grass and straw in the fields to the hole in an old dead tree or a fence post.

John began his spring plowing by breaking up the garden plot first. Then he turned to the cotton and cornfields - their plenteous growth of blackberry vines and young saplings his most formidable foes.

From the outset the weather cooperated and they made a good crop that first year, and by not buying anything that was not absolutely necessary, they were able to make their first mortgage payment on time.

The milk cow they had bought in the spring gave birth to a male calf, and after it was old enough to wean from its mother, they staked it in tall grass each day with drinking water in a wooden bucket nearby. When the weather started turning cool in the fall, and the corn ready for harvesting, John penned the calf up to fatten it on corn before slaughtering. Also, that same year, the sow that John had bought at the same time he purchased the cow produced a litter of five piglets. John kept three for meat and market and gave two to the Wheelers.

During their second year in Georgia, 1848, Melinda Sue was born. When the tiny dark-haired baby girl was laid in Elvina's arms, Elvina began to cry. Alarmed, John knelt by the side of the bed and cradled Elvina's head in his arm. "Darling, what's the matter?" he pleaded, greatly distressed.

"Because...because I'm so happy," she whispered hoarsely, tears running unheeded down her cheeks. John heard a sniff behind him and glanced over his shoulder to see Rosemary unashamedly wiping tears from her eyes.

"Women!" he growled good-naturedly, a big smile denying his impatience. Gently he touched the hand of the baby and as its tiny fingers curled around one of his, an expression of joy and amazement spread across his face, relieving the tired lines that had been so evident a moment before.

The crops were good again that year, and by continuing to practice their frugal lifestyle, they were able to pay their second mortgage payment without increased financial hardship.

As land-breaking time rolled around the third spring, John hitched the mules to the turning plow, whistling as he worked. As he followed the plow, his eyes riveted on the curling earth that peeled back from the blades, he felt a great surge of contentment. Just one more crop and the balance of the mortgage would be paid. Then, thank God, the land and the crops it yielded would be theirs to use as they pleased. Each time they had been tempted to buy some small luxury, or indulge themselves in new clothes that were not absolutely necessary, they had doggedly put aside the longings. Just one more year and the mortgage would be paid in full. Hopefully, everything would be different then. Silently, John once again began making plans for adding rooms to the cabin, working out the details while plowing or attending to some other chore. The crop year had started out, as the two previous ones, with conditions favorable. The early spring rains came in abundance and then stopped in time for the ground to dry out for early plowing and planting. But, then, the rain that could usually be counted upon to make the cotton and corn seeds sprout, didn't come. Day after day, the first thing they would do upon arising, was to go outside and search the skies, their eyes and hearts straining for the glimpse of a cloud that looked promising. By the time the rains finally came, it was too late to plant again, and they had to be satisfied with the scattered plants that had survived.

That fall the cotton yield was only about one-third of what it had been the two previous years, and the corn crop, that consisted mainly of nubbins, was not enough to supply their personal needs and the need to feed their livestock through the winter.

John and Elvina were intensely aware of the terms of their contract with Mr. Rawlings. But he had always been so congenial and accommodating. Optimistically they clung to the belief that when they went to him and explained the circumstances, especially since the conditions had been beyond their control, he would understand and extend the terms of their agreement for another crop year. After all, hadn't just about everyone in the whole county suffered severe crop failures?

But Mr. Rawlings had not been sympathetic with their plight. "Business is business," he quipped, his small eyes, which had been smiling and friendly heretofore, now hard and staring at them unblinkingly over his silver-rimmed spectacles. "I'm sorry," he continued, his impassive expression denying the sincerity of his apology, "but if you do not have the specified number of bales of cotton, or cash, as called for in the contract, then I have no other alternative but to foreclose." Unable to meet John's steely gaze, he lowered his eyes and started shuffling some papers on his desk. After a long moment of silence, he glanced up at them, his attempt at being pleasant resulting in a twisted smile that gave him the appearance of a grinning opossum. "However," he continued, still unable to look either of them in the eyes, "if you and your wife would like to renew the contract for another three-year period, this might could be arranged."

The contract was legal and binding. They had very little cash, and the bank's president informed them that because of the draught the bank had already over extended its funds and could not make any new loans. There was no one in Boston they could turn to, and John absolutely refused to even discuss Elvina's suggestion of asking the Wheeler's for a loan. Therefore, they were faced with two alternatives: move off the land or accept Rawlings offer of another three-year mortgage.

Hurt and angry, they were forced to accept. Everything they owned was tied up in the farm, and there was still another important factor to take into consideration. Elvina was expecting their second child in March of the next year.

The effect of Mr. Rawlings business dealings resulted in an immediate psychological change in John. To Elvina, observing him silently, heart aching, he seemed to become more embittered daily, and his usually pleasant disposition became moody and morose. Even the birth of their second daughter, Liza Gail, did not bring about any noticeable change in his behavior. If anything, it seemed to make him more despondent. Finally, Elvina had to accept the fact that it was not within her power to say or do anything to make John's burden lighter, and therefore, she occupied her days with the care of the children and her daily chores, exerting great mental effort toward not dwelling on their misfortune. Her life did take on a different perspective in one respect. She began reading her Bible more and spending more time in prayer.

It seemed to Elvina that an invisible wall had been erected between John and her, making their former warm relationship seem like a dream, an euphoric state that had existed in another world; another time. In her desperation and loneliness, she turned even more to God for comfort, praying for wisdom to cope with the blight that had contaminated their world. Day by day she painfully witnessed what hate was doing to her beloved husband, and she resolutely determined not to let their misfortune destroy her along with him. Outwardly she appeared calm and cheerful, but her heart ached. Being constantly on guard so as not to let John's irritability and impatience force them into emotional crises was beginning to make her a very intense and nervous individual. She found comfort from the Bible in that God's word promised "vengeance is mine," and was able to forgive Mr. Rawlings - even to the point of praying for his immortal soul.

The visits between them and the Wheeler's lessened. John's withdrawal into his world of silence and brooding caused a strain upon their relationship. Finally, feeling somewhat disloyal to John but at the same time disturbed over what was happening to their friendship, Elvina confided in Rosemary after church one Sunday what had taken place, begging her not to discuss it with anyone. But a heartsick Rosemary, unable to bear the burden alone, tearfully divulged the incredible story to James the next morning at the breakfast table.

James' immediate reaction was just what Rosemary had expected; explosive anger. Anger toward land sharks in general and anger toward John because he didn't come to him for help.

"Did he try for a loan at the bank?" James demanded, his voice harsh and demanding as if he held Rosemary accountable for what had happened.

"I think so... but for some reason the bank didn't want to risk a second mortgage, something...something about so many loans already made because of the drought."

"I'll be..." James stopped short of swearing and clenched his teeth. Then, defiantly hitting the table with his fist, blurted, "I'm going to John and offer him a loan!"

"No!" Rosemary retorted, eyes wide with alarm. "You can't do that!"

"And why can't I?" James demanded hotly, rising from the table and walking resolutely toward the door.

"Because...because I...I sort of promised Elvina I wouldn't tell! And, besides! He wouldn't accept your help! You know how stubborn he was about even taking milk without paying - when we had so much we were feeding it to the hogs! And another thing! Elvina said the contract has a clause in it preventing the loan from being paid off before the three-year period is up."

"D...false pride," Rosemary heard him mutter as he charged out the back door, letting it slam viciously behind him.

As the weeks stretched into months, John's frustration and bitterness became more apparent, made visible by the deep lines etched in his face. The plans he once talked about with such eagerness for enlarging the cabin were never mentioned, and his silence acted as a constant barrier between him and Elvina. It seemed to her as if everything that had been heretofore meaningful had come to a standstill, suspended in time, and they were just actors on a stage, dragging out the day-to-day drama of living. At times Elvina wanted to take hold of John and shake him hard, telling him, "John, stop it! Don't you see what you are doing to us, to me? Are material things that important to you that you would sacrifice all of us to your anger?" But she said nothing, oftentimes condemning herself as a coward - afraid to risk his anger, or even worse, pushing him even deeper into despair. Then, too, there was the indebtedness John had paid off in Boston. How long and how much did that take from his life? "Only you know, God, how deep this thing cuts," she prayed, compassion softening her hostility while her heart ached with love for him.

Then, when Liza was just a year and half, their son was born. They had named him John Robinson, a namesake for both of them.

There had been no further droughts or any other calamity during the second three-year period to prevent their paying off the indebtedness. Elvina and the children accompanied John on the trip into town to make the final payment. They waited outside in the wagon while John went in to pay Mr. Rawlings. Elvina's heart pounded so hard that it seemed to hamper her breathing. "Oh, dear Lord," she prayed silently. "Please don't let John lose his temper!"

To her amazement and profound relief, John was gone only a few minutes. He came back out of the office clutching a piece of paper in his hand, a dark scowl shadowing his face. He walked up to Elvina's side of the wagon and laid the folded paper in her hand. "It's over now," he said quietly, his expression impassive. Turning abruptly, he walked around the rear of the wagon to the other side and climbed up beside her on the seat. "I hope he rots in Hell," he lashed out angrily through clenched teeth as he picked up the reins and slapped the mules with the lines.

Elvina gasped, her arms tightening spasmodically around the sleeping child in her arms. "Oh, John," she moaned inwardly. She glanced furtively in his direction, dismayed by the clenched jaw, the half-shut eyes staring past the mules into nothingness. A wave of love and compassion swept over her creating a longing to place her arms around him and hold him tight and tell him that it was all over; that they were free from the worry and anxiety of the mortgage at last.

Supporting the baby with one arm, she reached over and gently pressed his knee with her other hand. "I love you," she said softly, unable to say more lest her voice break.

John's eyes, dark with misery, turned to stare at her. Slowly, some of the harshness of his expression faded and a crooked smile twisted the edges of his mouth.

"Everything will be better, now," she assured him lovingly, her eyes caressing his face. And to keep him from seeing the quick tears that she felt near the surface, leaned down and kissed the soft cheek of their sleeping son.

Elvina would recall the next few weeks as the beginning of the return of the husband she knew during the first years of their marriage. John began to talk again about adding another room to the cabin. "We probably should build it out of logs, just like the original," he concluded.

When he had harvested the last of the late corn and cotton and immediately started felling trees and hewing them into logs for building, Elvina could hardly contain her excitement. Occasionally she would surprise herself, and the children, by bursting into song.

John worked long and hard, a drive like nothing Elvina had witnessed since they had been living in Georgia. James Wheeler started dropping over to help John with his building project, and many times Rosemary came along, bringing their latest addition, a boy, whose arrival had been about the same time that Robinson was born. They had named him James, shortening it to Jim for easy identification.

When the crisp chill of fall settled in, the entire family went into town for a shopping spree, the first since the payments for the second mortgage had begun. They bought new shoes for everyone and work boots for John, as well as a new work coat, and not a mite too soon, for that winter would prove to be the most severe they had experienced since living in Georgia. Elvina selected yards of various materials for making new clothing for the family. For the older children's treat, they were allowed to select their own bag of candy, and John bought an entire hoop of cheese. Elvina's most thrilling treat came from the bookstore; a copy of McGuffey's Electric Reader "to teach Melinda, Liza and Rob later on," she explained to John, and a copy of <u>Jane Eyre,</u> a novel that Mrs. Lowell had said in one of her letters was "taking the country by storm."

They were all in a party mood and laughed a lot on the way home. But as they passed the Templeton Plantation, John and Elvina's expressions became thoughtful as they recalled the talk back in town; talk about the ever-increasing tension between the North and South over the slavery issue. Could it really be true? Was it possible that their country might be divided by war? And how would it affect the lives of her brothers who were now in their twenties, and her sisters' husbands.

And their anxieties were well justified, for the growing animosities between the northern and southern states had far reaching effects, touching their lives in subtle ways. Casual remarks loaded with hidden meanings about "Northern sympathizers" took some of the joy from church attendance, the social highlight of their lives. It became impossible for John to go into town without having someone approach him concerning his "stand," and they found, just as Mrs. Lowell had forewarned so many years back, that their New England dialect was fast becoming a detriment to their peaceful way of life.

The elements had seemed to be waging another war against them, too. Just prior to the turn of the sixtieth decade, in 1859, there was another severe dry growing season, and even though cotton sold for fifty cents a pound, their harvest was so scanty they sold it for barely enough cash to pay their taxes and bare necessities. And that same winter, both of their mules died within a two-month period, the replacement of which created an enormous drain on their meager savings.

In 1860, Abraham Lincoln was elected President without carrying a single southern state. Their neighboring state, South Carolina, seceded from the Union as soon as it heard of Lincoln's election, and on December 20, 1860, adopted the Ordinance of Secession. Within six weeks, Georgia was one of the six other southern states that followed South Carolina's example.

It was James Wheeler who brought them the news in the spring of 1861 that open hostilities had begun. He had gone into town for supplies and had ridden by their place on his way home to tell them the country was at war; that, on April 12, Fort Sumter, located in Charleston, South Carolina's harbor, had been fired upon by Confederate troops.

"John, how do you think all of this war talk is going to affect us," Elvina asked after they were in the privacy of their own room.

"I don't know," he answered slowly. "I don't believe it's right to own another human being and use him like some work animal, denying him the right to enjoy and use the fruits of his own labor. Yet, I don't feel that I want to go to war over this thing. How can I fight against the South, against our friends and neighbors? And… and if I survived, how could I come back here and hope to pick up my life and live at peace among people I had taken up arms against?"

But John never was forced to make that decision, and the talk of war and the general unrest throughout the country lost its immediate importance for Elvina due to a devastating personal tragedy. In the late fall of 1861, her beloved John died.

CHAPTER 6

Robinson was suddenly conscious of total silence; that his mother's voice had ceased. Her gray eyes, thoughtful and pensive, now focused on him. The fact that his reminiscing had prevented him from hearing one word she had read made him uncomfortable.

Elvina did not comment, just closed the Bible softly and rising, placed it back upon the mantle. "Guess we should get ready for bed," she suggested amiably. "Tomorrow will be here far too soon for all of us."

After Elvina and the girls had retired to the bedroom, Robinson slipped off his work clothes and lay down on his bunk in the far corner of the kitchen. The reminiscent mood that had been with him earlier returned, and as he lay staring into the dark, he began to relive the events leading up to his pa's death.

Even after all of the years that had come and gone it still seemed unreal. Impossible! One of those unbelievable occurrences that was inconceivable; yet, somehow had happened, and nothing had ever been the same since.

His pa had complained of not feeling well - that his arms and legs ached and his head felt tight and feverish. Overriding his arguments about having too much to do, Elvina finally persuaded him to go to bed and stay there.

After several days of fretting about all the work waiting to be done, John pushed Elvina's objections aside, insisting irritably that he felt much better.

It was raining that day, a cold penetrating drizzle that seemed to permeate even the inside of the buildings. John spent several hours in the barn repairing harnesses. The next day his fever returned. The hacking cough that had plagued him for a week had turned into a monster that seemed to rip his chest apart. The coughing spells left him weak and exhausted. Robinson overheard John tell Elvina that a tight band around his ribcage seemed to be squeezing the breath out of him.

His pa had developed double pneumonia and all the poultices, rubdowns, and home remedies that Elvina and sympathetic friends kept trying seemed to have little effect on the infection. One of the neighbors suggested the use of leeches to suck his blood, but Elvina rebelled completely against even the thought of such a thing.

Elvina sent into town for the doctor, but it was that time of year when illnesses of this type were paramount, and by the time Doc Evans finally arrived, there wasn't much he could do other than instruct them on ways they could keep him comfortable and solemnly warn those attending John to be careful about contracting the disease themselves.

John's temperature increased steadily until he became delirious. Helpful neighbors took turns sitting with him so that Elvina could get some rest. Occasionally John would cough up a reddish-brown phlegm, but as time went on, it became harder and harder for him to cough up anything.

All of those long days, and even longer nights, Robinson and his family moved about in a nightmare of anxiety. Melinda and Liza glided around the cabin like pale silent ghosts. Robinson had assumed the responsibility for all of the outside chores, welcoming them, in fact, for it provided him with an escape from the horror of his pa's suffering. The labored breathing, the hush tones of his ma, sisters, and others, made him even more apprehensive and afraid.

Late one afternoon while shelling corn in the crib, he became so obsessed with the fear that his pa was going to die that he began to shake violently. His legs refused to support him any longer and he fell across the pile of unshucked corn, clenching his fists. Great wracking sobs shook his thin shoulders as he pleaded over and over with God to let his pa live. Gradually his weeping ceased. Totally drained of emotion, he fell asleep to be awakened later by his mother's voice outside the crib door. Concerned by his long absence, she had come looking for him.

If she noticed in the dim twilight that he had been crying, she didn't mention it, and for this he was grateful. He stepped down out of the crib into the cold wind, reveling in the soothing relief it brought to his burning eyes. Elvina placed her arm around his shoulders as they walked slowly back toward the cabin.

"Ma," Robinson blurted, voice quivering, "Do... do you think Pa's going to be all right?"

Elvina looked down into her son's upturned face, and not able to bear the pleading for assurance that she saw in his eyes, looked quickly away, staring out over the tops of the dusk-tipped trees.

"I don't know, son," she finally answered in a husky voice, her arm tightening its hold on his shoulder.

"Isn't there something we can do?" he pleaded, a sob catching in his throat.

"The only thing we can do now is pray," she said softly, pausing and looking upward into the heavens.

Robinson's gaze followed that of his mother's and he noted that the stars were beginning to appear. "How cold they look," Robinson thought, shuddering.

Back in the cabin once again, Robinson tried to eat some of the food that a kind neighbor offered him, but it seemed to stick in his throat. The rasping struggle his pa was making for each breath in the next room seemed to echo and re-echo inside the small cabin. Finally, because it offered a fraction of privacy, he stretched out on his narrow bed in the back of the room, covering his eyes with the back of his hand.

"Please, God! Oh, please!" he begged silently, over and over again, his arm across his eyes to block the tears.

And outburst of loud sobbing brought Robinson straight up with a jolt. Melinda was coming out of the bedroom door with Liza close behind. They were both weeping openly. Robinson griped the side rail until his knuckles turned white, his eyes wide with fear and disbelief as he stared through the open bedroom door. His father's labored breathing had stopped and his head was no longer moving restlessly on the pillow. He could see his ma on her knees by the bed, her head buried against his pa's chest, her thin shoulders shaking convulsively with sobs. A kind neighbor helped her to her feet, while someone else pulled the sheet up over his pa's head.

Something seemed to explode inside Robinson's head and he jumped to his feet screaming "No! No!

No!" And, then, his ma's arms were around him and she was talking to him softly. He didn't seem to hear a word she said, but she kept holding him close until his body relaxed and the violent shaking ceased.

Mr. Wheeler came over and stood for just a minute, and then, softly speaking their names placed his arms around both of them. "Elvina, Rob. Rosemary and I want you and the family to come over to our house and spend the night. Some of the men and I will take care of things here."

His ma had remained perfectly still for a long moment not answering, then slowly shook her head. "Thank you, James. I'd appreciate you two taking the girls and Robinson over to your place, but I must stay here."

James was silent for a long moment then agreed. "If that's what you want, Elvina, then that's what we'll do."

The next day everything was hushed and subdued around the cabin, the sudden cackling of a hen, or a rooster crowing, sounding loud and obtrusive. Mr. Wheeler had bathed his pa and dressed him in his Sunday best. A pine coffin had been built by some of the men in the community, and now, it and its occupant overshadowed any and all other objects in the room. Volunteers had dug a grave in the cemetery adjacent to Big Spring Church.

Sympathetic neighbor women brought many dishes of food, which, under normal circumstances, would have been tantalizingly delicious to Robinson, but not this time. He could not eat.

For the funeral service at the church, the congregation sang "Sweet By and By," and then, a young preacher said a lot of nice things about his pa. Something was said about "the Lord giveth and the Lord taketh away," but all of this meant little to Robinson. The preacher kept talking about his pa being with the Lord and they would all see him again, if they lived right. Robinson didn't quite understand, or care, what the preacher was talking about. All he knew for certain was that his beloved pa was dead. He didn't care where he was; he just wanted him back.

The preacher led everyone in prayer and when he had finished, everyone that wasn't family filed by the open casket to take a last look at his pa. Then, the family was left alone except for the preacher and the Wheeler's who stood quietly in the background.

Later, as the pallbearers moved slowly across the small cemetery, stepping carefully as if they were trying not to disturb the one they were carrying, sadness like the slow moving mist of a cold winter day enveloped the cluster of friends that filed solemnly behind. When the pallbearers reached the graveside, they gently set the pine box on the ground. The preacher said more words, and then the coffin was lowered into the big gaping hole.

It was the first shovel full of dirt that hit the top of the box that was unbearable for Robinson. Just thinking about it now, caused him to spasmodically clutch his forehead in his hand and whisper agonizingly, "No! No! No!" That had been the worst part of the whole nightmare! Seeing his pa covered with dirt. Dirt! Just like his pa was nothing more than dirt! It seemed as if the pain in his chest was choking the breath from him.

Someone had led Melinda and Liza away from the graveside, but Elvina refused to leave. Robinson stood immobile beside her. She stood with her hands clenched tightly in front of her, and the expression on her face was so taut and strained that Robinson felt a moment of alarm. Once a massive sob raced like a tremor over her body, but she continued to keep her stoic zombie-like composure. Robinson felt as if he were strangely alienated from her. He longed to reach out and touch her, but somehow he didn't feel free to make the move.

Turning her head slowly in his direction, as if she had read his troubled thoughts, Elvina's sad gray eyes looked down into his. She reached out and put an arm around his shoulder, pulling him close. That was the way they stood, unmoving, until the grave had been filled. A red mound of red clay was all the evidence left of the events that had taken place there.

Robinson slept fitfully that night and awakened early before it was good daybreak. Easing into his work clothes, he slipped out of the cabin, picking up the milk pail on his way out. His head felt tight and his eyes burned, and he needed to keep rubbing his eyes to see clearly. The cold air helped clear his head.

The barn, as well as all of the other outbuildings, had always been friendly places to Robinson. He had helped his pa with the chores from the time he became large enough to follow him around. But, now, as he approached the barn alone, the dark yawning hole of the hayloft loomed ominous above him. He shivered, partly from the cold, partly from some unknown dread.

He went to the crib first, opening the door. The pile of corn was only a shadow in the early light. Robinson pulled himself up into the crib and quickly shucked some nubbins for the mules. When he had enough to fill the small basket left in the crib, he made his way to the barn hallway - hesitating only momentarily before walking into the dimness, the eager movements of the hungry animals reassuring him. After he had deposited several ears of corn through each opening in the wall that provided access to the troughs inside the stalls, he turned to the ladder to the hayloft. The opening at the top stared back at him, dark and menacing. A prickling sensation ran down his spine and his knees felt weak, discouraging the urge to run from the barn. "I'm the man of the house, now," he reminded himself shakily, "and pa wouldn't want me to be a coward."

Squaring his shoulders, he reached for a hold on the ladder and didn't pause until he had reached the landing. Looking neither to the left or right, he picked up the pitchfork leaning against the wall and plunged it into the pile of hay. When he had pitched enough through the opening to the ground below, he scurried back down the ladder, doggedly fighting the urge to look up. As his feet touched the ground, he heard the cow moo from her stall and the reassuring sound seemed to help relax his tense muscles. He picked up the pile of hay in his arms and carried it to the cow's stall, opened the door, and shoved the hay into the feeding bin – pushing it down hard so that the animal wouldn't scatter it on the ground. Returning to the hallway for the milk pail, he retraced his steps, and pushing the milking stool from its storage place in the corner of the stall to the right position beside the cow, sat down and began to wash each tit with the water from the pail.

Of all the places on the farm, the barn was the one that Robinson identified most with his father. They had picked peanuts off the vines in the loft, repaired harness in the hallway, shucked and shelled corn in the crib, and sometimes on rainy days, just sat and talked. Now, as he sat methodically milking the cow, the aloneness seemed to stifle him, and he felt as if the walls were closing in. Panic engulfed him, and he battled frantically against the urge to jump up and run. His hands ceased their rhythmic pulling. He sat motionless, heart pounding furiously. Suddenly sobs overcame him, and his shoulders began to shake convulsively as he leaned his head against the warm side of the cow and wept. The cow, sensing something out of the ordinary, stopped her munching to turn her head in his direction. But Robinson continued sobbing, totally unaware of his unsympathetic audience, and it was a sudden movement of the cow that brought him back to the job at hand. Not used to the pressure against her side, the cow moved sideways a step, barely missing the bucket on the ground with her foot. Retrieving the bucket and wiping his eyes on his sleeve, Robinson moved the stool closer. With shaking fingers that seemed to have lost most of their grip, he resumed the task of milking.

His ma had not allowed them to sit down and nurture their grief. Every day she had some new task for them to do. Gathering corn still in the fields, picking scattered cotton that had opened since the main harvest, digging potatoes and turnips, picking up walnuts and wild pecans. The girls grumbled a lot, to which Elvina had turned a deaf ear.

One day they had an unexpected visitor, Tom Provine, a fellow church member and a distant neighbor. Tom owned a molasses mill and he not only made molasses for his family's use but also for all his neighbors that grew sorghum and needed his services. John had helped Tom each year, taking his pay in syrup.

"Mrs. Stuart," he drawled, "I'm going to need some help with the molasses making. Yore boy, here, been comin' with his pa the last couple year, and he's a mighty fine worker." His gaze switched to Robinson who was standing near by. "Thought maybe you might help me out? Yore pay would be in lasses, ya unnerstand?" His glance flashed back to Elvina, his eyes searching hers for approval. She nodded, a gentle smile softening the tired lines that never seemed to completely fade away.

"How 'bout it, son? We start come mornin'."

Robinson turned to look at his ma. "Ma? What do you think?" he asked, face flushed with excitement.

"Well, if Mr. Tom needs you, I don't think it would be neighborly of us to refuse, do you?"

Robinson shook his head in agreement. "I'll be there in the morning, Mr. Tom," he agreed eagerly, "just as soon as I get my chores done."

"That be mighty fine, son," he concluded, tipping his hat toward Elvina. "Now, best I be on my way. Dark will be gettin' here soon."

As the horse and rider departed, Robinson turned eagerly to Elvina, "Ma, how about that! Mr. Tom wants me to work for him!"

"That's because he knows you're a good worker," she smiled, thinking how grateful she was to Mr. Provine. The molasses would be a Godsend.

The womenfolk had all missed him. Even Liza grudgingly admitted that she didn't like him being gone so much and even took over his milking chore at night.

The weather turned cold and the girls decided to work in the hayloft picking off peanuts. Elvina remained in the house to catch up on her mending. She had just sat down near the fire with her thread basket when she heard a man's voice call a loud "Whoa!" Peeking out the window, she gasped with delight. Her visitors were James and Rosemary and their young son, Jim. With joyful tears in her eyes, she hurried out the door and down the steps to greet them. Melinda and Liza came running up the pathway from the barn.

Inside, Rosemary hurried to the fireplace to warm her hands. "It's really nippy out there," she said, shivering.

"It wasn't so cold in the barn," Melinda offered, "we just burrowed down in the peanut vines."

"Where's Rob?" young Jim asked, looking around expectantly.

"Rob is helping Mr. Provine with his molasses making," Elvina explained, while dipping water into the coffeepot. "It was Mr. Provine's idea, and I'm so grateful that he could use him. It has helped Robinson keep his mind off ...things," she finished lamely, moving toward the fire with the pot. "Robinson and his Pa were so close... he misses him terribly." She paused momentarily to regain her composure, and then continued. "Robinson went with John the last couple of

67

years to help with the syrup making, so he's familiar with the work. He's surprisingly mature for a ten-year old. And, too, we can certainly use the molasses no matter how small Robinson's portion turns out to be."

Rosemary walked over to Elvina and placed her arm around her shoulder. "Vi, I don't want to be the one to add any more problems to your already burdened shoulders, but we felt that it's important that we tell you what we have learned in town. It seems that refugees have infiltrated the coastal area of our state and strangers are showing up in town. Now, the facts are, most of these people are just trying to find a safe place to get away from the war, but…"

James interrupted, somewhat abruptly, "Elvina, do you think you and your family will be able to stay on here without… without a man on the place?"

Elvina stood gazing at the fire, expression pensive. Turning slowly to gaze appealingly at her two visitors, she asked softly, "What else can we do? This place isn't much, but it's all we have! I have no training for any type of public work except housekeeping or washing clothes and that would mean that I'd have to leave the girls and Robinson alone every day. Besides? Where would we go? This terrible war is closing in on all sides. Who knows where it's safe anymore?"

"You could move in with us," Rosemary suggested. "You know the old saying … 'there's safety in numbers!'"

For a moment it looked as if Elvina would break into tears as she struggled to maintain her composure. "Thank you, dear friends," she replied, voice husky. "I know you sincerely mean what you just said. But we can't abandon our home. As for there not being a man on the place, I imagine there are far more homes without men folk around than with."

"You're right, of course," he agreed grudgingly. "But you all are so far away from everyone," he insisted.

"Well, maybe we're so far back in the woods no one will find us," Elvina countered hopefully. When neither of them said anything, she tried to be more reassuring. "We'll manage. We'll make it! I... I can't worry about what may happen. One day at a time is about all I can handle right now. Besides," she continued, "we're not entirely alone. We have the Lord."

"Vi, that sounds real good," James replied irritably, "and I don't mean to belittle your admirable faith, but where was the Lord when John was so sick?"

Elvina sat down on the end of the bench and sat looking at James thoughtfully for such a long moment that he squirmed slightly in his chair. When she answered, her voice was steady and confident. "We mustn't blame God for John's untimely death. John wouldn't stay in bed. There was nothing I could say, or do, to prevent him from abusing himself. For some reason, God didn't see fit to perform a miracle and spare his life, but I don't feel that God has deserted us."

It was Rosemary who broke the long silence that followed. "Vi, we don't mean to meddle, or interfere in your private affairs, but you and the children are like... like family. We can't help but be concerned!"

"And I understand," Elvina nodded, eyes filling. "I... I love you both for caring, and appreciate your concern more than we can ever tell you. But this is our home. There just isn't any better way that I can see. Besides... the children don't want to leave either," she explained glancing in the girl's direction, assured by the vigorous shaking of their heads in agreement.

James stood up rather impatiently and walked over to stand near the fire. Seemingly lost in thought, he stood gazing into the flames.

"We really must be going, Vi," Rosemary smiled, tone gentle. "It will be dark soon, and there are the chores to be seen after." The women embraced silently, both struggling painfully to keep their emotions under control. "I... I think I know how you feel, Vi," Rosemary said softly, pushing her friend from her to look deep into her eyes. "I wouldn't want to leave my home, either."

Elvina nodded, smiling her appreciation. "Thank you, dear precious friends. With the help of the good Lord and friends like you and James, we'll make it!" Then, remembering the sassafras tea she had put on to make, exclaimed, "Goodness! You can't leave without having a cup of tea. You're going to have a cold ride home!"

"I thought you'd never ask!" James smiled, his serious mood gone. "But it will have to be a quick one," he cautioned.

Elvina hurried to set out the cups. Suddenly she stopped dead still, expression grim. "Oh, my! I've been so concerned with my own troubles, I haven't even asked about Doug and Wray! Have you had any news from them lately?"

Rosemary just shook her head, eyes filling. "No, not since the last letter we told you about. We just know they are together, or were, which makes it easier, somehow."

Elvina nodded. "I'm so thankful Rob and Jim aren't old enough to go! John was so opposed to this war ... any war. If he had lived and they started recruiting older men, I don't know what his reaction would have been. It's unthinkable that here in our wonderful country, people are killing each other; yet, it's happening." She moved toward the table with the tea. "You two are remarkable people," she said softly, filling the cups. "Here you are, your boys off in the war somewhere... not knowing for sure where they are, or... or what's happened to them, yet, you come over here to see about us. You make me feel so... so unworthy!"

"Nonsense, Vi!" Rosemary objected, sipping the hot tea. "It's not going to make it any better or worse to sit down and worry about things all the time. Besides, when we are over here, we escape our own problems for a while. So, don't throw us too many bouquets," she admonished, attempting cheerfulness.

James finished his tea, then called to Jim who was talking to Melinda and Liza in the back of the room. "Come on, Jim! Time to go!"

They all walked outside to the surrey. "Tell Rob we're sorry we missed him," James called over his shoulder, assisting Rosemary into the vehicle.

"He'll be disappointed that he didn't get to see you," Elvina smiled.

James untied the reins and slapped the team lightly. In a matter of minutes they were rolling down the road toward home.

As the surrey passed from sight, Elvina turned to the girls who stood staring sadly after their departing friends. "Girls," she coaxed, placing an arm around each of them, "We need to get the chickens fed!"

"Ma?" Melinda asked, her voice trembling slightly. "Maybe Mr. James' is right! Maybe we can't make it without Pa." A sob caught in her throat.

"I... I wish Mr. James wouldn't talk like that," Liza wailed. "He... he scares me talking that way!"

"Now, you two listen to me!" Elvina scolded gently. "Rosemary and James are just concerned for us. We are going to be all right. Like I told them, we'll just take it one day at a time! And right now, the chickens are hungry! Now, off with you!"

Alone in the cabin, Elvina started preparations for supper. The trauma of John's death had pushed the war threat out of her mind, but James' solemn warning had brought it back with stark reality. "But we aren't any different from hundreds of other families whose men folk have gone off to fight," she reasoned silently, trying to bolster her courage. The latest news from town was that thirteen of the Southern states had seceded from the Union, and the Confederacy had elected Jefferson Davis as its President. "Yes," she said brokenly to the empty room. "Whether we wanted any part of it or not, war is upon us." She leaned her head against the mantelpiece. "Oh, John, how I need you," she whispered brokenly, the hot tears rushing unheeded down her cheeks.

* * * *

Robinson stood wearily watching Mr. Tom carefully skim the film from the last pan of syrup cooking over the furnace. The sun had just disappeared behind the trees in the west, silhouetting the man and the furnace. Night was fast approaching and Robinson was beginning to feel a little apprehensive about his long walk home in the dark. But he didn't want to mention leaving before Mr. Tom had given him permission.

This was the last day of the syrup making and all of the workers had pushed a little harder trying to get through early. But there were a few things that couldn't be hurried ... like the plodding mules trudging around and around the giant juicer, or the slow-bubbling syrup cooking over the hot furnace. Robinson proudly recalled that he had helped with just about every operation involved, from stripping the long leaves from the cane in the fields to feeding the stalks through the juicer.

Robinson shivered, suddenly aware of the encroaching night cold. He walked over to get his jacket from a fence post where he had hung it earlier. The mules had been unhitched and led away to the barn for food and rest. The only task uncompleted was the cooking off of the last pan of syrup and the clean up that followed. Sighing with relief, Robinson noted that Mr. Tom was walking to the end of the pan where the stopper could be pulled and the jugs filled.

"That's the last of hit, Son," he announced shortly. "Guess we can shut 'er down." He opened the furnace door and started pulling the coals out with a long-handled metal rake. "Bring me a bucket of water from that there barrel, Son. We don't want no live coals left here. Wind might cause some mischief during the night."

Before Mr. Provine had finished his instructions, Rob hurried to carry out the task. Bringing water to soak the pan had been one of his daily duties.

"We'll just let 'er soak tonight, Rob," Mr. Tom informed him, spitting a stream of tobacco juice to the side. "Hit's gettin' a mite late, young feller. Yore Ma's gonna be worried 'bout you. Best you hit the road. Don't you worry none 'bout yore 'lasses! I'll fetch them over later."

"Yes, Sir!" Robinson agreed much relieved. "Thanks, Mr. Tom!"

"You bet," the older man answered with a slight weary wave.

Robinson restricted his gait to a walk as long as he figured he was in hearing distance of Mr. Tom, but just as soon as he hit the main road, he took off at a fast run. There was still enough light to see the outline of the roadbed, but he thought with dread about the long stretch of pine forest that was ahead.

As he had anticipated, the road completely disappeared in the shadows of the wooded area. He had to force himself to a slow walk in order to find his way. A slight rustling in the bushes caught his attention, and he felt a tingling sensation up and down his spine. He stopped dead still, listening, his pulse thundering in his ears. Then, loud and clear, he heard a twittering and sighed with relief. "Just birds getting ready to roost for the night," he concluded as he started moving again. Unconsciously his pace quickened, and only when he stumbled on a rut and fell to his knees, did he slow his pace again. Burrowing his head down so that his coat collar came up around his ears, he hurried as fast as the deep ruts and holes would permit.

The autumn chill bit at his nose and face, causing his eyes to water and his nose to drip. He strained his eyes trying to see where he was going, but the hills that rose steeply on both sides and the limbs of the dense pines cut out even a flicker of starlight. The urge within him to break and run was close to panic and his teeth chattered uncontrollably - partially from cold but mainly from fear. How glad he was the weather was cold! At least he didn't have to worry about snakes crawling about.

A small animal, evidently frightened by Robinson's faltering footsteps, scurried away through the dry leaves, its movements creating monumental sounds in the sea of blackness that pressed on every side. His eyes ached from staring into the darkness, and he had to continually wipe the water from his eyes. The tingling sensation was running up and down his spine again, and he could almost feel something reaching out to grab him. Suddenly he thought he saw a faint light ahead through the trees. He wiped his sleeve across his face to clear his vision. What could it be? Who would be out this time of night? Was it refugees he'd been hearing about? Or even soldiers? He stopped dead still, his breath coming in shaky gasps. Should he continue or go back? But how could he admit to Mr. Tom that he was afraid to go home alone? Grimly he clenched his teeth together and a muscle bulged along the side of his jaw. No! He wouldn't admit that he was a coward! Resolutely he moved forward, one faltering step after another, his heart beating furiously and his whole body taut with anxiety and dread. He came to a curve in the road, and his spirits rose. He wasn't far from the open fields. As he moved cautiously around the bend, it took a full moment for him to realize what was taking place. There, peeping through the trees, glowing red in the darkness, was a moon as large as his ma's wash pot. As it climbed higher, it lit up the whole sky, and the road ahead resembled a ribbon of moonlight. With a yelp of relief, he took off at a gallop.

Later, sitting in the warm kitchen with his ma and sisters, his stomach full of baked sweet potatoes and fried meat, he told them about his trip home and even laughed a little in the telling.

And he was proud, too. Proud that he had been allowed to take his pa's place at the mill. Proud that he had been able to supply his family with molasses for the coming year. Somehow, he felt that his pa was proud of him, too, wherever he was, and that seemed to ease some of the pain he always experienced when thinking of his pa.

But, if he could have looked into the future, the fear of that dark road would have appeared next to nothing as compared to what was ahead. The War Between the States that had been creeping closer and closer to their world would become their war, too, sweeping across their lives and leaving pockmarks that would never be erased. A time when the peaceful activity of making molasses would become only a memory of something that happened in another world; another time; where death no longer struck as an indifferent act of nature, but as an instrument devised by man to wipe out thousands of lives with only one goal in mind; to destroy, to conquer, and to control. And all of it would be done in the name of justice and for the betterment of mankind

CHAPTER 7

Robinson was conscious of the clock striking. He had not counted all the gongs, but he knew there had been a lot. This meant that it was getting very late. His recall of past events had cost him needed sleep.

Restlessly he turned on his side. "I must get to sleep," he thought impatiently, punching the feather pillow into a more comfortable position.

Elvina was the first to awaken the next morning. It was still dark when she threw back the light cover, eased from her bed and pulled her nightgown over her head. She picked up her work dress from the back of the straight chair where she had spread it the night before and slipped into it. Stooping, she felt for her cotton stockings and high top shoes, finding them in the dark without any difficulty.

Easing her way toward the bedroom door she was careful not to awaken the girls sleeping in the large double bed on the other side of the room. Allowing them to sleep until she had breakfast ready was her way of indulging them a bit.

In the main room near the fireplace, she sat down in her rocker, quietly placing her shoes and stockings on the floor. The thick stockings went on first, and then she loosened the strings of her shoes. As the high tops slid over her ankles, she winced from the contact. Her feet had not yet toughened enough to prevent soreness. In a few moments the shoes were laced and tied without the benefit of light.

Sitting up straight in the chair, she reached into the pocket of her dress and brought forth the curved comb and hairpins that she had removed from her hair the night before. Pulling the comb through her long hair several times to remove the tangles, she then wound it into a tight flat bun on top of her head, pinning it securely. It would be cooler this way, as well as not hindering the smooth fit of her bonnet when she went to work in the fields later.

For a long moment she just sat in the rocker gently rocking back and forth. The clock on the mantle struck the half-hour reminding her of the passing time. Quickly she arose and walked over to the hearth. Lifting down the poker from its peg, she exposed the red coals from their cover of ashes and laid some kindling on the glowing mass. In a few seconds the kindling was blazing brightly.

She heard the familiar creaking of Robinson's bunk as he turned over, and she knew that he was beginning to wake up. Pulling a small splinter from a piece of wood, she held it to the fire until it was burning brightly. Moving over to the table she touched the wick of the candle with the flame. It caught immediately, the flame bulging yellow while smoke spiraled upwards. She blew out her small torch and threw it into the fire. The soft yellow glow from the candle encompassed the room, gently prodding Robinson that it was time to get out of bed.

Throwing back the thin coverlet, he sat up on the side of the bunk, the timbers groaning under the burden of his weight. For a few minutes he sat with his head in his hands waiting for the grogginess to go away. With sleep still making his movements slow, he reached for his pants where he had stepped out of them the night before. Mechanically he pulled them on over the short underwear, which had served as his sleeping clothes. He slipped into his shirt, leaving the buttons unfastened.

Walking across the room to the water bucket, he picked up the gourd dipper and partially filled the wash pan with water.

"Good morning, son," Elvina spoke cheerfully from across the room.

"Good morning," he mumbled as he bent over the pan to splash his face several times with the cool liquid. Reaching for the rough homespun towel hanging on a peg nearby, he rubbed his sparse stubble of beard vigorously until it was dry. He opened the cabin door, and picking up the pan, flung the remains of his mini bath into the yard. He replaced the pan on the shelf and then turned to remove the large milk bucket from its peg. He dipped several dippers of water into the pail before making his way out the door and down the path to the barn. It was not yet good daylight, but he had no difficulty in following the familiar path.

The ground was cold and heavy dew on the grass caused bits of dead leaves and trash to stick to his bare feet. Just inside the hallway of the barn near the ladder, he set the milk bucket down and started the climb to the hayloft, remembering the terror this job once held for him as a child.

Dawn was breaking in earnest as he made his way back to the house with the pail of milk. His gaze traveled to the nearby fields that were already planted and the plowed ones not yet bedded. Subconsciously his pace quickened.

Elvina had breakfast ready when he re-entered the cabin. The girls were up and dressed in their plain, long-sleeved dresses. They all sat down to their usual breakfast of biscuits, molasses and butter, washed down with cold sweet milk that had been cooling in a crock all night in the springhouse.

Robinson was the first to finish eating. Without comment, he arose and left the house again, this time to harness the mules.

"We must hurry, girls," Elvina prodded gently as she started clearing the table.

"Some day I'm going to be rich and I'll never have to work in the fields again," Liza pouted.

"We know," Elvina replied, forcing patience, "but for the time being, we need to get the corn planted, young lady!"

Melinda's reaction was to swing her long slender legs over the bench and stand up, stretching her arms above her head.

"How graceful she is," Elvina thought, her eyes reflecting a touch of sadness. "She's like a beautiful swan without a lake."

When ready for the field, the girls were protected from head to toe from the sun and soil. Gloves made from old socks, from which the ends had been cut off to allow more use of the fingertips, protected their hands. Their bonnets were elaborate pieces of headgear made from homespun material with the front section extending many inches from their foreheads. The headpiece was held erect by wooden staves inserted in inch-wide slits that had been painstakingly created by rows of tiny hand stitches. The staves were obscured from view by a small ruffle around the outer edge. For coolness and ventilation, the crown of the bonnet was buttoned to the stave sections, full enough to create a deep scallop between each button. A deep flounce around the sides and back came well below the high necklines of their dresses, the design of which was to keep the sun off their necks. Not one single ray of sunlight could touch their faces as along as they kept their bonnets on, and this was of utmost importance. A southern genteel lady would never think of letting her face and hands become sun tanned and rough to the touch.

From a nail on the storeroom wall in the barn, Melinda and Liza removed their work aprons that Elvina had especially sewn for them for planting seeds. Large pockets across the front provided a pouch for the seeds that they would drop by hand.

Melinda picked up a large sack of seed corn and handed it to Liza, then reached for the hoes. They had just started toward the field when they heard their mother calling, "Girls, wait a minute." They turned to see Elvina hurrying toward the spring, holding up a wooden water bucket as way of explanation.

"Liza, we forgot our drinking water again," Melinda groaned. "I'll run back and get it."

Melinda joined her mother at the spring where she was dipping cold water from the holding trough into the bucket. When it was full, she handed it to Melinda. "Thanks, Ma! We'll see you later," Melinda said cheerfully, her slender body bending slightly under the load.

Elvina nodded. "I wish my girls didn't have to work so hard," she thought sadly. But, then, her gaze traveled to the vegetable garden where young tender plants waved in the sun, and on to where the seeds planted in the fields were already pushing through the warm earth. A tremendous feeling of gratitude swept over her, crowding out her previous troubled thoughts.

"Oh, dear God," she breathed. "Thank you for our good health and all the blessings that are ours. Forgive, me, Lord, for daring to complain."

Turning in haste, she hurried back up the hill to the cabin. There were greens to be picked and washed, potatoes to be peeled and boiled, and bread to be baked before she joined the others in the field.

CHAPTER 8

Robinson had several rows bedded for planting by the time Melinda and Liza joined him in the cornfield. The unhurried movements of the girls irritated him, and as he passed them with his mule and plow, he was tempted to tell them "get-busy!" However, quarrels had erupted in the past by his so-called "bossing them around," therefore he stared doggedly at the ground peeling back from the tip of his plow and kept his silence.

They all worked steadily for some time with the heat from the climbing sun bearing down unmercifully. Liza pushed her bonnet back and wiped the perspiration off her face with her sleeve. "This heat is awful!" she grumbled. "My dress is already wet with sweat and sticking to my legs!"

"Better pull that bonnet back down or you'll be having to sleep with buttermilk on your face again," Melinda cautioned.

"I don't care!" Liza retorted. "Who's going to see us, or care, anyway?"

Melinda worked on in silence but a tirade of disturbing thoughts was troubling her. It was true what Liza had said. Most of the unattached males they knew were either much younger than they, or too old, or grass widowers like Will Rhodes whose wife had died in childbirth.

Liza yanked her bonnet back into place. "We're going to be old maids and have to work in these fields the rest of our lives," she wailed, viciously wiping away the angry tears.

It was Melinda's turn to stop and push her bonnet back, blinking against the salty perspiration that had seeped into her eyes. She rubbed her eyes with her sleeve. "Liza, you ought to be ashamed for talking that way! At least we have a home left and fields to work! You better not let Ma hear you talk like that!"

"I know," she whimpered defensively, stamping her foot more from frustration than anger, eyes filling with tears again. "It's just that I hate it so, Melinda," she finished lamely, defeat in her voice.

Melinda didn't answer, just pulled her bonnet back in place and resumed her digging. "Who would have me, anyway?" she questioned silently, agreeing with Liza. "Men like short women with large breasts," she reasoned sadly, glancing down at her front, dismayed, as always, that the contour of her small breasts was almost undetectable beneath her plain dress.

They heard Robinson's "Whoa" nearby and looked up to see him leaning against the plow handle, hat in hand, pulling a large sweat rag from his back pocket. "Where'd you put the water bucket?" he asked while impatiently mopping his face.

Turning loose of her hoe handle with one hand, Melinda pointed to a thick clump of bushes at the far end of the field. Robinson stuffed the rag back into his hip pocket, replaced his hat, and called "Giddy up" to the mule.

At the end of the row he stopped the mule again and wrapped the reins securely around the plow handle. He walked over to the bushes Melinda had indicated and removed the bucket from the shade.

Bringing the rim up to his mouth, he cautiously blew a leaf out of the way that had fallen into the water and then drank lustily. His thirst satisfied, he replaced the bucket and then dropped wearily to the ground in the shade, his gaze watching the rhythmical movements of the girls. Melinda dug the holes, Liza followed dropping in the seed and then covered the dirt firmly over them. Occasionally Melinda would dig with great vigor as she cut away some determined root that had escaped the sharp blade of Robinson's plow. As he sat watching the mechanical movements of the girls, his former impatience was forgotten. In its place was a deep yearning to remove them from the drudgery of the field, the stifling heat, and the grueling toil.

"But it's easy now compared to the years after Sherman gutted our land!" he thought bitterly, getting to his feet and heading back to the plow. His jerky movements as he untied the reins revealed the pent up tension within him. His eyes narrowed grimly and his jaws clenched in anger, as he recalled the terror and horror of the war imposed upon them. The deprivation and hunger it left in its wake. Remembering always kindled the smoldering anger within him that the passing years had not been able to quench.

As he turned the mule and started down another row, he recalled that it had been Leonard Mattison, the one-time local schoolmaster, who had provided them with advance warning regarding Sherman's plans to "sweep" across Georgia. Mr. Mattison had gone to Jonesboro on business and had come back with the terrifying news that Atlanta had been burned; that from Atlanta, Sherman had started his "march to the sea" and that the Union army had orders to cut a path of destruction all the way to Savannah, a gigantic sweep that was to break the fighting spirit of the rebels.

The day Mr. Mattison had driven by their place to bring them the news, he had remained in his buggy stating that he was not making a social call; that there wasn't time to get out and come in; that he had to notify as many of the local people as possible about the invaders and their intentions. So, the four of them had stood rigidly by the side of his buggy listening to the dreadful announcement while fear caused their heads to pound and their hearts to beat wildly.

The mental image of Mr. Mattison's tight-lipped expression as he relayed the message to them that day would remain indelibly stamped in Robinson's memory. How grim and set his face had been, pale except for a couple of bright splotches on each cheekbone, eyes calm, yet, dark with anxiety. Hands once strong and firm as he guided the youth steadily in learning to write the letters of the alphabet and in applying the switch of discipline when needed, now shaking noticeably as they held the reins of the horse that seemed to sense the urgency. Yet, Robinson perceived, even though he was only a boy that it wasn't fear that made Mr. Mattison's hands shake, but the man's keen sense of awareness of what was ahead for his friends and neighbors. And Robinson was terribly afraid.

Mr. Mattison had tried to appear matter-of-fact; his voice low and steady. "Mrs. Stuart, I hate to be the one to bring you and your family such disturbing news, but from the stories in town, the war picture is not at all encouraging for the South. Sherman is supposed to have ordered houses and brush burned along the way to indicate the progress the Yankees are making through Georgia. He has been quoted as saying that he intends to 'make the interior of Georgia feel the weight of the war.' Seems like those Yankees are determined to cripple the South by burning and destroying, and most cases, stripping the countryside of every smidgen of food they can lay their dirty hands on. There is some room for hope, though, in that it's been rumored that in hardship cases, the soldiers have been ordered to be lenient somewhat, sparing the dwelling house at least. Since... since you are a widow woman with a family, things might not go quite so bad for you."

He paused, and when none of them said anything, continued grimly. "Sherman is quoted as saying that 'he's going to bring the South to its knees,' and unless there's some change, it looks as though they'll march smack through our part of the state."

Again he was silent, staring out across the fields. Then his gaze shifted back to them, coming to lock with Elvina's.

"Mrs. Stuart," he continued, lowering his voice as if somehow this would make the information he was relating less menacing, "there have been reports, also, of mistreatment of the womenfolk. Since you have these young girls, I felt that it was expedient that you be forewarned." Picking up the reins, he said hurriedly, "Well, I must hurry on. There are others that I must get the word to."

"Thank you, Mr. Mattison," his ma answered quietly, as if she were thanking him for a ride home, or some other commonplace neighborly act. "Do you have any idea how much time we have before the ... before the soldiers will get this far?"

"I'd say three, maybe four days. According to the reports, which may be completely unreliable, the soldiers are making twelve, maybe fifteen miles a day. Of course, there's always the possibility of scouts showing up most any time, you know," he advised, marveling at the calmness of Elvina's expression. So many of the women he had talked to on his round had become hysterical.

Mr. Mattison nodded goodbye, tipped his hat, and tapping his horse lightly on the flanks with the reins, was soon out of sight around the bend in the road. As if transfixed to the spots where they were standing, not a person moved until the buggy and its occupant had disappeared from view.

The girls were the first to speak.

"Ma, what are we going to do," Melinda asked, her voice barely audible.

"I'm scared, Ma," Liza wailed, starting to cry.

"Now, stop that, Liza," Elvina commanded, voice stern with reproach. "Crying isn't going to help anything." Turning, she started walking briskly toward the cabin. "It's getting late," she called over her shoulder. "There are chores to be done."

Back inside the cabin, Robinson reached for the milk bucket. After dipping some water into the pail, he headed for the barn. As he walked down the familiar path, loneliness and fear engulfed him and the need to have his pa near was so strong that he felt he couldn't bear it. A choking sob caught in his throat. "Oh, Pa... Pa," he whispered into the encroaching twilight. "What are we going to do! Oh, Pa, if only you were here."

He tried to imagine what it would be like when the soldiers came; what their actions would be. Would they strip their crib of all their corn, and their barn of all the hay? Would they take their cow and mule? What if they burned their house? Where would his family go? What would become of them? With things the way they had been since his pa had died, it had taken all they could do just to make enough food and money to survive. It had taken every cent they could rake and scrape just to pay the taxes each year. His twelve-year-old mind was incapable of handling such tortuous questions, and the anxiety made his stomach churn and he had to swallow hard and run wash his face in the watering trough to keep from throwing up.

As he began to feel a little calmer and hurried to finish his chores, his anxiety began to turn to anger. "I wish I could take Pa's gun and shoot the last one of them," he muttered, "and if I get half a chance," he vowed through clenched teeth, "I'll do just that!"

Back in the cabin Elvina had started preparations for supper. Outwardly she appeared composed and serene, but she was far from calm within. Never in all of her life had she felt so entirely alone or known such helpless fear. Always before when danger threatened, she had been comforted by the fact that she could call upon her neighbors, but this time, her neighbors were facing the same enemy, the same problems, and they all stood to lose everything that was dear in their lives. But the possibility of losing the family's few possessions was not what caused the paralyzing fear that now griped her heart. It was the thought of what might happen to her children, particularly the girls. She had read about during times of war how soldiers, who would never think of maligning women in their own community, would oftentimes act like animals, brutally assaulting women and young girls. She glanced at Melinda who was busily peeling potatoes at the table. Tall for the age of sixteen, willowy in her movements, dark hair framing a cameo face that was made even more beautiful by large gray eyes outlined by long black eyelashes that turned up slightly at the end. Shy, gentle Melinda, whose only association with the opposite sex had been sitting in church with a neighborhood boy.

In spite of the tension of the moment, glancing at Liza standing before the fireplace slowly stirring the contents in the black pot, her face still showing the traces of recent tears, brought a smile to Elvina's pale face. Dear, dear Liza, the highly emotional member of the family; the one who cried when she was angry, happy, or sad; quick to show anger, but equally eager toward reconciliation. Liza, with her mass of reddish brown hair that was as hard to tame and control as her spirit; fourteen years old, and yet, still such a child in so many ways. A child with a figure developed already like that of a mature woman. The horror of some brute mistreating either of them made Elvina's head pound with every pulse beat.

Her helplessness and the hopelessness of it all began to crowd in on her and she felt her control slipping. "I mustn't! I mustn't!" she kept telling herself over and over. "If I let go, the girls will become hysterical." If only she could just open the door and start running, and run and run until she fell exhausted and never had to get up again.

To hide her desperation, she walked to the back of the room, pretending to look for something, but instead, she turned to the only source of strength she had ever been able to fully rely upon. Silently, she began to pray.

"Ma?" Melinda called from across the room.

Elvina turned toward her daughter. "Yes?"

Melinda stared across the room at her mother's face for a long moment, then apparently satisfied that nothing was amiss, asked. "Ma, Mr. Mattison said the Union soldiers were taking all of the foodstuff. If this happens to us... to everybody, we won't have anything to eat this winter, or seed for planting next spring?"

Liza, her voice still quivering, was the next one to speak. "But, Ma! Where... where in the world can we hide anything? If we move our corn and peanuts into the woods, then the rain will ruin it, or rats and squirrels will eat it?"

Elvina walked back to stand before the fireplace, gazing thoughtfully into the fire. Silently the girls moved to stand on either side of her.

"Ma, what are we going to do?" Melinda asked anxiously.

"Now, girls, we must not panic. We'll think of something."

"But, what!" Liza insisted.

Elvina was relieved from having to respond to Liza's insistent questioning by Robinson coming through the door with the pail of milk. "Here's Robinson with the milk," she said, forcing cheerfulness. "I'll just strain it so we can put it in the springhouse right away to cool. Then, we'll get on with supper."

Robinson moved forward to hand the pail to his mother. As his arm reached out toward her, their eyes met, and the calmness that he saw there suddenly made him feel less frightened, but his stomach still felt as if it had a hard knot right in the middle.

Usually they took turns saying the blessing before meals, but this time, without waiting to inquire whose turn it was, Elvina bowed her head and in a calm voice, free of emotion, laid their petitions before the Master's throne of grace, asking for His guidance, mercy, and protection during this dark hour. She asked especially that the Comforter would take away their fears and grant them peace.

The prayer seemed to calm the womenfolk somewhat, but it brought little comfort to Robinson. Hadn't he prayed for his pa when he was so sick? Hadn't his ma prayed, too? Hadn't his pa died? No, he didn't put much confidence in prayer. He just didn't know for sure if there was a God out there somewhere, and if there was, would He really do anything about their trouble?

Hours later, while the others slept, Elvina tossed and turned restlessly, trying to conceive of some plan whereby she could protect the girls and salvage their food and livestock. Sending the girls away was out of the question. Where could they go? Travel to Boston through a war-torn country? Never! And besides, she hadn't heard from anyone back East for quite some time, now. And there was the problem of expense. Where would she get the money?

"Oh, dear Lord," she prayed fervently, her pillow wet with helpless, silent tears that ran unchecked down the sides of her face. "What are we doing to do?"

Finally she dropped off to sleep. But it wasn't a restful sleep, and she was awake long before dawn began to break, her head aching from tension.

"Where could the girls hide?" That was the question that tormented her as she turned restlessly from side to side in her bed. There was no cave or shelter in the woods, and even if there were, she would be uneasy unless they were discovered and completely at their captors' mercy. The outbuildings were completely out of the question for that would be the first place the soldiers would pillage.

She was certain from what Mr. Mattison had told them that every inch of the cabin would be ransacked from top to bottom. The bottom of the cabin! Under the cabin! Why, of course! That was the answer! "Thank you, Lord," she breathed.

She had breakfast on the table by the time dawn was breaking. There had been no problem of getting the others awake that morning. Elvina waited until they had all finished eating before she approached them with her idea.

"Children, I laid awake most of the night trying to figure out some way, or some place, that you girls might be safe. Now, you can't hide in the barn, or any of the outbuildings for the soldiers will surely ransack that first ... possibly burn them. We can't look to our neighbors for help for they are up against the same problems that we face. Hiding in the woods is out of the question because of no shelter, and besides, the risk of being discovered out there alone is too great!"

"Ma, I'm so scared," Liza wailed. "I... I wish Pa was here," she sobbed, tears running unheeded down her cheeks.

"I know, dear," Elvina consoled. She stood up and walked around the table to put an arm around each girl's shoulder. "I... I wish your pa was here, too, but even if he were alive, he might be off fighting in the war. We'll make it," she assured them, patting them on the shoulder, and pulling them close to her for a long moment. Walking over to the fireplace, she stood with her back to the fire, her hands clasped tightly, the only visible evidence of her own anxiety. In the early morning light, the pale faces of her family stared pathetically back at her, pinched and drawn, eyes dark with apprehension.

"Now, here's my idea," she ventured, forcing a casual approach. "You know how high the floor of the cabin is off the ground at this end. Your Dad and I hauled rocks and underpinned the house to make it warmer in the winter. Now, the soldiers will surely find the opening and search under the house. But, what if we stacked rocks and build a second wall across a few feet back from the fireplace? It would be close quarters for you girls, but you could hide there with ample food and water until the soldiers pass through. It's high enough under there that you could sit up, as well as lie down." When there was no immediate response from any of them, she asked, "Well, what do you think?"

Melinda was the first to speak. "But, Ma? Mr. Mattison said... well, he said that the Yankees were burning and destroying homes, too. What... what about you... and Robinson?"

Touched deeply by the young girl's concern, Elvina had to turn quickly and pick up the poker to stir the fire so that the others wouldn't see the quick tears in her eyes. "What's the matter with me?" she thought angrily. "I'm getting as emotional as Liza!" Over her shoulder, she replied almost flippantly, "Oh, they won't harm an old lady like me." Emotions under control, she turned to smile at them, a response that had become less frequent in the past few weeks. "And they would think twice about meddling with a big boy like Rob!" she assured them resolutely. Embarrassed by the attention suddenly focused upon him, even in loving jest, Robinson quickly changed the subject. "Ma, what about our corn... and other stuff?"

"Well, I've been trying to figure out something there, too," she replied. "If the soldiers are striping the countryside, and that's what the reports have indicated, not only will there be a shortage of food now, but we will have no seed for planting in the spring. There are quite a few empty jugs in the smokehouse that we could fill with seeds, but as yet, I haven't figured out a safe place for storing them. Too bad we don't know of a cave somewhere!"

Robinson jumped up from his chair, overturning it behind him. "Ma, on the side of the hill where our creek winds through the next hollow, there's a huge rock that sticks out just like a giant table. Jim and I dug a big hole under it last year for our secret hide-a-way. We could hide a few jugs there!"

"That might work," Elvina agreed thoughtfully. "Well, we won't find out sitting here. Girls, you start gathering large rocks, after you have fed the chickens and finished with your chores."

"There's a lot of rocks down by the spring," Liza suggested, crossing the room to get the dishpan.

"Let the dishes go for now, Liza," Elvina commanded sharply.

"I'll hitch the mule to the wagon after I've fed him," Robinson volunteered.

"We must hurry," Elvina prodded, as though it were necessary. "Now, girls, keep a sharp lookout at all times. Remember what Mr. Mattison said about scouts!" Walking over to the mantle, she removed John's big gun down from the rack and handed it to Melinda. "You know how to use this. Now, you keep it in the wagon at all times," she cautioned, her tone implying "no argument."

"Ma!" Robinson called excitedly from the doorway. "The Wheelers are here!"

Elvina, joining Robinson at the doorway, saw James helping Rosemary from their surrey, and then the two came hurrying toward the house. Elvina hurried down the steps, greeting them warmly.

Inside, Rosemary and James moved toward the fire to warm their hands. Usually, these two friends were always calm; seldom unruffled about anything. But that day, there was an air of nervousness about them that made the room tighten with tension.

"You two are out mighty early," Elvina remarked, trying to sound casual. "Your boys Doug and Wray? Have you heard from them?"

"No, there hasn't been any word at all. The last we heard, they were somewhere in East Tennessee," Rosemary replied, voice breaking.

"Thank you, Elvina, for your concern," James offered. "But we came over to check on you all. Have you talked with Leonard Mattison?"

"Yes... yes, he came by late yesterday afternoon."

"Then you know the Union Army's plans are to sweep across Georgia?"

"Sounds like some kind of horrible nightmare, doesn't it?" Elvina responded.

Rosemary interrupted. "Elvina, we... well, James and I, we don't like the idea of you and the others staying on here, with all the trouble that's brewing. We would feel a lot better if you'd come over to our place."

Elvina shook her head in disbelief. "Now, isn't this something! Your own home and lives, possibly, threatened, the same as ours, and you take the time to come over here to check on our welfare? What in the world have we ever done to deserve such love and loyalty?"

"It's because we do love you and are concerned for you, especially the girls," Rosemary replied softly. "Now, how about it?"

"I don't want you to think that I'm ungrateful, Rosemary, and you, too, James. But this is our home. We... we just can't walk off and abandon it. It's all we have in the world. But, thank you, dear precious friends, for offering."

"Elvina, you've got to be realistic!" James sputtered, ignoring her arguments entirely. "There's safety in numbers, and there's less chance of anything happening to y'all if we are together." James' normally ruddy complexion flushed even darker. "I don't think you fully realize just what...well, just what the situation might be for you and the girls!" he insisted, glancing furtively in the girls direction.

Elvina stood quietly, not answering, thinking sadly, "How white his hair has turned." Aloud, she said, "Again, I want you to know how much I appreciate your concern, James, more than I can ever put into words. But we are making plans to protect what we can... and ourselves. But actually, when you come down to the bare facts, what's one or more when you're facing an army?"

Rosemary, face pale and drawn, moved over by Elvina and placed her arm around the younger woman's shoulders. "Elvina, please change your mind, for our sakes. Come home with us. I beg you!" Lowering her voice, she whispered anxiously, "You must remember the girls!"

Elvina stood quietly gazing into the fire. "I don't want you and James to think me ungrateful," she re-emphasized, "but I've never believed in running from trouble."

"But this isn't just... trouble, Elvina! This is war!" James retorted.

"I know. But again, this is our home. If it isn't worth defending, then, how can we expect to be worthy of it? I'm sorry. I have to stay."

Rosemary wasn't ready to give up. Turning to the girls and Robinson, she asked, "What do you all think about your Ma's decision?"

Liza's chin quivered slightly as she locked her gaze on a knot in the floor, but for once said nothing. Melinda glanced at her mother, then without hesitating, said quietly, "If Ma thinks it's best for us to stay, then I'm with Ma." Robinson's response was brief but emphatic, "I'm with Ma!"

An uneasy quiet filled the room. Elvina was the first to break the silence. "Let me tell you about our plans, then maybe you won't be so worried." Hurriedly she told them about the planned hide-a-way under the house and their plan to hide the seeds.

James picked up his hat and headed for the door. "Well, it's plain to see we can't change your minds.

I'm going to check out this hiding place and see what I think. Come on, Robinson, let's go see if this crazy plan is possible."

"We should have been making more preparations than we have," Rosemary said thoughtfully as the door closed behind the men. "But we believed that it was just a matter of time before the South would win this terrible war and the boys would be back home."

Nodding, Elvina leaned her head on her arm against the mantle. "You know, Rosemary, when John died, I thought, 'This is the worst thing that could happen to anyone - to lose your mate, to be left with children to care for all alone.' But at least, someone else didn't cause John's death! This horrible war! Neighbor against neighbor! Brother against brother! Thousands of our countrymen killed and our country torn apart! And we all wonder, 'How did we let this happen? Why couldn't something be worked out to avoid bloodshed?' Up to now, my greatest concern has been to provide the needs for my family, but that's been overshadowed by the fear of my own countrymen coming in and plundering and stealing what livelihood we have been able to hold on to and that my daughters are in danger of being ravished. What happens to men that turns them into animals bent on destroying each other? Do they really believe the cause they fight for so nobly justifies such inhuman behavior? And people like you and me, who have never hurt anyone deliberately in our lives, who are content to live and let live, are caught up in it just as much as those that perpetrated all of this madness. Probably, when the last shot has been fired and the smoke has settled, few will realize that it wasn't so much a cause of justice as it was a cause of greed. Greed caused this war in our country, and greed will not let go until our nation is drenched in blood. Oh, Rosemary! Where is it all going to end?"

Rosemary shook her head slowly, expression somber, her face suddenly drained and old. "I don't know," she said, voice desolate, eyes filling. "I know my boys don't believe in slavery, but, they had a deeper loyalty to the South."

The door opened and James stuck his head inside. "We've checked the space out under the cabin and I believe this plan of your just might work. Come on, Melinda and Liza. Let's haul rocks!"

With the four of them working it didn't take long to haul enough rocks to build the enclosure. When it was finished, there was room enough for the girls to sit upright, or to stretch out to sleep. The entrance faced the low end of the cabin so that single large rocks could be pushed across the opening once the girls were inside. Robinson brought hay from the barn, spreading a thick covering over the entire ground area of the enclosure.

The Wheelers could not be persuaded to stay for lunch. The good-byes among the womenfolk were tearful. James covered up his anxiety by hurrying Rosemary with the caustic remark that she was as "slow as molasses on a cold winter morning."

"God bless and keep you both," Elvina whispered as she embraced them.

CHAPTER 9

The large table-rock was located less than a half mile from the cabin but in order to get to its location, it was necessary for them to descend the hill on which the spring was located and follow its stream to the creek below. The table rock, according to Robinson, was located about half way up the hill on the other side of the creek and could only be reached by climbing another steep incline.

The journey up the rocky hill was of no consequence for Robinson. However, the womenfolk, encumbered by their long dresses, managed the climb by grasping the trunks of small saplings growing in the shade of the larger trees. The last part of the climb was especially precarious because of the huge slabs of slate colored rocks that made up the hillside between the creek and the table-rock.

The dirt beneath the table-rock was porous and crumbly which made it easy to loosen and remove. They were able to deepen the cavity by a couple of feet before their shovels hit solid rock. They concentrated then on widening the excavation area to the width of the rock. When they had finished, there was enough space beneath the rock to accommodate several jugs.

Early the next morning they headed for the rock, all of them loaded with jugs that they had filled the night before with dried-shelled peas, beans, corn, peanuts, wheat, and even some dried pepper pods. The most time consuming task had been removing the lint from the cottonseed so that less storage space would be required. They had used pieces of corncobs for stoppers, and as an extra precaution against moisture, placed corn shucks over the top of each jug, tying them securely with strips of corn shucks.

After they had finished pushing all of the jugs back under the rock, they piled large slabs of rock across the opening, working them into the hillside to resemble the rest of the area as much as possible. To hide any clue that digging had taken place, they piled leaves and debris over the fresh dirt that had been excavated. Then dead brush was placed over the area so that it would appear undisturbed.

The rocky hillside was familiar territory to Robinson, and when their task was completed, he was the first to start back down the precarious incline. Jumping lightly, while bracing himself from sapling to tree, he seemed totally unmindful of any danger of falling. Suddenly, his foot slipped, and he hit the ground on his backside. The loose rocks offered no resistance, and he started sliding down the bank feet first. The heels of his thick soled shoes struck a large slab of dark gray rock, and without any warning, the rock scooted forward, leaving a gaping hole in the side of the hill into which Robinson dropped out of sight before the others' horrified eyes.

Frantically calling Robinson's name, all three women scrambled down the hill as fast as their long skirts would permit, and upon reaching the opening, kept calling his name while peering anxiously into the darkness below them, "Robinson?" Elvina called sharply, her tone revealing her fear. "Are you all right?"

"Yeah, I… guess so," he replied in a trembling voice.

As their eyes became adjusted to the dark interior below, they could see Robinson slowly getting to his feet.

"Just stay right there," Elvina ordered. "We'll find a pole or something to pull you out."

"Here, Ma," cried Melinda, "use the shovel!"

As Robinson's eyes became accustomed to the dark, he looked around him in wonder. He seemed to be in a giant hole in the rock. His scalp prickled as he thought of snakes that might be hibernating in the crevices, and there was a large dark object in one corner that filled his young heart with fear. He stood perfectly still, not moving a muscle. There was movement overhead, and in a few moments he saw the spade end of the shovel descend through the opening. It took the combined strength of Elvina and Melinda to pull him out of the hole.

Once over the top, Robinson crawled over a few feet and sat down. He hugged his knees close to his chest to steady himself.

"Do you know what it looks like down there?" he asked breathlessly. "A small room! I'm going back to the house for a lantern and rope. I want to see what's down there!"

"Robinson, we don't have time for that!" Elvina reminded him anxiously.

"But, Ma! It's dry down there. It might be a hiding place for some of our other foodstuff."

Elvina hesitated, trying to decide what to do. Robinson took her silence as consent and scrambled to his feet. "I'll hurry," he called back over his shoulder as he made his way down the hill.

The women sat down on the rocks to wait. Robinson's disappearance had been terribly frightening. The girls chattered nervously, describing their reactions to the incident. But Elvina had only one thing on her mind. There was an army of Yankee soldiers headed their way. Time was running out.

Robinson must have run most of the way, as much as the rough terrain would permit, because it wasn't long before he was climbing up the hill again, panting with every breath.

"Sit down and catch your breath," Elvina cautioned as she tied the rope to the lantern's handle.

"Let me, Ma," Robinson begged, his breath still coming in gasps.

Robinson lowered the lantern into the hole while the others hovered close by. It was a small underground room of sorts, carved from the rock by some curious act of nature that had been occupied by human beings in times past, evidenced by a large grass mat in one corner, and some earthenware jugs lined up against the wall.

"Ma, I'm going back down," Robinson said, excitement kindling his voice. He pulled the lantern back up and untied it, handing it to Elvina. He reached behind him and tied the rope to a nearby tree, then slid back down into the hole, holding on to the rope. "Hand me the lantern," he called to the ones topside.

"It is a room," he verified as the flickering candlelight exposed the area. He walked cautiously around the space, holding the light high, investigating the walls, the ceiling, describing his findings to the three pairs of eyes peering down into the hole. He pulled the corncob stopper from one of the jugs and poured out some of the liquid. "The jugs are filled with water," he informed them, his excitement growing. Propped lengthwise against the wall was a makeshift ladder, its rounds held fast by leather bindings. Robinson moved it over against the wall near the opening in the top. Gingerly testing each step for stability, he climbed up the ladder, and finally handed the lantern to one of the girls. He had no difficulty in pulling himself over the topside this time. Carefully they pushed the large flat stone back over the hole, marveling at the way the tight fit would not allow water to seep into the pit.

Momentarily the marching enemy was forgotten as they headed for home, their conversation centered on the underground room.

"I don't think it's been used for some time," Robinson surmised. "I can't believe it has been there all the time! We've played around it and near it many times."

"I noticed a musty odor," Elvina added. "Was it very damp down there?"

"No. It was cool and dry. I didn't see any water signs, either. I believe we could store stuff in there."

"What if the ones that used it return and find our things and take them?" Liza asked.

"Well, I can't see that we have much to lose," Melinda countered.

Hurriedly they ate a midday meal of cold bread and molasses. Then, their task began of transferring what they could of their corn, potatoes, turnips, and wheat to the new hiding place. The terrain was too steep and rocky to use the mule, so they loaded cotton sacks with as much as each person could carry on their backs. They decided against putting any meat in the hiding place for fear that a flesh-eating animal might somehow uncover the opening.

Sleep did not come easily for Elvina that night even though she was exhausted both physically and mentally. Her mind kept racing wildly. If only there was someway to save their meat. She could think of no place except to bury it, and if some animal didn't dig it up, it would soon spoil. If they hid it under the house, some dog might come sniffing around and give the girl's hiding place away. Where would the most likely place be that the soldiers might miss and where the meat would be safe from predators? The smokehouse, of course! We'll bury it under the meatbox. She was so excited that it was hard not to get up right then and wake the others. Finally she slept, but at the first light of dawn she was awake. Quickly she got out of bed and started pulling on her clothes.

"Melinda! Liza! Wake up girls. We have a lot to do!"

In the kitchen she walked over to Robinson's bunk and touched him lightly on the shoulder. He sat up so quickly that it startled her. He must not have been sleeping very soundly either, she thought as she turned back.

"What is it, Ma? Are the soldiers coming?" he asked anxiously, throwing back the covers and reaching for his pants.

"No! I'm sorry if I startled you. But I need your help. I think I've figured out a place where we can hide what meat we have."

While Robinson finished dressing and putting on his shoes, Elvina uncovered the hot coals from the ashes and laid some wood on the fire.

"What are you going to do, Ma?" Robinson asked, shivering from the early morning chill in the air.

"The only place I can think of that our meat wouldn't be found is to bury it, and the only place that it would stay dry is in the smokehouse. We'll bury the two cured hams in the smokehouse under the meat box.

Elvina already had her coat on and was heading for the door. Robinson followed, reaching for his coat hanging on a peg near the doorway as he passed by. "You get the shovel from the barn and I'll get some shucks from the crib," she directed over her shoulder as she hurried out into the dew-covered world.

It took a great deal of tugging and pushing from both of them to move the heavy wooden meat box away from the wall. There hadn't been any meat in it for a long time for there wasn't any salt to be had in which to pack the meat. What meat they had was hanging from the rafters where they had cured it with hickory smoke.

Robinson placed the sharp end of the shovel against the dirt floor and punched hard with his foot. Nothing gave.

"Ma, this dirt's as hard as a rock," he grumbled.

"You keep working at it while I go get the pick," she said, disappearing through the doorway.

When the hole was finally deep enough, they lined the bottom carefully with several layers of overlapping shucks. She untied the hams from the rafter and placed them, along with the smoked sausage, in a cotton sack.

107

After the meat was arranged in the hole, they placed another thick layer of shucks over the meat.

"Let's find some flat rocks and lay them on top of the shucks," she suggested. "Maybe the rocks will help keep the dirt from sifting down through the shucks."

Finally they filled in the hole with dirt, packing it down firmly. More flat rocks were placed on top to camouflage the fresh digging. Then Elvina rubbed the tops of the rocks with some of the greasy dirt from the meat-smoking area.

They heard the door to the cabin slam and saw Liza walking toward the smokehouse, eyes puffed from sleep, a puzzled expression on her face. She gazed at the tools in their hands and the pile of dirt on the smokehouse floor.

"What have you been doing?" she asked, rubbing her eyes.

Before they could answer, Melinda appeared behind her, shivering from the cold.

"You'll both catch your death out here," Elvina scolded. "Go back inside and get some warm clothes on. We'll be in directly and tell you all about it."

They shoveled the rest of the loose dirt into buckets and scattered it in the garden. The final act was to push the heavy meatbox back to its original location.

They brushed the loose dirt from their clothing. A low "moo" came from the direction of the barn.

"I think the old cow is telling you something," Elvina said, glancing at Robinson, and for just a moment their eyes met. Even though neither of them said a word, the question was there, as if it had been verbalized. "How long will we have a cow to milk?"

The aroma of fried ham met them at the door.

"Do you think the meat will keep in the ground?" Melinda questioned after hearing what they had done.

Robinson echoed his mother's words from the day before. "Well, we don't have much to lose. The soldiers won't leave it hanging in the smokehouse."

"Do you think they will get here today, Ma?" Liza asked, face pale.

"I don't know, dear," Elvina replied, voice heavy with weariness. "Guess we'll know soon enough," she replied as she poured some water in the wash pan. "That ham smells good. Robinson and I have worked up a good appetite," she added, faking cheerfulness.

"I... I don't think it's fair," Melinda blurted, surprising everyone by breaking into tears. "We haven't done anything to them, or... or anybody!"

"No, it's not fair," Elvina agreed quietly. "But whether it's fair or not isn't going to change a thing."

CHAPTER 10

The waiting had been the worst part. They had worked feverishly for what seemed like weeks, but which in reality had only been a few days, trying to protect themselves from an enemy they had never seen, and the knowledge of whom had been acquired by rumors and stories told by refugees who had come into town. Remembering her earlier years in Boston and the trip South with John, it was difficult for Elvina to grasp the full extent of the situation. It was inconceivable to her that the people of the United States were so divided; that they had become mortal enemies; and that they were killing each other by the thousands. All of the war talk preceding the actual outbreak and the last four years of war had not helped her to understand the necessity for it. Now, in a matter of hours, unless God intervened, the war would envelop her family, too. She didn't allow herself to dwell on the possible consequences.

It was the middle of the afternoon of the fourth day following Mr. Matheson's visit. A heavy blanket of clouds had obscured the sun all day. A cold wind whipped the leafless limbs of the trees and the family's dejected spirits matched the bleakness of the landscape.

A bright fire burned in the fireplace, its flames bathing the four of them with warmth. The iron teakettle made a hissing sound as steam escaped through its spout, the noise intermingling with the soft thud of corn kernels falling into pans.

The family had objected to the corn shelling. "What's the use?" they had wailed. "The Yankees will take it all, anyway!" But Elvina had argued that they could put it in the loft of the cabin. Just, maybe, the soldiers would think the corn in the crib was all they had.

But Elvina's motive for keeping them busy was far more subtle. Keeping them occupied at some task helped relieve the tension and stress.

Abruptly Robinson set his half-filled pan aside and stood up, his hands impatiently whisking the cornhusks off his pant's legs. "Ma, I'm going to ride up the road a ways on Ole Mat to see if I can find out something!" There was a long silence as the startled womenfolk stared at him with wide-eyed concern. "I'll be real careful," he added lamely, seeing the dark anxiety in their eyes.

"Ma! Don't let him go!" Liza begged.

Elvina hesitated; questions running riot in her mind. How near were the troops? How dangerous would it be to let him go? Surely no harm would be done to a young boy? Since Robinson was so dependable and mature for his years, shouldn't she trust his judgment? Her maternal instinct recoiled against letting him out of her sight, yet she knew he was wise beyond his physical size or chronological age.

"All right," she agreed skeptically, "but be very careful," she cautioned. Then, as if to justify her decision, added, "It would help to have some advanced warning."

In less than an hour they saw Robinson and Ole Mat returning around the bend in the road. Ole Mat,

111

not used to being slapped on the flanks with such rapidity and force was laboring along at an ungainly gait, ears laid back, eyes rolling wildly.

The womenfolk hurried outside to meet Robinson. Ole Mat had not come to a full stop before Robinson was sliding off his back. "They're coming!" he gasped. "They're only a few miles away!"

Melinda, clasping her hands over her mouth as if to stifle a scream, stood gazing at Robinson, eyes wide with fear.

Liza burst into tears.

The only visible reaction from Elvina was a tightening of the muscles around her mouth and eyes. "After you've fed Ole Mat, Son, and tied him in the woods again, please check on the cow to make sure she hasn't broken loose from her stake. After you've fed and watered her you might see if you could milk her. It's early but it might be your only opportunity for a while."

Robinson nodded. Grasping the reins, he hurried toward the barn.

"All right, girls, let's get a move on! They might send scouts ahead," Elvina cautioned, trying to appear calm.

"Ma?" Melinda questioned, anxiety making her voice sound low and unnatural. "What if they set fire to the house?"

Elvina started walking briskly toward the cabin, the girls close behind. "We've discussed that possibility before, Melinda, and we'll just have to cross that bridge when we come to it," she answered matter-of-factly, fighting hard to suppress the panic that threatened to overcome her. Hoping to conceal her own fear, she barraged the girls with last minute instructions. "Liza, open the gate to the pig pen and turn the pigs loose. Shut the gate so they can't get back in. Just maybe they will go into the woods and the soldiers won't be able to catch them. Melinda, close the hen house door. If the hens can't get inside, they'll fly up in the trees to roost."

As the girls ran to carry out their assigned tasks, Elvina hurried back into the cabin. Quickly she brought wool blankets from the bedroom. In a clean white cloth she wrapped baked sweet potatoes, cold corn pone, and fried pork. Lastly, she included a half dozen small fruit tarts, sweetened with molasses. Picking up the clean jug she had ready, she rushed outside hurrying toward the spring.

The girls were back in the cabin when she returned, their faces flushed from the vigorous activity. She handed the jug of water to Liza.

"Your blankets and food are over there," she said, jerking her head toward the table. "Don't forget your bucket for relieving yourselves. And, here, take this with you," she added, reaching for the musket above the mantle.

"No, Ma!" Melinda objected vehemently. "You keep the gun!"

"It would only be taken! Now, let's not waste precious time arguing!" Elvina retorted impatiently. "Now remember, girls. You're not to come out unless they set fire to the cabin. If possible, I'll check with you occasionally by rapping twice on the floor to make sure all's well with you. You'll answer the same way. All right?"

Nodding stiffly, the girls headed toward the door. Suddenly Melinda turned abruptly, and dropping the blankets and food on the floor, threw her arms around her mother. Liza, setting the jug of water on the floor and placing the gun beside it, did the same. For a long moment the three of them stood quietly holding fast to each other. Elvina felt quick tears burning her eyes. With a gentle shove and a kiss on each girl's cheek, she pushed them away. "Hurry, now," she urged, patting them reassuringly on their shoulders. "I don't want the soldiers to know there are two beautiful young ladies here!"

"Ma," Melinda said in a hushed tone, "I... I can't stand to leave you alone!"

"I won't be alone. Robinson will be with me, and we will all trust in the good Lord to bring us through safely. Now, try not to worry. Thank Heaven the weather is not freezing cold," she added matter-of-factly, trying desperately to hide her feelings of apprehension and outright fear.

After the girls had disappeared into their hide-a-way under the cabin and had pulled the rocks across the opening, Elvina circled the entire cabin; peering underneath from all sides, making sure the hide-a-way could not be detected. Satisfied, she returned inside to find that Robinson had returned.

"I didn't get as much milk as usual from Ole June. I don't think she's going to be satisfied staying out of her stall all night, either."

Elvina nodded absently. "She's not used to being milked this early," she said as she busied herself with straining the milk into the churn, her nervousness causing her to spill some on the floor.

"Ma, listen!" Robinson rushed over to the small window and peered up the road.

She hurried across the room to join him and the two stood gazing in the direction the soldiers would come. The sun, shining through a slit in the clouds, was just above the top of the trees when the first troops came into view.

"Soon," Elvina thought numbly, "all of the terrifying questions that have tormented our minds these past few days will be answered and we will know if our home is to be ransacked and our meager possessions taken or destroyed. Will they take all of our food, leaving us totally desolate? Will they harm us physically?"

Suddenly the cabin door flew open with such force that it banged against the inside wall. Gasping from surprise and fright, the two of them stared unblinkingly at the soldier standing in their doorway, his musket leveled in their direction. As they stood motionless, staring at the intruder, another soldier appeared. The first soldier moved to one side and the second one entered the cabin, moving around the small interior checking under the beds and behind doors. The loft was checked, and through the back window, they caught a glimpse of soldiers opening their smokehouse.

Beneath the cabin floor, stretched out in their small quarters, Melinda and Liza lay perfectly still, their ears straining to catch sounds of the activity overhead - the heels of the soldier's boots sounding loud and brash to their frightened senses.

"Do you think they'll hurt Ma and Robinson?" Liza whispered frantically.

Melinda didn't respond, just burrowed her face harder against her arm. "I should have stayed with Ma," she thought miserably. "But this was the way Ma wanted it. Dear, Lord," she prayed silently, "please, please, don't let anything bad happen to Ma or Robinson!"

Overhead they heard a strange masculine voice ask, "You and this boy alone here?"

"At the present time," Elvina hedged, hating the lie.

"Where's the man of the house?"

"My husband died several years ago. I am a widow, and this is my son."

Evidently satisfied there was no one else in the house, the two went back outside. Robinson headed for the door.

"Robinson, come back here!" Elvina demanded, alarm causing her voice to be high pitched and unnatural.

Robinson hesitated, then leaned resignedly against the doorframe; face pale, eyes flashing with anger. "They're tearing our place apart, Ma! They don't have any right to do this!"

"Oh, yes, they do!" She shot back at him. "The right of might!"

"But we haven't done anything!"

"That has nothing whatsoever to do with it! This is war!"

"But, Ma!" he objected, hitting his fist against the doorjamb, "I... I just can't stand here and do nothing! Pa wouldn't!"

Robinson slumped against the doorframe, swallowing hard to keep the angry tears back. Elvina walked over to stand beside him. The two soldiers who had searched their house had stopped to talk to a man on horseback, evidently an officer.

Robinson suddenly straightened. "Ma, look! The man on horseback...the one with the fancy uniform...he's riding over here!"

As the rider's horse approached the cabin, a soldier stepped forward to hold the bridle while the officer dismounted. Another soldier, gun in hand, stepped forward, saluted sharply, and then preceded the officer into the cabin. Elvina and Robinson had to step aside quickly to keep from being brushed out of the way.

"He must be important," Elvina thought noting the stars on his shoulder.

With not so much as a nod in their direction, the officer looked around the room, and then headed for the bedroom door, glancing briefly inside.

"This will be adequate," he said to the guard as he came back across the room. Acknowledging Elvina with a nod, he said, "I am General Sherman, Madam. I have some important work to do. The room in there seems quite satisfactory. It will be my headquarters for tonight."

Speechless, Elvina stood staring at the man before her. So this was the notorious General Sherman - the one who had vowed to bring the South to its knees; the one whose name had become synonymous with destruction and death. Prickles ran up and down her spine as she noted the strange glitter in his eyes and his seemingly preoccupied manner, even while speaking.

The guard walked to the door and gave an order to the soldier holding the horse. In a few moments two soldiers came in carrying a satchel and several small metal cases, and following the General's instructions, placed them in the bedroom. Then he had them drag the bedside table to the middle of the room and bring in one of the dining chairs.

General Sherman dismissed the soldiers and closed the bedroom door. The guard walked over to the table, pulled out the other chair and sat down, propping his mud-caked boots on the table.

"Well, what are you gawking at?" he demanded arrogantly.

"Close the door, Robinson," Elvina said softly, ignoring the man's crude question. She walked over to the woodbin on trembling legs and picked up a log to put on the fire. At least they wouldn't burn the cabin with General Sherman in it, she reasoned, greatly relieved.

Later on another soldier came through the door carrying a tray of food. He tapped lightly on the bedroom door. "Your supper, Sir."

Evidently the General wasn't hungry for he mumbled something to the soldier without opening the door. The soldier turned to go back outside.

"Hey!" the guard stopped him. "I'll take that," he commanded as the front legs of the chair he had been leaning back against the wall in hit the floor. Placing the tray across his knees, he began to stuff the food into his mouth with his grimy hand. "You got any coffee?" he growled, not missing a bite.

"We haven't seen or tasted coffee for a long time," Elvina answered stoically.

"Then, get me some water," he demanded.

Elvina removed a tin cup from the safe and filled it from the water bucket. But before she could place it on the table, the soldier snatched it from her hand.

Above the noise, loud talking and cursing outside, they could hear the frightened squawking of the chickens. Once they heard pigs squealing and said goodbye to their meat supply for the next year. The fields came alive in every direction as bonfires were lit. They watched helplessly as soldiers started dismantling the smokehouse and throwing the split logs on a large fire they had built in the backyard. Elvina winced painfully each time a log was yanked loose and pitched on the fire. She had helped John split the logs to build the smokehouse.

Suddenly, without any warning, Robinson ran to the cabin door. Despite Elvina's frantic, "Robinson where are you going?" he ran outside and headed straight for one of the soldiers who was prying a log loose from the smokehouse wall. Robinson grabbed the man by the arm, yelling, "Stop tearing down our smokehouse! It doesn't belong to you!"

The soldier, highly amused, gave Robinson a big shove, sending him sprawling backward upon the ground. Nonplused, Robinson got up and ran headlong into the soldier again, pummeling him with his fists. Laughing uproariously, the soldier grabbed Robinson in a bear-like hug, lifted him off the ground, and walked toward the cabin door as if Robinson were no more consequence than a sack of flour.

Elvina, rushing outside, shouted, "Put him down! Put my son down!"

Ignoring her completely, the soldier walked to the cabin door, and with a giant swing of his arms, deposited Robinson none too gently on the cabin floor.

"You'd best keep that young whippersnapper out of our way," the soldier warned.

Elvina hurried back inside, closing the door behind her. "Are you all right?" she asked anxiously, helping Robinson to his feet. "That was a very foolish thing to do!" she scolded.

Without a word, Robinson walked slowly to his bunk and sat down. Grimly he held his hands against his ears, trying to block out the hateful sounds of the activities outside.

Elvina, heart still beating wildly, picked up her knitting.

The bedroom door opened and the General stood staring at them for a few moments. The guard, even though taken by surprise, was on his feet in seconds.

"You're dismissed for now, soldier," the General snapped.

As the doors closed behind both of them, Elvina tapped twice on the floor above the girls hiding place. Immediately two answering taps assured her that they were safe.

Elvina sat in the rocking chair all night – napping occasionally. Early the next morning, long before daybreak, she heard the loud talk of soldiers and much stirring about. Campfires blazed high again, and horses neighed somewhere. "Probably feeding time," she decided. "And with our corn, too, more than likely," she grimaced.

A light rain had fallen most of the night and had softened the red Georgia dirt in the fields. It clung to the boots of the soldiers and their loud complaints and swearing could be heard above the other sounds of the camp.

Elvina, never having slept soundly during the night, believed that the General had been awake most of the time. She had heard him moving about at all hours. It wasn't long before he came out of the bedroom. Nodding curtly to her, he went outside to join his men.

Elvina quickly tapped the floor twice with her heel. Like a resounding echo, two taps came back immediately. "Thank you, Lord," she breathed.

Robinson's bunk creaked as he sat up on its side. "I'm hungry, Ma," he said, eyes red and swollen.

"And might you well be!" she agreed. "I thought about it after you dropped off to sleep. With all that was happening, we never did eat anything."

Robinson walked over to the window. Dawn was breaking. Speechless he stood gazing at the place where the smokehouse had once stood. Every trace was gone, even the meat box. Elvina walked over to stand behind him, tears momentarily blurring her vision. A pile of shucks and dirt was all that remained as evidence of the treasure they had buried there.

"They found our meat," Robinson said grimly, fists clenched.

"Oh, no!" Elvina gasped, straining to identify the animal coming across the field from the woods. "Isn't that Ole June?" The cow, her utters strutted from not having been milked for so long, had somehow escaped her shackles and, from all indications, was heading toward the barn. But she never made it. She was led

121

away by one of the soldiers to be added to the rest of their confiscated herd.

"They tore down and burned the rail fence around the barnyard," Robinson fumed, voice loud with anger.

"And probably all of the rest of them," Elvina added, rushing to the front door, throwing it wide.

It was true. In the ghostly gray of the early dawn, made even more dismal by the fog and rain, there was not one sign of a rail fence anywhere - around the garden, pasture; nothing!

"The swine! The dirty, thieving dogs!" Robinson stormed, pushing past her.

"No!" she cried, grabbing hold of his shirt. When he yanked himself free and continued on anyway, she panicked, "Robinson, come back here!" she all but screamed. Then, for the first time, broke into sobs.

That was what brought him to a halt. He turned to look back at her. The terror in her eyes and the anguish twisting her face had a sobering effect. Slowly he walked past her back into the cabin. Elvina followed. When she trusted herself to speak, she said softly, voice breaking, "I can make it without the things the soldiers have destroyed and stolen. I couldn't make it if something happened to you, or the girls."

They heard footsteps on the porch and looked around to see one of the soldiers who had searched the loft of the cabin the day before coming through the door with a large gunnysack in his hand. He headed for the ladder to the loft.

Robinson lunged toward him. The soldier, with one foot on the ladder, turned to shove Robinson with his other foot, causing Robinson to fall backwards on the floor.

"Robinson, let him be!" Elvina screamed.

She ran outside. Maybe she could find the General. She looked frantically in every direction. Finally she spied him over near the road sitting on his horse talking to a group of soldiers. Holding up her long skirt above her ankles, she ran as hard as she could, weaving in and out among the soldiers, turning a deaf ear to their crude remarks.

"General Sherman," she gasped when she reached his side. "Your men have taken all of our pigs, chickens, and our cow. They've stolen our meat and our corn!" She had to pause momentarily to catch her breath. "Now, one of your soldiers is in the loft of my house stealing what wheat we have left!"

The General glanced in the direction of the cabin. At that moment, the soldier came through the door, a sack of wheat thrown across his shoulder. General Sherman tapped his horse lightly on the flank and rode toward the soldier who was headed for one of the covered wagons. The General pulled his horse up short in front of the soldier.

"Private, take the wheat back into the house," he ordered. "We'll leave this widow woman some bread."

After what seemed like an eternity, the Union soldiers moved on. Elvina and Robinson watched silently as the last segment of the army disappeared from sight. Trailing behind the troops, their children scurrying about trying to keep up, was a host of Negro men and women. And for the vast majority of the ex-slaves, the small bundles tied to the end of long sticks balanced across their shoulders contained the bulk of their earthly possessions.

"They'll be gutting Rosemary and James' place in a little while," Elvina said grimly, eyes swimming with tears.

When they were certain no one else was around, she hurried to tell the girls. "Melinda! Liza! You can come out now!"

As the girls crawled out from under the house, Elvina helped them to their feet, hugging them close to her. "Thank God, you're safe," she said over and over, choking back the tears.

But the girls stood mute, their horrified gazes staring unbelievingly past their mother.

"Ma!" Liza wailed, "our smokehouse is gone!" The girls ran to the corner of the house, stopping abruptly at the scene confronting them.

"Our fences," Melinda cried in disbelief. "They're all gone. And the corn crib!"

"They took all of our chickens, the cow, our corn, hay, everything," Robinson reported stoically, struggling manfully to keep from crying.

There was an eerie silence everywhere except for a stall door in the barn creaking in the wind. No pigs squealed for food, no hens cackled, no rooster crowed. Hugh black spots of smoldering ashes mocked the remains of what had been their rail fences. Debris, muck, and trampled earth met their gazes in every direction. Nothing was left to identify where the fences around the vegetable garden had been. All of the fruit trees in the orchard had been cut for firewood. Stumps glaringly new along the edge of the woods gave mocking evidence of the freedom taken by the invaders to cut what they pleased.

"How could they?" Melinda sobbed, moving down the path toward the barn with Liza close behind.

"It isn't fair," Liza fumed. "We never did anything to them!"

In despair they turned to walk back toward the house. Elvina was still standing where they had left her, completely motionless, the damp wind causing the soft curls about her face to move in lazy rhythm. Melinda thought her heart would break at the sorrow she saw written on her mother's dear face. Sobbing brokenly she ran stumbling back to Elvina, falling into her arms.

"Oh, Ma," she sobbed against the familiar shoulder. "I hate them. Oh, how I hate them!"

Absentmindedly Elvina patted the shoulder of the sobbing girl. Liza had followed, standing a few feet away, sniffing loudly.

"It's no use to hate them, Melinda," Elvina said, her voice husky as if it took great effort to speak. "Hate only hurts those who indulge in it." She reached out for Liza and held the two close to her for a long moment, then placing her hands on their shoulders, pushed them away so that she could look into their eyes. "It could be much worse. If General Sherman hadn't decided to sleep here, we would have probably lost our house and everything in it. We still have our home, the barn, and some food. And above all else," she added, reaching out to pull them close again, "my children are unharmed."

"But why did they do this to us?" Liza stormed, eyes glinting angrily through her tears.

"They believe what they are doing is right," Elvina answered as calmly as her aching throat would allow.

A few feet away Robinson stood stone faced and silent, his emotions and thoughts all mingled and confused. His young mind seemed incapable of grasping the totality and reason for it all. Up until a few days ago, the war had been something they only heard about in town, something happening way off somewhere to someone else. Now, in one night, an enemy had moved across their land, plundering and destroying. Things they had spent their lives building had been destroyed and trampled as if of no value. The sacred laws of possession had meant nothing at all. The weeping of his sisters disturbed him greatly. Anger toward those who had done this to him and to his family made his head pound. "The swine!" he muttered under his breath, suddenly possessed with an inane desire to start running. Without a word to the others, he headed toward the woods as fast as he could run. Then, remembering Ole Mat, he changed his course, running across the pocked fields, his feet becoming heavier with every step with accumulated mud.

He had hidden Ole Mat in a secluded cove along the creek, a place where the water curved around a high mass of dirt and stone upon which grew a clump of small bushes. When he was within a few yards of the hiding place, a loud bray echoed through the woods. Robinson stopped abruptly, eyes wide with disbelief.

"Ole Mat!" he yelled, starting to run at breakneck speed through the undergrowth. Then, he saw him, standing in all of his lop-eared glory in a circle beaten into the earth by his restless hooves. Robinson ran up to the old mule and threw his arms around his neck.

There, in the quiet woods, the young lad, who in many ways had become much more of a man than a boy in the past twenty-four hours, laid his head against the mule's hairy neck and wept.

But the tears didn't last long for he was eager to tell the others. With shaking fingers he hurriedly unfastened Ole Mat's shackles. Once the two had cleared the dense woods, Robinson leaped upon Ole Mat's bare back and dug his heels urgently into his sides.

"Giddy up!" he commanded sharply, leaning forward eagerly, his eyes toward home.

CHAPTER 11

The four of them toiled for days hauling away the debris left by the departing troops. Their wagon had been taken, too, so they devised a makeshift sled, the runners made from small trees. Eventually, all of the hateful reminders of their unwelcome visitors that could be removed had been hauled away and dumped into a deep ravine.

But there was always present in the back of their minds, especially the women, the underlying fear that more soldiers would come. They were always looking over their shoulders, and the slightest unidentified noise could cause their hearts to constrict with fear. Their home and farm that had always been a haven before now produced a feeling of isolation and lack of protection. The once peaceful woods now loomed dark and ominous.

The Wheeler's home had not been burned, either, but nearly all of their foodstuff that they had been unable to hide had been taken. The Templeton plantation had received the full brunt of Sherman's wrath. The beautiful mansion with its stately columns had been burned to the ground. Only the tall chimneys remained standing, providing a ghostly reminder of its past grandeur. The slave quarters and outbuildings had been spared, and it was rumored that Sherman had ordered this, hoping that the slaves would stay on and not follow after the Union army.

It was several days after Sherman's troops had camped on the Stuart's land that they were visited once again by Union soldiers. It was nearing noonday and the family had gathered inside for their sparse meal. Robinson and Liza were seated on one of the benches facing the door, and Elvina and Melinda were busy at the fireplace. Suddenly, the door was flung wide and a swarthy soldier in a Union uniform strolled arrogantly inside.

Elvina gasped, her eyes staring unblinkingly at the intruder, a mixed expression of surprise, fear, and anger robbing her face of all color. Melinda stood transfixed; one hand gripping a large cooking spoon, the other clasped tightly over her mouth to stifle a scream. Liza, shrieking shrilly, jumped to her feet, and staggering backward, leaned against the wall near the bedroom door, her palms pressed against the logs, eyes wide with fear. Robinson sat as still as death, his hands gripping the edge of the table. There was a sudden movement behind the first intruder as another soldier pushed his way into the house.

'Well, what do we have here," the second soldier smirked, his eyes taking in the room and its occupants.

"Looks like a cozy family gathering, Corporal," the first soldier replied.

"Well, now, ain't that real nice, Private Keathey," he smiled, the hard glint in his eyes decrying his friendly manner. Then, his tone abruptly changing to one harsh and demanding, he asked Elvina, "Where's the man of the house?"

Elvina's shoulders straightened. With a dignity that in no way revealed her surging fear, she answered calmly, "My husband is dead. I am a widow. These are my children."

"Well, well! A widow, huh? And how come yore a widow, Ma'am?" he taunted. "Did yore dear departed lose his life for the cause?" he mocked, his lips curling into a cruel sneer.

"No," Elvina answered quietly. "My husband died several years ago from pneumonia."

Ignoring her response, the Corporal turned to the other soldier. "Private Keathey, search the house!"

"You will find no one else here," Elvina assured the Private, "and the soldiers have already been here. They took away most of our food and livestock." Fear was making Elvina's throat ache and her heart was pounding so hard she was sure its beating could be seen.

"Is that a fact, lady? Well, peers to me like they just might have overlooked a few things. We'll make our own inspection, if you don't mind, eh, Corporal?"

The Corporal nodded slightly while moving over near the outside door. "McBirdie," he yelled over his shoulder. "Get the H--- in here!" Then, turning his attention back to the others, pretended to apologize. "Begging yore pardons," he offered, his expression cruel and jesting.

Shortly a stocky soldier of medium height appeared at the entrance. His ruddy complexion, his bushy hair and unkempt beard, his uniform dirty and ragged in places, reflected the appearance of one that had been living in the woods instead of a soldier in the Union army. Impatiently he turned to go back outside.

"Keep yore eye on them there," McBirdie ordered, jerking his head in the family's direction, "whilest Keathey inspects the place." Impatiently he turned to go back outside.

"All right, Keathey," McBirdie snapped, "Git busy!"

"Who you giving orders to?" the private retorted, his face turning red.

"You, that's who," McBirdie growled, pointing his musket in a threatening manner. "Directly from Corporal Finley."

Keathey sauntered over to Elvina's trunk and lifting the lid started pawing through the contents of the tray. Evidently disappointed, he picked up the tray and dumped its contents on the floor. Flinging the tray aside, he started pulling the special dresses Elvina kept in the trunk out one by one, making an elaborate display of each article of clothing by holding them up against his body and making a few choice remarks.

"Pretty fancy duds for a dirt farmer, don't you think, Private Keathey?" McBirdie smirked; his attention focused more on Melinda than the clothing.

McBirdie turned next to the pie safe. The small china cups and small treasures that were used only for very special occasions were dumped carelessly in with the dresses. Unable to watch, Elvina turned toward the fireplace.

"Hold it there, you," McBirdie snarled, "what you think yore doing?"

"Just stirring the rabbit stew," she answered, forcing a casual response while moving the iron bar until the pot hung directly over the flame. "Wouldn't you and the others like something to eat?"

Elvina had remained outwardly calm, expression stoic, until the soldier came to the shelves containing her books. With mulish indifference, he pulled the precious volumes one by one, pawing through them, sometimes ripping out the pages. Satisfied that there were no valuables hidden among the books, Keathey started toward the bedroom door, but was stopped by McBirdie who had been hawkishly eyeing Elvina.

"Let's take the books along," he ordered, his black eyes watching Elvina tauntingly. Plainly exasperated, Keathey started stuffing the books into another gunnysack.

"No! Stop it!" Robinson fairly shouted, rushing upon Keathey and pounding him with his closed fists. "Leave my Ma's things alone!"

It took only a second for Keathey to overcome his surprise, and laughing boisterously, grabbed the front of Robinson's shirt and flung him against the wall where he landed only a few inches from Liza's foot. Liza screamed, covering her face with her hands.

With a soft cry Melinda ran around the bench to where Robinson stretched prostrate upon the floor, his head held partially erect by the wall. Elvina rushed over, too, ignoring the loud threats from McBirdie. Melinda dropped to the floor and cradled Robinson's head in her lap, her shaking fingers pulling his hair aside to see if there was any blood. Robinson's eyelids fluttered, then opened, a puzzled expression clouding his eyes. For a moment he lay quietly, trying to figure out where he was, then remembering struggled to get to his feet.

"No!" Elvina whispered fiercely, holding him against the floor. "You stay right where you are! There's nothing we own worth getting hurt, maybe killed, over!"

"But, Ma," Robinson argued weakly, struggling to sit up. Elvina's only response was a steely grip on his shoulder, its very intensity defying him to disobey her.

As Keathey made his way into the bedroom, McBirdie moved over to the table, pulled out the chair at the end and sat down.

"You mentioned something to eat, Ma'am?" he stated casually, as if nothing of any consequence had taken place.

Elvina hesitated a second, then taking hold of Robinson's hand, directed her words toward Melinda. "Melinda, help me get him over to the bunk."

"Let him be!" snapped McBirdie.

"Come along, son," Elvina insisted, ignoring McBirdie, while assisting Robinson to his feet.

"I said, leave him be!" he growled through clenched teeth.

Still holding to Robinson's arm, Elvina turned toward the irate soldier. "And what will you do, Corporal? Shoot us?"

Without waiting for a reply, Elvina and Melinda escorted Robinson to the bunk. "Melinda, you stay here with him," Elvina directed. "Don't let him get up."

Melinda sat down on the edge of Robinson's bunk, her arm cradling his head.

At first, McBirdie's expression was one of cynical amusement as he sat watching Melinda's attentiveness toward her brother. Then, his eyes traveled down her slender body and the expression in his eyes became steely. His face slowly flushed to a deeper tone of red and his breathing became rapid.

"Hey, you!" he said loudly in Melinda's direction. "Quit coddling that brat and git over here and help yore Ma fix some vittles!"

Melinda glanced anxiously toward her mother.

"Did'ja hear me, gal?" McBirdie all but shouted. "Move!"

Melinda's legs threatened to fold under her as she slowly got to her feet. Cautiously she started back across the room walking as far away from McBirdie as the room would allow. McBirdie threw back his head and bellowed with laughter.

"Hey, you!" he snarled, but this time in Elvina's direction. "Dish me up some of that stew." Elvina, heart beating wildly, moved toward the fireplace. "And, you," he said mockingly toward Melinda, "you get me something to eat it with." When Melinda hesitated, his expression became mean, eyes hard. "Move, I said!"

Keathey came out of the bedroom. "Ain't nothin worth anything in there," he grumbled.

"Well, check the loft," McBirdie ordered. "There's bound to be something to eat, somewhere!" Muttering under his breath, Keathey started up the ladder.

Shaking visibly, Melinda made her way to the safe where the only remaining dishes were some tin plates and cups Keathey hadn't bothered to take. Picking up a plate and cup she moved slowly toward the table, placing them on the opposite side from McBirdie. Suddenly with catlike swiftness, McBirdie lunged across the table grabbing Melinda's arm. Terrified, Melinda tugged frantically to free herself. Laughing gleefully he moved around the table and with a quick jerk brought Melinda sprawling against him, crushing her with the arm and hand that held the musket.

Elvina stood gripping the large soup ladle in her hand, mind whirling, trying frantically to decide what to do. In the back of the room she saw Robinson struggle to sit up, then fall back weakly. Before she had time to make any move, however, Keathey came hurrying down the ladder.

"What's going on," he demanded over his shoulder, and then when he saw Melinda struggling in McBirdie's embrace, threw back his head and roared with laughter. "Well, Mac, yore making time with the women, as usual!"

McBirdie grinned broadly, revealing teeth yellow and brown streaked. "You keep an eye on things for a little while, won't cha, Buddy?" he wheedled, handing the musket to Keathey.

"Shore, thing!" Keathey grinned. "And when you get through, I just might try that sweet little thing over there," he added, nodding in Liza's direction. "She looks like she might have a little more to offer than that skinny one yore holding." McBirdie swooped Melinda up in his arms as if she had been a sack of potatoes and headed for the bedroom. Melinda tried desperately to hit him on the head and in the face with her fists but he just pinned her arms down in a vice-like grip. Her wildly kicking feet encountered only air.

Robinson, struggling once again to a sitting position, lost his balance and fell off the bunk. Keathey whirled, gun pointing at Robinson.

Elvina quickly dipped the large ladle into the hot stew, inadvertently touching the side of the iron pot. Keathey jerked around to see what was happening, only to come face to face with flying hot stew. With a cry of pain he fell backwards, dropping the musket to the floor. Quickly Elvina snatched the weapon, bringing it to cradle against her shoulder.

The bedroom door opened with a bang and McBirdie came charging into the kitchen, stopping short when he saw Elvina pointing the muzzle end of the musket in his direction and Keathey bending over the water bucket splashing water in his face. Elvina gripped the gun barrel with her left hand, pulled back the hammer, and pulled the trigger. Realizing what was about to happen, McBirdie flung himself to the floor. And just in time, too. The shot barely missed his head.

The outside door flew open and Elvina whirled, thinking it was the Corporal. But instead, it was a tall young man Elvina had not seen before. Instead of stripes on his sleeves there were small gold bars on his shoulder.

"What in the devil is going on in here?" he demanded, his puzzled gaze slowly encompassing the room.

Elvina, visibly shaken, answered through lips that trembled, "that... that animal," she said hoarsely pointing to McBirdie who was struggling to his feet, "tried to..." she hesitated, not able to bring herself to say the word rape, "that... that animal attacked my daughter!"

The officer turned to Keathey. "What happened to you, Private?"

"That bitch threw hot stew in my face, Lieutenant!"

"All right, you two," the Lieutenant snapped. "Gather up those gunny sacks and get outside." He turned to Elvina, holding out his hand. "You can give the gun to me, Ma'am. There'll be no further harm done to you or your daughters." When Elvina hesitated, an amused expression softened the hardened lines in his face. "Have you forgotten, Ma'am, that it has to be reloaded before it can be fired again?"

"But I'm hongry!" McBirdie whined from the doorway.

"Get moving," the Lieutenant growled. As he started toward the door, he turned around just in time to see Melinda stagger from the bedroom, a large bruise on her face starting to swell, her long black hair hanging loose, framing her face like a cameo. "Are you all right," he asked gently, thinking to himself what a beautiful girl she was.

"Yes," she said hoarsely, her hand gingerly touching the bruise on her cheek.

The Lieutenant turned to Elvina. "You can be thankful that I have sisters of my own, Ma'am," and turning abruptly, walked through the door, not bothering to close it behind him.

Elvina ran to bar the door, then turned to Melinda. "Are you really all right?"

"Yes, Ma." Then she began to sob.

Liza rushed over to embrace Elvina and Melinda. "Don't cry, Lindy," she consoled, between her sobs.

"Robinson," Elvina cried, pushing the girls aside.

"I'm all right, Ma," Robinson responded weakly from the back of the room. "Just a little dizzy, that's all."

Before they went to bed that night, Elvina read the ninety-first Psalm, and then led in a prayer of thanksgiving for God's watch care. For several minutes after she had finished, Robinson sat staring at his Mother, expression pensive.

"Ma? If God looks after us and protects us during times of trouble, then, where was He today?"

For a long moment Elvina didn't answer, her expression thoughtful, poignantly aware of her family's eyes focused upon her, waiting for her reply. Then, a gentle smile touched the corners of her mouth, relieving some of the tautness of her face. "You didn't see Him?" she asked softly.

"Ah, Ma!" Robinson retorted resentfully, somewhat confused. Could his mother possibly be teasing about something so sacred to her?

Elvina's expression became very grave as her eyes traveled quickly from Melinda, to Liza, and back to him. "I'm not teasing you at all, my dear, or being flippant. God was here today, as always. He was the love in that Lieutenant's heart. Because of the love for his sisters back home, we were spared a terrible tragedy. You know, the Bible tells us that 'God is love...' and something else... because of all the confusion, the soldiers forgot to take our wheat in the loft."

Robinson wasn't sure he understood completely just what his mother was trying to say, and he didn't try to figure it out any further, either. His head was pounding something fierce - hurting too much for him to struggle with any heavy thinking.

The next morning before the womenfolk awoke Robinson made his way outside. His head still ached something awful, and his legs were wobbly, but he felt compelled to set his traps.

Sometime later, his excited calls awoke the others. "Ma, Ma," he fairly shouted as he ran toward the cabin. Elvina came outside, pulling her faded robe around her. Melinda and Liza, expressions fearful, followed close behind.

"Ma," Robinson called again, his breath coming in gasps, "come see, come see!"

It was the gunnysack full of books. "No doubt they found them too cumbersome to fool with," they heard her say wonderingly as she knelt beside the sack.

But their joy was overshadowed later when Robinson went to the barn to check on Ole Mat. The soldiers had taken him away.

"Why, God? Why?" he whispered as he leaned in bleak despair against the stall door.

A new emotion was born in him that day - one that he had never experienced before; pure unadulterated hate. It didn't erupt like a violent volcano but started with a deep smoldering anger. "I hate them! I hate them! I hate them all!" he cried into the silence. In frustration he turned and beat the barn wall with his fist, and in the way of a young boy, who had not yet learned how to conceal his emotions, he began to cry. And the silent stall where his old friend had once resided only increased his despair. Finally, emotionally exhausted, he returned slowly to the house. In a voice dead of all emotion, he told his mother and sisters, "They took Ole Mat."

Seemingly oblivious to the cries of despair from the womenfolk, he walked over to his bunk to lie down and cover his eyes with his arm.

(Author's note: The bitterness and resentment that was born in Robinson that day would not ever entirely fade, even with time, but would live on as the horror stories of that terrible time in America's history were passed down from generation to generation.)

CHAPTER 12

Melinda beat on the handle of the butcher knife with her fist hoping to push it deeper into the ground near the base of the dandelion plant she was trying to uproot. The cold ground made her hands ache, and the north wind penetrated her shawl causing her teeth to chatter and her thin body to shiver.

In the pail beside her were a few roots; dandelion, she hoped. The cold wind stung her face causing her eyes to water and blur her vision.

She peered around furtively, suddenly aware that she was out of sight of the house. Her ma was forever warning her and Liza not to venture very far from home; that there was always the threat of some soldier passing through.

"We've been fortunate so far in that we've escaped being physically harmed," her ma had remarked just that morning. "Reports are that many women have been molested, not only by the Union soldiers but also by freed slaves. So, girls, stay close. Don't venture out anywhere alone. It seems that there is not much safety anywhere for anyone, anymore."

"Oh, Lord," Melinda prayed fervently. "Help me find something that we can eat." Her empty stomach churned from hunger and anxiety. "I feel like some giant claw is tearing at my insides," she moaned.

A movement in the nearby woods caught her eye. She rubbed the back of her hand across her eyes to help clear her vision. Then, she heard a horse neigh.

She did not know how long he had been standing there at the edge of the clearing holding the reins of his horse. Melinda's heart began to pound and the terrible weakness that came over her when she was frightened caused her legs to start to tremble and her hands shake.

"What will I do?" she thought frantically. "It's useless to try to run; the briars and weeds would only trip me. Besides, he could overtake me in moments riding his horse. I'm too far away from the house for anyone to hear me if I scream. Oh, dear God! Why did I come so far?"

She remained statue still for a long moment, trying to decide. "I know! I'll just pretend that I don't see him, and I'll walk slowly toward the house. Maybe he'll just go away." Slowly she managed to stand up, but her legs felt as if they would buckle any moment. "Dear God," she moaned weakly, "please help me!"

She heard the sound of the horse's hooves crunching the dry weeds behind her and she knew the soldier couldn't be far away. She turned to face him, eyes wide with terror, tears fresh on her cheeks. Transfixed she stared at the approaching rider, thinking dazedly, "there is something familiar about him," and then, remembering, her free hand flew to her mouth, smothering the cry of horror that was threatening to burst forth. It was one of the soldiers that had raided their home; the one who had kept the others from molesting her. She stood still as a statue, relief flooding over her, yet still terribly afraid. She clutched the butcher knife in her right hand as the bitterly cold wind wrapped her full skirt around her ankles.

When he was within a few feet of her, he reined in his horse. For a long moment he sat very still, just gazing down at her, expression impassive.

"What…what are you doing here?" she asked faintly. "You should know we have nothing more for you to steal?"

"Just carrying out my duty, Miss," he smiled "And you, Southern Belle? What are you doing out here alone? Don't you know these are perilous times?"

She continued to stare at him, not quite sure whether or not he was mocking her. "When you're hungry, you become braver," she said dryly, voice faint.

Effortlessly he dismounted, still holding the reins in his hand.

"I… I was trying to find something for us to eat," she explained lamely, offering the bucket for his inspection, relieved that the intruder was the Lieutenant. At least he was kind to them before. He moved forward, and she stepped backward, the hem of her long dress catching on her foot almost tripping her.

"Steady, now," he advised kindly, eyes friendly, appraising the girl before him, thinking, "she's suffering from extreme hunger and malnutrition." This wasn't anything new to him. It was everywhere! And being a Union soldier didn't make his job any easier. The official orders for him and his men were to scour the countryside for any foodstuffs that might be left. His quick appraisal didn't miss the dark circles under her eyes that caused her large gray eyes to monopolize her facial features. Her skin, which should have resembled the blush of a ripe peach, was colorless and dry, the high cheekbones most prominent beneath its surface. She swayed ever so slightly, and then before he could reach out and steady her, she crumpled unconscious at his feet.

He draped the reins of his horse over one arm, then stooped and gently picked her up in his arms, astounded that she was so light. He swore quietly. "She wouldn't weigh eighty pounds soaking wet!"

Before he reached the cabin, the door flew open and the older woman came hurrying out, her steps breaking into a run.

"What's happened to Melinda?" she demanded, her eyes frantically searching his for reassurance.

"She was digging for roots in the field over there," he said, jutting his head in the direction from which he had come. "I surprised her. I don't know whether I frightened her into a faint, or she collapsed from exhaustion."

"It could have been either," Elvina answered, relieved. "Please," she said, turning toward the house, "will you bring her inside?" She ran ahead, opening the door wide. "Here, lay her on the bunk."

Elvina poured a dipper of water in the wash pan and wet the end of the towel. Hurrying back to the bunk she began to bathe Melinda's face. Slowly, Melinda's eyes opened, and as her vision cleared, she saw the Lieutenant standing not far from her. She lay motionless, eyes wide with fear.

"It's all right, Melinda," she heard her ma's voice close by, and then she realized that she was home.

"Ma? How did I get back here?" she asked in a voice barely audible, while struggling to sit up.

"Everything is all right, Melinda," Elvina assured her again, pressing her back gently on the pillow. "The

Lieutenant, here, brought you home. You shouldn't have gone so far away from the house, dear," she scolded softly.

"I… I know, Ma," she agreed in a voice still shaky, attempting again to sit up. This time, Elvina let her go, assisting her to a sitting position. "I… I wasn't aware that I had wandered so far until… until he came along. I was looking for wild onions and dandelion greens and roots." She shook head sadly. "I'm afraid I didn't have much luck."

"Well, you're safe, and that's the important thing." Elvina turned to the soldier who was still standing near the end of the bunk quietly observing the two women.

The uniform the Lieutenant wore was hateful to her for it represented all of the terrible devastation and horror that had been inflicted upon them and their neighbors. "But," she reminded herself silently, "the Lord said 'if your enemy hunger, feed him,'" and so she pushed aside her feelings of hostility that kept trying to surface and asked kindly, "Sir, could I fix you a cup of sassafras tea?"

"That would be most kind of you, Ma'am," he replied, his relief evident, and not revealing by so much of a blink of an eyelash that he had never tasted sassafras tea in his entire life.

The door opened and Liza and Robinson came into the room, stopping short when they saw the Lieutenant.

"It's all right," Elvina quickly assured them. "The Lieutenant is going to have a cup of tea with us."

When the two stood as if transfixed, Elvina rebuked them gently. "Come in and close the door. The house is getting cold."

Liza moved cautiously toward the fire, never taking her eyes off the one she considered an enemy. Robinson remained near the door, his thin face flushed, thoughts wild and angry. He pushed the door shut with his foot, not too gently, thinking, "What's that Yankee soldier doing here? Isn't he one of those who came and raided our place before...the ones that stole Ole Mat? Didn't he try to hurt Melinda? Why was Ma treating him like a welcomed guest?"

"Robinson, come on over to the fire and warm yourself," Elvina coaxed, sensing his hostility. Reluctantly he moved across the room and sat down on one of the straight chairs near the fire.

Elvina poured each of them a cup of the steaming brew. "Sassafras tea is not as good without sweetening, but it still warms your insides," she explained, trying to make the atmosphere less hostile.

"I'm sorry I gave you such a fright," the Lieutenant apologized to Melinda who had eased across the room to sit down on one of the benches. He sat down at the other end. "You really should be more cautious about going out alone. Next time it might be someone like McBirdie that you would have to contend with."

Melinda shivered at the mention of his name. "As I told you earlier, Lieutenant, hunger will cause you to be less cautious sometimes."

"I'm sure," he answered gravely, his expression totally void of the coldness he had portrayed during his former visit. He sat the cup on the table and rose to his feet. "Thank you for the tea, Ma'am. Now, I must be on my way."

No one said a word as the door closed behind him. In a few moments they heard his horse galloping down the road.

"I don't like him coming here," Robinson blurted, his boyish face flushed with anger.

"Well, none of us do, son," Elvina retorted. "But just how do you suggest we prevent it?"

Robinson stood up and leaned his head on his arm against the stone fireplace. "If only I could do something!" he fumed silently. "If it wasn't for leaving ma and the girls alone, I'd join up with the Rebs. Maybe I could carry water or help some way! Anything to help get rid of these damn Yankees!"

There was a knock on the door. Everyone froze, not making a sound. The knock came again, and this time, there was a familiar voice with it. "Anybody home? It is I, Leonard Mattison!"

Robinson, nearest the door, quickly opened it. The others hurried to greet him and make him feel welcome. Elvina shook his hand warmly. "Oh, Mr. Mattison, it is so good to see you again!" She pulled the rocker closer to the fire. "Please sit down, but first, wouldn't you like to remove your coat?"

Nodding, Mr. Mattison slowly unfastened his coat, his hands trembling noticeably as he fussed with the stubborn fasteners. Elvina's heart ached at the gauntness of his face, the dark circles under his eyes. "The same as we," she thought pityingly, "skin and bones."

"How is Mrs. Mattison?" Elvina inquired politely.

"Well, I suppose she's fairing about as well as most. Like the rest of us, a good square meal would heal a lot of woes."

"And it doesn't get any better," Elvina replied angrily. "They keep coming back." Then, remembering her manners, asked, "Would you care for a cup of sassafras tea?"

"That sounds real good, Mrs. Stuart." Elvina poured him a cup, apologizing for the tin cup.

"Do you have any news about the war?"

"Have you heard that Sherman took Savannah?"

She nodded, expression grave.

"Well, it's been reported that Sherman sent the President a telegram presenting him Savannah for a Christmas present. Reports are that he's headed up the coast toward the Carolinas."

"Is the entire state of Georgia in the same condition as we are?"

"I'm afraid so. They say Sherman had his army divided into four parallel columns - all marching on different roads, and they cut a swathe of devastation twenty to twenty-five miles wide for over three hundred miles, destroying cotton mills and cotton gins, saw mills, and businesses of all kinds. Their wrath seemed to bear down harder on those who showed any hostility toward the Union soldiers. Reports are that Sherman told his men to favor the poor. But I haven't talked to any that have been particularly favored."

"He was kind, when he stayed here. And he did order the soldiers to leave us some wheat. But it's the others that keep showing up, that makes it so bad. We had a visitor just before you came - but he left empty handed because we didn't have any thing worth taking."

Mr. Mattison nodded sadly. "People are dying everywhere from hardship; especially the elderly and the very young."

"Mr. Mattison," Liza broke in, "how is Kallie?"

"Kallie's all right, I guess, thank you," he answered politely. "She sent you her regards, by the way."

Mr. Mattison sat staring into the fire for a long moment. "I'm afraid that I've not come for just a social visit, Mrs. Stuart."

"I suspected as much," Elvina responded, suddenly apprehensive. "Does it concern the war?"

"Yes, I'm afraid so, but not in the sense you mean. I... I know that you and the Wheelers are real close friends, and I have some bad news about their two boys. I felt that I needed someone to go with me to tell them."

All color drained from Elvina's face. "What news, Mr. Mattison?" she asked through stiff lips.

"You know how slow news travels? Well, seems like it's been a long time coming, but according to the casualty list posted in town today, Doug and Wray were killed at Cedar Creek in the Shenandoah Valley."

"Oh, dear God, no!" Elvina cried, burying her face in her hands. Soft whimpering sounds came from the girls.

Mattison sat staring into the fire, saying nothing, respecting their grief, thinking, "Oh, Lord, how I hate to tell the Wheelers." He thought about all the years that he and his wife had gone childless, and then when, in their later years, they had been blessed with a little one and it was a girl, how disappointed he had been. If she had been a boy, probably he, too, would have been taken in the terrible war. His family had suffered, but so far, all were still alive.

"Mr. Mattison," Elvina said quietly, "we haven't eaten anything really substantial for days. I would like for us to visit Jim and Rosemary, but I doubt if we have the strength to walk there and back."

"I managed for a wagon. I'll be glad to drive you."

Elvina didn't sleep much that night. The grief-stricken faces of her friends kept returning to haunt her. "Oh, dear God," she prayed relentlessly. "Please have mercy and give them peace."

As the first light filtered through the window she climbed out of bed and dressed. "The best antidote for a worried mind is work," she reminded herself sternly as she placed some logs on the fire and blew on the coals to get the flame going. She reached for her mending basket and moved her chair closer to the window where the light would be better. Suddenly she stiffened. Was that a sound outside the door? Surely the soldiers wouldn't raid this early in the morning?

She sat motionless, scarcely breathing, straining to hear, but only the crackle of the fire broke the silence.

"I'll just see!" she decided resolutely, picking up the poker and walking reluctantly toward the door. For a moment she stood with her ear against the door, listening, but there was no sound. Carefully she removed the heavy bar, and then opened the door a crack. There was nothing that she could see. She swung the door open further and moved forward to have a better look in all directions. That's when her foot hit the gunnysack. She stooped to feel along its bulging sides. "Dear, God," she breathed, "I do believe it's food."

She dragged the heavy sack inside and closed the door, making sure she replaced the safety bar. Hurriedly she dragged it over by the fire and as fast as her trembling fingers would permit and untied the grass rope that was wound around the top.

"It is food," she breathed. She caught hold of the bottom of the sack and emptied the contents on the floor, her eyes blinking unbelievably. There was a slab of cured pork, at least a peck of potatoes, a packet of dried beans, and of all things, a small pouch of sugar.

She could contain herself no longer. "Girls! Rob! Come see! Someone has left us some food."

"Where did it come from? Who brought it?" they asked, with all three of them bombarding her with questions at the same time.

"I don't know," she cried joyously as she removed the skillet from its nail on the wall. "But it's real! O, thank you, dear Lord! Thank you!"

And, Robinson, unable to wait, picked up a potato and rubbing it on his undershirt to brush away the dirt and grit, took a big bite, peeling and all.

CHAPTER 13

Preacher White tested the rock protruding above the water level with his foot to make sure it was resting on a solid foundation. The rock, if stable, would serve as a perfect stepping stone to the other side of the creek. He didn't want to make a slip and get his feet wet, not with them as cold as they were already.

He had been following the small creek for miles through flat lands and in the valleys between the hills. The side of the narrow creek on which he had been traveling had become too steep for walking comfortably, making it necessary to cross over to the other side. According to what he had been told by one of his fellow ex-slaves, he couldn't be too far from the "room in de ground," a hideaway used by many of the blacks in their attempts toward freedom before the emancipation.

It would be a safe place for him to hide for a few days. He reckoned it hadn't been very wise for him to speak out the way he did concerning the rights of the freed people.

"But a man has to do what de Lawd tells him!" he mumbled, "and Lawd? You knowed dem white peoples warn't doin' right by us!"

If his calculations were right, then the place ought to be around the next bend in the creek. He pushed aside the small undergrowth of vines and bushes, his ragged coat sleeve catching on a vicious brier that had curled in and out among the branches.

"Humph!" he grunted. "Dat mus be de debil's walkin' stick I don got tangled up wid." He worked as quickly as his numb fingers would allow freeing himself. "Lawd, but my hands an' feets is cold!" he mumbled out loud again, rubbing his hands together and stamping his gunnysack wrapped feet to improve the circulation. The preacher stood a long time gazing up at the hillside. "Dat seems rightly de place, awright, but someting ain't quite right!" The rocks weren't stacked the way he'd been told. Moving as fast as his cold limbs would allow, he made his way up to the place where the opening should be. He pushed some big stones out of the way, then several large tree limbs buried in leaves. He picked up a forked stick and started pushing the leaves aside, and that's when he saw it. "Dat's hit!" he cried jubilantly, "de big flat rock dat looks like a table top!" He pushed hard on the rock and felt it slide. There it was - a big gaping hole in the ground.

He squatted beside it for several minutes gazing down into the hole, trying to make out what was down there. "Looks like dar is someting stored in dar," he reasoned, straining to see. As his eyes became accustomed to the darkness, he was able to make out what it was. "Lawd hab mercy! It's some cone, still in the shucks! What I gwine do? I'se bound to be found out sooner or later, an' dem folks will think I'se stealin' der cone!" While he was trying to decide what he should do, he heard someone chopping with an axe. Hurriedly he slid the tabletop rock back in position and carefully replaced the covering of small limbs and leaves. He stood up and listened again. It was chopping all right, and it seemed to be fairly close by. He made his way carefully down the steep bank, crossed the creek again, and headed in the direction of the chopping. When he reached the crest of the next knoll, he could hear voices; voices of young people. That's when he saw them, two young girls and a boy.

Carefully he made his way toward them, keeping low. As he drew closer, he noted that they had only one axe and were taking turns cutting up a small tree that had blown over during a windstorm. Nearby was a makeshift carryall made from poles lashed together.

Back at the cabin the cold wind moaned around the corners, its pitch rising and falling repeatedly with the coming and going.

Elvina sat near the fireplace by the small window mending a garment that had received many such repairs before. The wind makes such a mournful sound," she mused, shivering. Four sweet potatoes lay in the ashes baking for their supper. A pot of unsweetened sassafras tea was ready for drinking. Robinson and the girls had gone to cut wood for the fireplace. The tea would help warm them when they returned. She glanced at the clock on the mantle, frowning. Dark would be closing in before long. "I wish they'd come on home," she sighed.

She was always more than a little anxious when they were out of sight of the house. The soldiers had not raided their place anymore but there was always that underlying fear that others would suddenly appear.

Food had been their greatest need since the night the Yankees had camped on their place. Realizing their meager supply would not last long, Elvina had insisted on strict rationing from the beginning. As their supplies dwindled, they had gone to bed night after night with their stomachs pinching from hunger, saving their meager rations for the waking hours when their hunger pains were harder to endure. They had combed the woods for nuts and acorns, and occasionally, were fortunate enough to trap some game.

Elvina leaned over and moved the coffeepot closer to the fire. She had learned to make a fair coffee substitute from parched acorns. Rosemary, who had managed to obtain a cookbook printed by the Confederacy, had passed along the recipe as well as many other helpful survival techniques.

She heard familiar voices outside and knew her family had returned. Sighing with relief she used the poker to turn the potatoes baking in the ashes. These were the last of the potatoes except for the few she was hoarding to grow setting plants from in the springtime.

The door opened and the girls came inside, their thin gaunt faces creating a sharp contrast against the cherry-red ends of their noses.

"Where's Robinson?" Elvina asked, replacing the poker to its holder.

"He's out at the woodpile talking to a Negro man," Liza stated matter-of-factly.

Elvina managed to conceal her irritation. This was a familiar habit of Liza's, the telling of just enough facts to arouse curiosity.

"Did you say a Negro man?"

"Yes, Ma," Melinda added quickly, "and he's nice. He helped us cut wood."

"But where did he come from? How did he know you were there? What was he doing in the deep woods on a cold day like this?"

Melinda shrugged her shoulders. "I don't know, Ma. He just walked up, said he heard our axe. He stood around for a while, and then he started helping us with the wood. And he was a big help!" she hastened to add. "He cut up the small tree we had been working on into fireplace logs and helped us haul the logs home. He said he is a Baptist Preacher. Preacher White is his name."

Elvina stood staring fixedly at the girls for a moment, thinking, "Probably hungry and hoping we have something for him to eat."

The door ·opened again and Robinson stepped inside. Pushing the door closed behind him, he stood leaning against it. "Ma, there's a Negro man outside. He helped us cut and haul the wood."

"So the girls have been telling me," she nodded.

"I thought maybe I'd divide my supper with him," Robinson finished lamely. "He—he's not wearing shoes and his clothes are really ragged."

Elvina glanced at the four potatoes in the ashes and then back at the three pairs of questioning eyes quietly returning her gaze. Without comment, she walked over and raked one of the potatoes out of the ashes onto the hearth.

"Pour him a cup of sassafras tea, Melinda," Elvina requested quietly. "Some of that ought to help warm him."

Silently Robinson took the potato his mother was holding out to him and the cup of sassafras tea from Melinda. Liza hurried to open the door for him.

Preacher White was sitting on the pile of wood, his shoulders hunched against the cold. As Robinson approached, he looked up. A big smile spread from ear to ear when he saw the steaming cup. Quickly he got to his feet.

"I'm sorry, Preacher White, but this is all we have to give you," Robinson said in an attempt to explain the meager rations.

"I unnerstands, Mistuh Rob, and I'm thankin' you mightly. Tis hard times eb'where. My! Dat chaz-raz tea sho do smell good, sho nuff! You be sho and thank yo Ma kindly for me."

"It doesn't have any sweetening, I'm afraid."

"Now, don neber yo mind. Hits hot and hit sho nuff hits the spot," he smiled, cautiously sipping the hot liquid. Then he carefully placed the cup on one of the upturned short logs. He sat down again and reached for the potato Robinson was holding out to him, turning sideways so that the wind would blow against his back. As Robinson turned back toward the house, he saw Preacher White bow his head for a moment as if praying, then bite into the potato, peeling and all.

Elvina placed four plates on the table and a fork by each. Then she divided the potatoes equally, placing a portion on each plate. A bowl of parched corn was the only other item on the table except their cups of sassafras tea.

After the blessing was said, Robinson asked, nodding his head in Preacher White's direction, "Ma? Do you suppose it would be all right if Preacher White slept in our barn tonight?"

"It's awfully cold outside," Liza added sympathetically.

Elvina didn't answer right away. She had been wondering about the same thing. Where could the man go this late? However, it was dangerous times with slaves freed by Sherman roving the country. One never knew what to expect, or whom to trust. But, he had seemed harmless enough and had been very accommodating. The children were certainly taken with him, and it was awfully cold.

"I suppose it would be all right," she said thoughtfully. "Here, Rob, take him a handful of corn and some more tea." Then, hesitating a moment as if trying to make up her mind about something, she arose, and telling Robinson to "wait a minute," went into the bedroom to return with a quilt.

"Tell him he can wrap up in this," she said quickly, as if not real sure she was doing the right thing. "Tell him... tell him we'll warm a rock for his feet."

The next morning Elvina was dressed and had a lively fire going when there was a light rap on the door. Glancing toward the bunk where Robinson was sleeping soundly, she moved hesitantly toward the door. She lifted the heavy safety bar from its cradle and slowly opened the door a crack. Standing back several feet from the entrance, a big smile lighting up his broad face, stood a middle-aged black man. Nodding almost continuously and still smiling he lifted his arm high in the air and there dangling from his clutched fist was a fat o'possem.

"I whopped him in de face and he all sullied up," he explained happily. "He nice and fat, too. Sho will make some fine eatin'!"

"Why, that's just wonderful, Mr....?" she stammered, realizing she didn't even know his name.

"Joshua White. Mos folks what knows me calls me Preacher White."

"Oh? Then, you are a preacher?"

"Yaz, em," he nodded emphatically. "I'se a Baptiz preacher."

"Well, thank you, Preacher White. This is a Godsend. We'll have a feast," she added, voice breaking slightly with emotion.

"Yaz em" he agreed, his head bobbing up and down vigorously. "He come sniffing round de barn," he chuckled, "but he ain't gonna do no more of dat. I'll look ta de cleanin', Missus," he added, turning to go.

"You can clean and wash him below the spring down there," she said, pointing. "Wait a moment and I'll get you a knife and a pan."

Elvina closed the door and leaned against it.

"Ma! What is it?" Robinson asked, sitting up in his bunk, alarm in his voice? When she didn't answer right away, he threw back the covers and bounded out of bed. "Ma? Are you all right?"

"Yes! Yes, son," she answered finally, shaking her head in wonder, eyes filling with tears. Softly, prayerfully, he heard her say, "Cast thy bread upon the waters; for thou shalt find it after many days."

Preacher White stayed on. Elvina and the girls improved his sleeping quarters by making a mattress cover out of odds and ends of material and stuffing it with clean straw.

And he taught them a lot about living off the land. He showed them how violet and wild strawberry leaves could be used for greens. That dandelion roots peeled, roasted until dark brown and coarsely ground made a fair substitute for coffee. He seemed to know where the wild onions grew the thickest, and there were times when boiled onions was all they had to eat. Preacher White helped Robinson build more traps,

159

fastened together with willow branches, and they gathered wild grass seeds for bait. They weren't choosy, either, about what they ate. If it could be used for food, it was eaten.

Preacher White helped split rails to restore some of their fences, particularly around the garden area. And it was his suggestion that Elvina make a harness for him and "Mistuh Rob" so that they could pull the turning plow and start preparing the cornfield and the garden plot for early planting.

Pulling the big plow was slow, grueling work, especially in their weakened condition. So, they all pitched in, doing their bit.

In the first months of Preacher White's stay, Elvina had tried several times to cautiously feel him out as to where he had come from; something about his past. But he was always evasive, the expression on his broad black face strangely impassive.

"Preacher White?" she asked one day. "Why do you stay on here? You know I have no means to pay you for your labor? We can't even offer you decent food or quarters?"

"Yo tooks me in, Missus, when I didn' hab no place ta go. You'se been my friends. Hit gabe me a feelin' of belongin'. I'se mos grateful, Missus."

His explanations had never sufficiently satisfied her curiosity. "Takin' him in," had meant his sleeping in the barn on a straw bed. It meant long hours of self-imposed labor with no pay, with barely enough food to survive. "He must be hiding from something, or someone," she concluded. "But he has been a Godsend for us." Then, as if a revelation was being born, she thought again about her own words, "A Godsend."

Didn't the Bible say, "For He shall give His angel charge over thee, to keep thee in all thy ways?" Could it be? she thought, overwhelmed by the implication. "Oh, God," she prayed, her heart full of wonder and praise.

It had taken a lot of restraint to wait until all danger of frost had passed to plant the vegetable garden. But the possibility of a late frost wiping out their entire food crop demanded patience. So, they waited until the middle of April before opening the rows. They dropped the precious seeds into the ground, not knowing, as yet, that General Lee had surrendered his army to General Grant at the Appomattox Court House in Central Virginia; that before the seeds had sprouted and pushed through the ground the terrible struggle between the North and South would officially end; and that the national leader who had proclaimed heroically in his second inaugural speech March 4 - "with malice toward none, with charity for all," would die on April 14 by an assassin's bullet. And even though these were great national events that were heard around the world, nothing really changed for the Stuarts and their neighbors. The most important thing still remaining uppermost in their lives was the means wherewith for survival.

Every weekday, weather permitting, they were in the fields by good daylight, digging, hoeing, raking. They still did not have any work animals, so most of the time Robinson and Preacher White pulled the plow. There were times when it was necessary for the womenfolk to take a turn, and this always upset Robinson even though he did not voice his objections. Every time he saw their thin bodies straining against

161

the weight of the plow, his hate for the "damn Yankees" welled up, and in his young mind and memory, they were all McBirdie's and Keathey's.

As food became more plentiful, their bodies became stronger, and the ghostly pallor of their faces slowly faded. But their lives were far from peaceful. Famine was a devastating problem in rural Georgia, and there was a constant threat from marauding whites and blacks that took food wherever they could find it.

During the week their only time for relaxation and being together that wasn't a work situation was in the evenings. After supper, they would sit outside, or lie on the cool grass. Sometimes they would sing and Preacher White would join in. And sometimes, with their urging, he would sing alone for them, his rich baritone bearing down on "Swing Low, Sweet Chariot."

One evening they were all sitting outside, cooling off after picking cotton all day. Preacher White had already retired to the barn. Elvina's work dress was damp with perspiration and the slight breeze that was stirring made her suddenly chilly. Shivering slightly, her thoughts turned to the coming winter.

"You know," she said thoughtfully, holding her arms close to her chest for warmth, "we've got to start thinking about when the weather turns cold again. Preacher White needs a warmer place to stay."

Robinson was quick to agree. "I've been thinking about that, too, Ma."

"Yeah," Liza chimed in eagerly. "He still wont come in the house, or eat at the table with us. It would be nice if he had a real room with a fireplace."

"Liza," Elvina reproached softly. "It's not ladylike to say 'yeah.'"

There was a long moment of stony silence, then Liza retorted. "I don't see that it makes all that much difference whether I talk 'ladylike' or not! Who's going to hear, or care, anyway, in this place the backside of nowhere!"

Ignoring Liza's caustic reply, Elvina continued. "I thought perhaps we might rebuild the smokehouse after we get through with the harvest. One of these days we just might have some meat to go in it, again." When there was no response, she suggested further. "We could petition off one end of the smokehouse for Preacher White. And, Liza, I don't see why it couldn't have a fireplace."

"Why don't we ask Preacher White what he thinks about it in the morning?" Robinson chimed in enthusiastically.

Preacher White's response was not disappointing. "Yas, Missus," he agreed with gusto. "An' I'se a pert good builder, too, Miz Stuart. Jez soon as we gits de cone and cotton in, I'll starts on dat!"

"We'll start on it," they replied in unison, breaking into happy laughter.

Preacher White, feeling accepted and needed, swung his hoe up on his shoulder. Pushing his old battered straw hat back on his head, he said jubilantly, "Come on, Mistuh Rob! We'se got work ta do! Yas, Sus! We gots cone and tatters ta look about fo we starts cuttin' dem logs." And throwing his head back, began to sing joyously, his bare feet keeping perfect step as he marched off toward the fields, "Oh, happy day! Oh, happy day! Since Jesus washed my sins away!"

Robinson had to trot to catch up with him. When Preacher White finished his song, Robinson asked, "Preacher White? Do you believe in Heaven?"

"Does I believ' in Heben? Why, cose I dos, boy! I'se a preacher, ain't I? How come yo ax a thin' like dat?"

"I don't know, except my Ma says my Pa's in Heaven."

"An' yo Ma is right!"

"But why didn't God let Pa stay here when we needed him so much?"

"Well, now, I reckon dat be's God's business, boy," he replied tenderly. "But one thing I does know! God don't eber make no mistakes!"

"Ma says that God loves us and cares for us."

"An' yo Ma sho is right bout dat, too!"

"Then, why did he let the war happen, and Doug and Wray get killed? And why did he let all those bad men come steal our food, and burn our fences and smokehouse?"

"Mistuh, Rob, dar's a lot ob bad in dis worl', but it ain't God's fault."

"Why, not? He made the world, didn't he? And everything in it?"

"Cose He made de world! Cose he did!"

"Then, he had to make the bad, too, didn't he?"

Preacher White stopped working and stood propped upon his hoe. Pushing his hat back, he scratched his head thoughtfully. "Mistuh Rob, I don' know why de good Lawd don gone let all de ebil loose in dis world! But He gwine take care of eberting' - just like he brought de childun ob Israel to de promised

164

land! And de walls of Jericho come tumblin' down! And he don sen' us his son, Jesus, ta make us clean!"

"But I haven't killed anybody! I haven't stolen other people's food. I didn't start that awful war!"

"I know dat, and the Good Lawd knows dat! But yo is a sinner, anyway!"

"How come?"

"Hit all started back in de garden of Eden … wid Adam and Ebe - and dat's when de ole Debil got his foot plum in de doh!"

"But what's that got to do with me?"

"Yo is a man, ain't cha? Well, all de peoples in de world is sinners cause Adam and Ebe sinned an' dey was de fust peoples on de earth."

Robinson stooped down and pulled up a bunch of grass growing near a stalk of corn. It was all so confusing. Somehow Preacher White made him feel like he was in some way responsible for the terrible things that had happened.

"But how could I be?" he thought miserably.

But hard work, deprivation, and death weren't the only problems they would have to contend with. Some of the neighbors seemed to resent the Stuarts because they hadn't suffered more loss during Sherman's raid. Subtle remarks were made in town and at church meetings about "some people not losing all their seeds and not being burned out like other folks." But the rumor that really hurt was the one that "maybe there were some Yankee sympathizers in the neighborhood." The fact that Elvina had shared their precious seed for planting with many of them did not seem to make any difference. She cautioned the family repeatedly not to dignify any such gossip by trying to explain, or even

165

acknowledging such crude and ridiculous charges. James and Rosemary had come to their defense, so they were told. But Elvina went to them and asked them not to do it anymore.

"It will only cause you trouble," Elvina insisted when they refused. "I can take it as long as I know that I'm not guilty of what they are saying. I can live with it."

Taking Preacher White in had not helped the situation, either. Along with some of the other name calling, they had acquired the name "nigger lover." Perhaps it was this type of hostility that caused the incident that drove the Preacher out of their lives.

It was late fall and they had worked hard to get the smokehouse and Preacher White's room finished before the weather got real cold. They would have finished it earlier only Preacher White wouldn't consent to work on it until there was plenty of firewood cut for the winter. Preacher White's room had a fireplace, and the women had made a new straw mattress for the bunk bed. "I'se gonna make me a table and bench one ob dese days," he said happily.

That tragic night, the girls had turned in early. Robinson had just taken off his shirt and was sitting on the side of his bunk. Suddenly, there were loud noises outside and a lot of commotion. Elvina rushed to the window, framing her face with her hands to block out the light from the lamp. All she could make out in the pale moonlight were men on horseback carrying torches, their faces obscured by large white pieces of material that had slits for the eyes, nose and mouth.

"What's going on, Ma?" Robinson asked trying to see over her shoulder.

Pushing him aside without answering she rushed over to the table and turned down the wick as low as it would go safely. Moving back to the window she stood peering over Robinson's shoulders to determine what was taking place. Two of the men dismounted and headed toward the room at the back of the smokehouse.

The bedroom door burst open and the girls, dressed only in their long nightgowns, rushed into the room, eyes wide with terror.

"Ma, what's going on?" Melinda whispered, her face drained of all color.

Elvina didn't answer, her attention riveted on the men outside. "Oh, dear Lord," she gasped as she saw the two men returning, dragging Preacher White between them. A seething rage swept over her.

"Liza! Melinda! Go back into the bedroom and put on your clothes," she ordered sternly.

"Ma! What are those men going to do to Preacher White?" Robinson all but shouted.

"I don't know," she retorted, mind whirling. She pushed Robinson aside so that she could get a better look through the window. In the flickering light from the torches, Preacher White's eyes looked like two balls of cotton. He stood rigidly between his two captors, his horrified gaze traveling around the group. Suddenly Elvina's mind was made up. She didn't know what the Preacher was accused of, but this was all wrong. She had no intention of letting someone who had been so good to them be treated this way. She ran over to the mantle, taking down the one gun they owned. Robinson, realizing what his ma's intentions were, yelled frantically, "Ma, what are you going to do? Ma! You can't go out there! They'll hurt you, Ma! Ma, Preacher White wouldn't want you to get hurt!"

Elvina, working feverishly trying to load the gun, did not answer.

Robinson's voice became frantic, "Ma! Pa taught me how to shoot! Let me go! Ma! You're loading it all wrong!"

"Robinson, be quiet," she stormed. Then, more controlled, "You're right. Quick! Help me!"

The girls, dressed in their work dresses, came rushing back into the room. Both were crying. "Please, Ma. Please don't go out there!" they begged, their voices bordering on hysteria.

"Now, you listen to me," Elvina retorted grimly, angrier than any of them had ever seen her. Her glance swept over the three pale faces staring at her. "Nothing is going to happen to me. They wouldn't dare hurt a woman. But that's our friend they are mistreating out there, and I won't stand by and see him hurt! Now, I want you all to promise me that you will stay inside."
A stricken silence was their only response.

"Did you hear me?" Elvina demanded, her voice a deadly calm, her face like graven stone.

Slowly the three nodded, sobs catching in the girls' throats.

"Ma?" Robinson started to speak again, but stopped short at the steely look she gave him.

"Robinson, I meant what I said," she hissed. "Stay inside! Now, unbar the door for me."

Robinson ran to remove the safety bar. Elvina walked out onto the porch and down the steps, one hand holding up the barrel of the gun, the other holding the stock against her shoulder, her finger resting on the trigger.

The men had not noticed her coming out of the cabin, and because of their loud talking and shouting she had to walk up fairly close to make them hear her. Her position was advantageous, too, for she was directly behind the two men on foot holding Preacher White captive.

"All right! That's enough!" she shouted, her face pale with anger.

Suddenly all activity ceased and there was a deathly quiet except for the flickering torches and the nervous movements of the horses. The two men holding Preacher White turned to look back at her, never releasing their grip on his arm.

"Turn the man loose," Elvina commanded

"Well, what we got here?" one of the men on horseback called out jeeringly. "Why, if it hain't Miz Stuart?" he mocked. "Why air you so interested in protectin' this here no good nigger? Maybe you just might have a real personal-like interest in 'em, huh?"

"Yes, I do," Elvina answered, her words falling like chips from granite. "I don't know what you think he is guilty of, and I don't know why you think you should make yourselves his appointed judge and jury, but this I do know. This man came to us when we were near starving, and for a straw bed in the barn and what meager food we had to share with him, he has worked hard to help us survive from what the Union soldiers did to us. He has been our friend and helped save our lives. Now, as to your insulting remark," she continued, shifting her gaze to the spokesman on horseback, "you must live around here since you know my name. So, you know, also, that I am a survivor, and I warn you. This man has been a friend to our family. I repeat! He helped save our lives. Now, this is my property and you are trespassing. This gun has only one load in it, but I assure you, I will make it count! Someone's going to get hurt if you don't turn him loose, so get on your horses, and get off my property, now!"

There was a long uneasy silence. The gun wavered just a little in Elvina's hand.

"Oh, come on men," one of the riders called out. "Let the nigger go. There will be another time. No use upsettin' the uhhh... lady, here."

"But, man! We've got to learn this'un a lesson," one of the men on foot whined. "If we let him go, he'll probably skip the country!"

Elvina pointed the gun at the one who had been speaking. One of the riders whose mount was slightly behind all the rest spoke for the first time. He must have been the leader. In a voice that was disturbingly familiar to Elvina, he said matter-of-factly, "All right, men. Let him go. We can take care of this matter some other time." Turning his horse without so much as a backward glance, he rode toward the road. The two holding Preacher White let go of him and hurried toward their horses. Preacher White's legs refused to support him and he slumped heavily to the ground. Elvina stood motionless with the gunstock against her shoulder until the hoof beats of the horses could no longer be heard.

"Ma! Ma!" the others called as they ran from the cabin. "Are you all right? Did they hurt Preacher White?"

"I'm all right," Elvina assured them shakily, feeling as if her knees were going to buckle. She looked down at Preacher White who was sitting dejectedly on the ground, his face in his hands.

"Preacher White," she said gently, "you know what this means?"

There was a long silence, then Preacher White's bowed head nodded slowly.

Robinson dropped to the ground beside him. "Preacher White, why did those men want to hurt you?"

But if Preacher White knew, he wasn't talking.

Slowly Elvina turned back toward the cabin. "Come, girls," she said quietly. Then, in Preacher White's direction, she added, "I'll pack you some food."

"Where will he go?" Liza demanded tearfully.

"He must go away from here. His life is in danger."

This time it was Melinda who voiced her objections. "But why? What has he done?"

"I don't know," Elvina responded sadly, "and it doesn't matter all that much that we know. The important thing is that we help him get safely away."

But Preacher White didn't wait for any supplies. When Elvina and the girls took the food out to his room, he was gone. The fire he had built in the new fireplace was still smoldering. Robinson, his head bowed and biting his lip to keep it from trembling, was sitting on the edge of the bunk bed that Preacher White had not been privileged to sleep in.

"Would he not wait, Son? Elvina asked gently.

Robinson, unable to answer, just shook his head. Anger and defiant thoughts made his head feel as if it would explode.

"I hate them! I hate them! They're just as bad as the damn Yankees! I hate them all."

Elvina stood for a long moment looking down at her son. Her immediate parental instinct was to chastise him for expressing such hatred against anyone. But instead, she sat down beside him on the bunk bed and laid her arm across his shaking shoulders, thinking, "How can I fault him when the rage within me is like a consuming fire?"

When she trusted herself to speak, she suggested quietly: "You know the Bible teaches that we must love our enemies and pray for them."

Robinson pushed her arm from around his shoulders, and quickly getting to his feet, rushed angrily out the door.

* * * * *

Robinson's reverie was interrupted abruptly by Liza impatiently calling his name, "Robinson, didn't you hear Ma ringing the dinner bell?"

"I'll be there just as soon as I get to the end of the row!" he yelled. Then, because he felt guilty for having taken out his frustrations on Liza, he managed a half-hearted "thanks" to her retreating back.

CHAPTER 14

Robinson sat on the hard straight-backed pew with his arms folded - face expressionless. His piercing blue eyes stared straight ahead, focusing on the preacher in the pulpit. From all outward appearances, Robinson was a young man intently absorbed in what the man of God was saying. However, his thoughts were evolving around the young lady sitting sedately next to him.

He could feel the warmth from her body, and frequently his nostrils picked up a whiff of something perfumery, the essence of which made him think of fields of clover in bloom, and piles of new cut hay with Kallie and him running through the fields holding hands. In his imagination they stopped running and the two of them stood breathlessly gazing into each other's eyes. Slowly he pulled her to him, and he could feel the softness of her body next to him as he held her close.

Now, by turning his head slightly, he could let his gaze shift downward until it rested on Kallie. This unguarded moment gave him a rare advantage of just feasting his eyes upon her. The top of her head, crowned with a mass of light brown hair, was just level with his shoulder. Her hands, folded in her lap, were small and delicate, and Robinson longed to reach out and cover them with his own. He could see the slight rising and falling of her breasts as she inhaled and exhaled, and strange emotions churned inside him; emotions that were new and disturbing.

Kallie must have sensed Robinson's eyes upon her for without warning the lashes lifted and she was gazing up into his eyes. A warm glow seemed to envelop him and he longed to reach out and touch her hand. But Kallie's gaze shifted quickly back toward the pulpit, her own conflicting emotions betrayed by a flush that worked its way up the contour of her face to her hairline, turning her creamy complexion a deep pink. Robinson suppressed a smile that threatened to engulf his entire face, and forced his gaze back toward the speaker, the excitement in his eyes betraying the emotions surging beneath his outward calm.

Struggling mentally, he tried to bring his thoughts back to what the preacher was saying. It had something to do with repentance and forgiveness and the threat of Hell fire. Robinson shifted his weight, repositioning himself on the hard bench, and wondered vaguely why it was necessary for him to repent of anything. Offhand, he couldn't think of much that he felt he needed forgiveness for, unless it was an occasional flare-up of temper toward his sisters when they tried to boss him around, or when it was necessary to cope with an occasional stubborn streak in one of the mules.

His thoughts didn't tarry long with the preacher. It was hard not to think of anything but Kallie with her so near. It was doubly hard to try to associate this lovely creature by his side with the Kallie that used to visit Liza occasionally. At that time, her long hair and been tightly secured in two pigtails that bounced when she ran like misplaced tails on a long-legged colt, and she had just about as much grace as one of their gangling female calves.

But the gap between those early years and the present had been miraculously closed one night, a year before, when during the summer revival, Liza had invited Kallie to spend the night with her. Sitting across the breakfast table from Kallie the next morning, Robinson had found it most difficult to identify this petite, well-mannered gentle beauty with the little girl he remembered before the war, and embarrassed them both by staring at her so much.

That was also the summer that Robinson began to show an unusual interest in revivals and church going in general. Some years back he had joined the church during one of the revivals, and had been baptized in a river along with many other converts, mainly because most of his friends had taken the step, and because he knew it would make his ma happy.

He had a deep respect for the Scriptures, however, partially because his ma took such great stock in them and her unfailing faith in the goodness of God. But he wasn't too sure, though, how much God could be depended upon in time of real trouble. If he were the kind of God that protected and looked after those who loved him, how come He had let his pa die? And why did He permit the Civil War, and all the misery, starvation, and death that went with it? It made him highly uncomfortable and anxious to try to find a reason, or an answer to such perplexing questions, and he usually pushed them aside as quickly as possible. At the moment, it was far more pleasant to let his thoughts dwell on Kallie.

Movements around them alerted Robinson that the service was drawing to a close, evidenced by the congregation standing and the hymn of invitation being sung. As he stood with his head bowed and eyes closed, his thought were on the activity to follow, namely, dinner on the ground.

Robinson and Kallie walked out of the church together, the same as they had for months, and stood off to one side of the church yard waiting for the ladies to spread their homespun tablecloths on which the dishes they had prepared with such care and pride would be placed.

The Reverend blessed the food and then everyone was free to wander up and down the long line of food, taking portions of whatever appealed to their vociferous appetites.

After Robinson and Kallie had finished eating, they walked down the long path to the Big Spring to get a drink of water, painfully ignoring the sly looks and knowing smiles of those who recognized the symptoms of young love. People were walking to and from the spring continually, as it was the only source of drinking water for those attending church services.

Kallie had brought along a small crystal cup that was shaped like a man's top hat that had been a gift from her father. Robinson took it from her hand and filled it for her from the bubbling spring. While she drank, he squatted down and, dipping the cold running water with his cupped hands, drank lustily.

Their thirst satisfied, they stood near the spring for a while exchanging greetings and comments with others who came by. After a while they strolled off to the edge of the clearing to sit on the trunk of a large tree that had been uprooted by the wind some time in the past. Robinson brushed off the top of the log with his hand and then stepped back to bow ceremoniously, offering the grand seat to his lady. Kallie laughed gaily as she sat down, spreading her full skirt with its many hidden petticoats daintily around her.

Jim Wheeler came by and after chatting with them for a few minutes about nothing of any importance, moved on to join some other young men congregated in the churchyard under a large shade tree. Jim liked Kallie, but he had felt somewhat abandoned since Robinson had been spending so much time with her lately.

Kallie seemed to sense an unusual air of controlled excitement about Robinson, or could it be, she reasoned, that she was the one excited, which wasn't unusual. Just being near Robinson made her feel as if she were floating on a cloud.

But, then, why did Robinson keep staring at her that way? He kept acting as if there was something he wanted to say but couldn't bring himself to utter the words. And when their eyes would meet, Robinson's gaze would cling to hers, so intense and searching that Kallie, feeling flustered and strangely elated, would quickly shift her gaze, while making small inane attempts toward conversation.

"How sweet she looks," Robinson thought, his hungry gaze taking in every inch of her face. Feeling his eyes upon her and unable to help herself, Kallie's gaze inevitably returned to his.

The urge to reach out and touch Kallie's hand was almost unbearable, but he knew that this would never do; that it would be totally unacceptable to any watching eyes. He had not verbalized his feelings for Kallie, and any advances by him before declaring his intentions as honorable would be considered socially unacceptable.

Robinson wished desperately that they could be alone. The things he wanted to say to Kallie were very personal, and it was extremely difficult for him to tell her how he felt with people milling about and children running and playing nearby.

Embarrassed by so much attention, Kallie looked away, pretending to watch a group of children playing tag. Her heart was pounding, and she felt the blood stinging her cheeks. Then, softly, just loud enough for her to hear above the surrounding noises, she heard him whisper, "Kallie, I love you so very much!"

It was such a simple statement, made quietly, in the middle of the afternoon with dozens of people and children milling about, but Kallie felt as if a trumpet had broken the stillness between them. The blood pounded in her ears, and it seemed as if she could only breathe in short shallow breaths.

Robinson sat very still, body rigid, waiting for her reaction. It seemed an eternity before Kallie gave any indication that she had even heard him. Had he been mistaken in believing that she felt the same way about him? Was she offended? Would she tell him she wasn't ready to get serious with anyone?

Slowly she turned her head in his direction and her gaze locked with his, her lips forming the beautiful words that he had longed to hear for so many months. "I love you, too, Rob."

To Robinson, it seemed that some invincible barrier between them had evaporated. There was so much to say - so much to talk about. But Robinson's main objective for the near future was to obtain permission from Kallie's pa to come calling.

"I'll talk to your Pa and get his permission to come calling," Robinson declared, feeling much bolder and more confident now that he was assured of Kallie's feelings for him. He felt brave enough to tackle most anything.

"Rob, I think I should talk to Pa first."

"But why?"

"I don't know ... except, Ma and Pa have such old-fashioned ideas."

"But don't you see? If you talk to him first, then I'm afraid he'll think I'm scared to ask myself?"

"Rob, please," she begged, eyes pleading. "I... I just think it will be a lot better if you let me talk to my parents first."

"All right," he agreed skeptically, not sure at all that he was doing the right thing. He'd rather fight his own battles.

"I'll talk to Pa this week and let you know next Sunday," she suggested, expression cloudy.

Robinson nodded, still not entirely convinced. "It's going to be one more long week," he grinned, languishing in the smile that replaced her dark concern.

Leonard Mattison, despite his austere manner and bushy beard, was a gentle soul. Years of occupying the position of private schoolmaster before the Great War had, by reasons of survival, caused him to assume an air of almost military authority. He had learned in the early years of his profession to be invulnerable to adverse criticism, both from the students and from their parents, unless, of course, it was justified. Being a devout Christian he worked at being fair and understanding, but at the same time, believed without reservation, that sparing the rod absolutely spoiled the child.

Kallie was not afraid of her pa, exactly. She just didn't know how he would react to her telling him that Robinson wanted to come calling. "He still thinks of me as a child," she fumed silently, her love and respect for him restraining her.

She knew that her pa set great store by book learning. When the war had made it impossible for the school to continue and her pa had to be away a great deal "doing his bit for the Confederacy," he had admonished her to "keep up with your reading." Kallie was certain that Robinson's lack of classroom instruction was going to be a big point against him as a suitor as far as her pa was concerned. But Kallie knew from her close association with Rob's sisters that Rob's ma set great store by book learning, too, and had seen to it, despite poverty and hardship, that her children had learned to read and appreciate good literature, even to some of the classics. But Kallie wasn't sure this would be a good argument in Robinson's favor, for he was dirt poor and there were his mother and sisters to consider. Kallie knew full well her pa would take this "calling" business seriously, for that was something else that he had cautioned her about repeatedly. "Never keep serious company with any man, my child, that you wouldn't consider marrying."

Kallie secretly believed his reasoning somewhat harsh for there were a number of boys in the community that she thought would be a lot of fun just to keep company with at church and at socials.

She approached her mother with the problem first, feeling more comfortable with her, and was excited to learn that it wasn't a surprise at all, in fact, it was no more than she had expected. "After all," Mrs. Mattison responded, eyes dancing, "do you think your keeping company with him at church for over a year, now, has gone completely unnoticed?"

Kallie's face turned a rosy pink. "Then... then you don't think Pa will object?" she pressed.

"Now, that, my dear child, is something you are going to have to discuss with him yourself," she answered blithely. Her reaction puzzled Kallie. Her mother was acting as if the whole matter were of little consequence instead of one of the most important things in the world.

It was the latter part of the week before Kallie summoned enough courage to approach her pa. Supper was over and Kallie had helped her ma wash and put away the dishes. Kallie slipped out of the kitchen before her ma had quite finished tidying up and found her pa on the veranda, rocking slowly back and forth in one of the high-backed cane bottomed rockers, gazing out over the fields in the fading twilight. Kallie slipped through the door and crossed the veranda to sit down on the top doorstep. For several minutes neither of them said a word. Finally, mustering up her courage, Kallie blurted, "Pa, there's something I need to talk with you about."

Mr. Mattison's rocking ceased. "Could it be that you want to ask if Robinson may come calling?" he questioned gently, understanding her anxiety.

Taken aback by her father's straightforward question, Kallie was silent for a few moments. Then, simply, "Yes, Pa."

"You must be serious about this young man, then?"

"Oh, yes, Pa!"

There was a long silence and her pa once again resumed his gentle rocking back and forth. In the fading light she could see him stroking his beard thoughtfully.

"Why didn't Robinson come to me, himself?" was the next question.

Kallie was quick to come to his defense. "He... he wanted to, Pa, but I asked him not to. I... I didn't know how you'd feel about it." Her voice became almost inaudible. "I... I convinced him that it would be best to let me talk with you first."

Another long silence followed. Kallie knew from past experience not to try to rush her pa. She knew her wisest course of action was to be patient and wait for him to speak.

"Kallie, have you seriously considered this young man's circumstances? He not only has himself to think about but his Mother and sisters as well?"

"I know," Kallie answered in a voice barely above a whisper.

Kallie heard her pa take a deep breath. She had no way of knowing the thoughts that were beating against her father's mind and heart. That for some time Kallie had been taken with this young man - a man practically penniless, with a widowed mother and two unmarried sisters to look after. But, on the other hand, he argued with himself, he was from good stock. He had a fair education for the times, and he was a hard worker.

From all accounts he was not a wild boy and had never been in any kind of trouble. He drew in another deep breath, thinking, "Oh, well, the young man just wants to come calling. It's not as if he is asking for her hand in marriage." But deep down he knew this was hollow reasoning. He figured he knew his little girl fairly well and she would never act casually or flippant about anything this serious.

"I have no objections, I suppose, to Robinson coming to call, my child. But just keep this in mind. This is your life, and the decisions you make concerning your future, especially the husband you choose, will be far reaching and will have a lasting effect on your life and on many others."

To Robinson, involved with the routine work on the farm, the week seemed to drag endlessly. He still had strong reservations about not talking to Mr. Mattison first himself. He hoped Mr. Mattison wouldn't think him a coward.

Sunday morning finally arrived. The Stuart family had been up since dawn making preparations for the big day. Robinson had fed the livestock, later hitching the mules to the wagon. For some time now, Melinda had taken over the chore of milking the cow weekdays. But on Sunday mornings, Robinson took care of the milking, since it took the girls so long to get dressed and their hair groomed to their liking. Too, there were always last minute duties in the kitchen because of the dishes they would be taking for the "dinner on the ground."

The service was just before officially starting when the Stuart's slipped in quietly, taking their seats near the back so as not to disturb the others. There was no visiting preacher to bring a sermon. Therefore, Reuben Wyatt, a relative newcomer to the area who had recently joined the church, had been invited to speak.

Robinson glanced quickly over the congregation, locating Kallie sitting up near the front. The long wait would soon be over, and he would know her father's decision. His heart began to beat wildly, and he felt his face getting hot. The room all at once seemed awfully close and stuffy.

Finally the service was over and Robinson waited near the aisle for Kallie. They walked out of the church and into the sunshine. Robinson wanted to grab Kallie's arm and shout, "Well, what did he say?" But he contained himself, nervously guiding her off to one side. When they were a discreet distance from the others, he turned to ask her, but was stopped short by the look in her eyes

"When?" he asked softly, happiness bathing him like warm water.

"Next Saturday afternoon," she smiled happily, eyes shining.

"Saturday," Robinson nodded, smiling broadly, suddenly ravenously hungry.

Just before the noonday meal Saturday, Robinson filled the black iron wash pot with water and built a hot fire around it. He brought one of the big tubs from the spring and placed it in the room that was to have been Preacher White's. It served him well as a private bathhouse.

Robinson ate his meal hurriedly; seemingly unaware of the light conversation carried on by the womenfolk. If he had not been so preoccupied with his own thoughts, he might have noticed the amused glances that passed back and forth across the table between the girls.

Melinda and Liza were busy with their regular Saturday afternoon task of scraping small shoots of grass from the shell-white yard when Robinson came down the doorsteps, dressed in his Sunday best. His gaze shifted uncomfortably from one to the other before asking, "Where's Ma?"

"In the garden," Melinda answered, nodding in that direction.

"Ma," he called loudly, heading for the team and wagon he had left earlier in the shade of the big oak. "I'll be home in time to do the chores."

Liza giggled and Robinson's face turned red. Undaunted, he vaulted into the wagon and onto the seat.

Ordinarily, riding eight miles in the wagon wasn't too much of a bore for Robinson. Usually he found it enjoyable for it was a welcome change from the grind and monotony of the farm. But today, the July sun seemed to bear down unmercifully, and each time the mules took a step, dust puffed upward, some of it rising to settle on his clean clothes. For a while he tried to keep it brushed off, but in despair soon discovered that the dust was not easily dislodged from his damp shirt and trying to remove it only made matters worse.

To his relief, Kallie opened the front door to his knock, and the moment both of them had anticipated for so long had finally arrived. At last they would have some time alone together - away from prying eyes.

Mrs. Mattison came in to speak to Robinson, asking politely about his family's welfare, and after making a remark or two about how hot the weather had turned, asked to be excused and returned to her baking activities in the kitchen.

Now that Robinson was actually alone with Kallie in her parent's parlor, he found himself at a loss for words. Kallie, eager to make him feel comfortable and at ease, smilingly invited him to have a seat, and in the tradition of a well-bred southern lady, asked him if he would enjoy something cool to drink after his long ride. Robinson nodded gratefully, smiling his thanks.

Kallie excused herself, returning shortly with two tall glasses of cold cider. They sat down side by side on the deacon's bench, sipping their drinks. From the time Robinson had entered the front door, he had hardly taken his eyes off Kallie while she was in his presence. It gave him indescribable pleasure just to sit and look at her. He was utterly captivated by the way she smiled, her facial expressions; her mannerisms; the way she cast her gaze down demurely when teased.

Kallie placed her glass on a nearby table and stood up. "It is so terribly hot," she complained, walking over to the open window. "There's a breeze over here."

Robinson placed his glass on the table beside hers and followed her to the window, coming to a standstill just behind her. He towered over her, and from his advantage point, could look down upon her mass of shining hair piled on top of her head. Cautiously, he reached out and touched a curl at the nape of her neck. He feasted his eyes upon her, not missing a single detail of her calico dress fitting snugly around her tiny waist, its yards of skirt falling softly around her ankles. Gently he touched her on the shoulder. Without a word, she turned and stood looking up at him.

"Kallie," he whispered gently, cupping her face in his hands. "Will you marry me?"

Eyes wide with wonder and love, Kallie was incapable of uttering a sound, so she just nodded. Slowly, as if in a trance, he slipped his arm around her waist and pulled her toward him, deftly stepping backward out of the view of the window and any prying eyes. Their lips met as if a magnet were drawing them together.

It was the first kiss for both of them, and Robinson could never remember experiencing a thrill such as this before. It seemed as if something vitally alive had raced over his body. Urgently he pressed his lips harder and she responded, reaching up to hold him close with her arms, and the kiss that had begun with such tenderness suddenly enflamed them. With their bodies pressed close together, lips searching and demanding, the pent-up desire that had been so carefully concealed for so many long months could now be expressed.

The kiss left them both visibly shaken. Robinson, conscious of strange emotions stirring within him, fought hard to keep from pulling her to him again and kissing her over and over. Hungrily he longed to kiss her face, her throat, her lips again.

Kallie's legs were trembling, and she found it somewhat difficult to breathe. Slipping her shaking fingers into his, she led him back to the deacon's bench where they sat down, bodies touching.

The afternoon seemed to melt away for there were so many things new to talk about. Familiar sounds drifting through the window of late day activities reminded Robinson that it was getting late in the afternoon, and he, too, had chores waiting. He kissed Kallie once more at the door, holding her close for another long moment.

"I'll speak to your Pa, soon," he promised, his calm expression in no way revealing his dread and apprehension toward carrying out such a commitment. They walked out into the hallway and down the porch steps. Robinson lifted his hand in a half wave and then hurried toward his team and wagon. As he headed out of the yard and out onto the road home, he remembered that in passing the Mattison's barn earlier, he had noted that there was a well for watering animals near the road. He stopped long enough to water the mules, waiting impatiently as they drank long draughts eagerly. Climbing back onto the wagon, he realized with dismay that the sun wasn't too far above the tops of the trees. He urged the mules to a faster pace, admonishing himself for not leaving sooner. It would be late into the night before he was finished with the feeding. But the memory of Kallie's tender response to his kiss returned to excite him, and his anxiety lessened as his mind turned toward his plans for their future.

He hadn't intended to blurt out his proposal that way! It was in stark contrast to all of the pre-planning and rehearsing he had done during the past week. Over and over again, while working in the fields, or doing his chores, he had gone over just what he would say. He would start by explaining that it would be a while before he could work out a plan for a home of their own; how his family obligations weighed heavily upon him; that it would be necessary for her to wait for him, if she loved him.

Throughout the next few weeks, Robinson wrestled with the problem. He knew that sooner or later he was going to have to have to break the news to his family, but he wasn't ready just yet. It was all still too new and private to discuss openly with anyone, even his ma.

When he approached the problems that would face him if he and Kallie were to get married right away, he would find himself clutching the plow handles in such a vice-like grip that his hands would cramp. Oftentimes, instead of turning the mule when he would reach the end of a row, he would stand gazing off into space, lost in thought.

Realizing that her young son was wrestling with a man-sized problem, Elvina respected his privacy, saying nothing, except to discourage the girls from teasing him.

Eventually, in near despair, Robinson had to admit that there simply was no way that he could marry Kallie any time in the near future, even though she was pressuring him for them to set a date. He couldn't bring her to his ma's home because of the limited space. There were only two rooms - the great room that served as kitchen, dining, and family room and the place where he slept on a bunk in the corner. The one bedroom was where his ma and sisters slept. The only other spot that afforded any privacy in the cabin was the loft, accessible only by a ladder at the backside of the kitchen. How could he ask Kallie to come live in a hole like that? Kallie's parents had offered to share their home with them, but this was totally out of the question where Robinson was concerned. First of all, it would be admitting that he couldn't provide a home for Kallie. Secondly, leaving his mother and sisters alone was something he refused to even consider. It took all four of them, working from sunup until sundown, to make a living and save enough money to pay their taxes in the fall. Elvina and the girls worked long hours during the summer chopping corn and cotton, working in the garden, cutting off fruit to dry, and thrashing dry peas and picking off peanuts in the fall. Soap had to be made, and collards pickled in brine. The women even helped him chop and haul wood. And, not only was the farm work to be done, but there were socks to knit and sewing that never ended. No! It was impossible. He could never leave his family to fend for themselves, especially after the way they had suffered.

Occasionally his preoccupation with his personal problems would get him into trouble. Once while plowing he came to the end of a row. Instead of turning the mule, Robinson looped the reins over the plow handle and walked over to a nearby clump of small trees growing along the edge of the ditch bank. Removing his old hat, he sprawled on the green grass, leaning his shoulders against the trunk of a small tree. Suddenly, the peacefulness of the moment was shattered by his realization that the mule, having devoured all of the available weeds and grass from its original position, had ventured down the ditch bank, dragging the plow which had fallen over sideways across the end of several rows of corn. Robinson sprang to his feet spontaneously yelling "whoa!" In a matter of seconds he was grabbing the reins, tugging angrily at the ropes. In dismay he looked back over his shoulder at the damage that had been done. Several mutilated stalks of corn were the result of his daydreaming.

"I've got to get hold of myself," he mumbled, expression grim.

Elvina was not at all surprised one afternoon in late summer when Robinson brought up the subject while they were picking cotton. The girls were not in hearing distance, providing a rare opportunity for them to talk privately.

"Ma, there's something I need to talk over with you," Robinson said nervously, standing between two cotton rows, aimlessly pulling at a wad of cotton he was holding in his hands.

Elvina straightened up from her bent position and stood quietly stretching her tired shoulders for a few seconds. Getting a firm grip on her cotton sack, she pulled it closer to her so that the weight would not pull against her shoulders. The sun was low in the west, so she pushed her bonnet back, exposing cheeks wet with perspiration, the dampness causing her hair to stick close to her head. Wearily she brushed a loose strand back with her hand.

"I can't say that I'm surprised, son," she answered gently, weariness also reflected in her voice. "I would have had to be blind as a bat not to notice the odd way you've been acting lately."

Robinson's face reddened as an embarrassed grin spread over his face. "I guess I have been acting a little strange at that. I've... I've got a lot on my mind."

"It wouldn't have anything to do with Kallie, would it?," she asked, her glance tenderly caressing his face, her heart aching at his troubled expression.

"Ma... I, that is..., we, Kallie and I, we... we want to get married!"

191

Elvina reached down and absent-mindedly picked the cotton from a bowl. "That's a mighty serious undertaking, Rob, especially for a couple as young as you and Kallie." When he said nothing, she continued, "Have you made any definite plans?"

"Well, not exactly. I tried to explain to Kallie that it would be some time before I could provide a place of our own and I suggested that we wait a couple of years, but Kallie didn't take to that at all. She wants us to go ahead and get married and move in with her folks." When Elvina said nothing, he continued hesitantly. "I... I don't want to do that. First of all, I wouldn't leave you and the girls alone. Besides, moving in with her pa and ma would be like admitting I couldn't provide a home for her myself."

"Well, there's the loft in our house," Elvina suggested. "It's a trifle hot in the summer, but the winter wouldn't be too bad. Or, we could possibly manage for a double bed and put it in the corner of the kitchen where your bunk is now."

They stood for a long moment, both silent, both unconsciously observing Melinda and Liza emptying their cotton sacks onto the wagon parked in the center of the field.

"There are many things to be considered, Rob," she said thoughtfully, placing a hand full of cotton in her sack. "As long as it was just you two, you could make out fairly well. But what if there are children?"

When Robinson finally answered, his response was totally unexpected. "Ma, have you ever regretted that you and Pa waited so long to get married?"

Elvina stood for a long moment in deep thought. A soft, dreamy expression replaced the tired lines of her face. "Yes," she said finally, "in that we could have had so many more years together. But on the other hand, if I had insisted on us getting married earlier, we might not ever made it South. That was your pa's great dream. I loved him too much to deny him that."

"But what about your dreams, Ma?"

"My dreams were his. It was just that simple."

Catching hold of her cotton sack at the top, she shook it vigorously, packing the cotton toward the bottom. "There's no sure answer to anything in life, Rob. We just have to pray about our problems and then trust God to show us the right path to follow." Stooping over, she began to pick cotton again.

"Why did she have to bring up religion?" Rob thought irritably. "She is so practical and level headed about everything else." It just didn't make sense how she could believe that God had been taking care of her all these years, considering all the hardships and tragedy. But he didn't comment. It would hurt her deeply if she suspected his true feelings on the matter and he respected and loved her too much to do that.

"Ma?"

"Yes?" Elvina answered, straightening up again, pressing her hands hard against the lower part of her aching back.

Robinson looked away from her gaze, his face flushing slightly.

"Ma, why have you never married again?"

Startled, Elvina stood gazing at her son for a long moment, thinking, "What in the world made him ask that?" Aloud, she said, "When you love someone the way I loved your Pa, you remain married to him or her in your heart. It wouldn't have been fair for me to marry someone else."

They had reached the end of the row and both of them automatically picked up their sacks, hoisting them across their shoulders. They headed for the wagon that was piled high with the day's pickings.

"If only Pa could have lived," Robinson commented wistfully.

"Yes, I've thought of that, too, hundreds of times over the years."

They walked along in silence, the heavy sacks of cotton limiting their breath for talking.

Robinson's thoughts returned to his ma's comments regarding the loft. It had possibilities. Actually, there just wasn't any other way.

There was no church service the following Sunday, and this meant that Robinson and Kallie could spend the afternoon together. He was excited, yet reluctant to tell her about his ma's suggestion. She surprised him by being receptive to the idea.

"I was afraid you wouldn't take to the idea, too much, Kallie," he said, scarcely believing what he had heard.

"Of course I'd rather have a place of our own," she answered softly, absentmindedly moving the toe of her shoe back and forth across a rough place on the porch floor as the swing moved slowly backward and forward. "I want to cook for you and look after you all by myself." She paused, then turned her head to look up at him, gazing at him intently, expression unusually serious and thoughtful. "But there just doesn't seem to be any other way! I love you so much I'm miserable when we're apart." She raised her hand to reach out toward him, then remembering the rules for modesty, quickly clasped her hands together in her lap. "Besides," she continued thoughtfully, her eyes searching his, "we'll have our own place someday."

Happiness like an incoming ocean tide swelled up within him. The last few months had been torturous. He had struggled against misgivings, doubts, concern for his family, and worst of all, the fear of losing Kallie. With Kallie gazing up at him with such quiet confidence and adoration, he felt as if something inside him had sprouted wings. At that moment, he felt as if there wasn't anything they couldn't face together. No problem he couldn't master.

"I love you so much, Kallie," he whispered gruffly. "I wish I could offer you everything. But you know what I am, and what I have. I can't even promise you a home of your own, yet; maybe never, for that matter," he added lamely, remembering his pa and ma's unfulfilled dreams. Cupping her face between his large hands, he gazed for a long endearing moment into her eyes. When he spoke again his voice was husky and somewhat shaky. "But one thing I can promise you, my darling, I'll love you like no other."

They decided on a late fall wedding for many reasons. There were the crops to harvest. Mrs. Mattison needed time to make Kallie's wedding dress, and by then, the weather would be cooler, making the loft more tolerable.

The wedding plans were kept simple because of the limited financial situation of both families. However, there was one item that Kallie's mother refused to compromise on. It had to be store bought, and not from the local country store, either. It had to come from town. This meant a long trip involving hours of riding in the wagon over roads often pitted with deep holes and ruts. Weighing all the issues and circumstances, Mrs. Mattison decided that the trip would be too difficult and impose too many problems for all of them to go. Therefore, Mr. Mattison found himself in the awesome position of being responsible for one of the most important decisions in Kallie's life, or at least, that was the way the womenfolk seemed to think. But being a kind-hearted soul in spite of the austere impression inferred by most folk, he clinched his teeth firmly together and kept his feelings of anxiety and frustration well concealed. He insisted, however, that the first bale of cotton would have to be picked before he would take the time off to go to town.

Later, early one morning, while they were eating breakfast, he announced that he would be going into town that day to take a wagonload of cotton to the gin. Mrs. Mattison's list had been made for weeks. Throughout the morning meal, she and Kallie bombarded him with instructions that sent his head into a whirl and made him wish fervently that he could just go to the barn and clean out the cow stalls, or perform some other uncomplicated task.

Later, as he guided his team pulling the wagon loaded with snow-white cotton out onto the main road and headed for town, it wasn't long before ghostly reminders, both small and great, rekindled his terrible memories of the war years. Partially burned buildings, even though covered with vines and nearly obscured by small bushes and trees, still provided credence to the devastation and horror that had taken place. He dreaded these trips into town for it brought hostilities to the surface that he managed to put aside and not dwell upon while plowing his fields. Even though it had been years since Sherman's march through their part of the country, near poverty conditions still prevailed for most of the rural populace. "When one family is struck with disaster, such as a fire or tornado," he mused, "then the neighbors can pitch in and help the victims back on their feet. But in this case, we were all down at the same time."

But, it was gratifying to see that progress, even if it were slow, was being made. With meager tools, many had restored their lives to a form of normalcy. For the need of hasty shelter, many had felled medium sized trees and split them in half. From these the walls of their cabins had been built, with red clay daubed in the cracks to keep out the cold wind. Fireplaces, crudely constructed from rocks and clay, provided a constant reminder of the urgency that had been behind their formation.

Occasionally he would pass a house whose inhabitants he knew personally, and they would wave, or come out to stop him for a few minutes of talk.

"It was the hard work that was the salvation of their souls and prevented many from going mad with hatred," he decided, remembering how survival had meant weeks, months, and years of backbreaking toil. Crops made with crudest of tools and outmoded methods; men and women serving as work animals to pull the plows, when a family was fortunate enough to have a plow left. But the greatest threat had been the total breakdown of government, and the feeling of security brought about by protection by the law no longer something to be taken for granted. There were plenty of men in uniform, but they weren't local protectors. They were Federal troops sent in by the Freedmen's Bureau to supposedly keep law and order and to protect the rights of the freed slaves.

When he arrived in town, his first destination was the cotton buyer. After he had sold his load of cotton, he headed for the gristmill. He could hitch his team and wagon there and also leave the bag of corn he had brought along to be ground. It was the miller who recommended a place selling the latest fashions in dress materials, and following his advice and directions, found the store without any difficulty.

Determined to get the dreaded job over with once and for all, he opened the door and stepped inside. Much of his apprehension soon subsided, however, by the helpfulness of a young lady working in the store who seemed to be knowledgeable on what the latest in fashions were. She showed him several pieces of material that were "soft of texture and the colors pleasing to the most discriminating tastes." When he explained that the material was to be used for his daughter's wedding dress, the young lady's interest increased delightfully, probing him with varied questions regarding the type wedding it was to be.

"What colah are your dawter's eyes, Suh," she asked in the most charming Southern accent, and when he told her they were a "kind of twinkling blue," the pale blue velvet was the only thing that would do. The saleslady recommended some tiny imitation pearls to be sewn on the dress, and asked him if he didn't want to purchase thread to match, and the whole matter seemed to be taken care of, leaving Mr. Mattison a little astounded by how painless it had been after all.

He was somewhat shaken by the total cost, however, especially the velvet, but his hostility and belligerence from having to make the decision entirely on his own caused him to feel a little reckless, so he told her he would take the material and the beads, too. It was when she asked him if there was anything else that he needed that he remembered the list his wife had given him. He pulled it out of his shirt pocket and began trying to make out the items. Impatiently he handed the list to the young lady, asking her to see if she could make any sense from it. Apparently she didn't find the list to be any major problem, and in a short while had added several items to his purchases.

Upon leaving, he thanked the young lady graciously, and once again out on the street, felt a relief so overwhelming that the prospect of buying the regular supplies, which he usually disliked, seemed unusually pleasant.

Mr. Mattison lost his last trace of resentment the next morning when Kallie unwrapped the material and held it up against her. Just like the saleslady had predicted, the blue enhanced the color of her eyes, causing them to appear almost violet, and Mrs. Mattison's "Oh, how perfectly beautiful," boosted his pride to the extent that he felt just a little smug with the success of his purchases. And when Kallie discovered the pearls and ran over to him, still clutching the pouch in her hand, hugging him like she used to when she was a little girl, a big lump rose up in his throat. He held her close for a moment, patting her awkwardly on the shoulder, then stated in a voice somewhat huskier than usual, "I must see to my livestock."

When the news spread throughout the Big Spring community that Robinson and Kallie had set a date for their wedding, the womenfolk began immediately to plan how they could pool their resources and send the young couple off with a good start.

Precious scraps of material were collected and two quilt tops were pieced. Homespun was woven for the linings. Green walnut hulls were used to make a dye that gave the linings color. A mattress cover was woven, ready to be filled with clean fresh straw.

The gifts ranged from bags of dried fruit, peas, and beans, to handmade items such as pillowcases with delicate embroidery and hand crocheted lace made from homespun thread. Somehow through the collective efforts of all the ladies, they had come up with two feather pillows and a featherbed.

The gifts were presented to the couple one Sunday afternoon after the church service and dinner on the ground was over. As the gifts piled up, Melinda noticed that her ma had become noticeably quiet. Concerned, she eased up beside her, whispering anxiously, "Ma, are you all right?"

The reassuring smile she flashed was so unexpected that Melinda was taken aback. "Oh, yes, dear. I'm perfectly all right," Elvina hastened to assure her. "It's… it's just… ." She stopped, unable to go on.

"It's what, Ma?" Melinda pressured, her concern deepening.

Finally, regaining her composure and smiling even though there were tears in her eyes, Elvina whispered, "It's just that everyone has been so good to us."

But what she didn't explain to Melinda was that for the first time since before the war, she felt the complete love and acceptance of the community again. "Thank you, God," she prayed silently. "Maybe, just maybe, it's finally over."

* * * * *

But the anger and distrust were not over as far as the South was concerned. However, to some extent, conditions had improved for the state of Georgia as a whole. The year was 1870; the year Georgia was readmitted to the Union. Mr. Mattison had come back from town reporting that there seemed to be less Federal troops. It was rumored also that all of the militia would soon be pulled out of Georgia. The Federal troops had always been a hateful sight to true-blooded Southerners, an irritating reminder that the South had lost the war. But the most caustic factor endured was that the officials in Washington didn't think Georgia was capable of handling its civil affairs. And even if the troops had been sent to supposedly keep law and order, especially where the rights of the ex-slaves were concerned, most of the local people didn't trust them. They looked upon them as aliens, foreigners on their home soil; invaders who didn't have any business trying to tell them how to operate their state business, even if the North had won the war.

Some individuals were terribly afraid of the military. To those who had suffered at the hands of unscrupulous Northern soldiers, during and after the war, the uniform signified oppression and danger, not safety; suspicion and fear instead of trust.

But all of the upheaval in state affairs, both local and Federal, had little effect on the lives of the rural populace, especially the poor, except that it made the meager price they received for their cotton and corn, after taxes or sharing with a landlord, a pitiful subsistence. It was a hateful, depressing way of life; an agonizing peace.

CHAPTER 15

The wedding ceremony was a simple one performed by Reverend Johnson at Big Spring Church immediately following the Sunday morning preaching service. Far from the norm, the church was crowded to overflowing by friends and relatives.

Robinson and Kallie stood with their backs to the congregation facing the preacher. Jim Wheeler stood to Robinson's right, serving as best man. Liza was Kallie's maid of honor.

Before beginning the ceremony, Reverend Johnson stood for a long dramatic moment waiting for absolute quiet. Then, in a voice that seemed to come from somewhere in the vicinity of his shoelaces, he began solemnly. "Dearly beloved." There was another dramatic pause. "We are gathered here today in the presence of God and these witnesses." His voice drawled on and on. The couple stood quietly, the calmness of their expressions not betraying the nervousness they felt. Robinson heard the preacher say something about Adam, and the creation of man, and that woman was created by God to be a helpmeet. The preacher's words echoed in Robinson's memory to a time several months prior to the wedding when he had struggled with the meaning of marriage and just what God expected of man.

Robinson had been the brunt of much kidding from Jim and some of the other young men after he and Kallie had announced their wedding plans. Some of the teasing had gone so far as to be crude and vulgar in its overtones, and Robinson, even though he knew it was all done in fun and no disrespect intended, had resented it deeply. His love for Kallie was such a tender thing, so dear and precious, that he could hardly tolerate their good-natured harassment. But it had caused Robinson to do some serious pondering along these lines - about the right and wrong of sex, and why it was only mentioned in hushed tones, and more often than not, referred to as something sinful. He wished his pa were alive so that he could talk with him. There was one point that kept nagging him. If sex were sinful, then why was marriage always referred to as "Holy Matrimony? In just listening to "talk," he knew that there were those who believed that even married couples should not indulge in sex unless it was for the purpose of bringing children into the world. Throughout his church-going experiences, he had heard many sermons relating to the creation story, particularly the creation of man and woman, and if he had interrupted the meaning accurately, God had instituted sex in marriage from the very beginning. Then, if God was a Holy God and could not look upon evil, then how could He bless something sinful?

"I'll find out for myself," he determined one morning while plowing the field where winter wheat would be planted. And so it was that after the family had finished the noon meal, Robinson took the Bible down from the mantle, and without comment, walked outside and sat down under the large oak, leaning his back against its massive trunk. Liza, never missing much that went on, quipped to Elvina and Melinda, "Well! Is Robinson going to start preaching?" But the withering look she received from Elvina curtailed any further comments on the matter.

Robinson started with the first verse of Genesis and read through the first chapter. He might have stopped with the twenty-seventh and twenty-eighth verses where it told about male and female being created in the image of God and that God blessed them and told them to be fruitful and multiply, except that by this time he found the unfolding of events strangely fascinating, especially the second telling of the creation story. He didn't stop until he had read through the third chapter as well.

By this time, lunch hour was over, so he closed the Bible and took it back inside. At least he was satisfied about what the Scriptures had to say. Certainly God had not called man and woman's relationship wrong when God blessed the union. He concluded that it was only after they had disobeyed God that their eyes had been opened to the evil side of the world. The way he saw it, man is conceived in sin because Adam and Eve disobeyed God. From that act forward, man's total nature was sinful in the eyes of God, not just the sexual relationship between man and woman. When blessed by God in Holy Matrimony, intimacy was not wrong.

Reverend Johnson paused and stood looking at Robinson, waiting expectantly for Robinson's response. "The ring!" he remembered, jolting into action. Face burning with embarrassment, Robinson turned to look at Jim who was to hand him the ring. Jim's expression was impassive except for the twinkle in his eye; a telltale brightness that Robinson recognized painfully as amusement. Robinson took the ring from Jim, his injured pride forgotten as he remembered tenderly that the gold band had been his ma's wedding ring.

The wedding was celebrated with dinner on the ground immediately following the ceremony. It was a long day for Kallie and Robinson, since both of them were basically shy and not used to being the center of attention. For once the multiple dishes of tempting food held little interest for Robinson, and he was hardly aware of what he ate. He kept looking at Kallie and thinking, "She's mine! All mine, for always!" And Kallie, apparently aware of what he was thinking, blushed often, portraying varying expressions of embarrassment and happiness.

The newly married couple rode back home with Elvina and the girls in the wagon. The women, with the exception of Kallie, chatted constantly about the events of the day. In the back of the wagon, flanked by the gifts and household items they had received that day, was Kallie's trunk; a wedding gift from her parents containing the sum total of most of her earthly possessions.

The sun was low in the west when they arrived back home. Robinson assisted Kallie from the wagon; then, removing her trunk carried it inside and up the ladder on his shoulder to their quarters. Kallie, following close behind, stood looking around her new home. Robinson, his eyes glued to her face, waited tensely for some indication as to how she liked the room. Her silence made him uncomfortable. He felt as if he should apologize, but the words wouldn't come. It had all looked so good to him before. The bed made up with linens that were gifts from the neighbors. The handmade dresser with a mirror and two small drawers on top that he had paid for with swapped labor; the hand braided rug made by Elvina. After what seemed like an interminable length of time, Kallie moved over near him and holding out her arms, whispered, "I never dreamed it would be this beautiful!"

Joyously Robinson pulled her into his arms, giddy-headed with relief. "Oh, Kallie, Kallie," he whispered over and over, kissing her eyes, her cheeks, her lips. "I wish I didn't have to take care of the chores," he whispered. "I don't want to leave you."

Reluctantly they made their way back down to the main room of the cabin. As he went into the bedroom to change into his work clothes, he heard Kallie exclaim, "Oh, Mrs. Stuart! Everything is so pretty. I love the rug you made for us."

It had been a long day and everyone was exhausted. Just as soon as the supper remains could be cleared away, Melinda and Liza went into the bedroom to prepare for bed. After Elvina had finished tidying up the kitchen, she kissed Rob and Kallie good night and disappeared into the bedroom also.

Robinson pulled a small strip of wood from one of the split logs in the woodbin and lit it in the fire to light a candle, then reached out his other hand to Kallie, noting for the first time how pale she was. When she took his outstretched hand, he was shocked by the coldness of her fingers. "Are you cold, darling?" he asked anxiously.

"A little," she admitted, shivering.

"It's warmer up here," Robinson assured her as they climbed up the ladder again.

Kallie walked over to the edge of the bed and sat down, trying to control her shivering. She had to clamp her teeth tightly together to keep them from chattering.

Robinson placed the candleholder on the dresser and turned to sit down beside her. He was at a complete loss as to what to say, or do. Here they were, on their wedding night, something they had dreamed of for months, and Kallie looked as if she might burst into tears at any moment.

He put his arm around her and pulled her close, his thoughts racing. What is the matter? Had he offended her in some way? When after some time she still sat rigid within the circle of his arm, he stood up and walked over to the window, opening the small wooden shutter. The moonlight streamed in.

"Look, sweetheart," he urged gently. "The harvest moon is beautiful."

Hesitating momentarily, she got up and walked slowly across the room to stand beside him, still shivering noticeably.

"Kallie," Robinson said softly, "I love you so very much." He put his arm around her waist and they stood looking at the way the road curved in the moonlight; the trees making shadows that caused the road to disappear in places. Robinson leaned his head down against hers for a moment, gently brushing her forehead with his lips. He noticed, greatly relieved, that she wasn't trembling quite as much.

Very gently he began to remove the combs from her hair. It tumbled down around her shoulders, creating an aura of moonlight. "Don't be afraid, darling," he pleaded. "We're man and wife, now. I belong to you, and you belong to me. I wouldn't do anything to hurt, or frighten you, for anything in the world."

Kallie stood gazing up at Robinson, her eyes two dark pools void of expression. He cupped her face in his hands and kissed her gently on the lips. "Darling, please don't be afraid."

It must have been his anxious tone that aroused Kallie's concern for him, her own fears forgotten. She didn't want him to be worried about her. Didn't he know that she loved him, too? Suddenly, the most important thing in the world at that moment was to reassure him and erase the doubt and anxiety from his face. Inhibitions gone, she reached up, softly touching the side of his face with her fingertips. He covered her small hand with his own and pressed it hard against his face. Standing on tiptoe, she kissed him tenderly on the lips.

"Oh, Kallie, Kallie!" he whispered hoarsely, burying his face in her hair.

In the bedroom below, the three women lay in bed, each locked in their own private world of thoughts. Melinda and Liza, protected from any intimate knowledge of the opposite sex, were caught up in their own imaginations of what this night would mean to Kallie. They looked upon her newly established position of bride and wife in awe and wonder, each silently wishing that they, too, were starting their married life with someone they loved.

And, Elvina, feeling an acute sense of loss in that her son was no longer entirely hers, lay quietly reminiscing her own wedding night so long ago, and re-living the terrible pain anew in that she would never hear John say "I love you," again, nor have him hold her in his arms.

The next morning Kallie awakened to the sounds of muted voices and the smell of frying meat. Slowly she opened her eyes. Daylight, sifting through the latticed shutters, made soft shadows on the rough rafters of the ceiling. Then, the memory of why she was here in this strange place came flooding into her consciousness, and she turned quickly to look at her husband. A sharp intake of her breath was the only indication of her disappointment that he was not there.

"Of course," she thought remembering, "he had to take care of the chores." Quickly she threw back the covers. "I must hurry," she prodded herself mentally. "I don't want Mrs. Stuart to think Rob married a lazy girl."

The loft was chilly causing her steps to quicken as she crossed the cold floor to her trunk. She lifted the lid and removed some underwear and a blue cotton dress. She slipped her gown over her head, her teeth chattering from the cold. The chill of the room increased her haste, and in a few minutes, her cold fingers were buttoning her dress. She removed a knitted shawl from the trunk and threw it around her shoulders, snuggling against its warmth. A pair of long cotton stockings was the next item of clothing she removed from the trunk before closing the lid. Once again she crossed the cold floor to sit on the edge of the bed where she began pulling on her stocking and shoes.

It had been strange waking up and finding herself alone. She had expected to reach out and find Robinson warm and comfortable next to her. In a way, it all seemed like a dream. Was she really married and had she spent the night in this room with her husband? Was her sheltered life that she had known back at home with her parents really over forever?

"This is my home from now on," she said to herself, her thoughts bordering on nostalgia. For a long moment she gazed around the room, which seemed a little alien without Robinson's presence.

Lost in thought her eyes moved from object to object. She walked over to the dresser, her fingers caressing the satin finish. This was the piece of furniture that Robinson had described to her with such pride; had told her about applying the finish and hand rubbing the surface until it was smooth and glossy.

Glancing upward she caught a glimpse of herself in the mirror and was dismayed by her reflection. "My hair!" she gasped, reaching up to smooth it in place. Hurrying over to her small valise that contained her toilet articles, she removed her comb and brush. When she had brushed all the tangles out of her hair, she plaited it into one large braid and then, after winding it firmly into a large oval bun at the nape of her neck, pinned it securely with hairpins. When she had finished she stood looking at the reflection of the room in the mirror. The small rocker with its ruffled cushion and skirt had been another gift from her ma and pa. Her gaze came to rest upon the counterpane on the bed, recalling how long it had taken her to weave it on her ma's loom. It also reminded her that she had not made the bed. Hurrying across the room, she started removing the covers and didn't stop until the featherbed was exposed. According to her ma, featherbeds should be plumped and turned every day.

She had remade the bed and was wishing fervently that she had a broom handle to smooth the humps from the feather bed's surface when she heard a door close below and Robinson's voice. "He's back!" she whispered joyously. It was only a matter of minutes before his head appeared at the top of the ladder. Grinning mischievously he called, "Hey, sleepy head! Time for breakfast!" Sprinting quickly over the top of the ladder, he hurried over to her, crushing her against him.

"I woke up, and you were gone," Kallie pouted against his shoulder.

"Did you miss me?" he teased, lifting her chin with his hand, his eyes devouring her.

"Yes," she admitted in a whisper, a slight flush spreading over her face.

"Good!" he laughed, pulling her back into his arms and holding her tightly against him. Hungrily his lips found hers.

"Breakfast!" Elvina's voice floated up to them. Kallie and Robinson slowly broke apart.

"I wish we didn't have to go," he whispered gruffly, crushing her lips against his again.

In a few minutes they had joined the others around the long table. Kallie sat quietly by Robinson, picking at her food. "I wish I could have cooked his breakfast," she thought wistfully. She became so lost in her musing that Elvina had to ask her twice if she would like some more milk, which embarrassed Kallie and made her even more self-conscious of her new status as a bride.

They all lingered around the table longer than usual that morning, reliving the events of the day before. But it wasn't long before Robinson pushed his plate back and announced that he had to get to work. Kallie's eyes reflected her disappointment. Pleased, Robinson placed his hand on her shoulder as he arose, his fingers pressing suggestively for just a brief moment, then he was gone out the door. Kallie sat staring at the closed door, a strange wave of loneliness engulfing her.

Impulsively Liza reached across the table and laid her hand on Kallie's. "Kallie, he's only gone to the woodpile," she reassured her mischievously.

Startled, Kallie's large blue eyes stared at Liza for a brief moment, then her warm smile that was so familiar swept over her face and she laughed softly, squeezing Liza's fingers in response.

Elvina, smiling happily, started stacking the plates. Melinda got to her feet, stretched lazily, then walked over to lift the dishpan from its peg. The workday had begun for them, too.

CHAPTER 16

Melinda stood before the dresser in the bedroom that she shared with her ma and Liza, giving herself one last appraisal before the small mirror. She straightened the bodice of her dress again and gazed in consternation at her reflection. Dark hair piled high upon her head, held firmly with a few precious hairpins, and a creamy complexion that was prone to appear pale. Leaning forward, she peered closely at one side of her face and then the other.

"It's the excitement, I suppose, that makes me look so pale," she worried, pinching her cheek slightly in several places and rubbing it vigorously. The other one received the same treatment. She stood looking first at one side and then the other, surveying the results of her mild assault. "That's better," she mused, turning to leave the room.

Liza had been dressed for over an hour. Since she was never overly concerned with her appearance, dressing for any occasion was only a matter of the necessary clothing and a quick hairdo. While Melinda was fussing with her hairstyle, Liza was outside helping Elvina with the last minute preparations for their housewarming party, which in reality was a "room warming" party. This social occasion was the result of a project initiated by Robinson the year following his marriage to Kallie. After the crop was laid by, Robinson decided to tackle adding another room on the cabin. It was agreed by all concerned that the new addition should be built from logs just like the original cabin.

When Jim Wheeler dropped by to visit Robinson one day and saw the pile of logs he had already cut, he passed the word around, and the neighbors pitched in and helped. A project that Robinson had hoped to get finished by plowing time the next spring was all completed in a matter of weeks, except for the inside sealing of the walls. To show their appreciation, the Stuart's had invited everyone that had assisted and their families to a potluck supper with square dancing in the new room later. Kallie's parents had received a special invitation.

Upstairs, Robinson struggled into his Sunday clothes while Kallie sat on the side of the bed waiting patiently. She looked about her at the small area that had become so much a part of her life. It would seem strange living in another room besides this one. After all, this nest of theirs, as they affectionately referred to it in private, held so many precious memories.

The winter months had not been nearly as bad as they had anticipated for the weather had been unusually mild. The lack of privacy had been the most difficult part for Kallie. Even though Ma Stuart and the girls were kind and considerate, there were times when she longed to get away for a little while - just some time alone. Kallie's severest testing did not come from being away from her family, or the confinement of close quarters. As a rule, the family atmosphere was peaceful and congenial with only an occasional flare-up of tempers, usually initiated by Liza. Kallie's burning need was a home of her own where she and Robinson could be alone. But this was her secret. She could never reveal her true feelings to Robinson. He had been totally honest with her before they married – and she had accepted the terms.

Sometimes when the discontent crowded in upon her and she felt that she must get away for a while, she would go for a long walk down by the creek and through the pastureland. The walks helped because they gave her needed solitude, a time to think, to breathe free, and to gather her thoughts together. She always found it easier to go back to the confines of their lifestyle after she had roamed the hills for a while.

She looked forward to nighttime for that was when she could be alone with Robinson and have him all to herself. In the winter, night came early, and after the chores were all finished and the supper things cleared away, they would escape to the one private spot in their world. Kallie had made the delightful discovery early in their marriage that her husband loved to have her read to him. On especially cold nights, they would warm large flat rocks near the fire, wrap them in pieces of cloth, and use them for foot warmers. Warm and snug, Kallie would read from Elvina's collection of books or from her own. Sometimes it would be a novel, a biography, or one of history.

She had a natural flair for oral reading and the womenfolk, as well as Robinson, enjoyed having her read to them. Oftentimes during bad weather when everyone was confined to the cabin during the day, Elvina and the girls would work at their individual tasks of knitting, piecing quilt tops, or mending. Kallie wrapped in a shawl and sitting near the window where there was more light, whisked them away into an exciting world of imagination. Unless the temperature was extremely low, the cold didn't keep Robinson from working outside, but on unusually bad days, he, too, would prop his chair against the kitchen wall, and leaning his head back, eyes closed, allowed himself to be transported to the world of the printed page.

Occasionally, when the weather permitted, they visited her parents, and these small excursions brought a welcomed change from the day-to-day routine. Not only was it a joy to be with her ma and pa again, but also the trip gave Kallie and Robinson a rare opportunity of being entirely alone for a while.

Loud laughter and the sound of several voices talking at once drifted up from the yard below, penetrating the silence of the loft and Kallie's pensive mood. Hurrying over to the tiny window, she saw that some of the guests were beginning to arrive.

"Hurry, Rob," she urged excitedly, "company's here!"

It wasn't long before the multiple sounds of wagon and buggy wheels could be heard, and the outer yard began to be filled with vehicles, nervous horses, and indifferent mules.

When all the guests had arrived and the food ready for serving, Elvina asked Mr. Mattison to return thanks. His "Amen" was the signal for those present to fill their plates from the delicious dishes of food the ladies had prepared.

Many of the guests had finished eating and were standing around indulging in small talk when a lone rider came into view. The sun was sinking behind the treetops and its dying rays picked up the reddish highlights of the hair of the rider's roan horse. The man sat erect, almost military in manner, except for the jaunty tilt of his hat, which gave him a rakish air.

Melinda stood transfixed, her eyes upon the approaching horse and rider. "That must be Garrett Anderson," she thought excitedly, her pulse fluttering in her throat like a butterfly caught in a spider's web.

Jim Wheeler and Garrett had first become acquainted when Jim's boss, a sawmill owner, had sent Jim to inspect some timber for sale in an adjoining county. The owner of the timber was Robert Anderson, Garrett's father. During the transaction of business at that time and in the months following, Jim and Garrett had become good friends. Jim had mentioned Garrett to Robinson several times, indicating how much he would like for the two to meet. It was Robinson's suggestion, therefore, that Jim invite Garrett to the party. "Besides," he thought, "it just might liven up the event for my two sisters who seem to rebuff all serious intentions of the available young men in our area."

Melinda continued to stand motionless as the rider brought his horse to a halt at the edge of the yard, his back to the guests. Then, suddenly aware that she was staring, she glanced around fleetingly to see if anyone had noticed. That's when she saw Jim hurrying over to greet the newcomer. To hide her embarrassment and excitement, Melinda busied herself with straightening the tablecloth in front of her and rearranging the near empty dishes of food. Any small task that would make her appear indifferent to the stranger's arrival.

She was kneeling with her full skirt tucked gracefully around her, busily rearranging some baked apples on a platter, when she heard Jim call her name from behind. She turned, looking upward, expecting

Jim to be there, but instead she found herself staring into dark brown eyes that were painfully familiar.

Melinda gasped, rising quickly to her feet, not even noticing the helping hand Jim held out toward her.

"You! What are you doing here?" she demanded, the old paralyzing fear surging through her even though she knew full well the man before her no longer posed a threat to any of them.

Before Garrett could answer, Jim asked, "Do you know this fellow, Melinda?"

"Yes," Melinda answered quietly, her composure regained. "We've met."

"You've met? You didn't tell me that, Garrett! Hey, just what is going on here, anyway," Jim demanded, evidently disturbed.

"Nothing, Jim. Really," Melinda answered somewhat evasive, her eyes never leaving Garrett's face. "We met during...during the war."

"During the war? How? When?"

Melinda's gaze shifted to meet Jim's quizzical stare. "This is the Yankee Lieutenant who kept his men from harming Liza and me."

"Well, I'll be...," Jim stopped short of swearing, expression grim. Turning again to Garrett. "You should have told me, Garrett."

Garrett shrugged. "It didn't seem important," he replied, trying hard to appear casual.

"Not important! Man, do you have any idea the position you have placed me in?"

"Maybe you're right, Jim. I suppose I just didn't think it through. I apologize." Turning toward Melinda, he said quietly. "It's good to see you, again, Ma'am. Now I'll just be on my way."

"No, Jim," Melinda objected quickly, reaching out to touch him lightly on the arm. "Mr...." she hesitated, not knowing his name.

"Anderson, Miss Stuart, "Garrett Anderson."

"Mr. Anderson is welcome here," she assured Jim graciously. "Now, Mr. Anderson, may I offer you something to drink? I believe the last time you were here all we had to offer was sassafras tea."

Garrett smiled weakly. "And I hope you have something to offer other than sassafras tea," he replied, grimacing good-naturedly.

The long thin notes of the fiddle started up in the new room. Still somewhat disgruntled, Jim excused himself and headed toward the sound.

"Tell, me, Mr. Anderson," Melinda requested as she poured a glass of cold apple cider. "Were you the one who left the food on our porch that morning?"

"Please call me Garrett," he corrected her again pleasantly. "Now, where would I get a slab of bacon and a peck of potatoes," he added, pretending innocence.

"You were kind to us," she said, shaking her head slowly as she recalled the horror. "We almost starved to death."

"There were many who did," he answered soberly, expression somber.

"Why?" she asked. "Why did the poor have to suffer so much?"

"The rich suffered, too, probably more, because they had more to lose. And, there always seem to be more poor people."

"Why did you come back down here?" she probed, handing him a clean plate and a fork.

"My father is a land speculator. I didn't want to make soldiering a career, so I came South with him and my mother and my younger brother, Keith."

"So! You've come back to swallow up what's left!" she concluded, fire in her eyes.

"No. You misunderstand. It's not like that at all! True, we're here to make money, but not to steal! We buy land at a fair market price. If the previous owner wishes to remain on the land and lease it from us, then he has that prerogative."

"Oh?" Melinda frowned, one eyebrow slightly raised. "Now, let me see if I have this straight. You people from up north came down here and destroyed our land, our homes, everything! And, then, after you've left us destitute, you come back and buy up our land, at your price, and let us live on it, for a price; your price, that is!" Her usually soft voice had become tinged with bitter anger. "I believe there's a not too nice name for those who do that! Carpetbagger!"

Garrett's face reddened. "You're making a judgment without knowing the facts, Miss Stuart," he explained patiently. "We didn't start the war anymore than you did. It was a terrible tragedy for both sides. I supported it because I do not believe that it is right for a man to own another."

When she offered no comment, he continued. "My Dad has never cheated anyone, nor taken advantage of anyone knowingly. Even though it might appear that we are one of the unethical groups, we feel like in time people will come to know and trust us as a friend. The war happened. It's over. Now, we have to pick up the pieces and go from here. My father feels that when he pays a man a fair price for a piece of land that the land sharks are going to rake in because the owner is at their mercy, he's done something to help that man. Every contract that my father draws up with a landowner has the stipulation in it that at any time the former owner wants to redeem the land, at the fair market price, he will have that opportunity. Most all of them welcome the chance to stay at home, so to speak."

"I'm sorry," she said thoughtfully. "It's hard to be objective when you've seen so much heartache and suffering."

"I know," he replied quietly, the grimness of his expression exposing the tired lines around his eyes and mouth.

"I'm sure you do," she agreed softly, eyes filling; seeing him for the first time from a different perspective. For someone of his sensitive nature, she gathered, it would have probably been easier to endure suffering that inflicts it on others.

Remembering her manners, she said apologetically, "You still haven't had anything to eat."

"You've changed," he said abruptly, and when she turned startled eyes to stare at him, he added hurriedly, "for the better, that is. Not that you could be more beautiful," he continued tenderly. "Even when you weren't anything but a rack of bones with skin stretched over it, you were still beautiful. You are another reason I eagerly accepted Jim's invitation. I wanted to see you again; to get to know more about you."

Blushing prettily, Melinda dropped her gaze and continued to serve his plate. "These baked apples are especially delicious," she suggested, trying to hide her confusion.

Garrett wasn't particularly interested in baked apples, or anything else to eat. He was too excited about seeing Melinda again. But, not wanting to appear rude, he consented. Besides, this gave him an opportunity to feast his eyes upon her. It was true, what he had said? She was more beautiful than he remembered. Her once gaunt cheeks were full, now, and her shapeless frame had filled out in the right places. She still wasn't what some would call a "full-bosomed woman," but she had the type of figure that appealed to him, tall and willowy, but feminine and dainty.

Later, as they entered the new room, the square dance caller was barking away and a set of square dancers were nimbly moving back and forth, or round and round, according to his instructions. Robinson and Jim were standing against the far wall watching the performers. Suddenly Robinson stiffened, and turning to Jim, demanded angrily, "What's that damn Yankee doing here?"

Not in the least surprised by Robinson's reaction, Jim hurried to explain. "Now, Rob, don't go getting all riled up. I invited him here."

"You invited him?" A slow flush covered Robinson's face.

"Yes. You told me it was all right," Jim hedged, feeling somewhat guilty.

"You... you mean that Yankee is your new business acquaintance?"

"Uh-huh! And a mighty good one, too! The best!"

"Jim," Robinson said quietly and evenly, his manner indicative of controlled anger that was about to explode. "If it should happen to make any difference to you, he was the officer that was in charge of the men who tried to rape my sisters!"

"The way I understand it, Rob," Jim replied, his own voice beginning to reflect agitation, "he was the one that prevented that very thing from happening to Melinda and Liza, and possibly your Ma!"

"He's still a damn Yankee!" Robinson all but spat the words.

"Rob, give him a chance," Jim coaxed. "He's a good guy, Rob. True, he's a Yankee, but he had a job to do. And he did it! But he still showed mercy toward the losing side. From the way I see it, you owe him a lot."

"I don't owe him a d---- thing," Robinson retorted through clenched teeth, face pale.

Jim said nothing. He'd never seen Robinson so upset. In fact, he couldn't recall ever hearing him swear before.

Across the room, Melinda turned to Garrett. "Do you know how to square dance?"

"No, I'm afraid not."

"It's easy," she smiled. "You'll pick it up in no time."

It was a glorious evening for Melinda. It hadn't taken Garrett long to learn the turns, and he laughed a lot, usually at himself when he would mess up. There had been a cool reserve toward him from the other guests at first,, but as the word passed around (initiated by Jim) that he was the one who had protected the Stuart womenfolk from the Union soldiers, the barriers were let down, and he was accepted cordially, if not warmly.

It wasn't that easy for Robinson, however. But before the evening was over he had cooled down to some extent, especially after he was reminded by Kallie that Garrett was an invited guest, and therefore, Southern hospitality demanded that he be treated as such with ungrudging cordiality.

And, too, he was happy for Melinda. Never had he seen her enjoy an evening with such enthusiasm. "I'm afraid she's hooked," he lamented to Kallie later. To himself, he thought bitterly, "And it would have to be a Damn Yankee!"

Melinda was still in a state of enchantment the next day. "I don't know why I never noticed how good looking he was before," she confided in the womenfolk while Robinson was outside.

"You were too overwrought to notice before!" Elvina reminded her. "He was the enemy."

"He said he has a younger brother, Liza," Melinda said, casually glancing in her sister's direction.

"Oh, now! Wouldn't that please Rob? Two Damn Yankees around!"

"Liza!" Elvina rebuked sternly. "There's no excuse for that kind of sarcasm!"

"Well? Isn't it true?" she demanded, eyes flashing.

"I think to be fair we should judge each individual on their own merit," Elvina interceded kindly. "We shouldn't just bunch them all together and label them as one."

"But he did help destroy the South!" she retorted, voice rising sharply.

"Yes," Elvina conceded patiently, trying to smooth the situation. "He did do that."

225

Kallie had remained silent, afraid that anything she might say would get her into trouble. Secretly, she thought Garrett extremely handsome, and it brightened her day just to see Melinda so happy. However, she wisely kept her opinion to herself because of Liza and Robinson's reservations.

But Liza's cutting remarks, which did have some merit, and Robinson's stony silence, weren't enough to destroy the magic of the night before for Melinda. Never had a man had this effect upon her emotions. Just being near him made her pulse quicken, and when their hands had touched while square dancing, she found herself wishing it could last and would have been mortally ashamed for anyone to know the thoughts that flashed through her mind. What it would be like to have him hold her in his arms? To have him kiss her? "Have I fallen in love?" she thought wonderingly, trying to keep her mind on the caller's instructions. "Was this the way it happened? One moment you were living a dull, at times almost unbearable existence, and suddenly, without any warning, your life was transcended into something so exciting that it made your head spin?"

And she would have been excited even more if she could have known Garrett's true feelings. To her dismay, her hair had kept slipping loose from its pins while she danced, and finally, at Garrett's insistence, she had let it hang free. As Garrett watched her slender body keeping time with the music, her hair swinging about her shoulders in a cascade of dark beauty, large gray eyes solemn and starry-eyed except when they met his, and then, the fleeting response of warmth he saw there; he thought she had to be the loveliest girl he had ever seen.

"Just as I remembered," he kept thinking happily over and over again. And for a little while, the war and all of its hideous scars were forgotten.

* * * * *

The multiple events that took place within the next couple of years following the "housewarming" were staggering to Elvina - both in number and importance. Garrett and Melinda had fallen deeply in love - which had surprised no one. And, then, to make it doubly exciting, a romance had developed between Liza and Keith - a whirlwind affair that seemed the most unlikely of all things to happen.

In the beginning, Elvina had been deeply concerned about Melinda and Liza's involvement with the Anderson boys. It wasn't that she didn't like them, or that she had any real objections to either of them personally, she just didn't know anything about them. If she could have had her way, the girls would have fallen in love with local boys from families they knew something about. And her concern was justified to a great extent. There had been many people pouring into the South since the war, and sometimes, they weren't too endowed with the virtues of honest and moral ethics.

But James and Rosemary Wheeler had helped quiet her fears. Friends of theirs who lived near the Anderson's had nothing but high praise for the entire family. That is, for David Anderson, the father, and his two sons, Garrett and Keith. Mrs. Anderson had died not long after their move to Georgia. From all accounts, the Anderson's were respectable and solid citizens who planned to make Georgia their permanent home.

As far as family resemblance and personalities were concerned, Garrett and Keith could have never been identified as brothers. Garrett, tall and dark complexioned like his father, was not a great talker but possessed a surprising talent for dry wit. There was an air of quiet self-confidence about him, and when he walked into a room, he seemed to bring a controlled strength with him.

Keith was just the opposite. His blond hair with red overtones was prone to curl and his deep blue eyes gave him a perpetual air of youthfulness. Short of stature and measuring only a few inches taller than Liza, he was a carbon copy of his late mother.

Keith and Liza had become friends from their first meeting, despite her inhibitions toward "Yankees" in general. He seemed to find her antagonistic remarks highly amusing. In time, Keith's attentions had become more amorous but Liza's attitude toward him remained aloof, treating him more like a lovesick puppy than a romantic suitor. It became increasingly obvious as they saw more of each other that Keith had come to adore her, basking in her caustic wit and oftentimes stinging banter. And, she seemed to grow fonder of him, too, in a sisterly sort of way.

But marriage? That had been a profound shock to all. No one had seriously considered Liza and Keith's relationship in the realm of matrimony.

Elvina wouldn't have been quite so apprehensive about Liza's and Keith's marriage plans if Liza's often repeated phrase hadn't kept coming back to haunt her, "Some day I'm going to be rich and never have to work in the fields again!"

Elvina had tried to talk to Liza over the years about the real values of life. "You may be letting yourself in for a lot of disappointment and unhappiness if you don't get your values straight," Elvina had warned her over and over.

"What does all this hard work ever get you?" Liza invariably retorted. "You struggle to plant and work the crops; then, there's the back-breaking job of picking the cotton, which I hate with a passion, and the gathering of the rest. The heat! The dust! For what, food on the table and a few measly dollars when the cotton is sold? And most of that has to go for taxes! Maybe enough left to buy a calico dress and a pair of shoes! No way! That's not for me! You'll see!" And even if she had dignity enough not to voice her cryptic opinions publicly, her family knew what motivated her refusal to take seriously any attention paid to her by any of the local young men. How she thought it would be possible for her to make this dream come true was something she refused to discuss to any great length. Therefore, the family just looked upon her outbursts as rebelling against a frustrating situation. One, they, too, identified with painfully.

Elvina had cautiously tried again after Liza had accepted Keith's proposal, explaining that the real important things in life centered on marrying someone you loved with all your heart. "I don't see why you can't have love and money!" Liza had replied, haughty in her optimism.

Dismayed, Elvina wondered what ever happened to the frightened little girl who used to cling to her skirts. And on the day of the wedding, which turned out to be a double one, Elvina had been torn between happiness for Melinda and apprehension for Liza. Did Liza really love Keith, or was she just using him for an escape?

"Oh, Lord," she prayed fervently. "Where did I fail with Liza?" Then, trying to find comfort, she had silently scolded herself. "Just maybe you're wrong, old girl! Now, quit borrowing trouble and torturing yourself!" But the announcement that overshadowed all the rest, including Jim Wheeler's forthcoming marriage to Salena Davis from Savannah, was the one made by Robinson shortly after Melinda and Liza were married. He and Kallie were expecting a baby.

CHAPTER 17

The leafless limbs of the trees stretched toward the heavens, swaying back and forth like the stilted movements of mechanical dolls. The sky was also gray, except when the low fast moving clouds separated. Occasionally a touch of blue beyond brought momentary relief through the overcast. Tiny sparrows hopped across the grass, their heads darting downward spasmodically to glean some tiny fragment of food.

Kallie opened the back door of the cabin and felt an immediate gust of cold wind against her face. The clouds parted for just a moment and the filtered rays of an unexpected burst of sunlight momentarily impaired her vision. "The birds are singing and it is only February," she mused. A saucy cardinal joined the sparrows, his bright red feathers providing a touch of cheerful relief to the somber landscape.

She had not told Robinson that she was with child. Time and time again she had been mistaken in the past. This time she was absolutely certain. They had been married for almost two years and both of them were beginning to be a little anxious about whether or not they could have a baby. However, it could be looked upon as a blessing, she reasoned. The crowded conditions under which they had started their married life would have made taking care of a baby extremely trying on the entire household.

Stopping at the woodpile, she picked up several small pieces of firewood and turned back toward the cabin. "I'll tell him tonight," she decided happily.

They usually read a while in bed before blowing out the light and this night was no different. Kallie could hardly wait to tell him but she wanted the timing to be just right - the mood perfect.

Kallie laid the book aside but did not blow out the light. The story had involved a boy and girl in a tender, tragic love story that had touched both of them deeply. She turned so that her head rested on his shoulder. Tenderly she kissed him on the neck just below his ear. Robinson pulled her hard against him, kissing her hungrily, and then their world narrowed to the dimension of the love they shared. Later, as they lay quietly savoring the wonder and joy of belonging to each other, Kallie knew that this was the special moment she had been waiting for. Snuggling her head close to his, her lips close to his ear, she told him her secret.

Robinson's surprised reaction was everything Kallie had hoped. He sat straight up in bed taking the covers with him, exposing them to the chill of the spring night air.

"Are you sure? Absolutely sure?" he questioned, not wanting to be disappointed again.

"Yes, yes," Kallie laughed softly, shivering partly from excitement and partly from the chill of the room. "I knew you'd say that, so I've made absolutely sure, this time!" Playfully tugging on his shoulder, she begged "Please lie back down before you freeze us both to death!"

"Well, how about that! I'm really going to be a Papa," he said wonderingly, lying back and pulling the covers close.

"When?" was the next question.

"Sometime in October."

"I can't believe it! Me a papa!"

"Well, don't forget I'm going to be a Mama," Kallie teased. "But, I… I have been a little worried," she confided, faking seriousness.

"Worried? Worried about what? Is something wrong?" he demanded, suddenly fearful.

"No, no!" she assured him quickly. "Not anything serious," she said softly, feeling guilty for teasing him about something so important. "It's… it's just, well, I'm wondering? Will you still love me when I get all out of shape and waddle like a duck?"

Grinning with relief Robinson propped himself up on one elbow again, intent on making a flippant remark. But something about the underlying expression in her eyes stopped him. Soberly, gently, he cupped his fingers around her chin, holding her face toward the light so that he could look into her eyes. "I'll love you even more," he whispered reassuringly, kissing her tenderly. "Don't you know that?" He leaned across her to blow out the light and then stretched out beside her again. "Just think!" he marveled. "I'm going to be a papa!"

Feeling completely safe and secure in his love, Kallie snuggled up against him. "I'll be glad when the baby gets here," she sighed happily.

Robinson had been totally sincere when he assured Kallie he was thrilled about the baby, but at the same time, he had many reservations, too. Doubts that he had never revealed to anyone. How could a man tell anyone, especially his wife who thought him fearless, that death held such a horror for him? That he thought it a form of cruelty to bring a human being into the world to face the inevitability of death? And, as if death in itself wasn't enough of an enemy, there was the hurt that man inflicted upon his own kind. But it didn't stop there! It was evident in nature as well.

There was enough of the artist in him to enjoy a beautiful sunset, or some rare wildflower. But death held an indescribable horror for him and he had never been able to overcome the resentment he felt when his pa's body had been lowered into the ground. Never would he forget the pain and ache in his chest as he heard shovel full after shovel full of dirt fall on the lid of that wooden box. How unreal it was that the warm, sensitive personality that had been his pa had been buried in the ground?

In his questioning he had tried to find relief in picturing his pa in Heaven, blissfully happy - removed from the cares of this world. But that didn't seem to help much. Death, the avenging force that could take a loved one away forever seemed impossible. But it was there - always the victor, except in the world of vegetation. Somehow it wasn't as final there with everything budding forth in the spring after dying down in the winter. "The difference, I suppose, is that man knows that he is going to die," he reasoned, not finding any relief to the perplexing questions.

He found himself becoming increasingly squeamish about killing animals for food. Oftentimes when he would observe a hawk falling with deadly swiftness to catch a small bird in flight, or a mouse trying to scamper to safety beneath a rock, he felt pity for the victim and a deep revulsion for the reality of it. Why was it that for so many creatures to live, another always had to die?

Once as he stood fascinated watching a spider spin its web, amazed by its expertise to create a symmetrical net so flawless in design, only to have his feeling of exultation soon turned to revulsion when a moth flew into the net and became entangled in its snare. The web trembled violently from the first impact and the frantic struggles of the moth that followed. The spider, perched high on the upper part of the web, waited patiently until the moth wearied and its movements grew less. Then, the spider began its descent along the web's surface until it reached its victim. There were a few more moments of struggle from the moth, but the spider overpowered it. Slowly the spider spun a wed around the moth until it resembled a cocoon. Back up across the web the spider dragged its helpless prey to deposit it somewhere beyond the edge of the eave of the house from which it had first attached its web.

But there had been an avenging side to the spectacle later on. A spider, having left the safety of its net, was captured by a dirt dauber. Evidently the dirt dauber stung the spider to paralyze it for it didn't struggle long. Then, clutching the spider with its tiny legs and feet, it flew to the small dirt tunnel it had molded form wet clay under the eave of the barn. Later on, when the dirt dauber's eggs hatched that it had lain in the tiny tomb, the spider would serve as nourishment for the larvae.

The whole scheme of the life and death struggle seemed cruel to Robinson, and he couldn't understand how a God of love could have created it so. Reasoning such as these tormented him when he thought of his unborn child and the uncertainty it would have to contend with in life. What if something should happen to him and his child had to claw and struggle for survival the way his family had? What if there were another war and the devastation came again to snatch away everything they owned except the determination to survive? At times his despair would become so intense that he would find himself regretting that his child was to come into the world. Then, immediately following such rebellious thoughts, he would feel deep shame in that he had dared question God, and he would ask forgiveness for his doubts and lack of faith, never finding any concrete answers to all the fears that plagued him. During these periods of depression, hard physical labor seemed to provide relief from his anxieties. Therefore, he would plunge into whatever task there was to be done with great vigor, relishing in the way it relaxed his muscles and gave his weary mind rest.

Robinson never mentioned his frustrations and doubts to Kallie. Sometimes after a meal, while lingering over a cup of coffee, he would watch her as she moved about her numerous household tasks. He envied the complacent attitude she seemed to have about life in general. When they attended church together, Kallie would sit in rap attention listening carefully to what the preacher had to say. She always seemed to come away satisfied and at peace. Robinson wondered, bitterly sometimes, if Kallie had found an answer to the dark unknowns that enabled her to face life with calmness and serenity. "Maybe she has never been faced with the stark realities in life that leaves one doubting and afraid," he reasoned. But he knew this wasn't true. She'd been a part of the war. So had his ma, and much, much more, and she had the same calm acceptance of life.

By mid-summer Kallie was beginning to look very much in the family way and resolutely refused to leave home for any reason. She wouldn't attend church and since neither Robinson nor Elvina wanted to leave her home alone, Robinson usually went by himself out of respect of his ma. He had much rather stayed home. Passively he sat through the church services, not revealing by so much of a flicker of an eyelash how strangely isolated he felt some times from the rest of those attending. He marveled at the confidence of the preacher in what he presented, and wished fervently that he could know the same kind of positive faith. When heads were bowed in prayer and hearts were turned to God in petitions, or thankfulness, he often prayed silently, "Please God, help me to understand. Help me to believe." There were times of desperation when he longed to talk with someone, but was ashamed to admit to anyone that he entertained such blasphemous and irreverent thoughts.

As the weeks came and went, Kallie, laughing good-naturedly at her increasingly grotesque shape, seemed to have no major concerns in the world except looking after Robinson and struggling with the discomfort associated with her condition. Weekdays, after the household chores were finished, she busied herself with making clothing for the baby. Having been forewarned by Ma Stuart and her own ma that winter babies were much harder to care for than those born in the warmer months, she was determined not to come up lacking in clothing for her child. There were gifts from friends and neighbors, too, seemingly happy for an opportunity to reciprocate the many acts of kindness shown them by the Stuart family. When Kallie would show the treasures for the baby to Robinson, her face radiant with happiness, he would find himself caught up in her exhilarating sense of expectancy, his anxieties forgotten for a time.

It was in the early morning hours while the entire household was still asleep that the baby decided to enter the world. Kallie awoke with a start, not quite sure what had awakened her. She lay still, waiting to identify just what had taken place. Had the baby just pushed unusually hard against her abdomen, or was it another type of pain that had awakened her? Daylight had not yet come, and the early October air was quite chilly; however, she felt restless and so thirsty that her mouth felt dry and parched. Moving cautiously so as not to awaken Robinson, she eased out of bed. Moving quietly she made her way through the familiar surroundings to the kitchen and the water bucket. She dipped some water with the gourd and had just brought the dipper to her lips when a sharp pain flashed across the entire width of her abdomen. Gasping audibly, she dropped the dipper back into the bucket. Grasping the shelf's edge for support, she stood rigid with pain. The discomfort lasted only a few seconds longer, and Kallie relaxed somewhat as the pain subsided. She succeeded in drinking some water on the second try, then made her way back slowly to the bedroom.

Robinson stirred as she sat down on the bed's edge, sleepily asking her if everything was all right. Not quite sure her labor pains had started and not wanting to alarm him unnecessarily, she answered as calmly as her fast-beating heart would permit, "I just went to the kitchen for a drink of water."

Slowly she eased back into bed and closed her eyes. She had dozed off again when another pain hit. She pressed her fingers firmly against her lips to refrain from gasping, and when it was over, she tried to remember what Elvina and her ma had told her about labor pains. They had warned her that the first baby might take a long time, so she tried to remain calm. She had no way of telling the exact time between pains because their only clock was on the mantle over the fireplace in the big room. Kallie counted slowly to sixty then counted each minute upon her fingers. She estimated fifteen minutes had passed before the next pain hit. This time, it was another severe one, and she gasped in spite of her efforts to conceal it. Robinson, who had been dozing fitfully, was wide-awake instantly. "Kallie! Are you sure you are all right?"

"I... I'm not sure," she confessed shakily.

"I'm going to wake, Ma," Robinson stated resolutely, pulling on his pants and heading for the bedroom door. In his haste he kicked his foot against the rocking chair, bending his little toe backward. Gritting his teeth to keep from swearing, he made his way to Elvina's bedroom.

In a few minutes Robinson returned to sit on the edge of their bed again. Then Elvina entered the room, her expression calm and reassuring in the flickering light from the lamp she was carrying. She questioned

Kallie about the pains and how far apart they seemed to be. While they were talking back and forth, another pain gripped Kallie, causing her to bite her lip and grip the side of the bed.

"Robinson, I think it's time to go into town for Doc Evans," Elvina stated matter-of-factly, smiling reassuringly at them both.

"Don't you worry, sweetheart," Robinson whispered to Kallie, kissing her tenderly. "I'll be back with Doc Evans in no time."

"Rob? Will you send word to my folks?"

"Sure thing," he assured her, kissing her again, and then heading for the door. "Ma," he called from the door, "take good care of her until I get back."

Later, Robinson and Elvina waited in the kitchen while Doc Evans examined Kallie. Elvina was putting on a pot of coffee to make when he came back out of the bedroom. "She's coming along nicely," he said matter-of-factly. "I don't think the baby will come for quite some time, though."

"Is anything wrong, Doctor?" Elvina asked, beginning to feel apprehensive.

"No, no," he hastened to reassure them. "It's just that your wife, Rob, is a small woman. But the baby's position is good and unless something unforeseen develops, it should be a normal delivery." He watched as Elvina pulled some hot coals closer to the coffeepot. "Robinson," he said casually, "it might be best if you found something to do outside."

There was a muffled groan from the other room and Robinson jumped up. "Not just yet, Doc," he said, hurrying toward the bedroom door.

Later, however, Robinson followed the Doc's advice. Every time Kallie cried out, he felt as if he'd been stabbed. Finally he went out to the woodpile to vent his frustration and anxiety on the logs. Kallie had begged him not to worry - but that was impossible. "How can she be so calm?" he wondered anxiously as his axe rose and fell, with chips flying in every direction.

But Kallie was far from being as calm as she would have the others believe. She had not voiced her anxieties to anyone but she was terribly afraid. As a child she had heard stories about childbirth whispered among her playmates. How some women had fits and chewed their tongues to shreds during childbirth.

Her strength began to wane as the pains became closer and harder. She was becoming so tired that as each pain subsided, she didn't think she could endure another one. But just about the time she would get her breath from one barrage, the pain would hit again and she was forced into another onslaught that seemed unbearable. There was an awful pressure in the lower part of her body that felt as if it were going to rip part of her away and she wasn't even aware that she was screaming. In the few moments between pains she kept thinking, "I'm so tired. I'm so tired!" and then it would hit again. One time she reached out frantically, clawing the air, and through the maze of pain, felt someone griping her hand, and as the pain subsided for a moment, Elvina's face came into focus. It was no more than a fleeting moment of recognition, however, for another pain engulfed her and she wasn't even aware that she was screaming again.

To Doc Evans, it was just another difficult childbirth. Not that he was callous and uncaring, but he had learned in the early years of practice not to become too emotionally involved. It was better for him and for the patient. But Kallie's screams were torture to Elvina who would have gladly suffered for her if it were possible.

Robinson had sat down on a log to rest for a minute when he heard Kallie scream the first time. He jumped to his feet as if some unseen object had pierced him violently. Slowly he sat back down, his face rigid. When the screams didn't let up but increased in number and intensity, he clutched his face in his hands and whispered brokenly, "Oh, God, please, please help her!"

But the screams continued. As time dragged by, a strange expression, cold and defiant, settled in his eyes and the muscles along his jaw worked spasmodically as he clenched and unclenched his teeth. "Why?" he thought wildly. "Why was Kallie suffering this way when she loved the Lord so? Didn't He claim to look after his own? Was it all brought on by the sin of Eve? That didn't make sense! Was his Kallie going through this horror because of the sins of some one else?"

"It's not fair!" he cried rebelliously, clutching his head tighter, almost wild with his own helplessness. He thought about the times he had witnessed seemingly easy births among the farm animals, and he grimaced with more bitterness. "Even the animals don't suffer this way," he muttered. The emotional pressure inside him seemed to explode and he turned his anger toward God. With anger crimsoning his face, he looked upward, and shaking his fist toward where he supposed Heaven to be, cried brokenly, "If you're any God at all, if you're a God of love and compassion, why does this have to be? You play with us like a cat does with a mouse!" His voice broke, and covering his face with his hands, wept great wracking sobs.

Robinson hadn't cried like that since the death of his pa. However, there was a difference in the pain he felt now and the sorrow he had experienced then. His pa's death had been something that was absolutely beyond his control, and if God had been a caring God and had control over life and death, and still let his pa die, then God couldn't care much what happened to them. So, he determined, he wouldn't count of God much for anything.

But this thing that was happening to Kallie! It was partly his fault. "If she dies," he thought desperately, "I don't think I can live with it."

There was a long piercing scream from the cabin and then total silence. He stood up, gazing in the direction of the sound, hardly breathing. In a few minutes the cabin door opened and his ma stepped outside.

Brushing his sleeve across his face to clear his vision, he tried to read his ma's expression. Slowly, like someone in a trance, tears still visible on his face, he started moving toward her, his eyes searching for reassurance. His ma moved on down the steps and into the sunlight.

"Kallie?" he whispered fearfully.

A tired smile softened the pallor of Elvina's face. "Kallie's going to be all right. She is awfully weak but Doc Evans seems to think she'll make it."

"Can… can I see her?" he asked, voice shaky.

"Yes," Elvina answered, following him up the steps.

Robinson stopped short inside the bedroom door, staring fixedly at Kallie's face. Her hair, dark and wet from perspiration, had been smoothed back from her face. Her dark eyelashes resting on her pale cheeks made her appear even more colorless. He waited, scarcely breathing, his gaze shifting to Doc Evans who was sitting quietly by the bed with Kallie's wrist in one hand and his pocket watch held in the other.

Slowly, like someone in a trance, Robinson approached the foot of the bed and stopped, standing motionless, his eyes never leaving Kallie's face.

"How is she, Doc?" he asked haltingly, as if it took great effort to speak.

"She's mighty weak but her pulse is getting stronger. What she needs now is rest."

Robinson nodded and moved to the other side of the bed. Quietly he dropped to his knees and gently picked up Kallie's other hand. It remained limp and lifeless.

Kallie knew Robinson was there. She felt his kiss on her forehead, but she couldn't seem to open her eyes or make any response. She was so tired it took a great deal of effort just to breathe. Her fingers refused to move when she tried to press his hand. It all seemed to take so much more effort than she could muster.

The doctor glanced at Robinson. "She's sleeping now."

Robinson carefully placed her hand on the coverlet and turned to walk out of the room into the kitchen. Mrs. Mattison had arrived and was sitting near the low fire holding something in her arms. "Don't you want to see your son, Robinson?" she asked softly, her expression a mixture of tears and joy.

Robinson stood quietly for a moment, expression blank. "There was a baby," he thought dazedly. Robinson moved over near Mrs. Mattison and looked down at the baby's face. Tiny lashes rested peacefully upon cheeks that were a dark red. Two ridiculously toy-like hands were clutched into fists and lay motionless outside the blanket. Without a word, Robinson turned and walked out of the cabin.

The two women's eyes followed him as he slowly made his way toward the barn with his head hanging down and shoulders drooped like a tired old man.

Robinson felt dazed, almost as if his mind were numb. He went into the cow's stall and reaching for the shovel stored in the corner, began scooping up the droppings left by the milk cow that morning. Over and over again the terrible screams of Kallie echoed and re-echoed through his brain. He winced inwardly as he recalled her tormented pleas as she prayed. Bitterness and anger made his head pound.

His thoughts flashed back to their wedding day and the two years they had shared since. Because both of them had been taught, and believed, that marriage was an institution devised by God for the perpetuation of the home and family, they had lived in a marital world free from anxiety about Kallie becoming pregnant. But now, he felt as if he had been tricked somehow. If this relationship of theirs could result into this kind of pain and horror, then it was a snare into an unreal world that defied all reason. "There won't be another chance for anything like this," he muttered, sending the scoop's blade plunging viciously across the dirt floor.

Robinson's bitterness did not lessen, nor soften, in the days that followed. Elvina noticed the change in him and it deeply troubled her. Not so much for what he said, but by his silence. Kallie, still weak and unable to move about much, plus the responsibility of the baby, wasn't aware of the difference in Robinson at first, except that she had noticed that he was unusually quiet and somewhat preoccupied. But with extreme physical weariness ever pressing down upon her, and the normal anxieties concerning the baby's welfare demanding most of her attention, she failed to recognize that Robinson was deeply troubled.

But Mrs. Mattison did. Robinson had driven her back home and if she hadn't recognized something was wrong earlier, she might have thought he was at naught with her during the trip. He didn't tarry, either, just came in long enough for some coffee and a short visit with Mr. Mattison.

"Well, what did you name that big boy?" Mr. Mattison asked proudly.

"John," Robinson replied, unemotionally. "John Mattison Stuart."

"Well," Mr. Mattison beamed, "that's a mighty big name to live up to!"

Robinson nodded. "We wanted to name him after you and my pa."

"I'm flattered," Mr. Mattison said, his smile denoting his pleasure.

Later, as the Mattison's stood watching Robinson's wagon turn onto the main road, their eyes dark with concern, Mrs. Mattison expressed her fears verbally for the first time. "I'm worried about Robinson."

"Worried? Worried how?"

"I don't know. It's not anything I can put my finger on. He just hasn't acted the same since the baby was born."

"Oh, he's just suffering from the shock of new parenthood," he replied jokingly, trying to relieve some of her troubled spirit.

Even though Mr. Mattison's answer was somewhat flippant, it was not a true picture of his inner feelings. He, too, was concerned about Robinson and his apparent withdrawal symptoms.

"Robinson will be all right," he assured her. "He's young and he has a lot of responsibility to carry. But he'll make it! Maybe by the time our grandson is Robinson's age the South will be back on its feet. Why, look at what's been accomplished already - the railroad from Atlanta to Savannah restored. And the Amnesty Act that's been passed! Do you realize that the Amnesty Act of 1872 pardons practically everyone who took part in the war against the Union?"

"But all of that doesn't improve our living conditions much," she replied grimly, plainly exasperated. "And besides, what's that got to do with Robinson's frame of mind right now?"

"You're absolutely right, but it's progress - and that's a lot to be thankful for when considering our children and grandchildren's future. Yes," he said, getting to his feet and heading for the door, "I believe things are going to get better."

But he wouldn't have been so optimistic if he could have looked ahead only a few short months when the country would be thrown into another panic caused by the depression of 1873.

CHAPTER 18

Kallie stood at her bedroom window watching the snow as it sifted down like minute pieces of white feathers, crisscrossing, dancing back and forth as if playing a game of tag. But all in all it was a lazy snow, taking its time about falling and even more deliberate in the way it settled on the grass and on the bare limbs of the trees. Occasionally a gust of wind would stir the light blanket on the rooftops of the outbuildings and tumble it along, creating a miniature image of a mighty windstorm.

The smoke from the chimney seemed to hesitate as it met the damp onslaught head-on, and wavering momentarily, curled its way up through the mist to become a part of the cold and to lose its identity entirely.

Only a few small sparrows gave life to the setting, adding nothing of color with their feathers of brown and gray. One came to rest on the window ledge, its feathers fluffed, making it appear more stuffed than real. Kallie, watching it strut along the ledge, thought how fat and healthy it appeared, seemingly lacking nothing for its physical welfare. "It doesn't have to worry about where its food's coming from," she mused, "or be concerned about getting enough warm clothes made, or having enough money to buy warm covering for its feet."

A sudden gust of wind hit the house, the unexpected movement and sound making Kallie acutely aware of the chill of the room. She gathered her shawl closer about her shoulders, and turning from the beauty that had a moment before captured her whole attention, hurried shivering from the bedroom into the warmth of the big kitchen. The baby was still sleeping in his crib near the fire, his fat cheek still and doll-like.

Elvina looked up from her knitting, her smile warm with genuine affection as she greeted her young daughter-in-law, carefully concealing her deep concern over Kallie's pallor and the dark circles beneath her eyes. Elvina seemed to detect a hint of sadness, too, bordering on melancholy but she was very hesitant about bringing up the subject for fear Kallie would think she was prying. Besides, she remembered from her own experience that depression was normal with most new mothers.

Kallie picked up the hearth broom from its place in the corner and swept what few ashes there were on the hearth back under the burning logs. The flames flickered from the sudden rush of air and a few sparks darted gaily up the chimney, adding a touch of animation to the quiet scene.

Robinson had not been back inside the cabin since breakfast. Kallie peeked out the window hoping to catch a glimpse of him. He would be coming in soon and more than likely his fingers and feet would be numb from the cold.

As if in answer to Kallie's thoughts, there was much scraping and shuffling of feet outside the cabin door. Robinson, his face red from the cold, opened the door and hurried inside, quickly closing the door behind him. Kallie, anxious though he wake the baby, cautioned him to silence with a soft "shhh," her forefinger pressing against her lips for emphasis.

Robinson removed his wool cap. Not bothering to remove his coat he picked up one of the straight chairs and placed its back toward the fire. He sat down, straddling the chair back, his arms resting on the top, his open palms toward the flames. His feet had long lost all feeling and could have been two blocks of wood as far as he could tell.

"You shouldn't stay out in the cold so long," Kallie reprimanded him gently. She pushed the coffee pot close to the coals, and walking over to the cupboard, took down one of the mugs hanging inside. When the coffee was hot, she filled the mug and handed the steaming brew to Robinson. His glance brushed her face quickly and then dropped to the cup she was holding out to him. He took the cup and slowly sipped the hot liquid while gazing thoughtfully into the fire.

Kallie returned to her chair and picked up her sewing. The room was enveloped in silence except for the click of Elvina's knitting needles and the simmer of the water kettle hanging over the fire.

"There's something not right between them," Elvina thought anxiously, "and if I weren't in here, they could possible talk it out." Unable to stand the heavy silence any longer, she stood up and moved to the fireplace. Taking down a long poker and a small shovel hanging from a nail, she turned the sweet potatoes baking in the ashes and blanketed them once again with hot ashes. She replaced the poker and shovel, then stood for a few moments warming her backside. Pretending to need some more thread, she disappeared into the bedroom.

Robinson continued to sit quietly, staring into the fire. He was acutely aware of Kallie sitting only a few feet away and his arms ached to reach out and crush her to him. When she had poured the coffee a few minutes before, his eyes had followed the outline of her body against the glow of the fire and his physical need for her was like an urgent, unsatisfied hunger. When she had handed him the cup of coffee, his body ached and cried out for her so intensely that his hand shook as if he were still shivering from the cold. He did not dare look at her for he was afraid his eyes would reveal what he was striving desperately to hide.

Kallie, too, was deep in thought. John was better than two months old and Robinson had given no indication of any physical desire for her. At first Kallie had not noticed, or even suspected any change in Robinson because of her weakened condition. Doc Evans had insisted that she stay in bed ten days to avoid the chance of hemorrhage, and his warning, coupled with concern and care of the baby, had kept her occupied. Robinson appeared dutifully proud of his son, showing him off to visitors and rocking him while Elvina took care of the household chores. But as Kallie became stronger, it seemed to her that Robinson had become increasingly restrained and withdrawn toward her. Apparently he was deliberately avoiding any physical contact with her because he would sit by the fire long after she had retired, or if he went to bed early, lie on his side with his face turned away. If she called to him, or moved close to him, he would not answer or give any indication that he was awake. Hurt and offended, torturous thoughts began to haunt her. "Did he find her repulsive physically now that she had borne a child? Did the baby's nursing annoy him? Was he jealous of the baby?" The anxiety had affected her appetite, too, causing her to lose weight. This factor, coupled with the need for breast feeding the baby, had resulted in extreme weight loss, and it was beginning to show in her face, creating a strained and haggard appearance.

Robinson, sitting quietly before the fire, his empty coffee mug on the floor beside him, was totally unaware of the turmoil he was causing in the hearts and minds of the two women who loved him. Having brought his emotions under control, he continued to stare into the fire, his mind absorbed with the events that had caused his dilemma in the first place. Embedded in his memory were Kallie's screams of pain as she had clawed the air, her eyes wild and her face contorted because of the pain. It seemed now that he could see her face pictured in the flames before him, the expression of pain flickering intense, then dying down, only to flare up again, larger and more threatening than before. The muscles along his jaw tightened and he griped his knees hard with his hands.

"I can't take a chance on causing that to happen to her ever again," he concluded bitterly. "I can't see her suffer that way, especially if I helped bring it about." Suddenly, as if driven by some spasmodic emotional impulse, he stood up, toppling the chair forward near the fire. The sharp noise awoke the baby and he began to cry.

Laying her sewing aside, Kallie stood up slowly, her eyes riveted on Robinson. Robinson, busily setting the chair upright, seemed not to notice.

The baby's crying culminated into full-fledged wails. Kallie slowly walked over to the crib. She reached for a dry diaper and began to change the baby. It was only after the door had closed behind Robinson that she looked up, her tearless eyes staring unblinkingly at the closed door.

Elvina's bedroom door opened and she came back into the room. Walking over to the cradle, she stood for a few minutes beside Kallie watching the jerky movements of the baby's arms and legs as he continued to let his displeasure known. "Let me hold him for a while," Elvina offered, and when Kallie handed him to her, walked over to the rocking chair and sat down.

"He's such a big fine boy," Elvina crooned as she rocked back and forth, her grandson, now satisfied, lying contentedly in her arms.

Kallie moved over to the fireplace and stood with her back to the fire, a tender smile momentarily replacing her strained expression as she gazed lovingly at her mother-in-law holding her son. Elvina's gaze suddenly lifted, and a look of warm affection passed between the two women. As Elvina's eyes dropped once again to the child in her arms, her countenance remained unchanged, but her eyes turned sad as she recalled the anguish on her young daughter-in-law's face earlier.

The afternoon dragged along for Kallie with Robinson only coming inside occasionally to warm. "I can't go on this way," she thought desperately. "I've got to know what's wrong with Robinson or I'll lose my mind!" That was when she began to formulate her plan.

When Elvina left to help with the outside chores, Kallie hurriedly made preparations for the baby's bath. Sitting near the fire, she bathed him on her lap, one part of his body at a time, so that he wouldn't get chilled. Very carefully she washed his face, arms, all part of his body, her thoughts on her plans for the evening. Robinson was not going to avoid her any longer without an explanation. If she hurried she could have the baby bathed and fed before Robinson finished at the barn.

She hoped Elvina wouldn't think she was shirking her share of the supper preparations, but she would risk this possibility rather than explain why she was changing the routine. By the time she had finished the baby's bath and dressed him in his long gown, his patience had completely worn threadbare and he was beginning to let his annoyance be known by lusty crying. After letting the baby nurse, she tucked him in his crib and then hurried to empty the bath water and start supper.

Later, after they had finished eating and the womenfolk had cleared away the supper dishes, they sat around the fire for a while with no one saying much of anything.

"Would you like for me to read for a while?" Kallie offered.

"Not tonight," Robinson answered, standing. "I think I'll turn in."

Kallie laid her handwork aside and stood up, too. Without comment, she lit the other lamp and followed him into their room. She didn't look in his direction but busied herself with getting ready for bed. Their bedroom was cold and she felt the chill as she slipped out of her dress and underclothes. She kept her back to Robinson; therefore, she couldn't tell whether he was paying any attention to her or not as she pulled her gown over her head. Quickly she removed the pins from her hair and brushed it several times to remove any tangles. She even daubed a little of her precious cologne behind each ear and on her wrists. Heart pounding, she sat down on a nearby chair to remove her shoes and stockings, stealing a glance toward the bed. Robinson, already in bed, had his back to her as usual, his face turned toward the wall.

Disappointment welled up within her and she fought hard against the angry tears that threatened to start. Not able to stand the pain of exclusion any longer, she rushed across the cold floor to his side of the bed and knelt on the floor, her face only a few inches from his.

"Darling," she whispered brokenly, the hot tears running down her cheeks in spite of her effort to control them. "Don't you love me any more?"

Robinson opened his eyes and thought he had never seen a more beautiful sight. He did not miss the fact that she was wearing the nightgown she had worn on their wedding night, nor that her hair framed her face like an aura of gold, the faint fragrance of her cologne taunting him with exciting memories. Her tear-filled eyes stared at him with such anguish and longing that it made his throat constrict.

"You're cold," he said gruffly. "You'd better get in bed," and in spite of his efforts toward self-restraint, reached out to touch her face with his hand.

Grateful for the first intimate touch in weeks, Kallie cradled his hand with hers and pressed it against her cheek. Robinson's rigid self-control crumbled, and turning back the covers, reached for her, pulling her onto the bed beside him. Over and over he whispered hoarsely, "Darling, oh my darling," as he kissed her face, her eyes, her lips. The emotion that swept over him was uncontrollable as he crushed her to him, and all of the weeks of denial that he had battled to maintain crumpled in the softness of her arms.

Afterwards, Robinson laid very still, eyes closed. Kallie lay quietly in his arms, just savoring the wonder of being a part of him again. She felt him take a deep breath, then let it go, ending in a massive dry sob. Alarmed, Kallie pulled away, her eyes searching his face. Robinson sat up in bed, holding his head between his hands.

"Darling! Darling!" Kallie whispered frantically, sitting upright, too. "What's the matter? Rob! Answer me! Are you all right?"

Robinson didn't answer, but continued to grip his forehead. Even more alarmed, Kallie tugged at his arm. "Robinson, for Heaven's sake, what is wrong with you?" she cried frantically.

"How could I have done such a thing?" he moaned.

"What do you mean 'done such a thing'?" she demanded incredulously. "Darling, you are my husband!"

"I swore I'd never risk you again to the suffering you went through when John was born. How could I have been so weak?" he groaned, his words encrusted with self-recrimination. He lay back on the pillow, his arm pressed across his eyes.

"Is that what's been the matter?" she cried, almost giddy with relief. She fell across him, laughing and crying at the same time. She kissed his cheek, his lips, and not too gently removing his arm from across his eyes, kissed those, too. Darling," she whispered hoarsely, "there's no pain on earth as terrible as being rejected by you."

Robinson, numb with self-loathing, thought accusingly, "I've betrayed her and myself as well."

Kallie scooted down under the covers and laid her head on his shoulder. When there was no response from him, she blurted tearfully, "I... I can't bear being pushed out of your life, darling! I can't live without you. I'm... I'm not a whole person anymore. My life has become frustrated and meaningless, even with the baby. You're such apart of me that being separated from you the way it's been since the baby was born is like having part of me cut away and set aside, to bleed and die!" Her voice broke and she began to cry uncontrollably.

Completely defeated, Robinson wrapped his arms around her, pulling her hard against him.

As Robinson went about his work the next morning, the memory of the tender moments the night before caused his heart to pound and his head ache. He yearned to go back inside the house and hold Kallie close again. But, then, the possibility of her being pregnant again erased the memory of their joy together and in its place, a feeling of dread and guilt engulfed him. "It's a trap!" he muttered bitterly.

The past few weeks had not been easy for him. Kallie had become his very life and shutting her out had been the most difficult thing he had ever faced. The only way he had been able to accomplish such rigid control was to recall the events of that awful day when she almost died. He had not even dared to discuss the matter with her for fear that what had happened the night before would take place.

What if she were with child again? The old horror rebounded, causing him to suspend in mid-air the forkful of hay he had started to pitch down from the barn loft. Slowly his arms relaxed and the pitchfork and its load came to rest on the barn floor as the impact of what might happen hit him again. "I am a weak, miserable piece of humanity," he muttered, clenching his teeth so hard that the muscles moved like marbles inside his jaw. Gripping the pitchfork viciously, he plunged it back into the pile of hay and sent the bundle flying out of the loft with such force that it scattered in every direction, showering on the ground.

There was no relief to be found from the anxiety that plagued him. All day, no matter what he was doing, his mind wrestled with it, draining him emotionally and making him feel tired and exhausted. As he probed and reasoned, his thoughts vacillated from memories of intense joy to deep depression. One moment he was glowing with the memory of their closeness the night before and Kallie's uninhibited response to him, and the next moment he was demeaning himself for being spineless, unstable, and without will power.

Emotionally exhausted, he admitted defeat. He loved Kallie to the extent that she was the most important thing in his life. He needed her; he needed her love. The stilted detached relationship imposed by him since John's birth had been torment for both of them. "We can't live that way," he determined resignedly, sinking his axe into the fireplace log he was splitting. For a long moment he stood staring down at the two halves of the log, not really seeing them. He stood the axe on the ground, leaning on its handle. "I really don't have a choice, I suppose," he mused, gazing off across the fields, eyes dark with emotion. "That's just the way it has to be."

Robinson's dread that Kallie might become pregnant again became a reality. John Mattison was only fifteen months old when the time came for their second child's entrance into the world.

It was not the best time financially for them to have another baby, but that was something they had no control over. The great panic of 1873 was in full force. However, the depression changed very little of their life style. It just meant more clothes made by hand, and very little food bought that was not grown on the land. They had managed to keep from going into debt. This was more than many of their neighbors and acquaintances could say who had fallen into the trap of mortgaging, necessarily, their expectant crops for seeds and supplies. Many of them lost their farms to unscrupulous merchants who overcharged them for their supplies, as well as tacking high interest rates onto their loans.

For Kallie's second delivery, she experienced no long painful hours of waiting, nor did she scream and claw the air as she had done before. The baby was born so much sooner than Robinson had dared hope that he could only stare in disbelief when Doc Evans came out of the bedroom and announced in his quiet unhurried manner that Robinson was the father of another fine boy.

"She made it a lot easier this time, Rob," he said, placing his arm in a fatherly fashion around Robinson's shoulder, a slight smile relieving the tired lines of strain around his eyes and mouth. "She won't be so tired and exhausted after this one. She's sleeping, now."

"Thank, God," Robinson said in a husky voice, rubbing his hand across his eyes, not actually aware of his acknowledgement of God's help.

"Any coffee left in that pot?" Doc Evans queried, reaching for his cup on the table.

"Sure... you betcha, Doc!" Robinson assured him, getting up with such haste that he almost toppled his chair over backwards. His legs, trembling slightly, threatened to fold under him.

They named their second son Robert Evans in honor of Doc Evans.

A year and a half later, in 1875, their third son, Nathaniel Wheeler Stuart, was born.

CHAPTER 19

"Will you go in with me, Rob?" Jim Wheeler asked, leaning heavily on one foot, gazing intently at his lifelong friend. The mischievous grin that was usually a part of his normal facial expression was noticeably missing.

Robinson stood quietly gazing out across his fields, thinking, "How many miles have I trudged behind a mule - up and down these rows, battling drought and rainy seasons; striving for the past ten years to recoup from the devastating cruelty of the war and never quite making it; not ever real sure if there will be enough food and money to supply the family's needs; pushing the hopelessness aside and striving on, always believing that the next year would be better; only, it never was much better," he thought bleakly. "Plows break, mules die, sickness comes, and the never ending dread of not being able to pay the taxes on the land."

Now, Jim was telling him that he had figured out a way, a plan, whereby they might overcome all of the hardships. And Jim was asking Robinson to join him - to be a part of its beginning. It all sounded so simple! But Robinson knew better. Nothing was ever simple, not anything worthwhile, anyway!

Deciding Robinson wasn't going to say anything, Jim continued. "I know where there's a sawmill for sale at a good price. Owner came down from the North expecting to get rich quick but couldn't take the climate and the labor problem. Wants to sell out tee-totally and go back up North. From the way he talks, he's so disgusted he would be thankful just to get his money back from the whole operation."

"I knew you had been away from home a lot, Jim, but I never thought about you working on a deal this big!"

Jim's grin widened. "The sawmill isn't the only plan I have in the making, either," he continued, his excitement building. "As you know, Salena's folks live in Savannah, and Savannah, as you may already know, also, is the largest naval stores center in the United States. Lumber and naval stores products come from pine trees. Look around you, Rob!" he demanded, moving his arm in a wide sweeping motion. "What do you see? Pine trees! And a lot of land that once grew cotton and corn is fast becoming pine forest again. And what comes from those trees?" He paused for emphasis, staring hard into Robinson's eyes, then continued, "Resinous sap; gum, that can be distilled into turpentine, tar, pitch, and many other products." Robinson, still not commenting, turned to look out across the fields. Jim paused again, studying Robinson's profile. When Robinson didn't comment, he continued. "Rob, I've been talking to a lot of farmers for miles around who own a lot of land that is reverting back to timber. They can't get help because the ex-slaves refuse to work unless paid high wages, and the farmers can't meet their demands. Most of the farmers are in the same boat we've been in, doing well to keep their taxes paid. Many farms are heavily mortgaged. They'd welcome any fair contract for timber rights."

"Jim," Robinson finally answered, trying hard to conceal his impatience, "this all sounds like a great idea, but man! Do you realize what you're proposing? Here we are! Two men, with families, trying to scratch out a living from the dirt! Where will the money come from to buy the sawmill...the equipment for tapping the trees...the storage tanks...the vats? And you say we'll need to locate the naval stores operation down state? Jim," Robinson laughed, a sound more of sadness than ridicule, "it's been hard for me to just scrape up enough money to buy shoes for my kids! Man! You're talking the impossible!"

"Now, wait, Rob," Jim urged patiently. "You haven't heard me out!" He was silent for a long moment, holding Robinson's gaze. "There's a man in Savannah, a Mr. Eschweiler, who is an investment broker. He's interested in backing someone in the lumber business and naval stores products. He says that with the expansion of the railroads in every direction and rebuilding going on in the South and North - there shouldn't be any reason why we can't make money. He already knows potential buyers in Europe for the naval products. And here's something else! Mr. Eschweiler has connections in Washington and he says it's only a matter of time before the South will be out from under Federal rule. If that happens, the economy should pick up. We'll be in on the ground floor," he finished urgently. When Robinson remained silent, Jim added, "Mr. Eschweiler is definitely interested in backing us."

"Us?"

Jim nodded. "Us," he emphasized, his mischievous grin suddenly appearing. "I told him we would be partners."

Robinson just shook his head, expression skeptical. "This Eschweiler... Eschweiler. He doesn't know anything about me?"

"Don't fool yourself! He's big business! He doesn't step into something blindly." Jim hesitated, then added, "Rob, I hope this won't have any bearing on your final decision, but we came highly recommended."

"By whom?"

"Robert Anderson."

"Robert Anderson!" Robinson exploded, flushing.

Jim nodded, waiting uneasily for Robinson's next reaction.

Robinson said nothing for a long moment, head pounding, partly from excitement, partly from anger. Why? Why did it have to be a Damn Yankee?

"Guess Mr. Anderson would like to help us get started in the business world," Jim stated matter-of-factly, shrugging his shoulders.

"I still don't see why a total stranger would put up money for us to use, especially two that have no experience in this type thing; even if we do come 'highly recommended.'"

"Oh, we'll have to put up some security, of course," Jim replied.

"Well, that lets me out!"

"What do you mean, Rob? You have this farm?"

"Of which I own only one fourth and that as an heir."

"Look, Rob!" Jim stated flatly, impatience evident for the first time. "I'm going to do something to better the circumstances of my life and for my family. I don't intend to follow a mule for the rest of my life. My pa's agreed to go on my note. It took me a long time to get up the nerve to ask him, but I believe this thing will work, and he has faith in me. In us!" he finished emphatically. "I believe we can make money; maybe, a lot of money. Not just survival funds, but enough so that once in a while we can have something store bought to wear. Something to eat occasionally that you didn't grow yourself! I want my kids to have more education that I got," he added quietly, voice subdued. "But I can't do it alone! I can't be out leasing land, or buying a lot of timber, and operating the mill at the same time. I've got to have someone with enough schooling to be able to add and subtract, someone who can figure a load of lumber or a stand of timber. I know you're a hard worker, Rob, and I know you're honest, and your ma did a good job with your schooling." He rubbed his palms together excitedly. "Together, we can go places!"

"This man in Savannah," Rob asked hesitantly, remembering his pa's experience with investment companies. "I don't want to offend you, Jim, but how do you know he's to be trusted?"

"Salena's pa knows him, and the firm he's with. They're no fly-by-night operators. They were in Savannah before the war and are known for their sound investments and honest dealings with their customers. I feel absolutely certain there's nothing to worry about there."

"How does Salena feel about your plans?"

"Welll… you know Salena! She's a great one for worrying, and she's not too happy about Dad mortgaging his place for us. She always wants a sure thing. But, when she starts with all the 'what ifs' and negative put downs, I just remind her of that fancy surrey she'll be riding in one of these days. How I'll take her to Savannah to buy all those fancy clothes and shoes. She just grins sorta weak-like and sighs in a big way…as if it's all decided anyway." Then, expression suddenly serious, added thoughtfully, "She's not too happy about the prospect of me having to be away so much. That doesn't set well at all. But she'll come around. She always does. That Ole Gal's a trooper!"

Jim's last remark sparked a short laugh from Robinson. "You'd better not let Salena hear you call her an 'Ole Gal.'" Then, thoughtfully serious again, continued. "Jim, I need some time to think about all this." His gaze traveled over the area of their farm. "This little hunk of land's not much, but it's all we have, and in spite of how hard the Feds have tried to make it rough for us, we've managed to keep it debt free. Ma has an awful fear of mortgages, and rightfully so. She'll have to be for it one hundred percent for me to seriously consider such an undertaking." He reached down and picked up a handful of dirt, letting it slip between his fingers. "This red dirt's colored with her lifeblood!"

Jim had never heard Robinson express such deep bitterness before, except about the "damn Yankees" and the war. His pulse quickened at what he considered an advantage. "Sure, Rob. I understand. But as long as we're breaking our backs anyway, it just might as well be for something more worthwhile than a few bales of cotton, and if the weather happens to go against us, not even that! Great balls of fire, Rob! Life's a gamble any way you go at it!"

Robinson frowned. "I know you're right. But, Jim, we've got to be realistic. You make it all sound so easy, but we're only two people! We couldn't possibly tap trees for several hundred miles, and run a sawmill, too! Do you realize how many men you're talking about?"

Jim popped his hands together, eyes shining. "That's where having capital comes in! We'll have the money to hire the hands we need, and the returns will be a nice profit. By the way! I've talked to Reuben Wyatt; told him about this setup. He talked like he might consider coming to work for us as overseer, or foreman, of the mill when we have to be away. But, mainly, he'd be in charge of the company books. In fact, he said he might be interested in investing a little money in the business."

Rob's pulse beat quickened. Reuben...? Stable, levelheaded Reuben...? the person the entire community looked to for counsel and advice on so many matters? This bit of information was certainly encouraging.

"Let me think about it for a few days, Jim," Robinson bargained, his cautious nature holding him in check; not revealing how excited he actually was.

"Sure, Rob, I understand," Jim agreed readily, greatly relieved. At least Rob hadn't turned him down cold. "I've hit you with this thing out of the blue, and you need some time to weigh the matter. Personally, as I've said over and over, I believe it's sound. But I need to know something in a few days. Don't want our prospective investors to think we aren't interested. Oh, by the way," he added, as an afterthought. "Mr. Eschweiler is well acquainted with someone already in the naval stores products. Said he'd arrange for him to help us in setting up our initial operation, if we needed him."

Robinson nodded. "That's very reassuring," he agreed. Jim's plan didn't seem quite so overwhelming with the prospect of that kind of help.

Robinson didn't mention Jim's plan to Kallie or his ma right away. Instead, he went to talk with Reuben. Somehow he had to get the whole picture more detailed in his mind before laying the entire scheme out to them. The thought that Reuben might be a sort of partner was certainly reassuring. Comfortable, solid Reuben was one of Robinson's closest friends. He and his wife, Jessie, had moved into the community shortly after the war, buying a small farm that bordered the south section of the Stuart land.

Reuben had been in his thirties at the time; about the same age Robinson's dad would have been if he had lived. An immediate friendship had developed, one that seemed unencumbered by any age difference. Robinson often leaned heavily on Reuben for companionship and advice. Reuben's slow, deliberate manner and piercing blue yes, shadowed by dark bushy eye brows, gave him an appearance of a man with great wisdom. He was educated, too, far more than the average person in the community, and this had made the local people a little suspicious at first, wondering why he would choose to settle on a farm in rural Georgia. But, with all of his social graces, he had never been accused of being "uppity," and he never culled anyone when it came to Christian service. He offered advice only when asked, and then, usually answered the person with a question, somehow causing the seeker of advice to feel he had made the decision on his own. He was deeply spiritual, however, and this was the only thing about Reuben that made Robinson uncomfortable. Reuben included the Lord in every phase of his life.

Following Jessie's directions, Robinson found Reuben replacing fence posts. Robinson explained to him about Jim's visit, while helping him with his work.

"Jim told me he had talked with you about the business," Robinson said after he had told Reuben about Jim's plan.

"Yes, and I don't know but what it sounds like a solid investment to me. In fact, I suppose Jim told you, I'd like to invest some money in it, too. Of course, any type of business venture is a gamble, but so is farming. And, like farming, whether or not it brings worthwhile returns depends largely upon how much a person is willing to work and sacrifice."

Robinson bristled somewhat. He didn't come to Reuben for a lecture. This wasn't like Reuben.

Sensing Robinson's withdrawal, Reuben apologized. "I'm sorry, Rob, I didn't mean to offend. Guess I was referring to myself more than anyone else. What does your ma and Kallie have to say?"

"I haven't told them, yet. Somehow I needed some time to get used to the whole idea. Sort it through, more or less. I just wish there was some other way besides mortgaging the farm."

Reuben plunged the blade of the shovel deeper into the earth, then stood leaning thoughtfully on the handle. "Do you believe that you and Jim can make a go of this thing?"

"Well, yes," Robinson responded hesitantly, expression cloudy. "If everything goes in our favor, that is."

"You have as good a chance at making it work as anyone else - maybe more. You're both hard workers. You're honest. You have, from all indications, sound investors behind you."

"But there's still a lot at stake," Robinson countered.

Reuben leaned his shovel against a nearby tree. Pushing his hat back, he stood quietly appraising the young man. "Rob, let me ask you something. When you start a crop in the spring, do you have any assurance that you'll make anything?" When Robinson didn't respond, he continued. "Well, from my experience, if you want a sure thing, you shouldn't be a farmer."

"But you have to admit there's a certain amount of security."

"Is security that important to you, Rob?"

"Not so much for me, but for Ma, and my family."

"Why don't you talk to your ma? You might be surprised. She had to have a lot of grit, a sense of adventure, and a tremendous amount of faith, to come South with your pa. She's a survivor and a fighter, Rob. So are you, for that matter."

Robinson's pulse beat quickened. Maybe Reuben was right. Was he assuming too much? His ma just might see it like Reuben suggested. Suddenly, he wanted to hurry home.

That night after Kallie and Robinson had retired to their bedroom, he told her about Jim's offer and his visit to Reuben's. Robinson had not been sure just what her reaction would be, but he certainly wasn't prepared for her exuberance.

"Oh, Rob! It sounds wonderful! A once in a lifetime opportunity! Who would have ever dreamed that Jim was working on something so big! That man! He knows just about everybody in the county practically!"

"County nothing," Rob laughed. "You mean from here to Savannah, don't you?"

"I...I just wish there was some other way beside mortgaging the farm, though. I hate to think of asking Ma Stuart to do that."

"I know. That's the only bad part."

"But just think, Rob! After the business gets going good and you pay off the loan, then - you can buy your ma some of the things you've always wanted for her! It's a cinch you'll never have anything plowing behind a mule!"

Robinson winced inwardly. This was the first time in their marriage that Kallie had been openly critical of their way of life. Even though it was true, it still wounded his pride.

But Kallie was too excited to suspect the reason for his silence. "Oh, Rob! If the business is a success, maybe we could add on to the house, and we'd have enough clothes for the children. Oh, Rob!" she said, excitedly hugging him hard, "it sounds like a wonderful, glorious dream!"

Robinson slept fitfully that night. He tossed and turned, and was awake long before daybreak. When he heard Elvina stirring about in the kitchen, he eased out of bed, and putting on his clothes in the dark, managed to leave the bedroom without awakening Kallie.

"You're up early," Elvina smiled, separating the coals in the fireplace from the ashes. "Don't tell me my habit is beginning to rub off on you," she teased.

Robinson walked over to the fireplace and stood gazing at the low flame. "I wanted to talk with you before the rest of the family waked up and there is so much confusion."

"Is anything wrong, Rob?" she asked, suddenly apprehensive. He sounded so serious.

"No, nothing is wrong. I just need to talk with you about...about a business matter."

"A business matter? I'm afraid I don't understand."

"It's a business deal that Jim has approached me with."

Puzzlement shadowed Elvina's face, but she waited quietly for Robinson to explain. She knew him so well. Whatever it was he wanted to talk with her about, he was having trouble getting it out.

"Jim came over two days ago while I was plowing the west field of corn. He wanted to talk to me about going in business with him."

"In business? What kind of business, Rob?"

"Sawmill...finished lumber, naval stores products, possibly later on."

"That's quite a lot of business, I'd say!"

Robinson nodded, expression grave. "You're right. I thought so, too, at first," he added, pulling up a chair and sitting down beside her. "But after I had listened to all of his plans, it didn't seem quite so impossible." He went over step by step what Jim had outlined to him. "It'll take quite a lot of capital. Jim knows an investment firm in Savannah that specializes in backing new business enterprises. They don't require enough collateral to cover the entire loan, but they do demand some. A kind of security."

After a long silence, Elvina asked quietly. "You're talking about mortgaging the farm, Rob?"

Suddenly the enormity of what he was proposing overwhelmed him. "I'm sorry, Ma," he blurted. "I thought all along that it was a crazy thing to ask you to do!" He got to his feet. "I'm sorry I even told you about it," he added apologetically.

"Now, wait a minute, Rob," she chastised gently, restraining him with her hand when he turned to walk away. "Don't go putting words in my mouth." She sat staring thoughtfully into the fire. When she spoke again, he noted a rare touch of sadness. "Your Dad and I had big dreams but life takes some cruel twists and sometimes our dreams just can't ever be. But that doesn't mean that I have lost my appetite for life and not ready to help better our circumstances if it is possible. I've always felt that you were capable of being something more than a dirt farmer, not that it isn't honorable work," she hastened to add. When he didn't respond, she asked, "Have you discussed this with Kallie?"

"Yes, and she was beside herself, urging me to tell Jim "yes" until she learned about the risk involved, for you especially."

"Not any more for me than for the rest of you," she replied.

Elvina sat silent again, staring into the fire. Her heart was pounding. She had spoken flippantly about the matter, but the idea frightened her. The only tangible security she had in the world, and the only thing she had in material wealth to offer her family, was the house and the small farm. If they lost it, where would they go? How would they live?

"Let me think about it for a while, Rob," she said, getting to her feet. "This is something I need to talk to the Lord about."

"Ma, I...I've known about this for a couple of days but just couldn't bring myself to mention it to you. I went over to see Reuben, to ask his advice, before I told you and Kallie. He was very encouraging; in fact, he's planning to invest some money in the business. He...he even offered me some money for expenses on the trip to Savannah." Seeing the puzzled look on Elvina's face, he hurried on to explain. "The broker who wants to finance the business lives in Savannah. Jim said it would be necessary for me to go with him to meet Mr. Eschweiler." All of a sudden the whole scheme of things seemed preposterous to Robinson. He headed for the door. "Oh, Ma," he blurted from the doorway. "It's all just too much! Let's just forget about the whole thing!" Without waiting for her reply, he hurried outside and headed for the barn.

Elvina walked over to the window and stared after Robinson. "My how tall he is," she mused, watching his long strides. "He's not a boy anymore, hasn't been for a long, long time. He's a man, and a man should have his chance. If I say 'no' to this plan, it might well be the only chance he'll ever have to fulfill some of his aspirations." She thought about her two grandsons sleeping in the loft, and the baby in Rob and Kallie's room. Things as they were didn't offer much hope for their future.

"Why, there's no question of what has to be done," she decided. "Rob and his family must have their chance."

And then, because she needed reassurance and was more frightened that she dared admit, she softly quoted one of her favorite passages from the third chapter of Proverbs: "Trust in the Lord with all thine heart, and lean not to thine own understanding; in all thy ways acknowledge Him, and He shall direct thy paths."

CHAPTER 20

Melinda smoothed the long slim lines of her velvet robe against her waist, denoting with satisfaction that the fullness of the skirt did not divulge the bulge just below her waistline. The gray eyes that stared back from the mirror were calm, yet the flush of her cheeks and the smile that played gently with her lips gave credence to the joy within her. She turned so that she could observe herself sideways in the long mirror and was pleased by her reflection, head erect, shoulders back. Her height that had been a source of dismay for many years of her life was something she now carried with pride. Not from vanity, but with an elegance belonging to a woman confident in the knowledge that she was loved and admired. Garrett was solely responsible for this metamorphosis of her self-esteem. If Garrett thought she was beautiful, then she must be. He was her world, and his opinion was the only one that mattered.

Her glance fell to the letter on her dressing table and a slight frown replaced her contented smile. It was a letter from Robinson, telling her that Jim Wheeler wanted him to become a partner in the lumber business. Initially, the partnership would require a certain amount of cash. The only way Robinson could buy into the partnership was to borrow money against the farm.

Melinda didn't care about the farm particularly, but what concerned her was how it would jeopardize her ma's ownership. She knew how important that small piece of land was to her ma. She glanced at the jeweled watch on her lapel. Garrett would be coming home soon. She would talk to him. "He will help me decide," she sighed gratefully.

As if in answer to her silent musing, the door opened and Garrett entered the room. Gasping with pleasure, she rushed across the room to be gathered in his embrace.

"You're early," she whispered happily as he kissed her over and over again.

Later while he was changing for dinner she told him about Robinson's letter. He listened attentively without comment until she had finished reading it to him. When he didn't respond right away, she asked apprehensively, "Well, what do you think?"

"It sounds like a golden opportunity for Robinson...and Jim," he agreed somewhat hesitantly, "but I hate to think of your ma being put in that kind of compromising position."

"I know. That's what bothers me, too. If something happened and Robinson couldn't pay back the loan, well..." her voice trailed off into a thoughtful silence.

Garrett stood before the small-framed mirror that graced his bureau, combing his dark hair. Finished with his grooming, he laid the comb down, and turned to put his arm around Melinda's waist. Playfully he patted her enlarged abdomen. "You won't be able to hide it much longer," he chided lovingly, kissing her tenderly on the lips. Suddenly, his arms enfolded her and he held her to him, burying his face against her hair. "I'm the luckiest man in the world," he concluded huskily.

The subject of the letter didn't come up again until after dinner and they were back in their room. While she was making preparations for retiring for the night, he picked up the letter and read it again. He sat for a long time as if in deep thought. Melinda made no comment for she knew that in his own time he'd give her his final opinion. Finally he looked up, his glance meeting hers. "Let me sleep on it," he smiled, folding the letter and replacing it in the envelope.

Melinda awoke the next morning to find the bed empty beside her. Hurriedly she arose and slipped into a silk robe that had been a present from Garrett. She wrapped its luxurious folds around her, marveling at its softness and beauty. There were so many wonderful things in her life since marrying Garrett. "Sometimes I wonder if I'm dreaming and I'll wake up to the way things used to be," she questioned silently. She walked over to the dressing table and picked up her hairbrush. Robinson's letter once again caught her eye. The joyous smile faded and a troubled expression took its place. "It's really not my decision to make," she argued with herself. "It's whatever ma wants to do." After a moment of reflection, she concluded. "But ma must have agreed, otherwise, Robinson wouldn't have written." Slowly she turned toward the door. "I wish Liza and Keith were home from Savannah," she sighed wistfully.

She found Garrett where she knew he would be - downstairs, sitting at the table in the breakfast nook with his father. They were both early risers and captured the early morning hours to discuss business matters with less frustrating interruptions. They both smiled a greeting when she entered the room.

"Good morning," she greeted them cheerfully, her warm smile encompassing the two men. She stopped to kiss Garrett lightly on the forehead, feeling the fleeting pressure of his hand upon her waist. She walked over to the buffet, poured a cup of coffee and returned to sit beside Garrett at the table.

"I've been telling Father about Robinson's letter," Garrett explained pleasantly.

Dismayed, Melinda's gaze held Garrett's for a long moment. She thought he had understood that this was a private matter. Why had he discussed it with his father?

Sensing her mild displeasure, Garrett reached under the table and pressed her knee reassuringly. "Dad thinks he might can help." he smiled encouragingly.

Mr. Anderson nodded. "What do you think about us offering to make Robinson a loan?" he asked, his piercing gaze never leaving Melinda's face.

"I...don't know?" she answered doubtfully, confused by this sudden turn of events. "Rob's...Rob's so independent," she finished lamely, not wanting to tell them he'd never accept "Yankee" money.

"You mean 'independent' when it comes to accepting aid from the enemy?" Mr. Anderson suggested, his tone kind.

Melinda nodded briefly, surprised and somewhat uncomfortable by her father-in-law's keen deduction of the problem.

"We've been talking about visiting your family before it becomes impossible for you to travel," Garrett broke in. "Why don't we leave tomorrow? Maybe, we can sit down with them and thrash this thing out."

Melinda nodded, smiling her gratitude, not trusting herself to speak. With the matter closed for the time being, as far as the two men were concerned, their conversation switched to other matters of business.

Suddenly ravenously hungry, Melinda picked up the little silver bell near her plate and shook it gently. Immediately the door to the kitchen opened and a tall middle-aged black man, who had been a slave to the former plantation owner, entered the room. "You rang, Miz Anderson?"

"Good morning, Daniel," Melinda greeted him warmly. "I would like some bacon and eggs, toast and jelly this morning."

"Yes, Ma'am," he nodded, smiling agreeably. "Will that be all?"

She looked questioningly toward the two men at the table, hesitating to interrupt their conversation.

"They already eat, Miz Anderson," Dan offered, answering her unspoken question.

"Then, that will be all, Daniel, thank you," she nodded, smiling.

Sitting quietly while waiting for her breakfast, Melinda's thoughts once again turned homeward. Garrett had made it all sound so easy, but she was very apprehensive. Robinson could be exasperatingly stubborn at times.

The thought of going home was exciting but also depressing; it wasn't the same any more. Going back to the small house where she was born, seeing her family crowded in the small dwelling, their needs so great, took away some of the joy of going home. She had to be very careful about presents, even, for fear of offending their fierce pride.

But back in her room looking over her wardrobe, her doubts returned. Dismayed, she realized that anything she owned would be elegant and expensive to her family. She decided upon a soft blue traveling suit. Hopefully, the full skirt would help conceal her condition.

"Maybe things will get better for them if Robinson goes into that business with Jim," she reasoned, her spirits lifting.

The baby leaped within her causing her to gasp with surprise. Wonderingly she laid her hand on the spot, and immediately, felt another small movement as if the child within her was responding to her gentle touch.

"Oh..." she sighed. "It's such a long time until I can hold my baby!"

CHAPTER 21

Garrett called "whoa" to the horses and tied the reins to the front of the surrey. He climbed down and came around to Melinda's side, extending his hand to assist her as she climbed down from the vehicle. She slipped her small gloved hand into her husband's unusually large one and arose a bit unsteadily to her feet. It had been a long tiring trip, and she had worried silently many times since their departure if the trip had been a wise undertaking. Her eyes met his, and momentarily she forgot her discomfort, reveling in the love and tenderness she read there. Slowly she stepped down, leaning heavily on his arm.

"Are you all right?" he asked, his expression serious.

"Yes," she answered cheerfully, trying to ignore the tightness in her abdomen and the annoying ache in her lower back. "I'll be all right after I've walked around a bit," she assured him, pressing his arm with her other gloved hand. She paused to look at the house, amazed that it seemed even smaller than she remembered. "It's not much larger than the tenant houses on the Anderson's plantation," she thought, immediately sensing a vague feeling of disloyalty.

The door opened and Elvina came hurrying down the steps, hastily wiping her hands on her apron. "You surprised us," she laughed, enfolding Melinda in her arms.

"I know," Melinda responded joyfully, returning her ma's embrace. "It was Garrett's idea. We came part of the way yesterday and spent the night in…," she hesitated, not wanting to mention the name of the luxurious hotel, "…in a hotel," she finished lamely.

Kallie came hurrying out of the house with Nat on her hip; a solemn-faced Robert trudging along behind. Melinda caught sight of Robinson, accompanied by John, hurrying up the path from the barn, the crooked grin she remembered so well lighting his face.

Later, after sampling some of Elvina's fresh baked molasses cake, Robinson asked Garrett if he would like to walk around the place and stretch his legs. Garrett readily agreed, welcoming the invitation because it would give him an opportunity to talk with Robinson alone.

Kallie sent the two older children out to play, cautioning them about hanging around Uncle Garrett and their pa. Closing the door firmly behind them, she turned back toward the other women. "Maybe we can talk without interruptions, now," she apologized. "They are so excited! We don't have a whole lot of company."

"Company?" Melinda laughed. "Just who are you calling company?"

"Well, you are to them."

Melinda leaned back in the rocking chair, her glance moving lovingly around the familiar room. "It's so good to be home with you all," she confessed, eyes glistening with quick tears.

"Well," Elvina said, pulling out one of the benches from the table and taking a seat. "How are Liza and Keith and why didn't they come with you?"

"Liza and Keith are in Savannah. Papa Anderson sent Keith down there on business and Liza went with him. Liza goes everywhere Keith goes, everywhere that it's permissible for a lady to go, that is."

"Does she seem to be happy?" Elvina asked guardedly.

Melinda sat with her eyes downcast for such a long time that Elvina was beginning to think she had not heard her question.

When Melinda did answer, her words were slow and studied as if she were weighing each one. "I don't know, Ma." Then, smiling brightly, added, "She's always involved in something. Goes night and day! She certainly has everything she said she was going to have some day." Unable to continue under her ma's unwavering gaze, Melinda turned to stare out the window. "I don't think she's ever really slowed down long enough to ask herself that question, Ma," she added thoughtfully.

"And, you?" Elvina asked cheerfully. "How are things with you, Melinda?"

"Oh, Ma!" she beamed, eyes shining once again with quick tears. "I didn't know it was possible to be so happy."

"You've fleshened up a bit," Elvina teased

Melinda blushed. "You noticed! And for a good reason, too," she smiled, eyes dancing. "Suppose you two already suspect?"

"That's something that's hard to hide from experienced women like us," Kallie laughed.

Later, after the men returned from their walk and all of them had eaten the meal Elvina had prepared before their arrival, they finally got around to discussing the thing most uppermost in all of their minds.

"We received your letter, Rob," Melinda said, as way of introduction. "We think the sawmill is a wonderful opportunity," she added, glancing toward Garrett for confirmation.

"Yes," Robinson agreed, pushing his chair away from the table and crossing his legs. "It was all somewhat frightening at first, but after I'd had some time to think about it and talk it over with others, it seems like a sound investment, particularly right now with the rebuilding and expanding that's going on. And," he continued, voice confident, "Jim says a lot of the products we'll produce, if and when we go into production, will be exported to foreign buyers."

"Rob?" Melinda persisted gently, "did Garrett tell you that his papa makes loans for this type investment?"

"Yes," Robinson replied hesitantly, moving somewhat uncomfortably in his chair.

"We discussed it to some degree," Garrett added.

Robinson uncrossed his legs and leaned forward, his elbows on his knees; his hands clasped tightly together, his eyes rooted to the floor.

"It's not that I'm not grateful for what your pa wants to do," he said finally, glancing first at Garrett, and then at the women. "It's...it's just that if I go into this thing with Jim, I'd like to feel that I did it on my own."

Melinda's hopes plummeted. "I just knew it!" she thought desperately, "and what a weak excuse!" Aloud, she argued softly, "But, Rob? I can't see why a loan from Pa Anderson would be any different than one from a total stranger?" She started to say something else about the unnecessary risks he was taking, but Garrett caught her eye and shook his head ever so slightly.

"I think I understand where Rob is coming from," Garrett intervened, speaking quietly. And then to Robinson, "I think I understand how you feel. But, Rob, our dealings would be strictly business. We'd loan you the money and charge you the going rate of interest just like a bank or any other loan agency. The difference is that if the business were slow at first, like most new ones are while getting established, then, you wouldn't be under stress from fear of foreclosure."

When Rob didn't comment further, Elvina arose and walked around behind Robinson, laying her hand on his shoulder. "You're independent just like your pa, Rob, and that's a good trait if you don't carry it too far. Sometimes we can be too proud, Son."

"Maybe, so," he replied staring at the floor, the muscles in his jaw working spasmodically.

Kallie and Melinda stared at Robinson in disbelief. For the first time in their married life, Kallie felt like shaking him. Garrett was offering him a loan without mortgaging the farm, and Robinson was stubbornly refusing.

Then, Elvina, who had been watching Robinson intently, turned to Garrett, speaking softly. "Garrett, I appreciate you and your pa wanting to help. It is most kind and generous of your father to make this offer. But Robinson is the head of this household, and the final decision is his to make."

* * * * *

"So, that loyal Rebel wouldn't accept our offer?" Papa Anderson said to Garrett, leaning back in his easy chair, one of his favorite pipes clenched between his teeth.

"I'm afraid not," Garrett replied, frowning his disappointment.

"Well, can't say that I blame him," the older man agreed, not failing to notice Garrett's frown of disapproval.

"I think he's risking a lot unnecessarily, and causing Mrs. Stuart to be in dread of maybe losing her home. She's the one I'm concerned about. He could have avoided worrying her with this."

The older man sat puffing on his pipe, deep in thought. "Mrs. Stuart is a remarkable woman," he said finally. "She has that rare quality of sensing the needs of others. She knows how deeply Robinson resents anyone from the North. And I have to admit that it's justified. He's seen a lot and has been hurt a lot. I've seen enough since I've been down here to understand a little of what the young man feels. He doesn't want any favors from anyone remotely connected with the 'damn Yankees' that ripped his world apart."

They both sat in silence with the crackle of the fire the only sound in the still room; Garrett weighing his pa's words, the other puffing on his pipe.

"No, I can't say I blame him," Mr. Anderson repeated, getting to his feet and walking over to the fireplace to gently tap the ashes from his pipe on one of the andirons. "Have to respect a man for having the courage to stand up for his convictions. He'll make it in the lumber business! He's straightforward and honest, not afraid of hard work, and he's determined! That's a combination hard to beat." Mr. Anderson's gaze fell on Garrett, who sat staring into the fire without comment.

"Think I'll turn in, Son. It's getting late."

As the older man turned toward the stairs, a slight smile softened the lines of his face. He thought contentedly, "I wonder what that stubborn rebel would do if he knew his financial backer was a 'damn Yankee'." But there wasn't the remotest chance of Robinson ever finding that out. Mr. Anderson had learned from long years of experience that if you wanted to keep something secret, you didn't tell anyone; not even the members of your immediate family. Only Mr. Eschweiler was in on the arrangement. And he had been sworn to secrecy under threat of being sued for breach of trust, if Robinson ever found out.

Alone, Garrett sat staring into the fire, remembering the war. "No," he agreed sadly. "I can't blame him, either, for being bitter. I was a part of it but I hated the death and destruction, too. Why do men always have to go to war to settle their differences?"

The sizzle of the dying fire was the only response in the silent room. The clock on the mantle struck eleven, reminding Garrett that the hour was late. Wearily, he, too, stood up and headed for the stairs.

CHAPTER 22

The music stopped and Liza and her partner came to a standstill on the dance floor. She looked around the ballroom, her glance quickly identifying her husband standing with a group of men near the refreshment table. A feeling of repugnance gripped her, but she stifled it to look up at her partner and smile demurely, accepting his compliment gracefully that he admired her as a dance partner. She glanced once again in Keith's direction, thinking, "I wager he's telling one of his often-told sordid stories to that group of men." His face flushed a vivid pink and the wide gestures he was making with his hands assured her that he was indeed having a good time. "He always does when he's the center of attention," she thought in disgust.

Turning her back to Keith, as if that would make him go away, she glanced again at her partner. Smiling down at her winsomely, he asked, "Would you like some refreshments?"

"Oh, yes, thank you," Liza replied pleasantly, her glance holding his for just a moment, then, dropping, the black lashes hiding the bewitching excitement in her blue eyes. He guided her to one of the velvet sofas and then, assuring her that he "would only be a minute" proceeded in the direction of the punch bowl.

Liza did not know the name of the young man with whom she had been dancing, and furthermore, she had no interest in finding out. She loved to dance; Keith didn't. Dancing helped her unwind, made her feel free. Uninhibited.

Her gaze slowly traveled around the large expanse of the room, appraising the gowns worn by the other ladies. Satisfied that hers was just as smart and beautiful as any in the room, she leaned back, her head tilted just a little, a small mocking smile making her full lips appear teasingly desirable. "Oh, how I love Savannah!" she breathed.

* * * * *

The carriage swayed sharply on the narrow cobbled street, causing Liza to lean heavily against her husband. This pleased him, and he encircled her with his arm, pulling her hard against him. He tilted her chin back with the back of his other hand, and kissed her hard, the smell of liquor nauseating her. "He always becomes amorous when I enjoy myself at a party," she thought hatefully. Liza sat motionless, thinking dispassionately, "His lips feel so hard and flat." She endured his caresses, wishing wildly that she could push him out of the door of the carriage. She loathed having him touch her! "And why?" she asked herself over and over each time it happened. Why was the thought of physical contact with Keith so repulsive? It wasn't that he was unattractive. Even though he wasn't considered handsome by most folk, he was certainly nice looking. Rather distinguished. He was fast becoming one of the best-known lawyers in the state, and his political acumen had gained him quite a reputation both in Washington and at home. Other women seemed to find him interesting; even flirting with him in her presence. Then, why?

Keith sensed her withdrawal and released her. Without a word he straightened up and sat staring out of the window.

"Now, he'll pout," Liza thought despairingly, "and my trip will be ruined!" Nevertheless, she made no move toward him, but remained on her side of the carriage, staring out of her window, grateful to be left alone. Finally, she leaned her head back against the cushioned upholstery of the seat, gazing out at the dark store windows. In a few moments the driver called "whoa" to the horses, and then he was opening the door. Liza gathered up the folds of her long silken skirt and stepped down out of the carriage.

Inside their room at the hotel, she kicked off her shoes and walked over to the massive armoire to hang up her wrap. Suddenly Keith's arms were around her again, his lips seeking hers hungrily, his hands caressing her soft body. When she automatically stiffened, he drew back, staring at her, eyes dark with anger. "Why, Liza? Why?" he demanded. "You laugh, dance and talk with mere acquaintances, yet, you are withdrawn and cold with me? Why?"

"I don't know," she whimpered, "except... except it leads to... to other things!"

"And what's wrong with that?" he all but shouted. "You are my wife, you know! Liza, you make me feel like a... a beggar, or even worse! Sometimes... sometimes I feel like I'm a molester!"

"Keith!"

"It's true, isn't it? What's wrong with us, Liza?" he demanded, eyes hard with anger, "or, me?"

"It's not you," she lied, dropping her eyes quickly to hide her deception. "I just don't like being touched that way."

"What do you mean 'that way?'" he asked, bewildered. "Liza, why in the name of Heaven did you ever marry me if that's the way you feel? Or, the way you are," he added, not bothering to hide his contempt.

Liza stood motionless, her heart pounding, staring at the floor.

"That's a good question," she thought. "Why did I marry you? Was it because Melinda was getting married...because I hated the farm...because I was looking for an escape...?" She shivered. She could feel Keith's angry eyes upon her, bearing down. Then, because he was afraid of his own anger and because he had an almost overpowering urge to slap her across her beautiful face, he turned away toward the door. With his hand on the doorknob he turned to stare back at her, and then he was gone, the door slamming shut behind him.

Relief and guilt flooded over her. Hurriedly she removed her dress and undergarments. She bathed her face hastily, and after removing the pins from her hair, gave it a few swift strokes with the brush. Then, she hurried to bed, pulling the covers high under her chin.

"Maybe he'll drink himself into oblivion," she thought angrily, and then, pangs of guilt swept over her. Burying her face in the pillow, she shook with great wracking sobs. Finally, emotionally dry and exhausted, she slept. She didn't know, or care, when Keith crawled into bed beside her hours later, his anger and passion having found satisfaction in the dark side of the city.

CHAPTER 23

Robinson sat next to the window of the Pullman car in which he and Jim were traveling to Savannah. It was still early and the passing landscape was shrouded in pre-dawn darkness, and the flickering light of the coach lamp made it difficult for him to see anything on the other side of the window. He stared through the glass straining to catch a glimpse of the unfamiliar landscape. The seat beside him was empty for Jim had gone back to the dining car to buy some coffee.

This was the first time Robinson had ever been on a train. The farthermost he had ever traveled from home. Subconsciously he touched his left shirt pocket where he had placed the money he had borrowed from Reuben, the crispness of the new material of the garment reminding him of the new clothes he was wearing. Jim had insisted that he go all the way; new shirt, vest, and tie, the whole works. But Robinson had held his ground, adamantly refusing to spend the money.

"No, Jim," he had refused stubbornly. "This is borrowed money. It will have to be paid back. My kids need shoes. If this deal doesn't go through, it will be rough just paying Reuben back for the shirt, pants, and my traveling expenses."

"It's just good business to look prosperous, Rob," Jim had argued, becoming impatient. "You know what I mean? Good impressions are important! Why don't you let me loan you the money?"

Robinson just shook his head. "What difference does it make who loans me the money? It still has to be paid back."

Now, sitting on the train among many that were well dressed, he wondered if he had been wise. Jim was right, he admitted grudgingly, about appearances. The clothes he wore judged a man. "But, if I had the money for that kind of outfit, I wouldn't be needing to borrow at all," he argued silently, trying to justify his decision.

He glanced down at his new grip that he kept securely between his foot and the wall of the coach. In it were the papers authorizing him to make a loan on the farm. This was the scary part. But his ma and sisters had been so insistent. Almost demanding. Thinking of his family and their loyal backing gave him a feeling of security and a resolve to make a go of the endeavor...whatever the cost in terms of personal sacrifice.

Jim dropped into the seat beside him. "The porter is making a fresh pot of coffee. Should be ready before too much longer." He slid forward in the seat, stretching his legs in front of him, his head resting against the cushioned seat; eyes closed.

"How can he be so relaxed?" Robinson thought, mildly resentful. "But then, I suppose if I'd traveled as much as Jim, I'd be used to it, too."

The conductor came through the door at the rear of the car, "Next stop Savannah!"

Jim swore mildly. "Well, there goes the coffee."

Robinson reached down and took hold of the handle of his grip. Jim, holding up his hand to halt him, never moved from his slouched position. "It'll be a while, yet, before we reach the station," he said.

* * * * *

Mr. Downer, Mr. Eschweiler's secretary, was a small swarthy man who evidently took his job seriously. He was well experienced at weeding out salesmen and undesirables who would waste his employer's valuable time. And the two standing before him, especially the blue-eyed one, appeared to be just that, if you could judge a book by its cover. For that matter, he thought, neither one of them judging by their appearance, would be remotely connected with the world of high finance.

"Yes?" he drawled, gazing at Jim and Rob over his silver rimmed glasses, his expression passive.

"Mr. Eschweiler is expecting us," Jim said courteously.

"Oh?" the secretary replied, one eyebrow elevated. "And what might the names be, Sir?" he asked, glancing down at his appointment book.

"Jim Wheeler and Robinson Stuart."

The secretary was on his feet immediately, extending his hand, an ingratiating smile flooding his face. The change was so obvious that it was somewhat disconcerting to both Jim and Rob.

"Oh, yes, Mr. Wheeler, Mr. Stuart," he acknowledged, his head bobbing to each of them. "Mr. Eschweiler is expecting you. Please be seated, gentlemen. I'll tell Mr. Eschweiler you are here." Nodding graciously, his expression in no way revealing his confusion, he headed for a large oak-paneled door at the far end of the room. Jim and Robinson had not even had time to get seated comfortably before the secretary was back, announcing that Mr. Eschweiler would see them.

Until Robinson had started on this journey, the only buildings he had ever been in, other than those of his home and farm, were his church, his neighbors' homes, and the stores in town. Highly polished floors, colorful area rugs, and elegant leather upholstery were completely new to him. To hide his feelings of discomfort and keen awareness of "not belonging," he maintained a stoic expression and decided he would let Jim do all the talking. "I should have listened to Jim and bought a suit," he thought miserably, painfully aware of his country bumpkin look.

But if these social standards were important to Mr. Eschweiler, he gave no indication. Very patiently and respectfully he went over the details of the enterprise in which they would be involved. He explained the terms of the loan, the margin of profit and loss to be expected by all parties involved, and the training and assistance that would be provided as they ventured into more difficult operations in the future. Robinson became so engrossed with the details and possibilities of their business venture that he became totally oblivious to his elegant surroundings that had intimidated him so painfully when he first entered the room.

Finally, after several hours, all of the details had been worked out to the satisfaction of all parties involved, and the necessary papers drawn up. "Gentlemen," Mr. Eschweiler said, rising and extending his hand, "I believe that just about wraps it up. I am looking forward to many years of pleasant, and profitable, business dealings with you both." He walked with them to the outer door of the office, granting them a safe trip home.

As the door closed behind Jim and Robinson, Mr. Eschweiler's glance met his secretary's. "Mr. Downer," he said with a twinkle in his eye, "appearances can be deceiving." And not waiting for Mr. Downer's reply returned to his inner office, closing the door quietly behind him. He walked over to peer out the window, his gaze following the two figures walking down the street.

"Mr. Anderson," he mused, nodding his approval, "I think you've picked yourself some winners, again!"

The ride back home on the train was far more pleasant for Robinson than the trip had been to Savannah. He was anxious to get home and tell Kallie and his ma everything that had transpired. Too, his former doubts and reservations about the partnership had been replaced with eager anticipation. He could hardly wait to get back home and put some action into their plans.

He was relieved the trip to Savannah was behind them, though. He wasn't a seasoned traveler, and besides, he didn't like being away from his family, even for a few days.

But he wouldn't have been quite so relaxed if he could have looked into the near future. A future that would be sending him back to Savannah to attend to company business, and this time, he would be entirely on his own.

CHAPTER 24

The train lurched to a stop and Robinson stepped down from the railroad car onto the depot platform. He felt as if he had sawdust between the collar of his shirt and the back of his neck. It had been a long, tiresome, cinder-blowing ride to Savannah.

He stood for a moment on the brick platform, gazing around him. This was his first trip to Savannah alone and the first time to be alone in any major city. He walked over and picked up his bag that the porter had placed, along with several others, on a nearby luggage rack. The porter moved toward him, smiling expectantly. "Yaz-suh, Boss! Could I hep yo, Suh?" he offered, smiling broadly, while reaching for Robinson's grip.

"No, no, thank you, it's not heavy," Robinson replied, thinking, "Why would he think I need help with this small bag?" He turned to walk down the platform to the depot when the thought occurred to him that the porter might have been expecting some kind of compensation. He turned back, only to see the porter heading down the platform toward the train's caboose. Shrugging, Robinson continued toward the depot entrance. "I'll catch it next time," he decided.

An appointment later on in the week with Mr. Eschweiler would hopefully result in some new accounts. Remembering his feeling of embarrassment at the previous meeting because of his wearing apparel, he was determined it would be different this time. His first objective was to purchase a business suit, and that would mean he'd need to find a tailor. Jim had given him the name of one he had used in Savannah, so that's where he decided to try first.

There weren't many people inside the train depot, only a few tired souls sitting on the high-backed wooden seats, evidently waiting for a later train.

Robinson walked slowly through the depot and out onto the street. He inquired of a passerby if he could tell him how to get to Zackery's Tailor Shop. The man responded by pointing down the street in the direction of the river.

Robinson hurried toward the business section, studying the houses and buildings that lined the thoroughfare. It wasn't long until he was walking along the waterfront, the dampness from the river causing a musty odor that seemed to permeate the buildings that created a barrier between the riverfront and the town that spread out beyond the bluff. Robinson had to make inquiries again before he found Zackery's - located in what seemed to be an affluent part of the business section.

As Robinson opened the door and stepped inside, a small bell above the door announced his arrival. Curtains over the doorway in the back of the room parted and a middle-aged man hurried to meet Robinson, his smile gracious and welcoming. A measuring tape hung loosely around his neck. Robinson also noted that his hair was gray at the temples, and the hand he extended to Robinson was as smooth as a woman's.

"How do you do, young man. My name's Benjamin Zackery. What may I do for you?"

Robinson nodded, deciding immediately that he liked the man. "My name's Robinson Stuart, Mr. Zackery. I need a good business suit. My friend, Jim Wheeler, from upstate told me to see you."

"Why, yes! I know Mr. Wheeler," he smiled, nodding several times. "Fine man, Mr. Wheeler."

"Yes," Robinson agreed readily. "Jim and I have known each other all of our lives."

"Is that so?" the man responded politely. "Nothing like good friends," he added as an afterthought. "Now, what kind of material did you have in mind, Mr. Stuart?"

Robinson inspected the bolts of material displayed, trying to make a selection. The proprietor, experienced with customers' indecisions, walked over to a bolt of material, suggesting, "This is a very popular material, here, Sir." He picked up the edge of the material, holding it up to the light. "It holds a crease very well, does not wrinkle easily, and it wears well. It would be a suit that would serve you well. One that would be very adaptable to many occasions."

Robinson's perplexed gaze traveled back and forth across the materials. The blood rushed to his temples and his head began to pound. He could buy only one suit and it had to be right. Totally frustrated, he turned to Mr. Zackery. "I think I'll follow your suggestion on this one here, but I don't want the black color. I believe the dark gray would be more to my liking."

"Certainly, Mr. Stuart. I believe you've made a wise choice. No disrespect intended, but most of my customers who wear the black are ministers and undertakers. As for the material, I sell more suits from the one you have selected. Unless you go into the very

301

expensive materials, you can't beat this for both wear and looks. Now, I'll need to take your measurements, Sir," he explained, slipping the tape measure from around his neck.

"May I suggest a vest from one of the coordinating materials, Mr. Stuart, or even from the same material as your suit? Most all of the best dressed men are wearing them."

Robinson stood mulling over the tailor's suggestion. A vest would up the cost but what Mr. Zackery said was true. He had noticed on the train that the men wearing dress suits wore vests with them. Mind made up, he nodded his agreement. "I'll take the vest, too. By the way, I'm somewhat pressed for time. I'm in Savannah for a business meeting the latter part of the week. Is there a chance you could have it ready by then?"

Mr. Zackery pursed his lips and stood rubbing the back of his neck. "I'll have to check with my assistant," he replied, heading for the back of the store and disappearing behind the heavy curtain that blocked the view into the workroom. In a few minutes he was back, a triumphant smile creasing his face. "Neither Mr. Leesburg, or myself, have anything with a deadline. We can have the suit for you in a couple of days. You will need to come by this afternoon around 3:00 for a fitting."

"Yes, yes indeed!" Robinson responded, smiling his relief. "I appreciate you helping me out this way."

"We're happy to have your business, Mr. Stuart, and we'll get on it right away. By the way, would you be interested in a nice hat, Sir? We have some very nice imported ones."

Robinson hesitated a moment, then nodded.

"Whew! I'm glad that's over," Robinson breathed as he left the shop, pulling the door shut behind him. He was pleased with his selection, but now, he was faced with the problem of shoes. "I should have asked the tailor the best place." After a moment's hesitation, he turned to go back inside. At the sound of the bell, Mr. Zackery appeared from behind the curtain. "Was there something else we can help you with, Mr. Stuart?"

"I'm sorry, Sir, but I'm new in town. Could you suggest a good place to buy shoes?"

"Why, of course," he smiled, pulling a slip of paper from his shirt pocket. He wrote the name of a store and the proprietor's name and handed it to Robinson. "Come, I'll show you," he said, walking to the front door and stepping outside, he pointed in the direction Robinson should go and gave him explicit instructions on how to get there.

Buying the shoes had been a simple undertaking - but the big problem facing him at the moment was finding a place to stay. He checked out the hotel recommended by the shoe merchant, but decided to try to find something less expensive. He'd stay there later, if prestige demanded, and funds permitted. There was always the pressing reminder that he was spending borrowed money. Suddenly, the feeling of panic returned. "How did I let myself get involved in this kind of operation? I'm way over my head. How can a greenhorn like me hope to do business with men who travel back and forth to Europe as easily as I'd go to town for supplies? Why, just buying an outfit of clothes has been a major undertaking." He began to sweat.

Then, like an echo in his brain, he recalled something his ma used to tell him, "Son, you don't know what you are capable of doing until you've tried, and if you don't try, you've failed already. Don't let the fear of failure rob you of becoming all that God intended you to be."

"All right, Ma," he determined. "I'll see it through - come what may! I couldn't quit if I wanted to. How could I ever look my family and friends in the face again?"

Acting upon information received from a law officer, Robinson had no difficulty in finding the rambling two-story Victorian style house with the sign out front - "Mrs. McAfee's Boardinghouse." After climbing the steep front steps, he turned the handle of the bell on the front door. Through the large oval glass, he could see a full-bosomed, plump, middle-aged woman coming down the hallway. She wiped her hands on her apron before opening the door.

"Yes?" she asked, expression friendly, though seemingly hurried.

Robinson touched the brim of his new hat. "Good afternoon, Ma'am. I'm trying to find lodging. An officer told me you might have a vacancy?"

Before answering, her quick glance inspected him from head to toe. "Yes, I have a room. It's small but comfortable," she informed him. She named a price that seemed reasonable. "Price includes supper and breakfast," she stated matter-of-factly with a "take it or leave it" air.

"Could I see the room, please?" Robinson inquired.

"Certainly," she agreed crisply, standing back for him to enter, then closing the door behind him. "It's upstairs."

The stairway was wide and curved, giving supporting evidence that the house had been used in times past for more prestigious living than a boarding house.

The room was small but comfortably furnished. "Probably a storage room converted to a bedroom," he decided.

"This will be fine, Mrs....?" he hesitated, realizing that she hadn't told him her name.

"McAfee! And if you be thinkin' me name's Irish, then you'll be thinkin' right, me young man. And what might your name be?"

Robinson smiled, suddenly realizing that her brusque manner was only a front. "Stuart, Ma'am. Robinson Stuart. I'm from out of town."

"You in town on business?" She queried, in her matter-of-fact manner.

Robinson nodded, reaching for his money pouch.

She took the money he held out to her, then headed for the stairs, pausing momentarily to inform him that supper was served at 6:00 sharp, and breakfast at 6:30.

CHAPTER 25

"Rob, there's this girl we want to fix you up with!"

Bill Holman's eyes glistened with excitement as he leaned slightly forward, elbows on the table, hands curved around the piece of stemware that contained his drink. They were all business associates of Rob's and they had all just finished eating a late dinner.

"She's new at Madam Etienne's," he continued, grinning knowingly. "A French girl and she hasn't been in this country too long. And, man! Does she know how to make a man forget his troubles?"

The men seated around the large round table varied in appearance and age; some younger than Rob, some older.

Bill's remark generated expressions on their faces ranging from small knowing grins to smiles that culminated into boisterous verbal agreement. Many of them were business associates of Rob's, and they were also well acquainted with what the city of Savannah had to offer in the way of entertainment for bored men away from their wives and families.

Robinson slid his chair backward from under the table so that he would have room to stretch his legs. Outwardly Robinson's facial expression had not changed, except for the slight lifting of one eyebrow, but underneath the calm veneer his heart began to pound. He worked closely with these men and their good will and support of Wheeler and Stuart, Inc. was an important financial asset. He knew he had to use caution and play this game with great care, or he could jeopardize months of hard work, time, and money that he and Jim had invested. Inwardly, he seethed with resentment for having to be put in such a position. Jim knew he was a greenhorn! That he was totally inexperienced in dealing with ways of the world.

"You need the experience," Jim had argued. "You might as well start now. You can handle it, Rob! If I didn't think you could, I'd go myself."

"If only I hadn't moved from the boarding house to the hotel," Robinson reasoned grimly to himself. It had seemed the wisest thing at the time, just in case some of the men had inquired as to where he was "lodging." Jim was such a stickler for prestige and these men had come a long way down the road from the smell of boiled cabbage and fried fat back - if they had ever been there in the first place.

"Well? How about it?" Bill probed; rubbing his palms together, his eyes bright with anticipation.

"I don't think so," Rob answered pleasantly, also rising, struggling to hide his indignation behind a pleasant facial facade. "I'm too tired to think of anything right now except a soft mattress and a good night's sleep."

The group's urging became more insistent. Rob realized that his safest and surest way out of this predicament was to make his exit as quickly and politely as possible.

Back in his room upstairs he lit the kerosene lamp hanging on brass chains from the center of the ceiling. Small crystal prisms hanging from a brass circle above the lamp chimney appeared to be girls dancing, glistening in the soft light. Robinson removed his coat and hung it in the oversized oak wardrobe, pausing momentarily to admire the beautiful finish of the piece of furniture. "Some day, Kallie, we're going to have furniture like this," he promised silently.

Walking over to the window, he stood gazing across the rooftops, automatically reaching up to unfasten his shirt collar. He thought about home and the kids and wished fervently that Kallie could be here with him. "She really would think this was something!" he thought, as his eyes moved slowly around the room, not missing a single detail of the luxurious furnishings. He repeated his vow again to the silent room. "Someday, she's going to have pretty things like these."

His thought returned to the offer the men had made. He grinned sheepishly wondering what a night with a French temptress would be like. The invitation had been tempting, he admitted, the thought being replaced immediately by an overwhelming feeling of guilt. Loneliness gnawed away at him like a hunger that couldn't be satisfied.

There was· a light knock on the door. A slight frown creased Robinson's forehead as he turned from the window and headed toward the sound. Expecting it to be one of his former men companions and dreading the pressure he knew would be applied, he was quite startled to see a young woman standing just outside the doorway. Without waiting for an invitation, she brushed past him and moved lithely into the room. Then turning to face him with a teasing smile playing provocatively upon her lips, asked seductively, "You sent for me, Monsieur?"

Speechless, Robinson stood with his hand still holding the doorknob. She was older than she had seemed at first, but very beautiful. The light from the overhead lamp shining down upon the crown of her head gave a sheen to her blue-black hair which was pulled back into a mass of ringlets and curls that cascaded down her back. The dress she wore was a brilliant scarlet that shimmered when she walked and clung to every part of her soft body, emphasizing her full bosom and hips, ending in a deep flounce at the hem. Her complexion appeared smooth and creamy, not at all rough like Robinson had always imagined women of her profession to be.

"Watz ze matter, Monsieur? You surprised, no?"

Tilting her head in a teasing manner, she laughed gaily, quite sure that his stunned expression resulted from the fact that he found her so desirable.

"Don't you think it would be more discreet if you closed the door, Monsieur," she purred as she moved within a few inches of him, her heavy-scented perfume permeating the air surrounding them.

Desire for her surged within him, adding to his panic. "Surprised?" he repeated quietly, not trusting himself to speak any louder for fear his voice would fail him. "Quite frankly, 'surprised' is putting it mildly. Who sent you to my room?"

For a moment her lovely face clouded. The brilliant smile flashed again. "You deed not know I was coming?" she taunted, laughing gaily, as she turned to parade around the room. "Then, I must be a gift from your friends," she chided, her eyes taunting him. "Your name is Stuart, is it not, Monsieur?"

"My name is Stuart, all right, but I have made no such arrangements of this kind with anyone, Miss...?"

"Just, Cherrie, Monsieur," she smiled, lips slightly parted, eyelids half-closed, her dark eyes appraising him invitingly.

"Look, Cherrie," Robinson stated firmly, fighting to maintain his stoic composure. "I don't know who made this arrangement, but it was none of my doing. Now, I'm afraid I must ask you to leave," he informed her curtly, moving to open the door wider.

"Oh, Monsieur, you must be one of those rare creatures inhibited with scruples? What a shame! I am sorree, Monsieur," she mocked, her tone light and unoffended as she glided toward the door. Pausing in the doorway, she turned to look back at him, still smiling tauntingly. "I'm just a wee bit sorree. I like men wez class." Turning slightly in his direction, she reached down into the folds of the top of her gown and removed what appeared to be several bills of large denomination. "The night has been most profitable for me, anyway, Monsieur," she chided gaily. "Your friends? They must be veery fond of you. They paid me veery well." With a grand sweep, she made her way down the hall.

Robinson closed the door hastily and slid the bolt across it, his face reddening as he heard her laughter still floating through the open glass transom over the door.

Disturbed by the lust the woman had roused in him, he plopped down upon the bed, still in his britches and shirt. He forced his thoughts toward home and Kallie. "Kallie, Kallie," he whispered tenderly. "If only you could be here with me!"

Hours later he awoke, disgusted with himself for wrinkling his good pants. Hastily he undressed and blew out the lamp. Crawling under the sheet this time, he thought miserably. "I suppose it takes this kind of living to make a go of this business, and if it does, then so be it! But I don't have to like it!" he decided grimly – giving his pillow several resounding blows with his fist.

CHAPTER 26

Elvina sat on a bench at the kitchen table with her oldest grandchild, John Matt, beside her, and a McGuffey's reader propped up in front of them. Patiently she waited as he struggled with his daily reading lesson.

John Matt squirmed. "Grandma! Do I hafta?" he whined.

"Yes, John Matt, you have to!" she stated in her unrelenting no-nonsense tone. "And the words are pronounced 'have to,' not hafta.'"

"Oh, aw right," he grumbled, reaching back to scratch an imaginary itch on the back of his neck.

"We're going over this page one more time, and if you get it all without a mistake, you may go outside and play," Elvina bargained gently but firmly.

Resignedly, John Matt started once again.

Lesson time for the two oldest boys was every weekday morning immediately after the outside chores and breakfast were over. Kallie relied on Elvina to teach the children since she seemed to have a gift for it and was far more patient than Kallie. Teaching the boys, especially John Matt with all of his nervous energy, was no easy undertaking.

"I'll take care of the morning chores around the house, Ma Stuart, if you'll just work with the kids on their lessons," Kallie had bargained with her mother-in-law. "Besides, they respond more to your teaching than they do mine," she admitted unashamedly.

John Matt was finally successful in completing his reading assignment without error, and with a shriek of joy, jumped up from the bench and headed for the door.

"Tell Robert to come in here," Elvina called after him. When several minutes had elapsed and there was no sign of Robert, she walked over to the door. The two boys were pitching a homemade ball back and forth.

"Robert!" Elvina called sternly, "Come inside. It's time for your reading lesson."

"Oh, Grandma!" he wailed, displaying his resentment by bouncing the ball on the ground with great force. "We're playing ball!"

"I'd hate to have to tell your pa that you didn't obey me," she threatened, her tone unyielding.

Robert pitched the ball to John Matt and turned to stalk toward the house. "I hate ole ABCs," he complained bitterly, big tears welling up in his eyes.

Lessons finally over, as much to Elvina's relief as the boys, Elvina joined Kallie with preparations for the noonday meal.

"I don't know how we're going to squeeze in time for Nat when he gets old enough for lessons," Elvina said despondently, shaking her head.

"If only we could get some kind of neighborhood school going," Kallie agreed. They talked about this often. She paused in her task of peeling a potato, eyes troubled. Casting a furtive glance in Elvina's direction, she blurted. "Guess I might as well tell you, now, Ma Stuart. There's going to be another one added to the future enrollment list."

Elvina turned quickly to look at Kallie, her eyes questioning. Kallie nodded.

"When?" Elvina asked, her calm expression in no way revealing her misgivings about the two of them being able to continue teaching the children properly with a new baby on the scene.

Kallie shrugged and turned back to her potato peeling. "Best I can figure it will be in early summer."

The two women worked on for some time in silence as if this last announcement required a while to digest.

"We need to get with the other families in the community and try to work out some kind of school plan for all the children," Kallie continued, not discussing her pregnancy any further. "Most of the kids around here can't even write their names."

"You're right," Elvina sighed. "But we women can't do much about it. In the first place, there's no adequate building for the classes, and all the men are so busy – they don't want to take the time to build a schoolhouse. And, too, so many of the men don't seem to think schooling is necessary for farm folk."

Kallie nodded. "It's not as bad as it was right after the war ended. Attitudes are changing somewhat. The people seem to have more hope and more interest in local affairs since the Federal soldiers have been removed."

"Have you had a chance to talk to Robinson lately about a community school?"

"No," Kallie answered hesitantly, with another shrug of her shoulders. "You know how he's been wrapped up in the mill and comes home too tired to eat, sometimes. Too, when he's not concentrating on the business, he's talking about enlarging this house. When he finds out about the new baby, I'm sure he'll want to start building as soon as possible. Not that I'd object, really," she added lamely. "Heaven knows we're walking over each other, now!"

They worked on in silence for a few moments.

"But the school's so important!" Kallie exploded, the urgency in her voice revealing the intensity of her feelings. "Time's something we can't ever make up! I haven't been able to get Rob really fired up about it, yet. Why don't you try talking to Rob, Ma Stuart?" Kallie pleaded. "Maybe you would strike a chord that I've missed so far."

"He already knows how I feel, my dear. It would only cause him to go on the defensive if I brought it up again. But you are right. Something does need to be done."

It was some time later before Kallie decided to bring up the subject to Rob again. They were alone in their bedroom and they were discussing their future addition to the family.

"If I have a little girl," Kallie stated emphatically, "her name's going to be Janie Elvina!"

"You've been saying that since before Robert Evans was born," Robinson teased, pulling Kallie close and stepping sideways so that he could see their reflection in the mirror of their bedroom dresser. Teasingly he patted her lower abdomen. "It won't be long before I'll not be able to hold you close to me - from the front side, that is."

"I know," she agreed despairingly. She looked up at him for a long moment, expression serious, gaze questioning. "This is one of the bad things about being in the family way. I always become so misshapen and grotesque. Too bad humans don't walk around on all fours; then, it wouldn't show so much!"

"Then, I couldn't hug you at all, and that wouldn't be any fun. I'll take you just as you are, thank you, Madam," he laughed heartily, kissing her affectionately on the neck just below her large bun of braided hair.

"Rob, I know we've talked about what I'm going to say many times, but since we are expecting another child, it's become almost an obsession with me."

"You're going to bring up the school again," he grimaced, his impatience evident. "Well, if we're going into that again, let's go to the kitchen and make a cup of coffee to help tackle it."

"All right," she agreed, working hard at being patient. "It's time to get breakfast started, anyway."

In the kitchen Rob uncovered the coals in the iron cook stove that he had surprised Kallie with upon returning from one of his trips to Savannah. In a few minutes he had a hot fire going.

"Rob, about the school," Kallie continued, while spooning coffee in the pot, "Ma Stuart said not long ago that if you and Jim don't take the bull by the horns to get the schoolhouse built, it will never be done, and she is absolutely right! In the first place, few of the other families involved have any financial resources to contribute."

Robinson didn't comment, just sat staring into space. Kallie, busy with breakfast preparations, was silent, too, for a while. Then, somewhat irritated because of his prolonged silence, blurted, "Rob, it takes all of Ma Stuart's time and mine just to keep things going now! What will happen when the new baby gets here?" Her voice broke. Knowing how upset Rob became when she cried, she was silent for a long minute – struggling to regain her composure. "I...I'm afraid it's going to come to the place where we'll have to give up the lessons, and that frightens me. I can't bear to think of any of my children growing up illiterate, not able to read or write! That would be a terrible injustice! Where would you be today if your ma had taken the easy way out and let you grow up without any education?"

"You're absolutely right," he agreed quietly, "but it's not just our problem, you know." He did not want to upset Kallie but he couldn't completely hide his annoyance, either. Didn't she realize that his time was limited, also? There were so many demands on him...the trips to Savannah, which were more and more frequent now... and the overseeing of the mill with Jim gone so much. It was paying off financially, too, for both of them had been able to repay the loans they had made, and there was enough capital in the bank to handle their operation independent of outside help. But the business was a jealous mistress, and success had not come easy.

They ate their breakfast in silence. Kallie, not trusting herself to say anything more for fear of antagonizing Robinson, sat quietly pushing her food around on her plate with a fork.

Robinson drank the last swallow of coffee in his cup. He got up slowly and pushed his chair back against the table. He stood for a long moment with his hand resting on the back of the chair, his expression thoughtful. "I know you are right, Kallie," he repeated.

"And I am concerned - far more than you realize. I'll try to find an opportunity to talk with Jim and some of the others." He turned toward the door. "It's getting daylight and I have to go."

Kallie hurried to follow and stopped him just inside the door. "Thank you, darling," she said softly, putting her arms around him while standing on tiptoe to kiss him.

"Be gone with you, woman," he chided, faking sternness. He brushed the underside of her chin lightly with his finger, his good-natured grin replacing the frown.

"Go on," she said softly, pushing him toward the door, eyes glistening suspiciously. "Get out of here!"

Inside the barn, Robinson hurried to saddle his horse. In a matter of minutes he was on his way, riding hard.

"Kallie is right," he agreed silently as he rode toward the mill. When a person couldn't read and write it imposed impossible barriers. War could wipe out everything a man had worked for all his life, but it couldn't take away what he had stored in his brain. And ignorance, when let run rampant, could be equally devastating as war in many ways. Didn't he see it everywhere he went? The South floundering under the burden of having had their local and state governments turned over to ignorant and untrained individuals placed in office by the Federal government. The killing had stopped, but what had followed, and was still going on to a great extent, had been equally as crippling. Maybe, worse, for the South's spirit had been trampled in the dust.

"And it's here to stay," he concluded dismally, "unless change comes about. And that kind of change has to come from the heart of the people, if any real progress was to be made. We must not sit placidly by and wait for the government to do something. It could go on for generations before help of any real consequence reaches the rural areas."

A profound resolve was born in Robinson's heart and mind that morning as he pondered the problem on his way to the mill. If there were to be any changes for the better, if there was to be any hope for the vast improvement in the educational and social welfare of the South he loved so dearly, then it had to begin at the grassroots with the children. "And that means we build a schoolhouse," he concluded, urging his horse to a faster pace.

CHAPTER 27

The womenfolk finished packing the remains of the picnic dinner, which had been prepared especially for the men working on the schoolhouse. The workday dinner had turned into a family affair. Children of all ages played in the clearing in the nearby woods. Their shrieks and laughter provided a sampling of many such noises soon to be heard during playtime at school.

Off to one side of the clearing, a large pile of ashes still smoldered. Thin wisps of smoke straggled aimlessly into the late afternoon coolness. Clearing the brush and burning the debris had been the women and older children's responsibility for the final workday.

The one room schoolhouse was near completion. Robinson, Jim, and a couple of other men were adding the last of the wooden shingles to the roof, while off to the side away from falling debris, another group constructed temporary benches to be used in the classroom. The offbeat rhythm of the hammers, mingling with the sounds made by the playing children, and the talk and laughter of the womenfolk, created a festive atmosphere totally opposite to the hard driving labor of the men. But there was good reason for celebrating by all of those present, both young and old. There was going to be a place where their children could learn their letters.

When the last of the baskets and boxes were packed away in wagons, the women gathered around the smoldering fire to visit. Since all of them lived miles apart, and their days were totally occupied with the care of their homes and children, socializing and visits were few, limited almost entirely to the all-day, dinner-on-the-ground preaching services at the church. And these only took place during the warm weather months. Even Kallie and Salena, who were the closest of friends, went weeks and weeks sometimes without seeing each other.

"That's it!" they heard Jim yell jubilantly as he climbed down the ladder from the roof. The rest of the new benches were carried inside and the men began to gather up their tools.

Later, as Robinson drove their team and wagon out onto the main roadway, Kallie turned to look back at the small building in the clearing. Her throat constricted with pride. "Oh, Rob," she breathed, "isn't it beautiful?"

"That it is," he agreed with a tired smile, glancing over his shoulder, too exhausted to show much enthusiasm. His gaze dropped to rest on his children in the back of the wagon. All of them were silently staring at the building slowly receding out of sight.

. "What do you kids think of your schoolhouse?" Robinson asked, straining to make his voice heard above the grinding wheels.

John Matt grunted. "It looks good, Pa," he responded, his lack of enthusiasm apparent.

Robert just shrugged his shoulders, indicating total indifference.

Nat said nothing.

Robinson turned back to his driving, an amused expression relaxing the tired lines of his face. "Giddy up!" he urged, slapping the team with the lines. "We should have headed home sooner," he remarked to Kallie. "We'll be way after dark getting home."

"Oh, the stock will wait until we get there," she said happily. "If you had quit before the schoolhouse was finished, there's no telling when all of you would have gotten together again. Just think! It's finished after all these months, now. Our children have a schoolhouse! I can't wait to get home and tell Elvina." Some of her exuberance faded at the mention of her mother-in-law. "I wish she had felt like coming today," she added, not verbalizing her concern that Elvina must have really not been feeling well to miss an occasion as important as this.

The noise made by the increased speed of the wagon made conversation too much of an effort, so they lapsed into silence. The children, tired from the long day, soon fell asleep on the quilt Kallie had spread on the floor of the wagon's bed, except for Janie Elvina who had nestled in Kallie's lap.

Robinson, engrossed in thought, recalled the day it had actually taken hold. He had left the house much disgruntled by Kallie's often-repeated phrase still ringing in his ears. "Rob, the children around here deserve an education."

"Our children were better off than most, I suppose," he mused. "Probably why I didn't really try harder to help get something done." His ma had started teaching John when he was only four, and as Robert and Nathaniel became old enough, she and Kallie had managed somehow, despite all the work to be done, to maintain a period of study each weekday during the winter months.

Robinson had approached Jim again that day about the school while they were eating their lunch. As always, Jim was receptive, but hesitant, about making any definite commitment. "I know the kids need a school, Rob," he agreed. "Other than yours and mine, I don't know of any around here who have had any schooling."

"And that bothers me, Jim. You know if it's going to be done, we'll have to ramrod it."

"Right again, Rob! And that's a lot of responsibility, as well as expense, and time, and a whole lot of work!"

"Well, with our combined broods, who has a better incentive, or responsibility?" he chided.

"Yeah, you're right, there," Jim agreed. "For that matter, we could have a private academy," he concluded good-naturedly.

Jim sat staring off into space for a long moment, his expression unusually quiet and thoughtful. Robinson didn't comment further, just waited. Robinson had come to respect those rare moments of seriousness of Jim's. When Jim quit clowning, he was ready to talk business.

Jim broke the silence with a question. "But even if we get the schoolhouse built, Rob, how could we pay a teacher? We sure don't want any help from the Federal government! I, for one, have had a belly full of Federal control."

"You already know where I stand on that, Jim," Robinson replied. "But we have to start somewhere. I say, let's get the schoolhouse and then go from there. Besides," he grinned sheepishly, "Kallie's not going to give me a moment's peace until something is done."

"Maybe if we donated the lumber, the men of the community would help with the construction." Jim offered. "I think it needs to be a community effort."

"I agree," Rob assured him. "And I don't think we have anything to worry about there. The community spirit has always been good."

Later on in the afternoon when they stopped for a work break, Robinson brought the subject up again. "What do you think about calling a meeting at the church next Sunday after everyone's finished eating?"

Jim nodded, expression thoughtful. "Don't know of a better time. Folks more agreeable after attending church and eating a hardy meal," he added, the familiar mischievous grin spreading across his face.

Since Robinson had been the one to approach the Reverend before the services started Sunday morning about announcing the meeting that afternoon, it seemed to be taken for granted that Robinson would be the spokesman for the group.

The response was most enthusiastic, which wasn't entirely a surprise to either Jim or Robinson. Kallie and Salena had been candidates for the school for years.

Several men offered timber, which could be used to replace the dried lumber used from the mill. Elderly Mr. Jenkins, wearing faded overalls and tobacco juice staining the corners of his mouth, announced with great gusto that he'd like to donate two acres of land because "it's a likely place for the youngsters and it has a spring that never goes dry, even in the hot weeks of August."

Then someone introduced the problem that was uppermost in everyone's mind. What about a teacher?

Most of those attending, with exception of a few who worked at the mill, were dirt farmers, renting the land they worked from a landlord who expected to be paid, in lieu of rent, one-fourth to one-third of their crops in the fall. A little chicken and egg money was about all the cash they saw during the year, and that usually went for snuff for the womenfolk, or an occasional slab of cheese.

A long silence prevailed. Robinson shrugged his shoulders. "That's the big question, folks, to which at the moment there is no answer. But, we just feel like the problem will be resolved once we build a schoolhouse."

Reuben Wyatt, seated on the back row, had not offered any suggestions, or commented on any matter so far. Slowly he stood up and walked to the front of the church. "Robinson," he said quietly, his words distinct, his eyes shadowed behind his heavy bushy eyebrows as he studied the faces before him. "I've had some experience in teaching. I'm not a learned scholar, but I am qualified to meet our teaching needs here. If it would be acceptable with the community, and arrangements can be worked out with you and Jim at the mill, I'd like to volunteer my services as your schoolmaster until arrangement can be made for a permanent one."

For a few moments complete silence prevailed over the room. Then, everyone seemed to start speaking at once. Someone was heard to say, "Why, I didn't know Mr. Reuben was a book man."

Robinson's pleasure and surprise were quite evident, also. Not that he was surprised, really, at Reuben's ability to teach. He had no way of knowing just what Reuben's qualifications were, but he knew he was a man of integrity, and if he said he could teach, then as far as Robinson was concerned, he was qualified.

When Robinson presented the question to the ones present, Reuben excused himself and said that he'd wait outside while they decided.

The vote was unanimous to accept Reuben's generous offer.

"How utterly amazing," Kallie remarked happily to Robinson later on their way home from church. "To think we were worried about a teacher, if we ever got the schoolhouse? And now we have a teacher before we get the building!"

Robinson had become so engrossed with his reminiscing that he didn't realize they were so near home until the team turned into their drive leading to the house. "Wake up, kids! We're home," he called over his shoulder.

In a letter to her parents several weeks later, Kallie happily described the unfolding events:

My dearest Poppa and Mama,

I have been intending to write to you for some time to bring you up to date on the progress of our school situation. I have been so long in writing, I'm sure you must think I've reneged on my promise to keep you informed.

The news is good. It is utterly amazing what Reuben has accomplished with the children. He has worked with each child individually these first months, determining their capabilities. He has separated them into groups according to the amount of schooling they have already (which is very little to nothing for some).

We are very pleased with the progress our brood is making.

Reuben doesn't seem to have any discipline problems, either. All he has to do is turn those bushy eyebrows in the larger boys' direction and they settle down. He is not a harsh disciplinarian; nevertheless, he does maintain control. He has the backing of the parents, too, and this is vital for a teacher.

His teaching methods remind me of yours, Poppa. Not only does he teach the children the basic fundamentals of reading, writing, and arithmetic, but he has classes in American history and geography for the advanced group. Also, a portion of the Bible is read everyday. The school day begins with the group pledging their allegiance to the Flag, and then the Scripture is read.

Our institution of "higher learning" is having a definite effect upon our community. The older children rebelled somewhat at first, being restricted for most of the day in the classroom, but they have adjusted surprisingly well.

My only contribution of any worth has been to make a large American flag for the school. There was some controversy at first over the flag. Many wounds from the war have not entirely healed. But Reuben has been very tactful and patient. From what I have been able to determine, it seems he has three major goals for the students: to make them aware of the goodness of God; to instill in them a love and appreciation for this great land of ours; and to create an interest and desire to learn. It seems to be paying off, at least where John Matt and Robert are concerned. They don't seem to fight learning quite as hard as they did at home. The

327

team spirit of competition and a touch of personal pride seem to have created a challenge with those two.

The school has been a good thing for our community as a whole. It has brought us closer together - striving for a common goal. And the gratitude and pride of the parents has been touching. Those who have no money to help financially have tried to compensate in other ways. They helped harvest Reuben's crop, and have cut firewood both for the school and for Reuben's personal use. But the most surprising thing of all has been the interest and pride in the school. It has taught me a lesson I'll never forget! That just because people don't talk about something, it doesn't necessarily mean they don't care. Hopelessness can have a devastating effect on a people.

And that reminds me of a problem that I'm afraid may cause serious trouble in our school. A few coloreds have asked if their children may attend classes. There are those who are violently opposed. Personally, it's a big problem with me. I keep asking myself, "If they have a genuine desire to learn, then how can we turn them away?"

Well, I hope I haven't worn you completely down with this epistle, but I knew you were eagerly awaiting news of the school's progress. Please remember us in your prayers.

I send love from all of us,
Your loving daughter,
Kallie

CHAPTER 28

Melinda gazed down at the child asleep on the carriage seat beside her, his head in her lap. Carefully she pushed the damp hair back that was sticking to the side of his face. "He works so hard when he sleeps," she said softly to Garrett while her love-filled eyes caressed her child's face.

She was going home! Home to her ma, to Robinson and Kallie and their family, and none of them had seen the son born to Garrett and her. Her delivery had been a difficult one, and she had not been able to get her strength back for weeks afterward. Her doctor had stressed that traveling was out of the question for a while.

Melinda had wanted her ma to come and be with her when her child was born, but that too, had not been possible. With Robinson away so often on business, Elvina had felt it not wise to leave Kallie alone, especially since Kallie was pregnant with her fourth child. Later, when Melinda received her ma's letter telling them of the baby's birth, a little girl, and they had named her Janie Elvina, Melinda's reaction had been a happy, "Oh, I like that! Named after the two grandmas!"

Garrett and Melinda had named their firstborn Stuart David Anderson. "Don't you think it has an aristocratic ring to it?" she teased.

"If you say so, my darling," Garrett had laughingly agreed, while gazing in awe at the tiny hand that was gripping his forefinger.

Melinda glanced up to meet Garrett's gaze from across the carriage. His look was so tender and loving it caused her to blush. She felt a warm glow under his steady gaze - a gaze that was telling her things that only the two of them could understand.

The last few miles of the trip were the hardest for Melinda. It seemed as if she could step out on the ground and run much faster than the carriage was traveling!

When the carriage finally pulled onto the road that ran across the farm, Melinda was all but sitting on the edge of her seat. "Look, Garrett! Robinson has built a tenant house! I hope he has added more rooms on the house!" she added eagerly, straining to see. "He hasn't!" she said dismally, falling back against the seat's back. "I don't see how they all find a place to sleep," she moaned as the carriage came to a halt under the big old oak tree.

Garrett opened the door and stepped down quickly, turning to take their son that Melinda held out to him, and then assisting Melinda from the vehicle.

There were excited shouts of joy from the direction of the house. Kallie came rushing across the yard with Elvina not far behind. After many affectionate hugs and some tears, there was much ado about the ways that the children had changed. Comments such as "What a beautiful child Stuart David was!" and "How much precious little Janie Elvina looked just like her namesake" were plentiful. Eventually they crowded into the old familiar kitchen to visit. For the three older boys this meant staying inside just long enough to partake of the tantalizing refreshments that had been in the making for days.

It was some time later, when the excitement had cooled down somewhat, that Melinda noticed for the first time the peculiar color of her ma's skin. Was it the poor light in the room, or the fire's reflection on Elvina's face that caused that awful yellow hue? Her ma seemed all right, or was she? Her movements seemed much slower. "But she is older," Melinda tried to reassure herself silently.

"How are Liza and Keith?" Elvina asked while pouring coffee into the cups.

"Oh, Liza is fine," Melinda responded, momentarily distracted from the concern for her ma. "Liza reminds me of a butterfly, somewhat, though. She just floats from one 'most glorious time' to another. She has no easy job trying to keep up with Keith! He's the liaison officer for Papa Anderson's company, you know. It would be an exhausting life for me but Liza seems to love it. Just the shopping she does to 'keep up with the latest fashions' would be an impossible task for me."

Elvina nodded. "They came by here for a few hours in the early spring on their way to the mid-west - Chicago, I think. It was wonderful seeing her. She's changed," Elvina added as an afterthought.

"Yes. Liza's a woman, now," Melinda agreed.

Elvina glanced at Melinda, trying to interpret her meaning. Did she denote a touch of sadness? But the bright smile that Melinda flashed when their eyes met allayed Elvina's fears.

"Rob?" Melinda asked, switching her attention across the room to her brother. "Please don't take offense, but I'd like to ask you something?"

"Fire away!" Rob smiled.

"I noticed the tenant house you've built. I'm sorry, I don't mean to sound critical, but why did you build that first? What I mean is..."

"Why didn't I add more rooms to this place first?" he interrupted. "Good question, Melinda. Well, the facts of the matter are that I've been so involved with the business that I've been able to spend very little time at home. There was no way I could keep up the farm. It was being overtaken with pine saplings and blackberry vines. This worried Ma. It bothered me tremendously, too. By building the tenant house I can rent out the place and furnish my renter with a place to live at the same time. Actually, it's worked out very satisfactorily." Robinson rubbed his hand slowly across his chin. "I...I just couldn't sit by and let Pa's farm disappear."

"That makes real good sense to me," Melinda agreed. "I knew there was a good reason. That's why I asked."

"We have plans in the making to add onto the house," Rob continued. "If things keep going well at the mill, we should be able to build some time next year."

Voices were heard outside. Adult voices mingling with those of the children. Elvina peered through the window. "It's James and Rosemary," she said happily while hurrying toward the door.

"We saw your carriage pass and I just knew it had to be you," Rosemary explained while kissing Melinda soundly on the cheek. "No one in these parts has a rig that fancy. And we wanted to see that big boy we've heard so much about."

"It's so wonderful to see you again," Melinda said with tears in her eyes as she hugged them both.

The Wheelers didn't stay long despite everyone's urging for them not to go. When Rosemary hugged Melinda to say goodbye, she whispered softly, "Melinda, I'm worried about your Ma."

Melinda moved her head back enough so that she could look into Rosemary's eyes. What she saw there frightened her. "Me, too," she nodded, a concerned frown creasing her forehead. The brief moment of secret communication was broken by James calling to Rosemary, "Come along, Rosemary. We don't want to wear our welcome out." The family walked outside to see them off.

As their buggy disappeared down the road, Kallie said to Melinda, "I'm going down to the springhouse to get some milk for the kids. Care to come along?"

Melinda nodded, grateful for a chance to talk with Kallie alone. She turned to hand Garrett their baby. "I'll be back in a few minutes," she explained.

When they were a safe distance from the others, Melinda touched Kallie on the arm. "Kallie, I'm worried about Ma! She's so... yellow! Has she been sick?"

"No...not really. Not sick in bed, that is. She has complained a couple of times of being tired. She explains it away by saying she's just a little bilious. She's been treating herself with some kind of tea she makes from bark, or something. Miss Rosemary mentioned to me the last time that we were at church that Ma's color was bad. Guess we hadn't noticed because we're with her all the time."

"I wish Doc Evans could check her."

"Now, that would really take some convincing. You know how your ma hates to go to the doctor."

Kallie opened the springhouse door and went inside. Melinda followed, the coolness and the familiarity of the place bringing back a flood of memories.

As they came back outside, Melinda suggested. "Kallie, Garrett plans to go back to Blyton tonight. He has an early business appointment in the morning. He could stop in town and ask Doc Evans if he would just 'drop by' to check on Ma."

Kallie didn't say anything for a long moment. Slowly she nodded. "That just might work."

Doc Evans did drop by the next day, but Elvina hadn't been deceived for one minute. After greeting him warmly and pouring him a cup of coffee, she asked straight out, "The children put you up to this, didn't they, Doc?"

"Well, I guess they did," he admitted. "But they are concerned and they have good reason to be. Not that I think it's anything serious," he hurried on to explain. "But it is something we need to keep a check on. I'm going to leave you some medicine to take. You should see some improvement in a few days."

Garret stopped by Doc Evans office on his way back to pick up Melinda. "Just thought you might have something you would want Melinda to know that you couldn't talk about in front of Mrs. Stuart," he offered as explanation.

"You've a very thoughtful young man," Doc Evans said, shaking Garrett's hand, "and right, to a certain degree. Mrs. Stuart is a sick woman. Evidently there's something wrong with her liver. Now, it could be serious, but I hope it will clear up with time. She needs to rest as much as possible. Give her body a chance to cope with what's attacking it."

"From what I've come to know of that woman," Garrett smiled, shaking his head, "rest is a dirty word."

"Work is all she's ever known," Doc Evans agreed. "It's been her means of survival. It isn't easy to change lifelong habits, especially with all those little children around. Don't mean to sound uncomplimentary," he hastened to add. "Those kids have been her life."

"I agree," Garrett said, getting to his feet. "Now, I must be on my way. Melinda will be anxious." Doc Evans followed him to the door. Garrett reached into his pocket, and turning around to face Doc Evans once again, stuck something in the Doc's pocket. "Just a small token of appreciation, Doc," he explained, putting on his hat. With a wave of his hand, he was gone.

Doc Evans closed the door and walked back toward his old battered desk. Absentmindedly he reached into his pocket and pulled out what Garrett had placed there. It was money, a bill of very large denomination. Doc whistled softly. "My, my," he murmured, shaking his head. "Little Melinda must have married herself a very wealthy young man."

CHAPTER 29

Doc Evans' remedy didn't correct Elvina's problem. One morning a few days later she had difficulty in getting out of bed and when she attempted to talk, her words were jumbled and disoriented. An alarmed Robinson rode into town for Doc Evans. After the doctor had examined her carefully, he called Robinson and Kallie into the other room to explain. "I'm afraid your ma is a very sick woman. My former diagnosis was correct. The trouble is in her liver. Unfortunately, medical science doesn't offer much information about treating diseases of the liver. We do know that oftentimes the liver can regenerate itself once the infection has cleared up. But in your ma's case, it has grown progressively worse. I... I must tell you, I don't like this confused state she seems to be in at times. That's an indication that the poison in her system has increased."

Robinson stared at Doc. "What are you trying to tell us, Doc?"

"That your ma is a very sick woman," he said simply.

"How sick?" Robinson insisted, fear griping his insides.

Doc Evans looked at Robinson for a long minute, then his gaze shifted to meet Kallie's. How often he had looked on the stricken faces of family members and had to tell them that someone they loved dearly was going to die. He had never found an easy way. It seemed the direct approach was often the less painful in the long run.

"I'm sorry," he said, his expression revealing his own sadness. "Unless there is some drastic change, a miracle you might say, I don't think she has much of a chance."

Robinson stood staring at the doctor too stunned to speak. It couldn't be true! Not his ma, too! Not again! Not Ma! He heard Kallie catch her breath in a sob, and he felt as if he were tearing up inside and choking all at the same time. Without a word he turned and hurried toward the back door. Outside, he crossed the open fields and headed for the woods.

John Mat and Robert, playing in the yard, called after him. "Pa, can we come with you?"

"No, boys," Kallie commanded sharply from the doorway. "Stay here!" Ordinarily, the boys would have haggled with her since their pa always took them along with him. But something about the expression on Kallie's face and the tone of her voice caused them to keep their silence.

Doc Evans had followed her across the room to the door. Gently he touched her on the arm. "Kallie," he said kindly, "there are certain precautions you must take. Sometimes diseases of the liver are contagious. Be sure to sterilize everything that is used for Elvina."

Kallie nodded. Then in a voice barely above a whisper, she asked, "Doc Evans, Melinda and Liza must be told. Would you... could you send them a message when you get back to town?"

"Most assuredly," he replied, patting her awkwardly on the arm, "you're going to need a lot of help from here on." Then noting the stricken look in her eyes, added gently, "Let's just take it one day at a time, my dear."

Kallie nodded again, unable to speak.

"Now, remember, Kallie," Doc Evans cautioned again kindly. "Anyone touching Elvina must be very careful to wash their hands thoroughly with hot water and lots of lye soap. Scald, or boil, the dishes used for her. Boil all the bedclothes and linens, etc. There can be more than one kind of liver ailment, but at this point and time, I can't tell, and may not ever be able to tell exactly, whether or not she is contagious. In the meantime, treat this disease as if it is contagious. That's the only way you can protect yourself and your family." He turned to pick up his hat and coat. Kallie hurried to write down how Melinda and Liza could be reached. Doc Evans' final instruction was for Kallie to give her the medicine he had brought. "It may, or may not, do any good," he said gruffly.

Kallie stood in the doorway watching the retreating back of Doc Evans. This can't be true, she thought, her throat aching. The children came running up, stopping at the bottom of the steps. "We're hungry, Mama. Can we have something to eat?" they asked in unison, running up the steps. Seemingly oblivious to what was going on around her, Kallie crossed the room to Elvina's door, pushing it open a crack. Elvina was sleeping peacefully. "It can't be true," Kallie thought over and over, her hand pressed tightly against her lips, eyes dark with misery.

The children, sensing something was wrong, stood in the kitchen watching her silently for a few moments, eyes wide and puzzled. Nat, unable to cope with the hunger pains any longer, ran over to the safe and opened the doors. "I'm going to get me a biscuit."

Janie Elvina joined in, chirping eagerly, "Can I have a biscuit, too, Mama?"

"Yes, yes, yes," Kallie answered quietly, walking over to the open door to stand gazing out across the fields, tears streaming unchecked down her cheeks.

And the children, biscuits in hand, stood munching and staring at their mama's back, expressions troubled. They had never seen their mama cry over biscuits before.

Robinson hadn't stopped until he reached the creek. He stood for a long moment gazing at the water flowing swiftly by. He remembered the time he had tied out the mule and the cow at this place - hoping the Yankees wouldn't find them. It had been rough; making it after the Yankees had left them destitute. "But it wasn't like this," he thought grimly. "At least we had hope of living, or remaining together." He burrowed his face in his hands and fell to his knees. "Oh, God! Now when it looks like I might do something for her to make her life easier, it's too late." He thought about the house plans he had drawn up at the mill; plans for a two-story house with white columns on the front. He'd been saving it as a surprise. He wasn't going to tell her until he had everything ready to start building. Now, she might never know; never see it.

He tried to pray. He hadn't really prayed since John Matt was born. But there wasn't anywhere else to go. God was his last hope. "Will you do it for her, God?" he begged pitifully. He talked to God about the woman in the Bible who just touched the hem of Jesus' garment and was healed. When he finally stood up and retraced his steps to the house, he felt some better.

Several days passed before Melinda was able to come. In the meantime, Robinson made arrangements at the mill so that he could stay home and help - mostly with the children.

It didn't take long for the news of Elvina's illness to get around in the community. Rosemary and Salena came over to take the children home with them. When Kallie tried to express her concern for her friends' safety, they pushed all of her objections aside. "We've been with you so much already, what difference could it make, now? We'll be all right." Many times during the day neighbors would drop by to inquire about Elvina's condition, oftentimes leaving some token of their concern at the door; usually a prepared dish of food.

When Melinda did arrive, Garrett was the only one with her. Liza, they explained, was away on a trip with Keith. She had been contacted, however, and was on her way. Garrett, upon Melinda's insistence, returned home to help care for little John Robert.

There were times when their hopes would rise - when Elvina seemed to mend and improve somewhat. Once she rallied and they could tell that she was trying to say something. Hovering near, they heard her whisper: "Though He slay me, yet will I trust Him." Robinson recognized it as Scripture, but didn't know which part.

By the time Liza was able to get home, Elvina had elapsed into a deep coma. Liza kept trying to get her ma to say something, pleading over and over, "Ma, its Liza. Ma, can you hear me? Do you know who this is?" But if Elvina could hear her, she was unable to respond.

"If only I could have gotten here sooner," Liza kept repeating brokenly. "I wanted to tell her I love her."

"She knew that you loved her, Liza," Kallie assured her gently. "She never once doubted that."

Melinda walked over and put her arms around Liza, holding her tight. "Don't torture yourself, Liza," she comforted, her own tears flowing. "Ma wouldn't like that."

Elvina, no longer aware of the functions of her body, had to be taken care of as if she were a helpless baby. Doc Evans had instructed them to turn her at least every hour to prevent fluid buildup in her lungs. The only way the girls were able to manage this was by turning Elvina on a sheet. Her skin against the background of the white bedclothes had the appearance of dark golden leather.

It was almost five o'clock in the morning when Elvina slipped quietly into eternity. All of her family was with her. She had been restless all night, more so than usual, moving her head constantly from side to side. Robinson and Melinda were on each side of the bed, attempting to make her comfortable. Liza was sitting on a chair at the foot of the bed.

There was no warning struggle when the end came. Elvina took a deep, deep breath, then lay completely still. Melinda looked across at Robinson, eyes wide with alarm. "Rob?" she whispered frantically.

"What is it?" Liza asked fearfully, rising to her feet.

Kallie, in the kitchen making coffee, heard the sounds and hurried to the bedroom. Just inside the door she stopped short, stilled by the scene before her. Everyone's eyes were riveted on Elvina's face. Slowly Elvina exhaled, and those looking on relaxed somewhat. Then, she took another deep breath, but this time, she didn't exhale and everything about her became frighteningly still.

Robinson picked up one of Elvina's hands and felt for a pulse.

"She's gone," he said, voice breaking.

CHAPTER 30

Elvina's illness, which had eventually resulted in her tragic death, was an experience that left its indelible mark on the entire family.

For Melinda, coming home again was never the same. Her visits became farther and farther apart. First of all, it was so painful. She missed her mother so terribly at these times. Kallie and Robinson were gracious and loving, but it just wasn't home anymore.

The break wasn't nearly as painful for Liza. She had crowded her life so full before Elvina's death that she didn't get home much, once a year at the most. She was soon back among her circle of friends again, suffering only short periods of depression regarding her mother and home, and these only came about on those rare occasions when she happened to be alone.

Robinson returned to the mill and from all observations by those who were close to him, adjusted well, working harder than ever to make the business even more profitable.

Kallie was the one that was faced with that dreadful, stark reality, of being alone; alone with the devastating sorrow that had been brought about by the loss of someone dear and precious; someone who had been such a vital part of her life.

Kallie's life had been intertwined with Elvina's from the day she had come to the Stuart household as a bride. Over the years, Elvina had become as dear to her as her own Mother. Not only had she been someone who was always there when Kallie needed help, she was that rare person in life that made Kallie's world complete. Other than Robinson, she was Kallie's dearest and best friend.

Kallie's parents had come for the funeral. But since there was such a crowd and the house was so small, they had returned home that same day.

Melinda and Liza had stayed a few days after the funeral to help dispose of Elvina's belongings and to take what they wanted of her personal things. Graciously they had included Kallie, giving her first preference.

Kallie considered the rocking chair that Elvina had brought South with her as a bride and rocked all of her children and Kallie's children in it. Robinson had asked for her Bible, which had seemed a little odd to Kallie.

Finally, she told them her decision, which wasn't in the least a surprise to Robinson. "I would like to have Ma Stuart's books."

Melinda hugged Kallie and told her, "I should have guessed!"

Liza could not have cared less. She never did like to read the way her ma and Kallie did, anyway.

Melinda took a few personal mementos and several pieces of her ma's handwork. With great reluctance she took the rocker, promising to send Kallie another one right away to take its place. "It's the one thing I associate most with Ma," she explained brokenly.

In the final outcome, Liza didn't take anything. "It would only be a reminder that would hurt. You keep her things here, Kallie, and if I ever decide I want something, I'll let you know."

And that's how it was. "The trunk would be nice," Kallie urged gently, "to keep your personal things in."

But Liza shook her head vehemently and hurried out to the carriage that she would be riding back home in with Garrett and Melinda. Garrett had come for the funeral but Keith did not come with him. "He had some important business in Atlanta," Garrett had relayed to Liza somewhat haltingly. Her response had been an indifferent shrug of her shoulders. She knew what it was all about. Keith was fast becoming known in the political circles. Georgia had adopted its first state constitution and one of Keith's close acquaintances had been elected Senator. It was a good time for aspiring, politically ambitious young men to get their foothold in the power structure, and Keith Anderson had no intentions of being left out, whatever the cost. And what was Liza's attitude? "More power to him!" She liked the feel of power, however trivial it might be at the present time. Prestige had its rewards and she enjoyed everything about it.

Then came that awful morning when Kallie arose the usual time to prepare Robinson's breakfast, kissed him goodbye, and turned back to a room of deathly silence. The children were still asleep, and it was so quiet. She could hear the clock ticking on the mantle. The spinning wheel, silent and dark over by the far wall, was a mocking reminder of the tragedy in their lives.

The milk pail, full of milk, remained where Robinson had placed it when he brought it from the barn. She must take care of that first. It had to be strained before the cream began to form on top. She had just finished straining it into the crock when she

345

heard Janie Elvina call "Mama" from the next room. Kallie hurried into the bedroom, hoping to keep Janie Elvina from waking the others. By the time she had finished dressing her, however, Nat was coming down the ladder from the loft, with Robert not far behind.

"Mama, I'm hungry," Robert complained, rubbing his eyes.

"Me, too!" Nat joined in, hopping upon the bench and walking up and down.

"Get down off the bench, Nat!" Kallie scolded.

She prepared breakfast for four, knowing that John Matt would be up soon, too, and thinking at the time she was frying the meat and scrambling eggs that she needed to have the water in the wash pot heating already.

By the time she had the biscuits on the table, John Matt was awake. He sat down at the table, propping his elbow on the table with his chin cupped in his hand. "I sure do miss Grandma," he said sadly, eyes glistening.

"I know," Kallie nodded.

"Will you be helping us with our lessons now that Grandma's never coming back?" Robert joined in.

Kallie fought back the tears. "Probably," she replied, not trusting herself to say more.

"I miss her," Nat declared woefully.

"We all miss her, dear," Kallie consoled.

"Ma, why did she have to die?" Robert asked beseechingly.

"I suppose God needed her in Heaven. Maybe he had something real special for her to do."

"Could we go to Heaven and see her some time?" Nat wanted to know while stuffing his mouth with a biscuit.

"Not right away," Kallie evaded, reaching for the biscuits and passing them to John Matt. "Here, Son, eat your breakfast before it gets cold."

"I'm not hungry," John Matt said, sliding off the bench and heading for the back door.

"Where are you going, John Matt? You had better eat your breakfast, now! I won't have time to fix it later."

She started to protest further when he just kept going, but stopped short. "I'm not hungry either," she thought dismally.

The hours seemed to fly by with very little accomplished. When Robinson came home late that afternoon, she was just hanging up the last of the clothes that she had washed, and there was no supper prepared. When they went inside the house, Robinson looked around in amazement and wanted to know what happened.

When Kallie retorted, "What do you mean, what happened?" he knew he'd touched a raw spot. And when Kallie discovered the crock of milk that she had failed to take to the springhouse, all soured and unfit to drink, she sat down at the kitchen table and sobbed. "I...I didn't know I depended so much on Ma Stuart," she confessed. "Rob, I just can't seem to get it all together!"

"You've been through a lot," he soothed. "There's been a big change in your life; in all of our lives. You'll be all right when you've rested up and get organized."

"Maybe, so," she answered dully, not really hopeful.

As the weeks passed, Robinson realized that the situation was not going to get better; that Kallie couldn't cope without some help. And that's when he went to talk with his tenant, Abe Johnson, about his wife, Sarah, coming to work for them. To his profound relief he learned that Sarah had been a slave before the war, born and raised on a plantation, and had served as one of the domestics in the "Big House."

They came to an agreement as to wages, and Robinson told her he needed her to come to work the next day, if she could. She was at their door the next morning before he left for the mill, and when she walked in and saw the pile of dirty clothes to be washed, turned without a word and went outside to start filling the wash pot with water, he knew he had a winner.

"Oh, Rob, thank you, thank you," Kallie exclaimed hugging him hard, not caring that the kids were watching.

And from that day on, Sarah became a vital part of the Stuart household, and was to remain so, as long as she lived.

From outward appearances, family and friends, alike, were relieved that Robinson had seemed to accept his mother's death so well. Reuben, remembering how bitter Robinson had been over his pa's death, was particularly relieved. In fact, Robinson seemed to have adjusted far better than Kallie, which was understandable. Robinson could go to work each day and escape the reminders.

But they wouldn't have thought it that simple if those concerned could have seen past the calm front he portrayed. A front he used as a shield to keep anyone from finding out just how deep the hurt and frustration had been; and was.

Robinson's reaction was controlled behavior that he had mastered. He knew that the world expected a man to appear strong and invulnerable; undaunted by what life might dish out; standing tall and proud. A man of worth was expected to hide his emotion, whether it was anger, hate, or grief, and even love, by a facade of dignity.

Alone with his thoughts, it was entirely different. He missed his ma with a hurt that never went away for long. And the bitterness was there, caused by the interminable question of why God couldn't have let her live; it would have been such a little miracle for Him.

If only he could erase the memories of those awful last days of her illness from his mind! She had loved her God so. Why would He let her be reduced to such a humiliating state, stripped of all pride and dignity and reduced to something less than human?

He had tried to talk to Kallie about it on one occasion, but she had not understood. Like himself, she did not pretend to try to understand the mysteries surrounding the workings of God, but it frightened her, as it always had, for him to voice such bitterness.

And he had his moments of anxiety, too, about criticizing God. The Bible was specific on this; that it was wrong and displeasing to God. But his hurt was so great that it overshadowed his fear.

Subconsciously he would delve into the past, reinforcing his bitterness. In times past, had God not let him down? He recalled that awful time when John Matt was born and how Kallie had almost died. God had seemed to turn a deaf ear despite their prayers and let her suffer such terrible pain for all that long time. To such an extent, that there was only a spark of life left in her. How God, in spite of all his ma's prayers, had let the Yankees pilfer and destroy just about everything they owned. And there was his pa. God had not helped there, either. Maybe a man would be much better off if he didn't expect anything; just stood on his own two feet.

Slowly, as the weeks and months went by, a new Robinson evolved. Kallie, subconsciously noted the change, but it was so slight, so indefinable, that she didn't give it much thought. When she did, she accounted it to what had happened to their family and to the growing demands of the business. What Kallie didn't realize was that Robinson had found an escape of sorts for the fears that haunted him, and that escape was work.

When he was busy, involved, he didn't have time to dwell on his personal problems. That same dread of the unknown that he had experienced as he walked home that night after the day of syrup making. The darkness had closed in around him, then, making each step precarious and frightening. Something sinister was lurking out there...something unnamed and indefinable.

Sometimes, at the most unpredictable moments, it would catch up with him, and he would have to face the ultimate question. What if there really is no God after all? No hereafter; no nothing? What if this is all there was to life...this life here on earth with its pain, its fears, its sorrows. What, then, would be the use of anything?

350

And immediately following these introspections a deep dark mood of depression would descend upon him, so heavy that it seemed unbearable. Hopelessness that was far worse than all the others. It made him want to beat his fists against the wall. Lash out in some way at the torment. For the most devastating thought of all, which inevitably crept in to bring him to the brink of despair, was "What if there really is a God? What if I should die and go to Hell?"

Thoughts such as these became more frequent; more painful, and work became his tranquilizer. Work, making money, and obtaining possessions became his purpose and goal in life. And he kept it concealed from those who knew and loved him the most by hiding behind the facade of a "church-going man."

CHAPTER 31

Robinson walked briskly toward the barn in the early dawn light. He needed to get to the mill earlier than usual this morning since Jim was still in Savannah negotiating for the expansion of their business.

All-out production of naval stores products had been part of their original plans - particularly by their financial backers. However, it was late in materializing. For one thing, for all practical purposes, they needed to locate the business further down state where the yellow pines were more plentiful and shipping wouldn't be as expensive. Another reason they had been slow in this decision was that it would necessitate either Jim or Robinson moving to that part of the state. But that problem no longer existed. Salena had been yearning to move closer to her parents who still lived in Savannah. Her enthusiasm for re-locating closer to home had made it much easier for Jim to decide to move. His moving, of course, would mean that Robinson would be solely responsible for the original part of the business. That was a sobering thought for Robinson; almost frighteningly so at times.

Abe had Robinson's horse fed and saddled. "What a luxury," he thought, smiling warmly at the black man who had become a friend as well as a hired hand. "Thank you, Abe."

"Yaz, suh, Mister Rob," Abe agreed amiably while handing Robinson the reins. "I aims to make good use of dis fine weather to get some of de corn pulled today."

"Looks like a good day for it," Robinson agreed, swinging into the saddle.

As he rode out onto the main road the sun had turned the eastern sky into a rich blushing pink. A few hundred yards from the house he turned to look back. As always, this view of his home compelled him to rein in his horse. For a long moment he sat gazing at the white two-story mansion.

"Is it real?" he marveled, taking a deep breath and exhaling. "How magnificent it appears in the early dawn light!"

He slapped his horse lightly on the flank. It took off at a gallop. "It was the right thing to do," he assured himself as he rode along. There was a large building loan on the place for he had bought his sisters' shares in the farm, too. But the mill was showing a good profit. In fact, had exceeded all their expectations

"And I've done a lot of growing, too," he admitted silently. His trips to Savannah and his part in the business meetings had opened up a whole New World for him; awesomely new at times. Too, he had acquired a broader concept and much deeper appreciation for his country. Poverty and devastation had been so much a part of his early years and of his known world. Even, yet, the scars were evident in any direction he happened to be traveling. And there was much traveling to be done in finding and buying timber.

But he had come to realize also, with pride, that even though his country was still struggling to overcome the ravages of war, both psychologically and physically, it was considered one of the top nations of the world in manufacturing. Since the end of the Civil War its railroads had expanded spectacularly. The increase in American industrial exports had amazed even the prognosticating experts and it had been his and Jim's good fortune to land in the main stream of it all.

Just before rounding the bend in the road that would block his view of the house, he reined in his horse and turned again to look back. The new part consisted of eight bedrooms, all large and spacious, two on each side of a wide hallway on the ground floor and a winding staircase to the upstairs hallway that separated four more rooms. The old part had been left untouched, and would still be used as the kitchen area, and possibly living quarters for household help. And on the front, extending from the veranda to the roof of the second floor, were six white columns. Not the huge round massive ones that had been a distinctive mark of pride for the pre-war plantation owners, but not anything to be ashamed of, either. "Your dream is here, Ma," he said aloud, as he turned and headed once again for the mill.

"It was time to build a larger home," he assured himself. Esther Melissa had arrived the next year after Elvina died. And less than two years later, Kallie had given birth to twins.

The twins were not identical. The girl, her head covered with a mass of black hair, was tiny and delicate. The boy, outweighing his sister by almost a half pound, was going to have light hair, if one could tell by the fuzz that was barely perceptible.

When the babies were brought to Kallie for the first time, she looked at the baby girl and exclaimed softly,

"Why, she looks just like Melinda. Rob, she has to be named for her!" She pulled the light blanket back from the baby boy and inspected him, too, from head to toe. "Rob, I'd like to name him Robinson." When Rob started to protest, she interrupted quickly, "Darling, you don't have a single namesake."

"And neither do you."

"But that doesn't matter. Please, I want one baby named for you." Her smile faded as she reminded him softly, "You know, Doc Evans has said there shouldn't be any more babies."

Reluctantly he agreed. "The names won't sound alike. I thought twins' names were supposed to match?"

"Who said so? We can dare to be different! Besides, they don't look anything alike. How about Robinson Anderson Stuart?"

"Whew! What a mouthful," he moaned, grinning, still skeptical. "But, you've earned the right to name them whatever you please," he decided, leaning over to kiss her gently on the forehead.

However, he wasn't at all surprised when she informed him later that she had changed her mind. "Instead of Mary Melinda, how about Rosalin Melinda? Robinson and Rosalin?"

"Anything that suits, you," he agreed, hoping it was settled.

As his horse trotted around the bend and the mill came into view, he could see smoke belching from the boiler's smokestack. This meant the mill hands were on the job. As he rode into the mill yard and over to the corral, he noticed that Jim's horse was inside. "He's back early," he thought excitedly as he quickly dismounted and guided his horse through the gate, hurrying to remove the saddle. He was anxious to hear what Jim had to report.

CHAPTER 32

The sun dropped below the treetops, its dying rays creating long shadows across the sawmill yard and the various storage buildings. It was late summer and the weather had begun to be much cooler, especially at the end of the day and early evenings. Bright patches of color dotted the woods from leaves that were beginning to turn, giving a hint that autumn wasn't too far away. A brisk breeze had been blowing intermittently all day and had loosened many of the drying leaves, causing them to sail through the air, or float lazily down to the ground, depending upon the velocity of the wind.

All of the crew had gone for the day except Jim and Robinson who were still pouring over plans for the naval stores enterprise. The mill hands always left early enough to arrive home before dark, mainly because of their wives being alone. Even though there had been very few threats of violence in their community from former slaves, tales of white women being molested were common, causing the women to be wary of being alone, especially at nighttime.

"That's just about the entire picture, Rob," Jim concluded, gathering up the papers spread on the desk and placing them back into his carrying case.

"When do you plan to start building?"

"Not for a while. There's a lot of preparatory work to be done on the site before that happens. Too, I must find a suitable place for the family to live. That's not going to be an easy job, either. Good housing is scarce in that part of the state. Rob, I'd like for you to go down with me for a few days when we get set up. I think it's important that you be there from the ground up."

Robinson nodded, frowning slightly. "Deciding on someone to be in charge of the mill while we are away will be our biggest problem. However, Reuben will be working full time until school begins."

"Reuben could handle things for a few days; no doubt about that," Jim agreed thoughtfully. "By the way, how's the new foreman working out?"

"Mike's doing a good job. I just don't think he's ready to take on the whole load, yet."

Jim nodded. "Well, let's go home," he suggested, turning toward the door. "I haven't seen my family much in over a week."

Once outside Robinson locked the office door and then walked over to join Jim at the corral, subconsciously admiring the huge yellow moon peeping over the treetops in the east. Jim already had the saddle on his horse and was tightening the girth. Robinson lifted his saddle down from its storage spot in the shed where they housed the horses when the weather was nasty. As he turned to place the saddle on his horse's back, he noticed a faint red glow just over the treetops to the north. At that moment the glow became much darker and tips of flames could be seen above the treetops.

"Jim, look," Robinson called, nodding in the direction of the fire, then realizing Jim couldn't see his nod in the twilight, said sharply, "Jim, to the north, there! What do you suppose that is burning?"

"Looks like it might be a house on fire, or a barn! That's the direction of the Lanson place! Come on!" he yelled, not waiting for Robinson's response.

Quickly Jim led his animal through the gate and then jumped into the saddle. Robinson followed and in a matter of seconds, both of them were urging their mounts at a fast gallop down the narrow drive that led to the main roadway. They turned west at the main road, goading their mounts as much as they dared down the unfamiliar course, thankful for the bright moonlight that enabled them to travel at a faster pace.

"It is the Lanson's place," Jim shouted to Robinson whose horse had overtaken Jim's and was now galloping abreast of his. In a few minutes they turned again onto a small dirt road leading to their right, so narrow that it was necessary for Robinson to check his animal's speed and fall behind again. Their horses rounded a bend in the road and the burning building was now in view.

"Oh, God," Robinson moaned, as he caught a glimpse through the trees of flames leaping through the upstairs window, and the overhanging limbs of nearby trees already charred and smoldering. They reined their horses to a grueling stop a safe distance from the fire and jumping to the ground, hurriedly tied the reins of their mounts to some nearby trees. They started running toward the house but stooped abruptly as the roof caved in, sending a whirling mass of sparks, smoke, and ashes into the dark sky above.

"Wonder where the family is?" Robinson shouted over the roar of the flames.

Jim shook his head. "Did you notice before the roof fell in that the front door was wide open?"

Cautiously they made their way around the house with the heat becoming more intense as the wind blew the flames in their direction. They circled the house, finding no one.

"You don't suppose they were caught inside?" Robinson asked.

"Maybe they are away from home," Jim answered, frowning; eyes dark with concern.

Neighborhood men began to arrive, some horseback, others in buggies with their wives. Their first question was always, "Where are the Lansons?"

They stood around in small groups, gazing at the blazing timbers, the reflection of the fire upon their faces magnifying the horror they suspected. No one had ever known the Lansons to stay away from home overnight.

A large pine that stood between the house and the barn suddenly caught fire, not only threatening the barn but the other outbuildings as well. Jim and Robinson found an axe at the woodpile and cut down the pine, utilizing their skill as timber men to direct it safely away from the smokehouse and other nearby structures.

Shouts came from the barn as several men worked feverishly to remove any livestock that had been penned up for the night - while the womenfolk worked frantically to contain the burning grass by beating out the flames with tree branches. The windlass on the well squeaked endlessly as men rushed back and forth carrying buckets of water to throw on the smokehouse and other nearby outbuildings.

What seemed an eternity to those fighting the fire was actually less than an hour. The fire spent itself and nestled down between the pillars to finish consuming the last remaining evidence of what was once a home. The chimney, blackened by the smoke, stretched starkly upward, a grim reminder that a house once shrouded its bulging stone sides.

As the flames died down, darkness moved in, making it difficult to see. It would be hours before the ashes and charred pieces of wood would be cool enough to be investigated.

"We might as well just go on home," a man drawled from somewhere in the encroaching dark. "Ain't no way we can find out nothin' 'fore morning."

Robinson and Jim had been the first to arrive; now they were the last to leave. Wearily they untied their horses and climbed into the saddles. They sat for a long moment - their gazes lingering on the smoldering mass.

Jim suddenly straightened in his saddle. "Hey! Did you hear that?"

Robinson's horse, eager to be gone, pulled anxiously against the reins. "Whoa, boy," Robinson urged soothingly, gently patting the restless animal's neck while straining to hear. "Hear what?"

"I thought I heard a low moan from over there," Jim said, pointing toward the woods. "There…there it is again!" Jim almost shouted, dismounting quickly and hurrying toward the wooded area. "Over here, Rob!"

Robinson dropped to the ground. Quickly he secured the reins - then hurried after Jim. The undergrowth on the outskirts of the woods was thick, making it necessary for them to move cautiously in the dark since the moonlight filtering through the trees provided only a spattering of light. Brier vines, curling over a bush, caught Jim across the face and he swore softly. Robinson moved guardedly to the right to avoid getting entangled in the prickly mass. As he lifted his foot to move forward, the toe of his boot caught on something soft - almost tripping him. "Jim...over here!" he called urgently.

Robinson squatted down beside the still form straining to identify who, or what, it was in the shadows. "It...it looks like a young girl," he said anxiously as Jim moved in beside him. Carefully they pushed the thorny vines back with their boots. As the moonlight penetrated the area, Robinson gently pushed the long strands of hair aside that were partially covering her face.

"It's the youngest Lanson girl," he said quietly, gently laying his hand against the side of her throat to feel for a pulse. "It's Zenna Lanson."

"Is she alive?" Jim asked, joining Robinson beside the still body.

"Yes," Robinson answered slowly, "but she has a nasty cut on her head. Must have tripped on the brier vines. Probably hit her head on that rock."

Robinson eased his arm beneath the small body and lifted her in his arms. "Her flesh is clammy," he remarked as they headed back toward the road and the horses.

Back in the roadway, Jim quickly removed his coat and wrapped it around the small frame in Robinson's arms - tying the sleeves together in front to keep the coat from falling away.

"Hold her for a minute, Jim, while I get on my horse," Robinson said. Jim complied - handing the limp body back to Robinson once he was in the saddle.

"I think I'll scout around a little more," Jim said solemnly. "Might be someone else out there."

"All right," Robinson nodded, "but make it quick. This one needs attention."

It wasn't long before Jim returned. "Nothing," he said grimly, swinging onto his horse.

They let their horses take the lead, each of the men lost in their own thoughts. When they came to the fork in the road where Jim turned, Robinson suggested that he take Zenna on to his house. "You've been away from home for quite a while and you need to be with your family."

"I'll come with you - if you think there's a need," Jim offered.

"No... I don't think that's necessary. After I get her to the house, Kallie will know what to do."

"See you in the morning, then," Jim answered, his tone reflecting extreme fatigue.

"See you," Rob answered, voice heavy, suddenly conscious of his own weariness. His head throbbed and his eyes burned from exposure to the heat and smoke.

Even though Zenna didn't weigh a hundred pounds, Robinson's arms were aching by the time his home came into view. He could see a light from his and Kallie's bedroom window. "She's still up," he sighed gratefully.

Kallie had been listening anxiously for Robinson, wondering why he was so late. When she heard a horse approaching in the drive out front, she hurried to open the door, puzzled why he had not taken his horse on to

363

the barn. In the dim moonlight she could tell that he was holding what looked like a child in his arms. Moving quickly out the door she hurried down the steps to meet him. "Robinson, who is that? What in the world happened?"

"It's Zenna Lanson," he explained wearily. "There's been a terrible fire. I'll tell you all about it later. Right now, just help me get her down and inside."

Kallie led the way to a bedroom on the main floor, quickly turning down the bed's counterpane and quilt. Very carefully Robinson laid Zenna's limp body on the bed. Blood had dried in her hair, causing it to mat over what was evidently a bad cut on her head. Quickly Robinson removed Zenna's shoes while Kallie checked her wrist for a pulse.

"It's weak but steady," she said, easing the limp hand back down and covering Zenna with the quilt. "I'll get some more cover," she offered, disappearing through the door and reappearing a few minutes later with another quilt that she doubled across Zenna for extra warmth. Tenderly she laid her fingers against the side of Zenna's neck. "Her pulse is stronger," she said, relieved.

For the first time since Robinson had arrived, she noticed his grimy face and clothing. "Rob...you reek of smoke! What in the world happened? Where was the fire? Not...not the mill?"

Robinson shook his head. "The Lanson's house burned," he answered grimly, his throbbing head causing his words to come slowly.

For a long moment Kallie's eyes searched Robinson's. "Rob?" she asked hesitantly, "What happened to the rest of the family?"

Robinson just shook his head, again. "We...we didn't find anyone else."

"Oh, dear God in Heaven," Kallie groaned, pressing her hand hard against her mouth, eyes filling with tears. "You don't suppose..." her voice trailed off never completing the question as he turned away and headed for the door.

"I have to take my horse to the barn," Robinson stated wearily from the doorway. "That is, if you think she's going to be all right."

"I believe so, for now. You go ahead. But...please hurry. When she comes to...?" Her voice trailed off into nothingness.

Outside again he did not bother to mount up but walked the distance to the barnyard gate leading his horse. Inside the gate he turned loose of the reins. The thirsty animal hurried to the watering trough and in a matter of moments was drinking lustily. Robinson followed, cupping his hands beneath the small stream that was piped in from the spring. He splashed the cold water on his face several times - relishing in its soothing coolness. Then, he, too, drank long refreshing draughts thinking that water had never tasted so good.

Robinson waited patiently for the horse to get its fill and then led it back to the barn's hallway where he removed its bridle and saddle. The horse trotted down the hall to its stall. Robinson brought a half-dozen ears of corn from the crib and pushed them through the opening in the wall to the feeding box. As he fastened the door and turned to leave, he heard the horse bite into an ear, the familiar crunching noise sounding loud and brash in the stillness of the night.

He retraced his steps back to the house. Once inside he removed his smoke stained jacket just inside the back door and dropped it to the floor. Wearily he made his way back to the bedroom where he had left Kallie with the girl. The scene had not changed. Kallie's quick glance in his direction reflected her relief. Slowly he walked over to the fireplace where he leaned his arm against the mantle. Exhausted, he laid his head on his arm.

Kallie stood up and moved across the room to stand near him. "Can you tell me what happened, now, Rob," she whispered anxiously.

Slowly Robinson raised his head to look at her. "I'm not sure," he said hesitantly. "Just as Jim and I were heading home from the mill we noticed a glow above the treetops to the north. We realized it was in the direction of the Lanson's place. By the time we got there, though, the house was a roaring inferno." He paused, his next words coming with great difficulty. "There...there was no sign of the Lansons, except Zenna, of course, but we found her in the woods just before we started home."

There was a low moan from the direction of the bed and Kallie turned quickly to her patient. Slowly Zenna opened her eyes, her face expressionless; eyes blank and staring. For a moment she laid quiet, just gazing up at the ceiling, then a slight frown creased her forehead.

"Zenna?" Kallie called softly.

Zenna turned her head slowly, her puzzled gaze coming to rest on Kallie. "Where...where am I?" she asked, attempting to sit up.

Kallie gently pushed her shoulders back down on the bed. "You are at our house, Zenna. Mr. Rob brought you here. You must lie quiet, dear. You've had a nasty fall."

Kallie, concerned that the blow to Zenna's head might have caused a concussion, tried to calm her, but Zenna's voice rose hysterically. "I saw him! I saw him! I saw him from upstairs! It was Lonnie Williams. He knocked Emily down with a stick of fire wood." Her voice broke completely and it was some moments before she could control her weeping enough to continue, her words a hoarse whisper. "I...I heard Pa's bedroom door open and Pa yelled something, and then there was a loud thud. When Lonnie came back out of the bedroom, he picked up the lamp and threw it against the far wall. Fire...fire was everywhere!"

Robinson had moved slowly across the room to stand at the foot of the bed. "Who did you say it was, Zenna?"

"She said it was Lonnie Williams," Kallie interrupted, eyes wide with horror.

"It was Lonnie! Lonnie Williams!" she cried, her words ending in another siege of sobbing.

"There, there," Kallie urged, attempting to console her. "You must try to be quiet."

Zenna didn't seem to hear. "I...I was so scared," she whispered brokenly. "Once I heard the baby crying downstairs, then, it stopped. Lonnie's clothes must have been on fire for I saw him run out the front door slapping at his legs." A massive shudder shook her small frame. "Fire was everywhere. "I...I made it down the stairs part way, but the fire was so hot. I caught hold of the handrail and swung to the floor. Somehow I got to the door and outside. Lonnie was over by the well pouring water from the well bucket on himself. He didn't see me, so I ran as hard as I could for the bushes at the edge of the woods. It... was so dark in the woods, I couldn't see where I was going. As I ran through the bushes, my foot caught on something. That's ...that's all I remember."

"You must have tripped on a saw brier," Kallie offered as an explanation. "There's a jagged cut across the top of your foot."

But Zenna hadn't heard, for suddenly her head dropped sideways and she became very still. Alarmed, Kallie quickly checked her pulse again. "Rob, she's fainted. You stay with her while I run get some fresh water to bathe her face."

"You stay with her," Robinson said, walking around the bed and picking the pan up off the floor. "I'll get the water."

As Robinson hurried to his task, his thoughts were racing wildly. Was it possible that Lonnie Williams' hate had driven him to this extreme? He recalled the last time he had seen Bob Lanson, Zenna's father. Robinson had gone to town for supplies and Bob had been in the general store where Robinson had stopped for some purchases. Bob had spoken friendly enough but left just as soon as his order was ready. This type behavior was highly irregular for Bob. Ordinarily he was friendly and talkative.

As Bob walked out the door, Will Knight, the storekeeper, shook his head - expression grim. "There goes a man what's all tore up. It's tearing his insides out what happened to his girl."

"What are you talking about, Will?"

"Why, Rob! Haven't you heard? His oldest girl, Emily, is in the family way and she's not married." Will shook his head sadly again, his eyes mirroring deep concern for his friend. "They say Lonnie Williams is the father. Anyway, Lonnie swears he's not going to marry her. He's engaged to some hoity-toity girl in the next county. Understand the wedding date has been set. If the bride-to-be gets wind of Lonnie's shenanigans with the Lanson girl, there wont be no weddin', I'm thinkin'!"

A few days following Robinson's conversation with Mr. Knight, there was a shotgun wedding. Since Reuben was the local Justice of the Peace, he had been asked to perform the wedding ceremony, and he was the one who related the tragic story to Robinson. Seems as if Bob Lanson had gone after Lonnie with a shotgun and had shown up at Reuben's with Lonnie, Emily, and a marriage license.

"Bob knocked on my door one night and when I answered, he said, 'Good 'enen, Mr. Wyatt. I got a couple 'ere what needs to git married. Wonder if you'd mind doin' the honors?'"

"Lonnie was as pale as death, possibly because he was so mad," Reuben surmised. "I've never seen a man's face so set, just like it was carved from stone, eyes like narrow slits of steel. Reminded me of the feeling I get when I see a rattlesnake coiled to strike."

Reuben paused - deep in thought. "Emily appeared calm," he finally continued, "but awfully pale, too. She looked as if she'd been through a lot – all dark under her eyes and cowed down. It was necessary for me to call Jessie in as a witness and when Emily's eyes met Jessie's, her eyes filled with tears. Emily didn't look up any more during the entire ceremony. Things got a little rough one time - when it came time for Lonnie to say 'I do,' he just flat refused at first."

Reuben stood for a long moment staring off into space as if it were difficult for him to talk and then continued. "I heard Bob threaten Lonnie. His teeth were clenched, his eyes were flashing and he said 'say I do, boy, or by Heaven, I will blow you to pieces right here!'" Reuben paused again, then continued slowly. "Lonnie just stood there - just like he was carved out of stone - a small twitch under his left eye the only thing that moved. Finally, he took a long deep breath and in a voice that was deadly calm, but perfectly clear, said 'I do.' When it came time for Emily to make her vow, her voice broke and her words were barely audible. As soon as Emily's vow was uttered, Lonnie turned abruptly and headed toward the door."

"I've never seen such fury in a man's eyes," Reuben continued after a brief pause - his words coming haltingly. "That boy didn't even look at Emily - just turned and stalked out the door."

A few months later Emily's boy was born. It was a boy. No one had seen or heard from Lonnie since the wedding.

As Robinson re-entered the room with the water, Kallie whispered excitedly over her shoulder. "Rob, she's coming to again!"

Zenna's detailed description of what happened that fateful night was later substantiated by the charred evidence uncovered in the ashes of what had once been the Lanson's home.

There was a memorial service later at Big Springs Church for all of the victims. Kallie had tried to discourage Zenna from attending - hoping to spare the young girl any additional emotional pain. But Zenna had been determined - her courage evoking the admiration of the entire community.

There never seemed to be any question by the Stuart family, or Zenna for that matter, that she would come to live with them - especially since her mother had died years back and there were no known living relatives. Later on, the court appointed Robinson and Kallie, upon their request, legal guardians of Zenna.

"You will be a great help to me," Kallie had assured Zenna repeatedly. "And besides, I've always wanted an older daughter to stand with me against all these menfolk."

Zenna, smiling her gratitude, her large sad eyes swimming in tears, rushed over to hug Kallie. Turning to Robinson, she solemnly shook his hand. "I'm thanking you both for your kindness to me," she said haltingly, fighting hard to keep back more tears. "I'll...I'll try hard not to ever cause you any trouble."

And Robinson, deeply touched by the intense sincerity of the young girl's declaration, stood silently remembering a time when as a child he had lost a loved one. "But I had Ma and my sisters to lean on," he reasoned pityingly. "Zenna's lost all of her family - everything!" Compassion and empathy for the sad-faced girl made his throat constrict. Silently forcing a big smile to control his own threatening emotions, he placed an arm around her thin shoulders - hugging her tightly.

CHAPTER 33

The law tracked down Lon Williams and brought him back to Georgia to stand trial. Multiple ugly scars on his legs substantiated Zenna's recall of seeing Lon's pants legs on fire the night the Lansons' house burned. His horrendous crime made an indelible imprint on the community as a whole, and they demanded quick justice. The Federal district judge was contacted and an early trial expected.

When the news first leaked out that Emily Lanson was in the family way and Lon Williams was responsible, the friends of her father and mother watched with despair as a once proud family slowly succumbed to the burden of shame. Emily stayed close, never leaving home, and Zenna, their youngest daughter, stoically bore the brunt of many crude remarks made to her by boys, and occasionally girls, of her own age. When Lon murdered the entire family, with the exception of Zenna, even those who had been guilty of making unkind remarks were angered and demanded retaliation.

Reuben and Jessie had been close friends of the Lansons. Bob Lanson had discussed the predicament Emily had gotten herself into several times with Reuben. Reuben and Jessie had felt so helpless. There hadn't been much they could do except stand by them, reassuring them of their love and friendship.

Even though Lon Williams had murdered one of his best friends, Reuben couldn't get the man off his mind. Reuben wasn't seeing the man who had murdered people he cared about; what preyed upon his mind was a man who now stood facing eternity utterly alone. As a Christian, concern for Lon's soul weighed heavily upon Reuben, and the burden followed him wherever he went. He would wake up during the night with the problem on his mind and would not be able to go back to sleep. Finally, he decided that if he expected to find any peace, he had to go to the jail and make some effort to talk to Lon.

When the deputy walked back to Lon's cell and told him he had a visitor, Reuben heard him say angrily, "I don't want to see nobody! I don't need nobody!"

Undaunted, Reuben walked back to the cell door. He stood for a long moment gazing sadly at the back of the man who stood staring out of the small slit that served as a window in the cell. "I'd like to talk with you a few minutes, Lon, as a friend."

"Don't need no friends! All I need is to get out of this Hell hole!"

A heavy silence hung between them. "Lon," Reuben tried again, "you're in deep trouble. I'd like to help."

"Can't nobody help me. I just want to be left alone!"

Reuben stood quietly a few moments longer. "Lon, I know there's nothing anyone can do as far as the law is concerned, but I know how you can find peace of mind." When there was no response from Lon, Reuben turned and walked out of the jail, not looking back. He felt that he had totally failed in what he had come to do.

When Zenna heard that Lon Williams had been found and was in jail, her heart pounded so hard it seemed to be affecting her breathing. Even though Lon was in jail, the thought of him being only a few miles away terrified her. What if he should escape and came looking for her?

That night the dream returned. She was running, trying to get away, but the woods were dark as pitch and she could not see anything. Eyes wide, straining to see, while briers and limbs grabbed cruelly at her face and hair, she struggled to find her way. So terrible was the fear that drove her, she didn't even think about any threat underfoot such as rattlers and copperheads that she knew sought their prey at night as well as in the daytime and could strike, when disturbed, with deadly accuracy even in the dark. Once she tripped over a log and fell sprawling into the undergrowth. Frantically struggling to get to her feet, she grasped desperately for something with which to pull herself up, only to close her hand around the limb of a devil's walking stick. The pain from the thorns seemed to paralyze her hand and arm. Half-crawling, sobbing wildly, she had clawed her way back to a standing position and once again, tried to escape, but then her legs sank into a deep hole up to her stride and she was powerless to pull herself out. And then, the dark shadow was hovering over her, large hands reaching for her, holding her powerless; arms pinned to her sides. She tried to scream, the pressure of the air against the walls of her throat painful. Finally, she was able to scream and the sound burst through, waking her, and for a moment she was staring into eyes that she thought were those of the enemy, and then, the screams came

375

in full force; terrible rasping screams fueled by uncontrollable fear. But, then, through all of her terror, she heard a familiar voice, low and demanding, calling her name over and over, and she felt the gentle but firm shaking of her shoulders. That was when she realized that it wasn't the enemy, but Kallie. Crying hysterically, she locked her arms around Kallie's neck, weeping convulsively.

"It's all right. It's all right," Kallie soothed.

Zenna's crying began to subside. "I...it was terrible! I couldn't get away!" she sobbed brokenly.

"But you are safe, now. Look at me!" Zenna slowly opened her eyes.

"See?" Kallie smiled tenderly. "You are surrounded by friends! No one is going to harm you."

Through tear-filled eyes, Zenna's gaze traveled from one pair of anxious eyes to another, finally resting upon Robinson. She was safe! Mr. Rob could take care of anything! A feeble smile fluttered on her lips.

Robinson and Kallie discussed it over a cup of coffee the next morning. "If there was only some way to protect her from it all," Robinson worried.

"I know," Kallie groaned. "She's tried so hard to be brave and put her fear aside. I doubt if I could have handled something like this when I was twelve years old."

As time grew nearer for the trial, Zenna had to be told and they were deeply concerned about what her emotional reaction would be. Kallie chose a time while Zenna was helping her in the kitchen to try to draw her out. "Zenna, my dear, has anyone told you that the date has been set for the trial?"

To Kallie's immense relief, Zenna's only reaction was a slight loss of color in her face. Kallie plunged ahead, trying to sound casual. "The court has decided that it will be necessary for you to testify, Zenna."

"Wha...what does that mean...testify?"

"Well, since you were the only witness, it will be necessary for you to tell the court what happened."

"What if I don't want to? Would they put me in jail?"

"Oh, no, dear. Nothing like that! But since you are the only witness, the case might be dismissed for lack of evidence."

Zenna stared wide-eyed at Kallie, fear making the pupils of her eyes dilate. "You...you mean he might go free?" she stammered, face ashen.

"I'm afraid so," Kallie agreed, her words gentle. "They have no actual proof except your testimony that he was there that night." Kallie walked over to Zenna, placing her arm around her thin shoulder. "You wouldn't be alone," she assured her, hugging her hard. "Robinson and I would be there, as well as many other friends." Kallie felt her start to shiver. "There is no way he could harm you, dear. But," she hurried on, trying to allay some of her fears, "the trial is several days away, and you don't have to decide right now."

It was Zenna who brought the subject up later on that evening. She had helped bathe the smaller children and get them to bed, even telling them a bedtime story. Zenna loved telling stories to the children, making them up as she went along. "Where does she get all those ideas for stories?" Kallie often wondered, for there seemed to be no end to her creative inventiveness. Many of the stories had become family classics, which her young listeners demanded over and over again, word for word, until one would think Zenna was reading them from some delightful storybook.

Kallie and Robinson were lingering over coffee in front of the kitchen fire when Zenna slipped into the room. Surprised, Kallie exclaimed, "Why Zenna! I thought you were already in bed!"

Zenna nodded. "I...I just wanted to tell you something," she said haltingly. "It's about the trial. I...I've been thinking about what you said, Miss Kallie, and I think my family would want me to...to testify." She turned back toward the door, eyes downcast. "That's all I wanted to tell you."

Robinson stood up and gently called her name. "Zenna?"

Slowly Zenna turned to face him.

"You are a very brave girl." He walked over to her and placed his arm across her shoulders. "I know you will do just fine."

He felt her small rigid body relax beneath his touch as she stood gazing up at him, adoration making her eyes shine. "I won't be afraid with you and Miss Kallie there, Mr. Rob."

"You'll be just fine, Zenna, just fine," he repeated, patting her on the shoulder. "Now, get yourself to bed, young lady, and no nightmares! You're absolutely safe here."

Zenna nodded. Unable to speak, she once again headed for the door. Abruptly she turned and walking over to Kallie kissed her on the cheek. Smiling brightly to hide the quick tears, Kallie hugged her close, kissing her in return. "See you in the morning," Kallie smiled, giving her an affectionate pat.

The trial had not taken long. Robinson and Jim were called to tell the part they had played in what had taken place that fateful night. Some of the other men of the community were asked to testify as to how the Lansons charred remains were identified the day after the fire and the location of the bodies. Zenna, who had been asked by the court to remain in the hall outside the courtroom until called, was the last to testify.

The judge even lost some of his austere aloofness as the young girl came forward, and surprised the courtroom spectators by admonishing her gently. "Don't be afraid, Zenna. No one is going to harm you."

Zenna had paused momentarily when he called her name, and then, managing a shaky smile, proceeded to the chair recently occupied by other witnesses. Even the court clerk who held the Bible for her to be sworn in by was gentler in his approach. Zenna answered, "I do" clearly and distinctly to the clerk's question of "Do you swear to tell the truth, the whole truth, and nothing but the truth, so help you God?" She sat down primly, keeping her eyes downcast, painfully aware of the man sitting in the front row of chairs off to her right.

She heard someone say, "Now, Zenna, if you will, just tell the court in your own words what happened the night your home burned."

Zenna swallowed hard and tried to speak, but no sound came. She felt the hot tears behind her eyelids and thought desperately, "I mustn't cry! I mustn't!" Her panic stricken gaze traveled to Robinson. Smiling gently, he nodded. With renewed confidence, she slowly took a deep breath. Haltingly, but clearly, the words came. Several times she had to stop to regain her composure but managed not to break down. When it came to the part where she had to tell about the baby, and her father, she couldn't go on. Then, she remembered what Kallie had said, "If you don't testify, he will go free." In a voice barely above a whisper, she continued her account of what happened.

The prosecutor asked her if the intruder she saw in her home that night was in the courtroom. Zenna nodded, her eyes fastened on the man standing near her.

"Will you point him out to the court, please?"

Zenna froze. She had not looked at Lonnie Williams throughout her testimony. Frantically her gaze shifted to Kallie, then Robinson. Reassured by their nods of encouragement, she took a deep shaky breath and hardly turning her head, pointed to Lonnie. For one brief moment her eyes met his. The scene of what took place the last time she had seen him flashed before her eyes. Rising to her feet and pointing her finger at Lonnie like an avenging angel, she testified in a quivering voice, "I saw Lonnie Williams murder my sister. He killed my Pa, too." At the mention of her father, her voice broke into a sob.

Zenna was asked kindly to step down and the judge gave instructions to the members of the jury. As the jury filed out of the courtroom, the judge announced a fifteen-minute recess. By the time the court reconvened, the jury had made their decision: "Guilty of murder in the first degree."

The judge pronounced the sentence. "Lonnie Williams, you have been found guilty of murdering three people. The penalty in this state is death by hanging. Do you have anything to say to this court before sentence is passed?"

Lonnie shook his head.

"Then, it is my duty to pass sentence. Lonnie Williams, at such a time and place to be established by this court, you will be hanged by the neck until dead!"

Zenna, sitting quietly next to Robinson, watched silently as the guard ushered Lonnie toward a door in the back of the courtroom. Just before he disappeared through the doorway, he turned to face the courtroom, his eyes focusing on Zenna. For a long moment, until the guard prodded him on, he stood gazing at her intently, his somber expression more given to sadness than hostility.

CHAPTER 34

Reuben opened the heavy wooden door of the jail and stepped inside, nodding cordially to the deputy sitting behind the desk.

"Howdy, Mr. Wyatt," Deputy Ben Johnson greeted him while unwinding his long thin frame to a standing position. "How you been gittin' long?"

"Very well, Ben. How's the wife?"

"Doin' jest fine! Jest fine! Mean as ever!"

They both laughed. There wasn't a gentler, kinder soul in the state of Georgia than Ben's Amanda.

"How about a cup uh good coffee, Mr. Wyatt? Made fresh this mornin'," he drawled.

"No, no thanks, Ben. Not this time."

"Guess you got word that feller back there in that cell wanted to see you?" Ben's friendly expression had turned into a dark scowl.

"Yes, that's why I'm here. How many days until the…" Reuben hesitated, reluctant to use the word.

"Till the hangin', you mean?" the deputy asked, his voice becoming intentionally louder. "Believe hits 'bout three days from now." Then, jerking his head in the direction of the cell behind him, drawled, "Hangin's too good fer the likes uh him!"

Reuben didn't answer. "Could I see the prisoner, now?"

"Shore! Shore thing, Mr. Wyatt! Didn't know there was any big hurry!" He walked toward the back of the room, calling over his shoulder, "I'll jist git the key offin' this here hook."

Reuben followed him down the narrow hallway. Ben fitted the key in the lock of Lon's cell, swinging it wide for Reuben to enter.

Reuben stepped inside and Ben closed the door behind him, locking it again.

"How are you, Lon?" Reuben asked quietly.

Lon stood with his back to the cell door, gazing out the small window. He remained in the same position until the deputy's steps could no longer be heard going down the hallway. Slowly he turned to look at Reuben.

Reuben's quick appraisal noted several days' growth of beard, dark circles under his eyes. Much thinner, too, than at the trial, but still a fine looking young man.

"Good morning, Lon," Reuben greeted him cordially. "I received word you wanted to see me."

Lon nodded, his earlier belligerence noticeably missing. "I...I need to talk to someone and you're the only one I could think of might...or, would, help me." He walked over to the narrow cot and sat down, both hands gripping the edge, eyes downcast.

Suddenly he looked up at Reuben appealingly, eyes hollow with misery. "Mr. Wyatt, you know what a horrible thing I done?"

"Yes," Reuben answered quietly, expression grave.

"I... I been doin' a heap of thinking, Mr. Wyatt. I got all fired up on rotgut whiskey. I got to thinkin' about Ole Man Lanson making me marry his gal, and I got madder and madder. I ne'er did take to nobody tryin' to push me 'round."

"There wasn't any mention of your drinking that night during your trial, Lon?"

"I know. I didn't tell nobody."

383

"For Heaven's sake, man why not? It might have helped your defense?"

"Nawww," Lon disagreed, shaking his head slowly. "I'd only git sent up fer life and that'd be worsen death. I spent time in the pen onct and I don't aim ta ever do it agin! Besides, I don't deserve ta live after what I done!"

"Lon, have you considered an appeal?"

"No!" The word fairly exploded from his lips. "No!" he said again, his tone less emotional. "Let's jest let things stay as they are. It...it was when I heard Emily's little sister telling about what I done that it hit me...hard! Such as me ain't fit ta live!"

"Why did you send for me, then?"

Lon just stared at the floor for a long time, so long that Reuben began to think he had not heard his question.

"I...I been pretty tough all my life, Mr. Wyatt, and I done a lot of mean things. I ain't never been scared of nothin' afore - up to now. But I'm scared, now; scared of what's goin' to happen ta me when I die. I ain't never been a church goin' man. I can't read neither. But my ma used to tell me about Heaven and Hell, 'fore she died. I...I've heard what some folks believe happens to the likes of me after they...they leave this world. Is...is there really such a place as Hell, Mr. Wyatt?"

"The Bible says there is. In the Bible Jesus had more to say about Hell than he did Heaven."

"Then, I...I guess that's what's goin' to happen to me."

"You don't have to go to Hell, Lon," Reuben informed softly, sitting down on the edge of the cot beside him.

Lon's puzzled gaze clung to Reuben's. "I don't understand, Mr. Wyatt. I killed three people, one of them my own kid. There ain't no way I can make that go away, or ever make up fer hit."

"You can't Lon, but God can." The puzzled look on Lon's face caused Reuben to hurry on. "That was taken care of for mankind for all time, a long time ago, on a hill called Golgotha. That's where Jesus, God's son, died for the sins of us all, all sins, Lon, big and small for you, and for me. All we have to do is believe that He is the Son of God and ask forgiveness for what we've done wrong."

"But how do you know that He was the Son of God?"

Reuben pulled a small Bible from his coat pocket. Gently, the way a father might explain something to a small child, he told Lon the story of Adam and Eve; how the Bible teaches that they were given a choice between good and evil, and how they chose to disobey God. Because of their disobedience, the penalty of death was placed upon them, and on all men that would follow them into the world. He explained to Lon how God selected a people, a chosen race, the Hebrew nation, to reveal himself to the world through them; the laws he gave them to live by; and the command for a blood sacrifice for the redemption of sin; how the Hebrew nation repeatedly broke the First Commandment, and all the others, and therefore, were exiled over and over again, many times into slavery. How God came to earth, in the form of man, a man conceived by the Holy Spirit of God and born of a virgin, and His name was Jesus; how Jesus lived, died, and was raised from the dead.

"Lon, Jesus proved to the world that He was the Son of God when He rose from the dead, and He has promised us that if we truly believe on Him, and are born again, we have the promise of eternal life with God in Heaven."

"Born...born, again?" Lon said, puzzled. "What does that mean. How can anyone be born twice?"

"Not born again physically, but born again in the Spirit. By trusting in Jesus, you may be born again spiritually, just like you were born the first time physically. It means that you are a new creature - with none of the old sin remembered anymore. Just like a new born baby, you are a new person in Christ."

Lon stared at Reuben. "Mr. Wyatt, how do you know all that is so?"

"Because the Bible tells us."

"But, who wrote the Bible?"

"Men, inspired by the Holy Spirit of God, recorded it for us. They also told us hundreds of things that would come to pass, and they did, and have, and there are yet things to come to pass that they foretold."

"Bu...but how do you know that Jesus really rose from the dead?"

"There were hundreds of witnesses that saw Him, talked to Him, ate with Him, after his resurrection."

"But how could God ever forgive me for all I done? Mr. Wyatt, I killed my own kid?" he whispered hoarsely, burying his face in his hands.

Reuben opened his Bible. "Lon, hundreds of years before Jesus Christ came to earth, a prophet by the name of Isaiah wrote: *'But he was wounded for our transgressions, he was bruised for our iniquities; the chastisement of our peace was upon him; and with his stripes we are healed.'"* Quickly, Reuben turned to the book of John and began to read: *"And there was an apostle of Jesus, named John, who was with Him before He was crucified, and after, who recorded these words of Jesus: 'Verily, verily, I say unto you, he that heareth my word, and believeth on Him that sent me, hath everlasting life, and shall not come into condemnation; but is passed from death unto life. For God so loved the world that He gave His only begotten Son, that whosoever believeth in Him should not perish, but have everlasting life.'"*

Reuben closed the Bible. "That means you, Lon, even a murderer like you. All you have to do is believe and ask for forgiveness. Jesus' death on the cross will wipe your slate clean and God will remember your sins no more. God promises that in the Bible."

"Even me?" Lon's hands dropped, revealing eyes filled with tears. "Even me?" he whispered brokenly.

"Yes, Lon. Even you! Even me." There were tears in Reuben's eyes, too.

Reuben placed his arm around Lon's shoulders. "All you have to do is confess that you are a sinner, and ask God to forgive your sins and to save you."

Lon suddenly gripped his head again with his hands. "Oh, God!" he groaned. "I am sorry, so sorry." He began to weep, great wracking sobs. "Have mercy on me, Jesus. Have mercy," he whispered brokenly, falling to his knees. Then, "Thank you, Jesus," he whispered again softly, the agony gone from his voice.

Reuben had slipped to his knees beside him, praying softly. Then he started quoting the twenty-third Psalm, not stopping until he had finished it.

"I...I heard the preacher read them words at my ma's funeral. It didn't mean nothin' ta me, then. I thought it was a lot of hogwash." Then quietly, as if he had made an awesome discovery, "If only I had listened to my ma, Mr. Wyatt, things might have been a lot different."

Lon was quiet for a long moment. "Mr. Wyatt, will you come back and read them words when...?" he stopped, unable to go on. Then, regaining his composure he continued. "You know, about walkin' through the valley... ?"

"Of, course, Lon," Reuben assured him. And he didn't wait until the day of the execution, but visited Lon every day, discussing spiritual truths, answering Lon's questions as best he could. Rejoicing in Lon's eagerness to know all he could about God's word right up to the very last day.

After time was all over for Lon in this world, Reuben was sharing his experience with Robinson and some of the others at the mill. "It was a terrible thing," he told them. "So many lives wasted. But Lon found peace in Christ before he died and I feel privileged to have been a witness to the transformation. God took away his guilt, and his fear. I'll never forget one of the last things he said to me: 'Mr. Wyatt, I just wish hit was possible for me to tell others 'bout Jesus. You keep tellin' 'em, Mr. Wyatt!'"

And Robinson listened, and wondered about that kind of peace; wondered why he had never found peace that satisfied, and the thought made him dreadfully afraid.

CHAPTER 35

"They say time heals all things," Robinson remarked weeks later to Jim as they were making a routine inspection of the mill. "But it sure is taking a long time for Zenna to get over her fear of Lon Williams."

"But the man's dead," Jim reasoned. "Has that not made any difference?"

"Some. But she still has nightmares."

"Probably will for years to come," Jim surmised. "That was just about the worst ordeal a grown up person could have to deal with, let alone a child."

"I know. And she's done real well. She stays busy helping with the children and that's kept the memories at bay during the day."

A vehicle approaching up the drive from the main road caught their attention. Robinson was the first to react. "Look, Jim, it's Zenna, and she's alone!"

Zenna pulled lightly on the reins as the buggy came abreast of them. Jumping lithely to the ground, she hurried to the back of the buggy to remove the lunch basket.

"I've brought your dinner, Mr. Rob," she called. "There's enough for you, too, Mr. Jim," she added smiling warmly.

"I'm sure ready for this," Robinson beamed, lifting the linen towel to take a peek. "Why didn't Kallie come with you?" he asked, reaching for a piece of warm cornbread and taking a bite.

"Oh, she was busy and she asked me to bring your dinner," she replied avoiding their gaze. Being the center of attention always embarrassed her.

"Well, why don't you stay and have something to eat with us," Robinson offered.

"No, thank you," she answered, a half smile disclosing flawless teeth. "I promised the children that I would eat with them," she explained as she climbed back into the buggy. She picked up the reins and with a gentle "git up" was soon turned around and heading back the way she had come. Zenna looked back and waved and it was then they realized that they were still standing as if transfixed, watching the retreating buggy.

"How about that!" Robinson chuckled, pride in his voice.

"She must be improving to come alone," Jim agreed, his smile as broad as Robinson's.

When Zenna arrived back at the house she drove the rig around to the barnyard gate. She knew the hired hand would take care of everything, so she tied the reins to the fence. She was elated to think she had made the trip to the mill alone. It wasn't bad at all. She wasn't even scared once. "But why should I be," she argued with herself. "Lon Williams is gone forever."

As she entered the kitchen where the kids were already seated around the table, she was met with their excited calls of "Zenna! Zenna!"

"Children, not so loud," Kallie scolded. "Well, Zenna, how did it go?"

"Fine, Miss Kallie. Just fine," she smiled, her eyes meeting Kallie's in a moment of silent understanding.

After everyone had finished eating and Zenna had seen that the younger ones were in bed for their nap, she returned to the kitchen where Kallie was putting things away. Removing the broom from its hook, she swept the crumbs outside that the children had dropped.

Usually Zenna took off just as soon as the chores were finished to play with the older children. When she stayed inside and answered their impatient calls with "just a minute," Kallie sensed that something was on her mind. "Is anything wrong, dear?" Kallie asked, breaking the silence.

"No...no, Miss Kallie," Zenna assured her, shaking her head. "Nothing's wrong."

"You just seemed to have something on your mind," Kallie persisted gently.

Zenna sat down on the end of the bench, her ankles crossed tightly beneath her, hands clenched in her lap.

"I'd...I'd like to ask you something, Miss Kallie."

"Of course, dear," Kallie assured her, crossing the room to place her arm around the young girl's shoulder, her calm expression completely hiding her apprehension.

Zenna's face turned red and then paled. She rubbed her hands together nervously. Kallie's smile slowly faded, concern shadowing her eyes. "Zenna, what's wrong, dear? You can tell me," she persisted kindly.

"Nothing's wrong, Miss Kallie," Zenna insisted unconvincingly. "It's...it's just that...well, I...I just wondered if maybe...maybe I could go to school," she finally blurted, her words tumbling over each other.

"To school?" Kallie repeated her voice incredulous, relief flooding over her.

Zenna just nodded her head, unable to say more.

One of the boys appeared at the door, calling loudly, "Zenna, come on." For once, Zenna seemed not to hear.

"You boys go find something to do for a few minutes," Kallie commanded in her no nonsense tone.

"Shucks," one of them was heard to say as they wandered away from the door.

"Zenna," Kallie said, turning her attention back to her. "You're almost thirteen. Do you realize, my dear, that even with the studying you've been able to do since you've been with us, you would still be in classes with the very small children?"

"I know, Miss Kallie," she cried softly, eyes dark with emotion. "But I wouldn't care! Please, Miss Kallie, I want to learn to spell, and read anything I want. I want to know how to figure sums. Pa didn't think book learning was important, for girls 'specially. I want to go so much! I'd keep up with my chores, and still help with the little ones?" Her voice had taken on a pleading note.

Kallie's arm dropped from around the frail shoulders. She turned to walk over to the window and stood staring outside seeing nothing, thinking - how unimportant some people thought education was, particularly for a girl. "What does a girl need education for?" was the usual comment. Or, "you don't need book learning to cook and keep house and raise kids." Kallie remembered how determined her pa had been that she receive all the education possible. "Get it in your head, my dear, and nobody can take it away from you," was his often-repeated advice. Her education had certainly made her marriage to Robinson more meaningful in that their love of reading had provided a whole new dimension to their isolated world. For selfish reasons she'd like to keep Zenna at home. It had been a blessed relief to have her tend the little ones. She turned to meet Zenna's gaze, dark with eagerness and longing. "I don't know any reason why you can't go to school, little Zenna, if that's what you want to do. I think it is a wonderful idea!"

Zenna came to life - rushing over to Kallie and hugging her fiercely around the waist. "Thank you, thank you, Miss Kallie! I'll study ever so hard…and I won't let my chores go undone, either. I promise! You'll see, Miss Kallie! I'll make you proud of me!"

"I'm proud of you already, dear heart," Kallie said softly, gently stroking Zenna's long hair.

"Zenna! Come on!" Robert yelled irritably from outside. "Ain't you ever coming?"

Impulsively Zenna stood on tiptoe and kissed Kallie on the cheek, her face radiant. Happily she turned to rush outside to join the others.

"You don't say 'ain't', Robert Evans! It's aren't!" Kallie overheard Zenna scold as she joined the others.

"Yeah," Robert spat, disgusted. Then, "Come on, Zenna! Let's go swing down some trees!"

CHAPTER 36

Earlier at the mill as Zenna had driven out of sight, Robinson and Jim turned toward the main office building where they would join Reuben for lunch. Reuben always brought his lunch from home.

They had almost finished eating when Reuben made his staggering announcement. "Guess Jessie'll want to kill me for telling you boys this. She wanted to wait until later to announce it. But I can't keep it any longer!"

"Tell us what, Reuben?" Jim prodded, puzzled. "Is it serious?"

"Well, in a way, but a good way, too. It's…well, Jessie's going to have a baby!" he finally blurted, trying unsuccessfully to appear calm.

"A baby!" Jim and Robinson exploded in unison, expressions incredulous.

Reuben nodded, reddening happily. "We weren't sure at first. Jessie's not a young woman, you know. But guess it's for real. She's been to see Doc Evans," he added as if to convince himself as well as the others.

"Well, bless my time!" Jim exploded. "If that don't take the cake! You ole son-of-a-gun!"

Reuben grinned, too moved to speak further.

Robinson congratulated Reuben warmly, asking about Jessie's condition. Reuben, composure regained, smiled happily. "Oh, she's fit as a fiddle. Making baby clothes as if she's expecting twins."

When Robinson told Kallie that evening she couldn't believe it, either. "Robinson? Is it really true?" she beamed, eyes wide with wonder, excitement dancing on her face. "Jessie's going to have a baby?" And not waiting for his response continued eagerly. "Oh, how simply wonderful! They have waited so long! Why, Rob! The two years we waited for a baby seemed like an eternity!" And still not giving him an opportunity to comment, began to plan what must be done for Jessie. "We will have a sewing bee! That's one baby that's going to be dressed to the hilt!"

Reuben took a leave of absence from the mill in the spring to make a crop and to be nearby just in case Jessie should need him. In his spare time, he made a cradle, fashioned out of walnut, its sides and ends constructed of small rounds, each one painstakingly sanded to the smoothness of glass. The rockers, which required a special skill, Reuben contracted for with a man who specialized in handmade furniture. The cradle, finished and occupying its place of importance weeks before the baby was due, provided tangible promise of the future occupant.

Excitement over Jessie's expecting was paramount throughout the community and there were several gatherings in the homes to sew baby clothes. When they all descended upon Jessie for a surprise baby shower, her reaction was all they had hoped. She laughed and cried at the same time, her gratitude warmly touching.

Finally, the long months of waiting were over and the announcement spread abroad that Reuben and Jessie were the proud parents of a big boy.

Reuben dropped by the mill to tell the crew his good news. "A boy, huh?" Robinson greeted Reuben, punching him affectionately on the shoulder. "Just what you ordered. Let's go tell the others."

They found Jim in the boiler room. "We're mighty proud for you and Jessie," Jim grinned, elated. "How about a cup of coffee to celebrate?" He offered, reaching for the smooty pot kept next to the boiler smokestack.

"Jessie make it all right?" Robinson asked guardedly.

Reuben's expression clouded. "She's doing fairly well, now. She had a rough time of it. Guess it was her age that made it so difficult."

"Maybe so, maybe not," Robinson countered. "Kallie's first one took an awful long time getting here."

Reuben nodded. "Well, I don't want to be gone from home too long. Mrs. Marshall's with Jessie, but I feel like I should get back. Just couldn't wait to tell you boys."

As they watched Reuben make his way to his horse tied outside the gate, Jim remarked, "Did you get the feeling, Rob, that Reuben was holding something back? Something he's not telling us?"

Robinson stood for a long moment staring at the retreating rider, nodding thoughtfully. "Maybe he's just tired. It's terrible to watch someone you love suffer like that."

"Yeah," Jim agreed. "Women sure go through a lot having kids. You're probably right. It's probably the strain he's been under."

The next afternoon Robinson came home to find Kallie upset - her eyes red and swollen from crying. "What's wrong, Kallie? Has something happened to one of the kids?" he demanded, alarmed.

"No," Kallie answered, voice shaky. "I...I went over to the Wyatt's today...to take some soup I'd made. Rob...something's wrong with their baby," she groaned, unable to keep the tears from returning.

"Wrong? Wrong, how?"

"It's...it's the baby's eyes," she answered tearfully. "They're shaped funny...like, like Bud Cason's."

"No! No!" Robinson groaned. "Are you sure? Could you be mistaken?"

"No, I'm not mistaken. And, yes, I'm sure. Oh, Rob," she moaned against his shoulder, "I came home and hugged everyone of our beautiful normal kids, and felt thankful and guilty all at the same time."

"I know," Robinson answered, throat aching. "And this is probably the only child they will ever have at their age." Gently he pushed her aside and turned abruptly to head up the stairs. "Why, God?" he asked silently, bitterness stifling him. "Why Reuben? Someone who has loved you and served you so faithfully?"

That evening from his place at the head of the dining table, Robinson studied the face of each of his children. All well. All normal. All healthy. He recalled something Reuben had said to him years ago - about the joy of his children. "You're right, Reuben," he agreed silently. "I've been so involved with providing the necessities of life that I've been blind to so much good; taken so many things for granted."

Robinson's reverie was interrupted by John Matt, who ordinarily was not concerned with anyone else's welfare. "Pa? Are you all right?"

Feeling as if his privacy had been invaded somewhat by John Mat, Robinson glanced furtively at Kallie. Slowly, as if in deep concentration, he picked up his fork and began to eat. After a few minutes he laid his fork down and sat looking first at one child and then another. Then, in a rare moment of sharing his feelings, he admitted quietly, "I'm fine. I was just thinking about how proud I am of you children."

A few weeks later Reuben dropped by the mill. After waiting for the right opportunity to talk with him privately, Robinson told Reuben there was something he'd like to ask him. "It's something personal, Reuben, and if you tell me it's none of my business, then we'll just pretend the matter was never mentioned."

"What's on your mind?" Reuben agreed quietly.

"It concerns your baby, Sam."

"What about Sam, Rob?"

"It's just that...well, Reuben, you're one of the finest Christians I know. Ever since I've known you, you've always put God first. Do...do you ever question why God let this happen to you and Jessie?"

Reuben sat for a long moment just staring into space, expression pensive. He took a deep breath and exhaled slowly. "I...I have to admit that I was hurt, Rob. The disappointment was almost unbearable. The baby's coming meant so much to Jessie and me. It was a miracle and it seemed that Heaven's doors had opened and filled our cup to overflowing. Then, when Sam was born and we realized that he...that he would never be normal, our hearts were broken. You...you think about so many things. How, in many ways he'll never be anything but a child. We'll never know the joy of watching him develop into a normal man. We'll never attend his wedding, and we'll never have grandchildren. Then, there's the responsibility...the wondering what will become of him later on if Jessie and I become unable to care for him." Reuben lapsed into silence, eyes sad.

"This is the thing that is so hard for me to cope with, Reuben! You've always been such a faithful Christian. If this could happen to you, someone who has loved and served God, even sacrificially, then how can you believe that He loves you? Can be depended upon?"

"God is dependable, Rob," Reuben said, his words coming slowly. "He just seems undependable when we try to run things our way instead of His."

"Then, you're saying it was God's way to let Sam be less than a whole human being?"

Reuben sat for a long moment thinking about what Rob had asked. "I believe that God created this world and the universe with sustaining laws; laws that control the stability of the planets, of the atmosphere, of birth, life, and death. God's not going to change those laws just for me, unless, of course, for reasons known only to Him he decides to intervene, and then it becomes a miracle." He paused, as if pondering his next words. "According to Doc Evans this type of birth defect happens quite frequently with older women; especially those who have never given birth before."

"I agree with you up to a point; about the laws of the universe. But what kind of God is it that repays love and devotion with pain and sorrow? It would have been such a little miracle for God to make Sam normal."

"Rob," Reuben countered, patiently stating his case as if explaining it to a child, "no where in God's word does He promise to protect us from the pain of this world. But He does promise to give us the strength to cope with it, if we rely on Him totally, that is. We can't deal with life on the basis of right now. We have to trust God with the bad as well as the good. The Scriptures tell us *'that all things work together for good to them that love God, to them who are the called according to his purpose.'* It's like I said before. We can't think in terms of just the present. We have to trust God with the whole picture that extends beyond this world and into eternity."

"But now is all I can see and know for real! I know that I'm here. Why, or where, it all began is more than my mind can fathom. I believe in a supreme being, and I want to believe in a God of love, but I look around me and I see death, heartbreak, calamities, and destruction happening to those who love God just the same as those who deny him; even worse, sometimes! The Bible says that we're not to worry, that God's eye is on the sparrow! But, Reuben! What boggles my mind is always the question…if His eye is on the sparrow, and He truly cares, then why the hawk?"

"Robinson, life is a great mystery. God is an even greater mystery. There is no way we will ever understand fully the mind of God while here on this earth. If we could bring God down to our level, then he wouldn't be a God at all. I don't know why God permitted evil and pain in the world. Nobody knows. The Bible doesn't tell us that. But it does tell us that

God gave man a choice...to choose good or evil, and that man chose to go the evil route. But God in his grace and mercy provided for us a substitute, a sacrifice, to atone for that evil, and His name is Jesus. But there is a condition! We have to repent of the sins in our life, and accept Christ on blind faith, Rob, the faith of a little child. This is what the Bible teaches."

"That's asking a lot."

"Yes, I suppose it is," Reuben agreed quietly. "But it works." The two men stood quietly for a long moment in deep thought. "Rob, I don't know why God didn't see fit to let my boy be normal. But my Bible tells me that '*all things work together for good to them that love God*,' and I know as His child, that even this can be used for His glory, if I will let it."

"Then, you're saying that what happened to Sam was God's will?" Robinson persisted.

"I believe that He permitted it."

"For your good?"

"Rob, it is recorded in the Bible, and down through history, where numerous men of great faith, of which I'm not comparing myself," he hastened on to add, "suffered horribly; many killed for their faith. Paul, that great spiritual giant, second only to Jesus Christ, had his 'thorn in the flesh' that God would not remove. But Paul said that the sufferings of this world are naught compared to the glory we have awaiting us if we are faithful. Then, there's that great Patriarch, Job, who God allowed Satan to take away almost everything meaningful in his life, yet he could still say, 'Though he slay me, yet will I trust in him.' Rob, I don't know all the answers but I believe that is the way God intended it to be. I just know that faith in Jesus

Christ gives me a peace that is beyond all understanding. That through His strength, nothing can destroy me; not even death."

Robinson stood quietly for a long moment recalling the day his ma had died. She had said those same words that Reuben had quoted from the book of Job: "*Though he slay me, yet will I trust in him.*" His ma knew that kind of peace.

"I don't suppose I'll ever know what it's like to experience peace like that," Robinson stated bitterly, eyes dark from inner pain. "There's something about all of this that I just can't pull together. Something that escapes me."

"You don't have to pull anything together, Rob," Reuben urged quietly. "Just accept it. Accept Christ as your Savior."

"But that's what I find so hard, Reuben," he admitted, confessing to something that he had never fully admitted even to himself before. "I can't believe." And as he turned to walk away, he felt once again that chilling feeling of dread he had experienced the night his pa had died; of being alone and adrift on a dark and stormy sea.

CHAPTER 37

Robinson slowly opened his eyes. Confused, he remained still for a few moments not knowing where he was. The bedroom was dark except for the pre-dawn light that filtered through the loosely woven curtains.

The confusion cleared and he realized that he was in his own bed. He did not move but remained in the same position, relishing the good feeling of warmth and nearness of Kallie breathing lightly beside him.

He knew a light rain was falling outside for he could hear its light tapping against the windowpanes. The sound of the rain in the night always brought with it his gratitude for having a warm dry place to live. And then his musings wandered to the cemetery where his pa and ma were buried. In his imagination he could see the rain falling on their graves; cold wet rain that seeped down, down, down into the earth.

Experiencing an acute sense of restlessness, he pushed back the covers and eased out of bed, moving cautiously so as not to awaken Kallie. The room was chilly because it was still early spring. Hurriedly he eased on his pants and shirt that he had left on a chair beside the bed before retiring. Picking up his boots he moved toward the bedroom door, eased it open and then moved silently down the hallway to the stairs and on to the kitchen below.

In the kitchen he slipped on his boots, leaving them untied. After lighting the lamp that hung in a metal holder on the wall near the fireplace, he soon had a warm fire blazing in the fireplace that had always been such a vital spot in his life and memory. He stood for a long time before the crackling flames warming himself, his expression solemn and thoughtful.

After a while he walked over to the metal food safe, and reaching back across the top, lifted down the writing materials he always kept stored there. He placed the items on the table and sat down on one of the benches. For quite a while he just sat at the table, deep in thought.

Slowly he dipped the quill in the ink and started writing, the combined sounds of the quill as it scratched across the paper and the crackling of the fire magnifying the quietness of the room. He continued writing for some time, pausing only to replenish the ink of the quill.

Seemingly, eons of time ago,
Fate decided that you were no longer needed
To create in this world a better way of life;
And, therefore, speeded up the process of death
Whereby,
Your mortal eyes went to sleep forever with the dead.
It was the simple things that made your heart beat free
And which,
At the close of that final day,
Laid bare the true goodness of your soul.
How deeply it hurts to think--
That through all the pain and toil
Your only monument is a veil of green;
Which, only for its eternal season
Can give hope and meaning

To what was once a form of greatness.

Exhausted and drained, his head dropped down on his folded arms.

"Why can't I put this darkness out of my mind?" he asked himself angrily. "It's like a curse, always there, lurking in my memory." As always, there was no answer, only the crackling of the fire and the sound of the rain. When Kallie came downstairs later to start breakfast, she found him still there, asleep, the words he had written hidden beneath him. She touched him lightly on the shoulder and he awoke with a start, sitting upright. He stared at her for a minute, his vision still blurred from sleep.

"Darling," she said, kissing him tenderly on the forehead. "Couldn't you sleep in bed?"

"No...," he answered quietly, slowly rolling up the paper. "I...I was restless. I was afraid I would disturb you."

She put her arms around him and laid her head against his thick hair. "Darling," she said again, her voice somewhat husky because of her concern, "can't you tell me what's troubling you?"

He sat still for a long moment savoring the nearness of her, enjoying her touch. "You wouldn't understand," he answered finally, a trace of melancholy in his voice. "No one could!"

The door opened and Sarah came into the kitchen looking fresh in her large apron, the numerous small braids of her black hair hidden beneath one of her many colorful cotton headpieces. She nodded to them, smiling her greeting, and walked over to the cook stove. Removing one of the iron caps from the top, she started building a fire from kindling. She had long since stopped being surprised to find Mr. Rob in her kitchen in the mornings.

Kallie smiled her greeting in return and reluctantly removed her arms from Robinson's shoulders. What was it that he couldn't share with her? She felt rejected, alienated from her beloved husband. Her remarks to Sarah as she started helping with the breakfast were warm and affectionate but her mind felt numb with an undefined dread.

As Kallie walked away, Robinson sat with his eyes downcast. He hated himself for shutting Kallie out that way. But he couldn't define to himself what was troubling him. Momentarily his gaze switched to the fireplace and the iron hooks extending over the flames. For a brief second he could see his ma standing before the open blaze, spoon in hand, stirring the contents of the pot hanging over the fire. Impatiently he rolled up the paper. Hastily getting to his feet, he picked up the articles that he had placed on the table earlier, and turning, walked out of the kitchen without a word.

Returning to the bedroom upstairs he walked over to the large chest-on-chest that contained his personal belongings. Opening the drawer that he reserved for his private papers, he placed the writing materials inside except for the ink, which he placed on top. Thoughtfully he pushed the drawer to and opened the one below that contained his socks. Moving over to the bed he sat down on its edge and removed his boots then pulled on the heavy woolen socks. When he had finished lacing his boots, he didn't stand up but remained where he was, head bowed, a dark scowl creasing his forehead.

"What is the matter with me?" he groaned, his angry words blocked by clenched teeth. "Why do I have this awful sense of dread that haunts me? Am I a total coward?" he sputtered savagely. His thoughts turned even further inward. "What if something happened to me? What would become of Kallie and the children?" He felt an overpowering impulse to bash his fist against something.

"This is ridiculous!" he muttered accusingly, getting angrily to his feet. Why was it that these awful moods seemed to occur in the early morning hours? Questions concerning the existence of God; the unexplainable aspects of life dealing with illness and death; why someone morally good and useful taken - while the meanest, orneriest evil-infected human being could seemingly thrive unmolested? So many inconsistencies! So many unexplainable things in life. So many mysteries.

If there is a God, why does He keep himself so far removed, and why did He allow evil in the world? If He is the creator of all things, then, why did he create evil, also? If so, then why is man held responsible for it? If he could know for sure there really wasn't a God, then there wouldn't be the mental torture of wondering if it were true; if He actually punished for wrong doing both here on the earth as well as in the world beyond? "Maybe the ancients had it together," he mused, as he recalled something he and Kallie had read one time about the philosophy of the Romans and the inscriptions they had carved on their tombs: 'I was not; I was; I am not; I do not care.' Pretty smart people, those Romans." And, then, remembering his ma and her unshakeable faith, he was filled with remorse and guilt.

"What if God is real? Will He punish me for my doubts and questions? My family, too?" Robinson sat for a long time lost in deep thought. Then, he muttered, "If there is no Supreme Being that loves and cares for us, then this life with all of its uncertainties and pain is all that man can hope for?"

In a gesture of hopelessness, Robinson dropped his head between his hands, his elbows resting on his knees. "It follows me everywhere," he thought desperately. "There is no escape. It even follows me to the woods," he groaned as he recalled the time a few months back when he had been alone in a deep forest.

He had gone to check out a large area of timber, marking the trees to be cut. Climbing a steep hill, he had dropped to the ground to catch his breath. The undergrowth wasn't very dense on top of the knoll, and he could look beyond to the surrounding valley and the upward sweep of the oaks and maples covering the hillsides. It was late fall and the few remaining leaves on the trees had been breathtaking in their bright array of colors. Far below he could just barely detect the glint of the sun upon a small pond.

He sat transfixed, trying to absorb the beauty. His feeling of elation had been so intense that his breath had caught in his throat. Oh, how he had longed for Kallie to be there to share the beauty with him. A shadow had passed overhead and he saw a large hawk swoop down through the trees, winging back upward with a tiny fury animal in its claws. His moment of reverie was shattered and in its place, reality, heartless and cruel, closed in.

He had gazed about him thinking of all the violence that existed beneath that seemingly sea of calm, and all of the creatures that lived in constant fear of some lurking menace, both on land and in the water. For all things to live, something had to die, whether animal or otherwise. Looking up through the dense foliage of a large pine, he reasoned that even the trees weren't safe from disease, violent winds, or lightning. And time, the death knell of all living things would eventually touch those that escaped the onslaughts, and their existence, too, would be no more.

If there was a God so great as to create such a world of beauty, so great as to fill the universe with wonders beyond the imagination, could He not, in all of His greatness, excluded pain and sorrow? Why was evil permitted in the world to plague man and beast, and especially man since he had been created with a conscience and the ability to reason?

The beautiful scene no longer held any fascination for him and he had dropped back on the soft pine needles, his arm resting across his eyes to blot out the filtered rays of the sun. "Is there no peace for me?" he whispered into the wind. "Am I alone in all of this Hell of doubt and anxiety? Do others feel as I do, and just as I do, remain silent, harboring their fears? Why can't I have the same kind of faith Kallie has, a child-like trust, believing that everything will be all right. But I know better! If there's one thing I am certain of in life," he muttered grimly, "it's the uncertainty of life."

And then his thoughts had turned to the children that he was responsible for bringing into the world. "I've brought them into this, to grow up in a world of fear and death. How could I have been such a fool?

Oh, God!" he cried, not even aware that he was praying, "I am so confused! Is there no peace to be found in this life? I'm so tired of all the whys and ifs. Oh, God, if you are there, please help me!"

But there had been no answer, only the wind moving softly through the tree branches overhead. He had felt empty, washed out, defeated. He sat up, a grim expression causing hard lines to form around his mouth. No longer was he even aware of the beauty around him. He lifted himself from the ground, moving slowly, as might an aged man. Picking up his axe, he continued down the other side of the hill.

A door slamming somewhere in the house brought him back to the present and he arose hastily, walking out into the hallway. Downstairs he removed his great coat from the closet just inside the back door and pushed his arms into its sleeves. He opened the door and walked outside, conscious of the cold morning air upon his face. He walked slowly toward the barn, his thoughts still manacled by anxiety. Robinson nodded to the hired hand's cheerful "Good-mornin', Suh!" - while pausing to rub the soft nose of his horse, all saddled and ready to go. He glanced back over the path he had just walked, his eyes resting on his house. How beautiful it looked in the early morning with its two stories and the smoke drifting out of the tall chimneys with much swirling and coiling.

The back door flew open and Robin came racing down the path. Robinson's first impulse was to chastise him severely for not having on heavier clothing and his shoes, but couldn't bring himself to dampen the joyful expression on the little tyke's face. Running as swiftly as a young colt, Robin streaked

411

toward the barn, pausing only long enough to scamper over the barnyard gate. All frowns of disapproval disappeared as Robinson swung his young son high into the air.

"Don't you know you should have your shoes on?" Robinson scolded. As usual, Robin chose to ignore such questions, and instead of answering, hugged his pa hard.

"What you doin', Pa," Robin inquired, leaning backward so that he could look into Robinson's face.

"Ooh, just looking around before leaving for the mill."

"Can I go to the mill with you?"

"May I?" Robinson corrected him. Then, "Not today," Robinson answered, whacking him playfully on his bottom as they turned toward the gate.

"But you say 'not today', every day, Pa!"

"Well, every day you aren't yet big enough to go with me," Robinson laughed as he swung Robin high onto his shoulders.

"But, Pa," Robin persisted, giggling playfully, and ducking his head as Robinson opened and entered the back door, "I want to go, now!"

Inside the kitchen Robinson swung Robin to the floor. "Wash your hands and get ready for breakfast," he directed, shrugging off his coat, the aroma of fried ham and hot coffee making him suddenly aware that he was ravenously hungry.

In the dining room a fire was burning brightly in the fireplace, and the rest of the family was straggling in and finding their seats around the table. Sarah was pouring milk into the glasses by each child's plate.

Kallie came through the swinging door with a large platter of biscuits. "All right, children, we're ready to eat," she announced cheerfully.

After everyone was seated, Kallie looked at Robinson expectantly. Bowing his head, he said the same short prayer that he had repeated hundreds of times before, "Dear, Lord, make us thankful for what we are about to receive. Amen."

Robinson raised his head and sat quietly observing his family. Sorghum molasses and hot biscuits were their favorite breakfast combination. As the pitcher of molasses passed around the table from one to the other, the golden syrup became a little pool in each plate. Large hunks of butter were laid on top of the molasses and mashed into it with a fork until it was as smooth as gravy. Then it was scooped up with a knife and smeared on a biscuit (John Mat and Robert taking a half biscuit with each bite).

Robinson heard Sarah quietly scolding them. "You chillun don't wolf down yo' food! Dat's the way hound dogs does." Robin and Lindy, one on each side of Zenna, received a gentle rebuke also from Zenna for sopping their plates. A slight smile tugged at Robinson's lips as he watched her with the younger children, noting how well she could control them. "She certainly has a way with them," he marveled silently.

Eventually everyone was finished and had left the dining room, leaving Robinson and Kallie the only two at the table. Kallie picked up her cup and moved to his end of the table. She pushed aside the dirty plates to make room for her cup and sat down in a chair beside Robinson. Sarah appeared with a fresh pot of coffee and refilled their cups. It was a rare occasion when they had a few minutes alone together.

Later, as Robinson headed for the mill, sitting tall and erect in the saddle, Kallie stood at the dining room window silently watching. Sometimes he turned around and waved. "How strong and handsome he is," she thought proudly. "He's no longer that long lean Rob that I married," she smiled. Then, recalling his mood earlier in the day, her blue eyes darkened with anxiety. Quickly she turned form the window as if to escape the troublesome thoughts. "I must check on the children," she murmured, to no one in particular, as she hurried out of the room.

Robinson breathed deeply and let his big roan set its own pace. He sat easily in the saddle, his eyes soaking in the beauty of the countryside. There was just enough chill in the air to make the wind brisk. His earlier mood of depression was gone, now, as he reveled in the freedom he felt. It was exhilarating to ride along and look over his property that now extended all the way to the mill. Furthermore, in the future he intended to invest every dollar that he could spare in more land.

Jim had no desire to possess large amounts of land the way Robinson did, but he enjoyed ribbing Robinson about owning so many acres. "Rob, you don't want to own all the land!" he would tease good-naturedly. "You just want to own all that borders yours."

It was true, Robinson smiled, recalling Jim's remark. He did enjoy owning land. It gave him a sense of power and security that was intoxicating. Land covered with stately pines and towering oaks represented something stable and tangible with which he could identify. There was a tremendous sense of pride in his farmland and tenant houses, too. His houses were small but comfortable, and he knew his reputation for dealing fairly with his renters was solid. Bad crop years, sickness and misfortune, with these Robinson was well acquainted and he was very tolerant with those who suffered such misfortune. But with laxness and dishonesty, he had no patience. No one remained a tenant of his very long who made a practice of either.

"Someday, all of this will go to my children" he reflected with pride. The thought always pleased him and he smiled into the sun. But thinking of the children reminded him of a conversation some weeks back, the subject of which had become a source of irritation between Kallie and him. She kept bringing it up. Just wouldn't let it rest! And that wasn't like Kallie at all.

It had all started with a visit from Reuben. He had dropped by the house to talk with them about furthering John and Robert's education. Reuben believed the boys should be sent to an academy, and to Robinson's dismay, Kallie was in total agreement.

Reuben had introduced the subject by complimenting the boys, elaborating especially on how intelligent both of them were, and how capable they were of doing far more advanced studies than he had the time, or expertise to provide.

"It's time I looked this thing squarely in the face," Robinson muttered. "I just don't want the boys to leave home. Anyway," he argued silently, "they have more education now than I received and I've made it. But that's not fair," he argued with himself. "I would be sorely lacking in education if it hadn't been for Ma and Kallie's patient persistence and tutoring."

And, Zenna! That had been the second awakening! "You know," Reuben had informed them at the same time, "that Zenna is a little pro. It's a shame she can't go further in school. She's that rare kind of student that has an insatiable appetite for learning, and too, she loves to help with the younger ones, particularly the slow learners. Has the patience of Job! To be perfectly honest, I believe she's a far better teacher in many ways right now, than I am."

Reuben's praise had not come as a surprise to Robinson and Kallie for they had become to depend upon her to help with their younger children's studies; but to leave home and go away somewhere to school? "She is so young!" Kallie had argued.

Reuben just shook his head, smiling his disagreement. "She's not a child, anymore, and quite mature for her age. I think she would make it just fine in one of the colleges for young women. But, of course, there's the expense, and you both have done so much for her already."

"The expense would be the least of the hurdles," Robinson assured him. "What money the Lansons had saved, which wasn't much, the court put in trust for her. We haven't even used what the court allowed for us as her ward. Too, there's enough timber on her deceased parent's home place to pay for her education. No, whether or not Zenna goes to college does not depend upon available finances."

Reuben had been jubilant. "Then, I hope you will see fit to allow her to go. It would be such a shame to waste all that talent and ability."

"We'll think it over and let you know what we decide" Kallie assured him. "My reasons for keeping her here are mostly selfish ones. She is my right arm when it comes to helping with the children. But...I don't see how we could, in good conscience, deny her the opportunity. My pa insisted on me having a good education in a time when most people thought educating a woman was a total waste of time and money. I've always been grateful to him."

"Well, I must be on my way," Reuben said, rising and walking across to the hall tree where he had hung his hat. Kallie followed him to the door and laying her hand gently on his arm, said softly, "You're very excited about all this, aren't you Reuben? These are your protégés, the fruits of your labor of love. Am I not right?"

Embarrassed, Reuben stared at the floor. Then, lifting his head to look her squarely in the eye, expression serious, he spoke with great earnestness. "There's a lot of potential in those three young people. Given the right opportunity, there's no telling what they might become. Yes, it means a lot to me. I'm a teacher, and they are all special to me. Well, I must hurry. God bless you both."

As the door closed behind him, Kallie turned to Robinson, her voice husky. "Were those tears in his eyes, Rob?"

"No doubt about it. Teaching the youngsters has been good for him."

"It's been his salvation," Kallie agreed quietly. "But heartbreaking, as well, I'm sure. You know they must be a constant reminder of his own child's handicap."

417

When they approached Zenna the next day about the matter, they knew from the way her face flushed slightly and her eyes widened that she had been anticipating their conversation. Reuben had laid the groundwork well, they surmised.

"Mr. Reuben has been giving us some glowing reports of your achievements in school," Robinson told her by way of opening the conversation.

"He says that you are a fast learner," Kallie added. "In fact, you've gone just about as far as our school can provide."

"Mr. Wyatt thinks we should send you away to school, Zenna," Robinson continued. "Has he discussed it with you?"

Zenna nodded vigorously, eyes shining.

"How do you feel about it, Zenna?" Kallie inquired gently.

"I...I think it would be the most wonderful thing that could possibly happen to me," she confessed, her words tumbling over each other. "But...but where would I get the money. It costs a lot to go to college."

"I don't think money would be the all deciding factor, Zenna," Robinson informed her. "You see, there is some money in savings that belonged to your family. It was put in trust by the court. Then, there's the timber on your parents' farm that you inherited. It could be cut and sold if the need presented itself."

"There's just one thing that makes me real sad," Zenna said.

"And what is that, dear heart?" Kallie urged.

"You and Mr. Rob have been so good to me. From the beginning you've always made me feel as if I belonged."

"Well, that's exactly how we feel," Kallie assured her. "You do belong to us. You're a very important part of our family."

"I...I know, and I love you both so much. And the children! They are my family, too. I...I don't know whether I could make the break or not - going so far away. Mr. Reuben said the girls' college in Atlanta would be his first recommendation."

"Well, it wouldn't be forever," Robinson smiled teasingly. "We would be right here when you get through. And who knows? You just might be our next school Marm. Reuben has mentioned more than once that he needs another teacher at the school. If you do go away, he's going to have his hands full."

Zenna nodded, blinking hard. Kallie put her arm around Zenna's shoulders, squeezing her tight. "Well, we can talk about it some more later. We just wanted you to know that whatever you decide, we're behind you all the way."

Robinson's reminiscing was brought to an abrupt halt when his mount turned off the main road and headed up the drive to the mill. Robinson never ceased to enjoy looking over the stacks and stacks of lumber that spread out over several acres. He took a deep breath and let it go slowly.

"It's good to be alive," he sighed contentedly, the black mood he had experienced earlier in the day completely forgotten.

CHAPTER 38

The passenger train, after many stops and jerks and long intervals of no movement, finally pulled out of the depot with the lights of Atlanta eventually disappearing from view.

Zenna sat staring at the dark window beside her, straining to catch a glimpse of the landscape rushing past. But, instead, it was her own reflection; eyes shining with excitement that stared back at her.

But it wasn't the train ride that was exciting. After completing her studies at the college in Atlanta, she was finally going home. She had never intended to stay away from home so long, or even thought she could at times, because she had been extremely homesick at first. She had missed the companionship of the children, and the love and friendship of Miss Kallie, especially their long talks. She longed to hear Sarah's affectionate scolding when the kids got out of line, and she missed the quiet sense of security Mr. Rob provided by just being there.

But once her classes had started, the demands of her studies occupied so much of her free time that the pangs of loneliness had less time to gnaw at her. Too, it hadn't taken many trips to class for her to realize that her limited educational background had not prepared her for the scholastic level she was trying to maintain, and this meant work; long tedious hours of study with little time for socializing.

Aunt Liza had helped make things a lot easier. She had met the train, just like she had promised Robinson and Kallie, and had helped get her settled at the college.

But Aunt Liza's direct, sometimes caustic manner in presenting her views, or opinion, had resulted in a devastating blow to Zenna's self-esteem. In her matter-of-fact frankness, she had informed Zenna that although her clothes were nice, if she expected to be included with the "in" crowd at the college, she would have to do a little better with her appearance.

Zenna had been crushed by Aunt Liza's remarks, for Zenna was very proud of her new wardrobe, much of which Kallie had painstakingly sewed. But she had managed to hide her hurt feelings and followed Aunt Liza obediently from shop to shop, dismayed by the prices of some of the outfits. Finally mustering up her courage, she had voiced her opinion about the purchases. "I…I don't think I can afford these things. I really don't care that much, Aunt Liza. I…I just want to learn."

"Nonsense!" Liza had laughed gaily. "You are going to find out that clothes are very important. People will certainly judge you by what you wear."

"But…but, I want to be sure I have enough money to stay in school. That's more important to me than anything else!"

"Rob told me to get you what you needed," Liza had stated emphatically, brushing her objections aside.

Zenna had written home later, explaining as best she could without sounding critical of Aunt Liza, about the spending spree, and offered to return the things. "I haven't worn many of them. I wanted to obtain your approval. I don't want to do anything to jeopardize my chances of staying in college."

Kallie had written her back immediately, stressing the fact that Mr. Rob had said for her to keep the outfits. They agreed with Zenna that the prices were a little steep, but they were sure the clothes were good ones and would serve her needs well.

Relieved, Zenna was quick to express her appreciation by return mail. "I want to thank you for permitting me to keep the purchases. Aunt Liza said that the clothes would help me be accepted by the "in crowd." I don't think the clothes have helped much. I've been studying such long hours there hasn't been time for socializing."

She hadn't told them the whole truth. How painfully aware she had become of her background when thrown in with young ladies from the large cities and prestigious families. How she just didn't seem to belong, not only from her lack of social niceties, but from most of the girls' liberal attitudes about moral values. How the classroom had become her oasis, and studying her escape. But she didn't really feel a tremendous sense of loss. Her excitement over learning overshadowed all other such concerns.

Her instructors had been quick to recognize in her a potential and a special hunger for learning that was a rare and precious thing in a student. Not only did they find her a joy in the classroom, but also it salved their ego to have a student that hung on their every word; one that soaked up knowledge like a dry sponge in water; and one that looked upon every subject as a new adventure.

A few weeks prior to the end of the first year, Horace Smitherton, president of the college, had approached her about working in the office during the summer months. Her duties, if she accepted, would be to transpose grades and records, and assist the professors with their clerical duties.

Zenna had been astounded by the offer and highly complimented. Her only reservation about accepting the job was that she would not be able to go home for the summer. But when she found out that there would be time for her to include a course or two of her studies, she decided to accept. A sacrifice now, would mean going home for good at an earlier date.

The job had been good for her. It had enabled her to come to know many of the teachers on an unprofessional basis, and Zenna found to her amazement that the impersonal mask they wore in the classroom was not a permanent fixture; that they could laugh and joke, and many were warm and friendly. Once she had shyly mentioned this observation to Elaine Doss, one of her co-workers. Elaine, laughing gaily, had replied, "Oh, but they have to maintain their dignity in class, or someone would be sure to take advantage."

Elaine's friendship had been good for Zenna, too, but not strong enough to break down Zenna's reservations about discussing herself. But there was no reluctance in discussing the Stuart family. In time, Elaine came to feel that she knew all of them personally because of Zenna's vivid descriptions. Robin's antics were conversation pieces, and just the mention of Rosalin Melinda always caused a rare and special smile to light up Zenna's dark eyes. Elaine knew that Mr. Rob was tall, with auburn hair that glinted when the sunrays touched it, and Zenna's expression always softened when she spoke of him.

'Miss' Kallie was short and "soft and plump with bright blue eyes and a smile that lights up her whole face." Sarah, the children's nurse, was kind, but firm with the children, making them tow the line when necessary, especially the older boys when they were still at home.

Sometimes Zenna's longing to see her adopted family was almost unbearable, and then, when she seemed to need it the most, one of Kallie's letters would arrive. After she had read the pages and pages of what had been going on, who had been sick, how much the children had grown, and somewhat reserved reports on the boys at the academy, Zenna felt almost as if she had visited with them. She would read and re-read each letter until she could almost quote it from memory.

Her letters home were always cheerful, and her descriptions of her friends and acquaintances always kind and complimentary. She gave glowing accounts of her exciting job in the administrator's office, and about the interest Dacus Smitherton, the president's son, had shown in her that summer; even to the point of inviting her to attend a concert with him. What the food was like at the college. Any bit of information that would make them feel as if they were sharing this part of her life.

What she didn't tell them was the hurt she endured because of the slight of some of the girls from the more prestigious families. How she had, without excuse, remained silent upon all inquiries concerning her real parents and family, with the exception of just stating that they had all died, except her, when their home burned and the Stuarts were her foster parents. How, one day, after she had attended the concert with Dacus, she had walked into the girls' lounge to hear Sylvia Lystrum relating the events leading up to the death of her family, and the trial of Lonnie Williams. That Dacus never asked her out again for Sylvia had made sure he knew all the facts, particularly the one about her sister having a shotgun wedding. How Zenna had walked into Mr. Smitherton's office later and offered her resignation, only to have him tell her that she was a "valuable employee and a fine student and he did not feel it fair for anyone to be held responsible for the indiscretions of some one else." And her esteem for him went even higher for she knew full well that the decision had been made under the most trying of circumstances for Dacus' mother maintained rigid rules concerning social prestige, even for the college, for which, evidently this time, she did not have the last word.

Nor did Zenna write them that young men who had not shown any particular interest in her before suddenly started asking for permission to come calling. That she had accepted a date with one who had been introduced to her by his sister, only to discover that because of the torrid stories, he had thought Zenna would be an easy take. After that, Zenna refused to go out with any of the young men.

Just before final exams at the close of her second year, she was made a permanent job offer at the college. The job would include administrative duties in the office, as well as being an assistant to one of the professors.

"I can't tell you what this means, Sir," she confessed to President Smitherton, struggling hard to maintain her composure. "I consider your offer quite an honor. But I want to go home to see my...my family. It's been two years. I can hardly wait!"

"I understand," he agreed kindly. "Tell you what! You go home, spend the summer with your folks. Think about our offer. You might change your mind later and decide that you would like to come back." He paused and then continued. "I might add, also, that you would be given the opportunity to pursue your studies further here at the college," he informed her, a boyish grin softening the tired lines around his mouth. "Now you know how much we would like to have you come back," he laughed. "I suppose you might consider that a bribe." Zenna had included the job offer information in her last letter home. "I didn't make any commitment other than I'd think it over. I'm so homesick right now, all I can think about is being with all of you again!" The rest of her letter was composed of the glowing details of Aunt Liza taking her shopping and home with her for lunch for the last time before Zenna left Atlanta. "Aunt Liza stays caught up in a whirl of activities all the time, more so now that ever, because of Uncle Keith's political involvement. I don't know whether or not she has written you, but Uncle Keith has decided to run for the office of state Senator."

Zenna leaned back in her seat trying to relax. It was going to be many long tiresome hours before she would be stepping off the train. She fished in her tote bag for the book she had brought along to read. But it was no use. The light was too poor, and besides, her thoughts kept returning homeward, making concentration difficult.

Maybe John Matt and Robert would be home from the academy. The thought of them brought a playful smile to her lips as she wondered how many pranks they had pulled at the academy. There had never seemed to be a limit to what their mischievous minds could conjure up for entertainment. Like the time they had set fire to a mule's tail. Ole Dan was a feisty animal with a strong will of his own. Sometimes when he got tired, he would lie down and no amount of prodding and lashes with the plow line could persuade him to his feet. This was a favorite trick of Ole Dan's, and because he was so lively, there was no reason to believe that he was sick, or hurt.

It was Robert's idea to tie a bunch of sage grass under Ole Dan's tail and set it on fire. There was no delay in Ole Dan's getting to his feet that time, but he also destroyed several rows of corn in the garden before he could be calmed down.

She remembered how they used to stand at the edge of the yard and throw hickory nuts into the air, shooting them with rocks from their slings. Nat was usually the winner for he was an expert marksman. "Nat was different from the other two," she recalled. There was something appealing about Nat that was lacking in the two older boys. Kindness, probably, would best describe it. Good-natured, slow to anger, always dependable, even as a small child. "He, too, will be leaving soon for the academy," she concluded.

Her smile softened as her reminiscing centered around Janie Elvina and Esther. Keeping peace between them had been a severe test of patience and intestinal fortitude; so near the same age, and so different in personalities.

427

When she thought of Robin, her heart beat a little faster. If someone had been observing her facial expression, they would have noted a sudden sparkle in her eyes and a lilt to her smile. "That Robin," she thought affectionately. She could almost feel the touch of his little arms clinging around her neck when she would tuck him in bed, or when he was hurt or frightened. Energetic, imaginative, and quick to observe the simplest change in the house, or someone's attire, he was a delight to the entire household; certainly to Mr. Rob, she confirmed. And, of course, there was Rosalon Melinda; quiet, never intrusive, content to ever be Robin's shadow.

Zenna moved impatiently in her seat. Time seemed to stand still. As a diversion she decided to walk back to the dining car and get something to drink but changed her mind when she discovered that it was occupied with men and tobacco smoke. Retreating hastily, she made her way back to her seat. On the way she stopped to chat momentarily with a lady with three small sleeping children. Upon introducing herself she found out that the woman's name was Mrs. Gentry, and to Zenna's delight, the lady's destination was the same as her own.

The two women seemed to take an immediate liking to each other and Zenna even enjoyed a makeshift breakfast later on in the dining car with Mrs. Gentry and her brood. After they had finished eating and had returned to their car, it wasn't long before Zenna was weaving one of her magical stories for the children, keeping them absolutely spellbound to the immense relief of their harassed mother.

As the end of their trip grew closer, Zenna walked back to the rest room to wash her face and smooth her hair. In the mid-morning light she was dismayed to see faint dark circles beneath her eyes brought about from lack of sleep. But she was greatly relieved that her dress hadn't wrinkled too much. She had selected her homecoming outfit with great care - spending with more abandonment than ordinary because it was money she had earned. Her dress was made from a multicolored print in earth-tone colors with touches of burnt orange and green that seemed to intensify the richness of her dark eyes and hair. The tight fitting jacket that buttoned snugly at the waist enhanced her tiny waist and full bust.

Time, which had seemed to stretch into eternity earlier, now was suddenly in short supply as she heard the porter announce her stop. Hurrying back to her seat she hastily pulled her belongings down from the shelf above. She was the last one in line at her end of the coach and she kept leaning over the empty seats to peer out the window to the platform below, searching for a familiar face.

"There! There's Mr. Rob," she whispered excitedly to Mrs. Gentry who was just ahead of her, a faint blush erasing the tired pallor so obvious a short time earlier. "And Miss Kallie! Ohhh, there's Janie Elvina and Esther, too! But where's Robin and Rosalin? Oh, there they are - off to the side! They're standing with Nat!"

At last she was stepping down the steps, the squeals of delight from the children bringing tears to her eyes. Robin was the first to reach her, and as he flung his arms around her neck, her hat which she had spent so much time on deciding the most becoming angle, wound up all to one side with only the long hat pin keeping it intact. Kallie, somewhat taken aback that she had to reach up to embrace Zenna, hugged her fiercely, then pushing her from her at arm's length, said unsteadily, eyes swimming with tears, "Is this my little Zenna?" And Zenna, too moved to speak, just hugged Kallie again. Then, the deep masculine voice that Zenna remembered and loved so much was saying gruffly, "Don't you think it should be my time, now?" and she found herself being crushed against Robinson in a bear hug. One by one she hugged the children. Rosalin Melinda was the last because she held back, suddenly overtaken with shyness.

"Oh, Miss Kallie - Mr. Rob!" Zenna exclaimed happily, remembering her manners and her newfound friend. "I want you to meet someone I met on the train. We traveled from Atlanta together," she explained as she turned toward the Gentry family waiting down the platform to tell her goodbye.

Those first few days back home were some of the most joyous and memorable in Zenna's young years. Just getting accustomed to the changes in the children was an exciting experience. Nat had grown much taller; his usually thin face somewhat fuller. Janie and Esther had grown, too, but had not improved much toward their inter-personal relationship. John Matt and Robert wouldn't be coming home for the summer. John Matt had decided to go into the medical field, and therefore, had accepted a summer job at the academy to help with the expense. Robert, impressed by his Uncle Keith's career in politics and aspiring to follow in his exciting footsteps, had shown a keen interest in law, and through business associates and acquaintances of Rob and Jim, had landed a summer job as a clerk in a law office.

Of all the adults, Sarah seemed to have changed the least. Kallie, somewhat plumper, was beginning to appear square-framed and matronly. Robinson, lean and tan from working outside in the sun so much, had changed very little except that his shoulders were much broader.

After a couple of good nights sleep, Zenna awakened early one morning and decided she would go down to the kitchen to once again be part of the familiar routine.

"There have been so many changes, Sarah," she remarked happily, removing plates from the shelves of the new cupboards that had been installed along the wall. "The children have grown unbelievably, and Miss Kallie has done so much to the house. Everything is beautiful!"

"My Chile, you done gone and done some changing a mite yo'self," she chided, her eyes glancing up and down Zenna's figure.

Zenna flushed prettily, causing Sara to burst out laughing.

"Ahh, chile, come on, now! Do' you go gettin' flustered wid me! Dis am yo ole Sarah, 'member? De one what's knowed yo since dis high!" She laughed softly, holding her hand in mid-air in line with her own trim waist.

Zenna glanced at her quickly, and then burst out laughing, too. It was this mood of gaiety that Kallie walked into, and it obviously made her very happy. Walking over to Zenna she hugged her tightly. "Dear, dear, Zenna, how wonderful to have you back!"

"It's wonderful to be back. So much so, that it seems like an illusion. I've returned so many times in my dreams."

And it was this mood of affection and gaiety in which they finished preparing breakfast, the joy overflowing at the table and including the rest of the family in its magic. Breakfast was a gala affair, climaxed by Kallie's announcement that a picnic and barbecue in Zenna's honor was being planned for the coming Saturday so that all their friends could welcome her home, too.

The day for the picnic dawned with a low overcast of ominous clouds that seemed ready to turn into rain at any moment. For a while it looked as if the festivities were doomed. But a stiff wind started blowing from the east and before long, the clouds had moved on, allowing the bright sun to shine.

Zenna dressed for the picnic with great care. The dress she decided upon was one of her favorites. The color of the material was a greenish-gray background on which tiny red rosebuds were sprinkled. The fashionable neckline framed the contour of her face, enhancing the rich color of her hair and eyes. The tight fitting bodice, the exaggerated fullness of the bustle in the back, all combined to make a striking picture of a beautiful young woman. She turned sideways glancing one last time in the mirror, thinking that bustles had done a lot for her slim hips.

Many of the guests had already arrived before she made her way down the long winding stairs and out onto the veranda. Robin and Rosalon came rushing to meet her. With Rosalon clinging to one hand and Robin the other, she made her way toward the picnic area. Robinson, standing with the men tending the meat roasting on the barbecue, looked up to see her walking across the yard. He stepped forward quickly to go meet her, and overheard several flattering comments from the men and women standing nearby. "Is that little Zenna Lanson?" he heard one woman ask in amazement.

And Zenna, beautifully poised, smiled graciously, though blushing from so much unusual attention did not really hear the applause or the flattering words. What she was painfully aware of was Robinson's hand upon her arm and the closeness of him making her heart beat so fast that it seemed to be cutting off the very air she was trying to breathe.

CHAPTER 39

Robinson was awake instantly, feeling as if he had never been to sleep at all. This had become a habit for him; going to sleep the minute his head hit the pillow, only to awaken a couple of hours later. Unable to go back to sleep, he would toss and turn, oftentimes until morning.

"I wonder what time it is," he thought. He heard a cock crow somewhere and decided it was either midnight, or some time just before daylight. Cautiously he eased out of bed, careful not to awaken Kallie, his destination the kitchen. In her room down the hall Zenna was slowly awakening. Not fully, but in that euphemistic state of not being totally aware of where she was or what she was doing. Somewhere outside a bird twittered, and then another, and another - until it seemed hundreds had joined in the awakening. She opened her eyes to darkness in the room but through the open window, she could see a faint tint of dawn breaking in the east.

She was accustomed to rising up early. Her first shift at the college office had begun at seven. Her schedule was such that she could work for a while in the office, leave for class, or classes, then return to work again. The only strict requirement was that she keep the posting up to date.

Restless and unable to stay in bed, she got up and slipped on her cotton robe and slippers. Moving slowly and very quietly, she eased out into the hallway and down the stairs. Maybe there was something she could do to help Sarah in the kitchen.

The kitchen door was closed, which struck her as rather odd since the weather was warm. She eased the door open, flinching slightly as one of the hinges squeaked. A lamp was burning on the kitchen table and Robinson was sitting at the table, some writing material beneath his hand, his head bowed as if in deep thought.

Startled, Zenna began backing through the door but was too late to escape detection.

"Why, Zenna?" Robinson said, surprised, halfway rising from his seat. "Come on in. You're up early."

"I'm terribly sorry, Mr. Rob. I didn't know you were down here." Smiling her apology, she started to close the door.

Robinson raised his hand quickly to halt her leaving. "You aren't disturbing me, Zenna," he assured her, sitting down again. "Come on in," he invited again warmly, while stacking the papers before him.

"I couldn't sleep," she explained, easing into the room. "I'm in such a habit of getting up early, it's hard to break. I thought I'd slip down here and keep Sarah company."

"It's not time for Sarah, yet. She should be coming in before long, though."

"Would you like some coffee, Mr. Rob?"

"That sounds like a winner," he agreed, smiling his appreciation.

She opened the cap on top of the stove and started adding kindling and pine stove wood. When the blaze was going strong, she replaced the cap. She picked up the coffeepot from its perch on the back of the stove and proceeded to make the coffee.

"What subject did you find the most interesting in college?" Robinson asked, subconsciously aware of her graceful movements.

Zenna placed the coffeepot on the stove and stood for a long moment deep in thought. "I...I'm not real sure," she confessed finally, walking over to the table and sitting down across from Robinson. "I liked them all." After another short interval of thought, she said slowly, "I...I liked working with figures; mathematics fascinates me. Courses in art, history, and music theory were interesting, too. I just like to learn. There wasn't anything that I studied that I didn't like. But I suppose the ones I really looked forward to the most dealt with literature; poetry, especially."

Robinson's interest quickened. "Do you have a favorite poet?"

"Well, yes in a way. Longfellow was one of my favorites. There's a quotation of his that has meant a great deal to me. It's from his poem "Hyperion," *Every heart has its secret sorrows which the world knows not, and oftentimes we call a man cold, when he is only sad.*"

She looked down quickly and then continued slowly. "He has another one entitled 'A Psalm of Life.'" I can't quote all of it - but it's one of my favorites. It speaks to me. Somehow, I identify with it, particularly the last verse. *Let us then be up and doing, With a heart for any fate; Still achieving, still pursuing, Learn to labor and to wait.*"

Robinson sat staring at her bowed head, Zenna's words ringing in his head. "That's what has carried you through, isn't it, Zenna? Your unquenchable optimism?"

She shrugged her shoulders, embarrassed by such close scrutiny of her inner thoughts. "I think my sustaining strength has been the love and support given to me by you and Miss Kallie and the children."

"My ma would have agreed with Longfellow," he said thoughtfully.

"Don't you, Mr. Rob?" she asked, rather hesitantly.

Her question seemed to make him uncomfortable and she wished fervently that she hadn't asked it.

"Up to a point," he admitted, rubbing the back of his hand across his chin. "It's... it's the uncertainty of life that's my biggest problem."

"But isn't that true with all of us?" she asked gently, hoping he wouldn't think her impertinent.

"Yes, I suppose you are right," he nodded. Impulsively he picked up the piece of paper he had been writing on and handed it to her, his eyes never leaving her face as she silently read the words:

Hungrily, the soul searches
For answers not to be found,
A hunger, almost anger,
Grasps the mind with a passion
Almost of defiance and,
A little madness.
Looking, probing, searching,
At times, forgotten
Because of duty demands.
But, there it is again,
At the most unexpected time --
And place.
Maddeningly probing the very

437

Depths of reason.
How, where, why?
And, then, what?

He sat quietly waiting for her reaction. Finally, when her gaze met his, her eyes were brimming with tears. She was thinking; "He's always seemed so strong; bigger than life, somehow." To him, she said softly, "Oh, Mr. Rob! I can identify with that, too!" She felt as if she had truly found a kindred spirit.

"I was afraid you would think me a little mad."

"Oh, no, not mad, Mr. Rob. Just hurting."

Their eyes met - clinging with understanding. No longer was he the father image and no longer was she the child, but a man and a woman recognizing in each other the need to be understood.

And they talked and talked. Thoughts thrown out by one - and caught by the other - back and forth like an exciting game - challenging each of them to higher and deeper levels of intellectual awareness.

And that was where Sarah found them when she came in. Smiling broadly, she chided, "Well, I sees you two done been havin' coffee. Couldn't wait for Sarah to make it fur you, I reckon."

"Good morning, Sarah," Zenna responded cheerfully, rising to remove the dirty cups from the table.

Robinson nodded to Sarah, picking up his writing materials. "I'm afraid I give Sarah a bad time with her kitchen," he grinned.

"Now, you don't do no sech of a thin', Mr. Rob!" she declared. "You come off dat! I likes findin' you in my kitchen."

Robinson, smiling broadly, headed for the door. Walking up the stairs, his thought returned to the morning encounter with Zenna. He was more comfortable with the Zenna wearing her faded dressing gown and her hair tousled from sleep than he had been with the sophisticated young lady that had stepped off the train. The conversation with her had excited him. He felt exhilarated; renewed. As if something new and exciting, almost mysterious, had touched his life for a moment.

Back in the bedroom that he shared with Kallie, he stood looking down at the round face on the pillow for a long moment, a tender smile touching his lips, thinking a little sadly, "We used to talk like that when we were first married - for hours at a time - before the children came. Our long talks had been exciting and exhilarating, then." Suddenly, without warning, it was there again…that acute sense of dissatisfaction, an unexplainable feeling of loss threatening to pull him down again into that dark valley of depression. "I've got to get out of here," he thought desperately, stooping to tie his shoelaces.

Hurriedly he made his way into the hall, careful not to make any noise with the door. Just as he started down the stairs, Robin came flying down the hallway. "Pa! Wait for me!" Robinson swung him up to his shoulder, squeezing him until he cried "Ouch!" while giggling joyously. As the two continued down the stairs, the tantalizing aroma of fried ham and coffee drifted up to meet them from the kitchen below.

Robinson didn't tarry long at the breakfast table. Jim was back and would be at the mill to discuss further expansion of the business. Once he was on the

439

way, he pushed his mount to an unusually fast pace, his thoughts returning briefly to his earlier discussion with Zenna. Zenna, waiting patiently while he struggled with some thought he was trying to verbalize. Her eager response, quick and to the point, stimulating his thinking in that she seemed to understand what he was trying to convey. Then, too, he recalled uncomfortably, how lovely she had been sitting across the table from him - the flickering lamp light upon her face creating an illusion that was almost angelic; how he had found himself wondering, to his shame, what it would be like to hold her in his arms; to touch her young body. And he felt an intense guilt, a loathing of self, because of the way his pulse quickened and for the aroused emotions the memory of her created down deep inside him.

As Robinson opened the office door and stepped inside, he heard Reuben say to Jim, "I think it's a real good idea, myself."

"I'm not so sure, Reuben," Jim countered. "A woman working here at the mill might ... well, you know, cause talk."

"Cause talk? About Zenna! Why, she's one of the family!"

"And a very attractive member, too," Jim argued, his voice loaded with skepticism.

"What are you two arguing about?" Robinson asked cheerfully while removing his hat and hanging it on the hall tree near the door.

"Good morning, Rob," Reuben replied pleasantly even though he was somewhat put out with Jim's attitude.

"Hi, Rob," Jim replied, his greeting cordial.

"Now, what's the big argument? Or, is it private?" Robinson added hastily.

"No, nothing like that," Jim hastened to explain. "Just a difference of opinion, really. As you know, Reuben is anxious to have the summer off, and we've been trying to come up with a solution for his temporary replacement. He suggested Zenna for the job."

Reuben nodded. "Zenna told me at the picnic that she had worked part time in the college office and that her duties had consisted primarily of keeping books. Since this job requires only a day or two a week at the most, she seemed the ideal solution; if she would consider taking it, of course."

"I doubt if she would be interested," Robinson replied thoughtfully. "For the most part, she's enjoying being with the family too much. And, besides, I don't think she has fully decided about returning to school this fall. If returning is a real possibility, then I'm sure she wouldn't want to sacrifice the time."

"Well, let's put it this way, Rob," Jim persisted. "If she were interested, do you think it would b...be permissible?"

"Permissible? Well, like Reuben said, she is family."

"But with the men out there in the mill, and Zenna the only woman...?"

Reuben intervened. "Mike, the foreman, and Robinson always make it a practice for one of them to be here at all times. If something should come up where both of them had to be away, then Zenna could switch her days. Besides, I don't think any of the mill hands would dare try anything offensive!"

441

Jim shrugged his shoulders in defeat. "Well, looks like I'm out voted. The next step is to find out if she would even consider the job."

Robinson introduced the subject at supper that night. "I know you've just gotten home, Zenna, and you probably won't even consider what I am about to ask, but there's an opening at the mill for a part-time bookkeeper for the summer. Reuben, after talking with you at the picnic the other day, has suggested you as his replacement."

Zenna stared at Robinson for a long moment, then her glance flew to Kallie. "I...I'm tremendously flattered," she replied slowly, "but, I...I just don't know. I really hadn't thought about working."

"I don't want you to think for one moment that this is a personal favor, Zenna. Nor do I want you to feel obligated. It is strictly a business offer."

"Do you think that's the place for a young lady?" Kallie intervened, breaking the silence.

"That's the same question Jim asked," Robinson smiled. The smile faded and his expression became serious again. "However, Reuben doesn't think there would be any problem, and neither do I for that matter. Mike, or I, would always be at the mill, and like Reuben suggested, if something came up where we couldn't be there, then Zenna wouldn't need to go to work that day."

"But she just got home a week ago," Kallie wailed, gazing appealingly at Zenna.

"Could...could I think about it, Mr. Rob?" Zenna inquired, her troubled eyes searching his face.

"Sure thing! Reuben told us back in the early spring that he'd like to be off for the summer but we haven't been able to find a replacement. Bookkeepers are hard to come by this far back in the sticks!"

"Robinson!" Kallie said sharply. "I resent that remark!"

"Why should you?" he countered, grinning mischievously. "How much farther back in the woods can you get?"

"Well," she sniffed indignantly, "I suppose it's true. I just dislike our part of the country referred to in that manner."

"I would, too, if anyone else said it," he agreed, laughing heartily.

Supper over with, Zenna read to the children from the new books she had brought them. After they were all bedded down, she joined Kallie and Rob on the front veranda.

"Miss Kallie, I...I've been thinking about what Mr. Rob said at supper about working at the mill?"

When Kallie didn't say anything, Zenna haltingly continued. "You and Mr. Rob, and Mr. Reuben, have been so good to me. I just don't see how in good conscience I could refuse to help. Mr. Reuben practically served as my private tutor when I first started to school. He would use recess and lunchtime to help me. Gave me extra assignments. He was my protector, as well. He wouldn't let any of the older children get away with disparaging remarks about me being so much older than the children I was in class with - not in his presence, anyway. I feel that I owe him a tremendous debt of gratitude. And you and Mr. Rob! I can't ever repay you for all you've done for me - an orphan you took into your home and you've made me feel accepted just like one of your own children!"

Kallie reached over and patted Zenna lightly on the knee. "I understand, dear heart, really I do. My reasons are totally selfish. I'm just not ready to share you for any cause right now."

When Zenna came down to breakfast the next morning, she was dressed and ready to go. "When Abe brings your horse, Mr. Rob, will you please tell him I'm going to need the buggy?"

Robinson nodded. "Then, I take it you have accepted the position? And you didn't even inquire as to the salary. That is not good business, my dear," he chided.

Zenna blushed prettily. "You know, I didn't even think about that," she smiled.

Robinson held up his cup for Sarah to pour him another cup of coffee, silently denoting, with relief, Zenna's conservative outfit.

That afternoon at quitting time, Reuben told Robinson he didn't think there was any need for him to come in the next day. "Zenna didn't have any trouble understanding our system. She's going to do just fine."

"You're the expert," Robinson replied, impressed. "Now, you can get to do some of the things you've been putting off. I don't know what we would have done without you, Reuben. You have been more than a friend and an employee. You have been like a father to me."

"Well, I enjoy it, and the money helps. Jessie and I try to put a little something away to help take care of Sam, if something should happen to us."

"How is Sam, Reuben?"

Reuben just shook his head, eyes sad. "He...he has developed enough use of his hands to feed himself, and he has learned enough words to communicate with us to a degree, but I'm afraid there is absolutely no hope of him ever being able to care for himself. Well," he said, abruptly changing the subject, "guess I'll be heading home. Thank you, Zenna," he called from the doorway. "You've done yourself proud at that school!" And tipping his hat in a gentlemanly fashion turned and walked briskly toward the corral.

CHAPTER 40

In the years to come Robinson was to ask himself over and over just how did it all happen. Just when did that point in time take place when he stopped thinking of Zenna as the little orphan girl they had taken in and made one of their own children; the time when he had begun to see her as someone else; a beautiful woman who was in love with him. Not that she ever told him. Never by overt word or action did she reveal her hidden feelings for him. He just knew. That was why he made a point of taking all of the jobs away from the mill that he could without imposing on Mike the foreman. Neither he nor Mike liked being confined for any length of time to an indoor job.

Jim thought Robinson's actions were a little strange since he knew how Robinson hated the trips to the cities. If Jim could have come up with any plausible reason to substantiate his suspicions, he would have thought that Robinson was running away from something.

Zenna was totally unaware of creating any problem whatsoever. Unfamiliar with the work routine, she had no reason to question what evolved. Happily she came to work, satisfied in the knowledge that she was doing a good job; that she was needed. But more importantly, she could be near Robinson and be a meaningful part of his life; his work. She was positive he didn't have the slightest notion that she was in love with him. How could he? Didn't he consider her one of his own children?

446

And Kallie, secure in her husband's love, never once thought about the possibility of any change. It did concern her somewhat that her sexual relationship with Robinson could not be the same that it had once been. Doc Evans had been emphatic about her not having any more children. He had talked to Robinson, explaining the grave danger. It well might mean her life, Doc had emphasized.

Their lifestyles were different, now, also. Robinson had the mill and seemed to be preoccupied with it and with acquiring land and more tenants. Her life was wrapped up in the children. Her brood had dwindled to five; four the coming fall when Nat would go away to school. But it was still a full-time job. She loved her beautiful home and delighted the entire family by devising new ways to make it more attractive and appealing. There was only one deep touch of sadness that never went away entirely - that Elvina had not lived to see it; never did know that her dream had come true through the love and devotion of her son who had dedicated it to her memory.

There were times, however, when Kallie had noticed rather strange behavior on Robinson's part; times when he seemed to withdraw into a world of his own - shutting her and everyone else out. Not as an offence - just preoccupied. And the way he would get up sometimes in the night to wander around the house. What was it that he wrote on those pieces of paper that he never allowed her, or anyone else to read? It had all seemed to start not long after Ma Stuart's death.

It was Kallie's daily prayer that God would somehow touch him. Remove the awful blackness that seemed to burden him at times. If only he would talk to

447

her about it. He was such a wonderful man. Others thought so, too. Unquestionably a devoted husband and father.

She suspicioned that it all tied in somehow with his faith in God, or his lack of it. She never could quite figure out where he was coming from, or what he really believed. It frightened her sometimes when she caught a glimpse of his bitterness. The thought was almost too painful for her to consider, but there were times when she was convinced that somehow Robinson had a grudge against God, and the thought left her with a dreadful sense of foreboding and doom. "That can't be it," she would argue with herself. "Not Ma Stuart's boy."

That fateful day of events, which would bring about definite changes in Zenna's close relationship to the Stuart family, happened in early August. There had been a lot of rain, which was highly unusual for that time of the year. August was famous for its blistering heat, dust, and dried grass. But not this August! Showers would appear unexpectedly, last long enough to soak everything, and then the sun would come back out again. The heat combined with the humidity made one's clothes stick to the skin and the air muggy and hard to breathe.

Robinson had made a trip to Savannah to meet with Jim the first part of the week. There were some new contracts to negotiate, which in turn would mean enlarging their operation and acquiring more equipment.

Zenna hated the days at the mill when Robinson was away. Usually, he seldom did more than stick his head through the doorway once or twice during the day, but that kept the days from being so long and boring.

It had been a long week, but it was Friday. There didn't seem to be any air stirring, especially in the office building. And Zenna, in keeping with her promise to Robinson and Kallie, seldom left the office. Her long skirts clung to her legs due to perspiration. The short hair around the edge of her face that escaped her upsweep hairdo was prone to curl slightly when the weather was damp, and today, it did just that, giving her a girlish appearance.

Robinson was due back today. The thought had kept her emotions on high key all day. Then, as the day slipped by, the devastating thought occurred to her that he might not come to the mill at all but go straight home.

And then her heart skipped a beat for she saw him riding up from the main road - sitting tall in the saddle. "How handsome he looks," she thought with pride.

She stepped outside the office door and waved. To her dismay, Mike, the foreman, came around the corner from the direction of the mill. "Well, I see the boss got back," he greeted her as he walked toward the approaching rider. Disappointed, Zenna turned and re-entered the building.

Mike opened the gate to the corral for Robinson and waited while he dismounted, then the two made their way back toward the office, obviously involved in deep conversation. Once or twice they stopped to give their undivided attention to some detail of their discussion.

The two men came into the office building together. Robinson greeted Zenna warmly, and Zenna, suddenly overcome with shyness, raised her eyes to his only momentarily, then looked quickly away. But in that brief moment when their glances met, Robinson had detected beyond any doubt the secret that Zenna thought she kept so well hidden. It disturbed him profoundly - but yet, left him strangely exhilarated.

Robinson turned to Mike. "Well, what have you and the men accomplished while I've been riding the rails?"

"We got that new vat put together, Mr. Rob, in spite of the rain!"

"Well, now, that I've got to see! It's all just a little hard to believe, isn't it Mike?"

"Yes, Sir!" Mike nodded. "Miss Zenna! 'Fore long we're going to need a full time bookkeeper. Maybe, two!" Not waiting for her to respond, he turned once again to Robinson. "I told the men they could go an hour early today, Mr. Rob. They all got soaked getting the new vat in." Robinson nodded his agreement and Mike continued. "If it's all right with you, Sir, I think I'll call it a day, too."

Zenna folded up the ledgers and placed them in the safe. Mr. Rob was home and she felt like singing! She pulled down the windows and closed the locks. Robinson was waiting to lock the door as she came outside.

Zenna hesitated. She would like to see what the men had done, too. Impulsively, she asked, "Mr. Rob? Could I come along? I've never been any farther than this office."

A small warning signal sounded somewhere in the back of Robinson's mind but he pushed it aside. After only a moment's hesitation, he smiled broadly, "Sure, why not? You're long overdue for a tour of our operation."

They walked swiftly down the roadway, carefully avoiding the mud puddles. "Looks like we might have some more rain," Robinson remarked, glancing toward a black cloud building in the southwest. Robinson pointed out the different buildings, explaining their use and purpose. Off to one side there were acres and acres of lumber, stacked just right so that it would dry. Then, there were also stacks, as far as Zenna could see, of crossties ready to be shipped to the railroad companies.

The new vat was located at the back of the lumberyard. Robinson inspected it carefully, evidently pleased. "The men did a first class job," he said.

Suddenly there was a loud clap of thunder and the wind came in a great gust, twisting Zenna's skirt around her knees. Lightning streaked across the sky and there was another violent burst of thunder.

"That cloud surely did come up in a hurry," Robinson shouted into the wind. Then, the rain started. Large scattered drops at first, then turning into a downpour. Mixed in with the rain were marble-sized hailstones that pelted them like small rocks.

"Come on," Robinson yelled to Zenna. "We'll take cover in the sawmill shed!"

Before they could reach the protective cover of the shed, both of them were drenched. The wind seemed to increase in velocity and then it was sweeping under the front of the shed. Instinctively they moved farther back until a pile of sawdust blocked them. The temperature had dropped rapidly, and Zenna, wet and chilled began to shiver; then her teeth started chattering. Robinson placed his arm around her shoulder, pulling her close to him for warmth. "Is that better?" he asked.

She glanced up at him, nodding, then, their eyes met and locked.

Robinson felt the heat rising within him. He knew the danger signal, but he couldn't move. Zenna turned in his arm to face him, her eyes never leaving his face. Like a man drowning, his lips met hers, and fire swept over him. Suddenly she was pressing against him, arms locked around his neck.

* * * * *

Zenna lay deathly still beside Robinson on the pile of sawdust. Slowly and painfully the full realization of what had happened began to dawn on her and she began to cry.

"Don't cry, Zenna," Robinson whispered hoarsely, gently brushing her hair in place.

"This must be the way it happened to Emily," she thought horrified. She sat bolt upright, pushing Robinson away. What have I done! What have I done! What if I have a baby! Fear, cold and hard gripped her and wouldn't let go. Her teeth began to chatter again, but this time it wasn't from the rain.

"What have I done?" Robinson groaned inwardly. "I've betrayed my wife, I've betrayed a young girl that I took into my home and accepted as my own daughter. I've ruined her! Robbed her of her maidenhood. What man would have her now? How could I have been so weak? All the times I've been tempted by women when I've been traveling and I've always been able to resist." And then the full impact hit him. What if she became pregnant and people found out he was the father? What it would do to Kallie, his family? "Oh, God!" he breathed. "What have I done?"

Zenna stumbled out of the shed and started running back the way they had come - giving no thought to the now drizzling rain, the mud and water in the roadway. Robinson staggered after her, his feet feeling like two pieces of lead.

Neither of them spoke as he brought her horse from the corral and hitched it to the buggy. Zenna climbed up and sat down. After Robinson had fastened the last trace, he stood with his hand on the footboard, his eyes searching Zenna's pale face.

"Please forgive me," he begged.

"It was as much my fault as yours," she said so low he could hardly make out what she was saying. "I think I've been in love with you from the very beginning."

Robinson shook his head. "I'm older and supposed to be wiser. I'm your foster parent. I have a wife and children. I am supposed to protect you and them from harm." His voice broke. "I...I never intended for anything like this to happen."

"Neither did I," she said through stiff lips. "It...it just happened." She dropped her eyes, fighting back the tears. "Mr. Rob," she said, the name sounding ridiculously formal after what had happened between them, "Miss Kallie, she must never know." Her face crumpled again. "I...I can't bear the thought of hurting her."

"I know," he agreed, his face void of color, saddened eyes searching her face. "Oh, God," he thought miserably. "How can a man be in love with two women at the same time?"

He walked around to the side of the buggy. "There's sawdust in your hair," he said gently, reaching up to brush it away.

Zenna sat in the moving buggy, unmindful of the reins in her hand. Not even noticing the route the horse took, letting him take the lead. When the buggy stopped, she realized with a jolt that the horse had arrived at the barnyard gate. She dropped the reins and climbed down, not even bothering to tether the animal before she started walking slowly toward the house.

The children came running to meet her, squealing with delight. "Zenna's home! Zenna's home!' She stooped down to hug them one at a time and they clung to her, unmindful of her wet clothing. She looked up to see Kallie standing on the back porch, her face wreathed in a warm smile. "You're a mess!" Kallie said, laughing. "What happened?"

"I...I got caught in the rain," Zenna explained, feeling the blood rushing to her face. Quickly she looked down, hugging the children tighter.

"Tell us a story, Zenna," Rosalin begged shyly, holding on to Zenna's hand.

"In a little while," Zenna agreed. "I'm going upstairs and get cleaned up right now."

Upstairs in her room, Zenna pulled the damp dress and her underskirt over her head. She would write President Smitherton tonight. She had to get away from this place before disaster came tumbling down upon them all.

CHAPTER 41

"Will you write often, Zenna?" Kallie urged while they stood on the depot platform waiting for the conductor to make the boarding call.

"Of course I will!" Zenna assured her, faking a big smile. She didn't feel like smiling. All she wanted to do was crawl off somewhere and be alone with her misery.

Robinson had already carried her suitcases aboard and her trunk was in the baggage car. Robinson had permitted the children to accompany him on the train. It was a thrilling experience for them since they had never been inside of a train before.

"Goodness, it's hot!" Kallie complained, beads of perspiration glistening on her upper lip. "This is terrible weather to be taking a trip on the train."

Zenna nodded absentmindedly. Her attention was centered on Robinson as he and the children came down the steps of the car at the far end of the platform and returned to join Kallie and her.

"Zenna, are you sure you are all right?" Kallie asked, her blue eyes mirroring her concern.

"I'm just fine, Miss Kallie," she assured her, forcing another fixed smile. "It's just this heat."

"Board!" came the conductor's warning.

"I must get on board," Zenna said, stooping to hug the children. "I'll send you some new books," she promised when Rosalin puckered up to cry. Zenna held Kallie in a long embrace, kissing her on the cheek. Turning to Robinson, she hugged him as she always

455

did, with her usual, "Bye, Mr. Rob!" No one would have ever guessed that things were any different from the way they had always been.

"Did Zenna seem a little sad to you, Rob?" Kallie asked on the way home.

"Of course she was," he replied. "It must be depressing to be going that far away from your family."

"Yes...yes. Of course! I know you're right. We are all she has. I would like to see her meet some nice young man and get married. She'd be a perfect mother. But, she's too interested in college right now."

Robinson said nothing. He was thinking about the farewell at the station.

The days following his and Zenna's moment of madness had been living torment for Robinson. The loathing and self-contempt he felt for himself was indescribable. Betraying his marriage vows was an awful sin, but to defile Zenna and ruin her chances for happiness, well - there wasn't anything much worse than that. Reminding himself of the fact that she was willing didn't make him feel any better, only worse. He had taken advantage of her love; or had he? "I didn't set out to seduce her," he would argue with himself - depression weighing him down. He remembered his ma reading the Ten Commandments and *thou shall not commit adultery* was right there along with *thou shall not kill.* I'm just as guilty as Lonnie Williams in breaking the Commandments," he decided.

Reuben came back to work at the mill after Zenna left for Atlanta. He noticed Robinson's preoccupation but decided it was caused by the pressure of their heavy workload.

"You're working too hard, Rob," he admonished him one day. "You know that old saying: 'All work and no play makes Jack a dull boy!'" When Robinson remained silent and didn't offer any comeback, Reuben had let the matter drop. He wondered if Jim knew what was bothering Rob.

Liza had surprised them with an unexpected visit. Keith was campaigning for Senator in their part of the state. Kallie had asked her right away if she had seen Zenna since she'd returned to college.

"Oh, yes!" she assured them. Liza then proceeded to describe in detail the fund-raising dinner Keith's political party had given in Atlanta and what a time they had persuading Zenna to attend as their guest. "I don't think she has much of a social life," Liza concluded, "and I really don't understand why. She is such a lovely girl. There certainly wasn't any lack of attention from young admirers at the rally."

Robinson's pulse quickened. "Take it easy," he warned himself sternly. "You don't have any right to resent attention paid her by someone else. But I do," he admitted guiltily.

Liza's visit had been reassuring for Robinson somewhat from another standpoint. If Liza were showing any signs of pregnancy, Liza's hawkeyed perceptiveness would surely have detected it. But it's only been a little over three months, he figured. There was still a possibility.

He tried to imagine what Kallie's reaction would be if she ever found out what had happened between him and Zenna but that was too painful to dwell upon.

"That just can't happen," he would moan over and over again. "To have that gentle soul find out that the two people she loves so much could betray her that way would be the worst form of cruelty."

He didn't worry about Zenna revealing the matter. Her love for Kallie, and hopefully for him, assured that. But things have a way of leaking out. "Oh, God," he thought. "Worms such as I don't deserve to live."

The possibility of Zenna being pregnant plagued him constantly. What would she do? Where could she go? How could she explain? Everyone knew that she did not go out with men. Then, there was the question of money. He wanted to write and ask, but was afraid that might prove to be incriminating, somehow. One morning he mentioned it to Kallie. "Kallie, some time when you're writing Zenna, will you ask her if she needs any money." When Kallie had looked at him questioningly, he had hurried on to explain, "You know, she hasn't used up all of the money that was put in trust."

"Of course I'll ask her if you want me to," she agreed readily. "But don't you remember? We went over all of that before she left."

"Oh, yes. We did, didn't we? Well, no need asking, then."

There had never been anything between him and Kallie before that they couldn't discuss. There was no one, not even Reuben that he dared confide in. He was totally alone in his Hell, "And it's all of my own making," he admitted, guilt blackening his soul.

* * * * *

458

That day at the train station Zenna had been able to hold back the tears until the train was well on its way. Then, her control crumbled and there was no holding them back any longer. She had not allowed herself the luxury of tears the last few days at the Stuarts. Her eyes would have swollen and Kallie would have demanded immediately what was wrong. But she could let down, now, so she turned her face to the window, buried her face in her handkerchief, and cried until there weren't any tears left. Exhausted emotionally she laid her head back on the seat, eyes closed, totally unaware of the other passengers.

"You must love them a lot," a male voice beside her said kindly.

Zenna's eyes flew open and she sat up straight, thinking indignantly, "How dare you invade my privacy!" But the words stopped short in her throat. The expression on the man's face beside her was too warm and compassionate to deserve an angry retort.

"Yes," she agreed softly, dropping her eyes modestly. "I...I do. They...they are my family and I won't be seeing them for a long time. I'm going to Atlanta to finish my college work."

"You are to be admired. Not many young women go to college these days - especially if it means leaving their home and family." When she didn't offer any comment, he continued. "Have you made any definite plans for the future other than college, of course. Wait a minute," he laughed. "I put that badly. What I'm trying to say is, have you decided what you're going to do after college?"

"No, not really. I'm working part time as an assistant to one of the professors at the college. I think

I'd like teaching. Sometimes I think I would like to be a writer. But there again, I'm not even sure I have any talent."

"Have you ever tried?"

"Only what's been required for my courses."

"One never knows what one can do until one tries," he said, grinning boyishly.

Zenna didn't answer. She sat staring out at the passing landscape. It was almost dark. The thought was depressing.

"May I introduce myself?" the voice beside her asked, intruding upon her pensive mood again.

When she turned to look at him and he didn't read any rejection in her glance, he continued. "My name's Byron Davenport." He extended his hand, smiling broadly.

Zenna stared at his outstretched hand. Men didn't usually offer to shake a woman's hand first. "I'm Zenna Lanson," she responded politely, not offering her hand.

Zenna didn't feel like talking. Her head seemed to have a tight band around it and it was hard to concentrate. She wished the man beside her would just go away.

Utterly exhausted, she laid her head back against the seat once more. The train lurched and Zenna awoke with a start. Her head had slipped to one side and was resting against Mr. Davenport's shoulder. Shocked and embarrassed she straightened up, apologizing. "I'm so sorry. I... I must have fallen asleep."

"You needed it," he agreed, expression kind. "I was afraid you would be embarrassed when you woke up and found your head against my shoulder, but I didn't have the heart to move, or wake you. You were sleeping so peacefully. And besides," he grinned, "I was rather enjoying it."

"Thank you," she offered, her embarrassment lessened.

"I think I'll go back to the dining car and get a bite to eat. Would you do me the honor of joining me?"

"Thank you, Mr. Davenport, but I'm not hungry. Besides, Miss Kallie, my foster mother, packed a box lunch for me. She knows how I hate eating in the dining car alone. There's usually only men back there."

"Well, I'd protect you with my life," he countered, his infectious grin appearing again.

In spite of herself she found herself smiling. "Thank you, Sir. I appreciate your kind invitation, but not this time. Really. I'm just not hungry."

"Could I bring you a cup of coffee?"

"Yes," she agreed gratefully. "That would be nice."

Byron Davenport walked toward the rear of the train - his expression contemplative. As a newspaper reporter he had looked into a lot of eyes - happy eyes, angry eyes, troubled eyes, and he had learned to read them rather accurately. You learned to note these things in the newspaper business. That young lady back there has been hurt, and hurt deeply, he surmised. What a shame. Wonder what it was? Not those people back there at the station that saw her off, he decided. They were too happy and caring.

"Lanson." He rolled the name over and over in his mind. "Where have I heard that name?"

He opened the door into the dining car and looked around the smoke-filled room. Miss Lanson's right, he agreed silently. "Only men. Jumping grasshoppers! That's it!" He stood still in the middle of the car as if thunderstruck. Williams versus Lanson trial! He'd been sent down to cover it years back. How long? Eight? Ten years? He was a cub reporter, then. That sad big-eyed young lady back there was the girl who had testified against Williams. He remembered marveling at her courage.

"Could I help you, Mr. Davenport, Suh?" the porter asked, a little puzzled by the well-known reporter's strange actions.

"No, no thank you, Jeremiah. Oh, wait a minute! I don't know what I'm saying. Yes, Jeremiah. I'll take two coffees and one of your famous ham sandwiches to go."

"Yaz, Suh," Jeremiah said smiling broadly. "You on to something hot, Mr. Davenport?"

"No...no, not really. I just thought of something I've been trying to recall for...for a while."

Jeremiah laughed heartily. "Reckon I knows how that is, Mr. Davenport. It don't get no better with age, either. Speaking of myself, Suh," he hastened to add.

Byron made his way back to their car and seat while complimenting himself on the fact that he'd only spilled a drop or two of the coffee.

Zenna was still staring out the window, or rather, at the glass. Nothing could be seen outside, now, but dark shadows.

"Here you are," he said proudly. "I made it!" He handed the cup to her, then sat down. "Brought my something to eat back with me," he announced with a grin. "If Mohammed won't go to the mountain...?"

She smiled, really smiled, for the first time. "My lunch box is up there on the shelf somewhere."

He handed her his coffee and in less than a minute was sitting down again with the box of food in his hand. "Feels mighty heavy," he grinned.

"I know," she smiled. "Miss Kallie feeds her family well."

"Miss Kallie? I believe you said that was your foster mother?"

"Yes," she nodded. "M...my family all died in a fire when I was twelve, except my mother, that is. She had passed away before...before the fire."

Well, I was right, he thought. To her, he said, "I'm sorry. I hope I haven't brought back painful memories. Here," he said, handing her the box, "let's see what Miss Kallie packed. Uh-oh," he laughed. "Didn't realize you only had two hands. I'll hold your coffee until you get the box open."

"My, goodness! Look at all this food," she exclaimed upon opening the box. "I could never eat all this! You'll have to help me." She took her coffee from him and sat sipping it slowly.

"You're not eating," he chastised.

"I'm not very hungry. Please, won't you help me? I'll never be able to eat all of this!"

When Zenna awakened later after many hours of restless napping, it was to find the seat vacant beside her, but not for long.

"Hey," he said jubilantly, returning from the direction of the diner, "I've got good news! The diner's practically empty. How about some breakfast?"

"Breakfast? Don't you think it's a little early?"

"Not if you want to beat the crowds!"

"Mr. Davenport," Zenna exclaimed, really laughing for the first time in days, "you're a hard man to…"

"…Get rid of?" he finished for her, laughing boisterously when she blushed.

When the porter came forward to assist them in the dining car and called her companion by name, Zenna was impressed.

"You must travel on this train a lot, Mr. Davenport. Just who are you," she asked after they were seated.

"Not anyone famous, nor notorious," he teased. When she said nothing, but sat looking at him expectantly, he answered. "I'm a newspaper man."

"A reporter?"

"I'm afraid so. Better than ten years."

"Well! That advice you gave me last evening about trying to be a writer? That's from the horse's mouth, wouldn't you say?"

"Guilty!"

"I'm impressed, Mr. Davenport."

"Now that we've shared something personal, like breakfast in a train's dining car, don't you think it would be permissible for you to call me Byron?"

"All right," she agreed shyly, "if you'll call me Zenna."

"Agreed!"

Liza and Keith were at the station to meet her. "How did you know?" Zenna stammered, evidently pleased.

"Oh, I have ways of finding out things," Liza beamed, hugging Zenna fiercely. "That brother of mine sent a telegram," she confessed.

"That was thoughtful of Mr. Rob," she murmured. "Oh, Aunt Liza, Uncle Keith, I'd like for you to meet someone I met on the train. This is Mr. Byron Davenport."

Keith extended his hand. "Any friend of Zenna's is a friend of ours," he assured Byron, smiling confidently.

They shook hands, Byron thinking, "Don't be too sure, about that! You don't know me, but I know you. You are the candidate for Senator with all the money bags behind you." The thought was revolting to Byron.

Turning to Zenna he smiled at her warmly. "Thank you, Miss Lanson, for making a trip ordinarily boring most delightful. Now, if you will excuse me, this reporter's got work to do." And without so much as a backward look, disappeared into the crowd.

"For goodness sake!" Liza quipped, tilting her head. "Is he always that rude?" Then denoting the troubled expression on Zenna's face said gaily, "Zenna! I have the most wonderful surprise! Keith's promised to take us to lunch later on, and he only patronizes the best places."

"That...that will be nice," Zenna answered politely, faking a pleasant smile.

During the following weeks it didn't matter where Zenna was, or whom she was with, or what she was doing, the fear and dread that she might be pregnant never left her waking moments long at a time. What had happened to Emily and the disgrace it had brought upon her family kept creeping into her thoughts to haunt her. The possibility of bringing any hint of shame upon the Stuart's good name made her cringe with pain. And Kallie, gentle loving Kallie who had

465

taken her under her wing and helped see her through all the dark times; who had actually been better to her than her own mother in many ways. So many people would be disappointed in her. Even the children would hear the whispers and no longer look at her with eyes of trust. And there was Mr. Reuben who had always regarded her as the epitome of virtuous womanhood. Then, there was Mr. Smitherton. The thought of him brought a stab of pain to her heart. She could just envision his wife standing in her most prestigious manner and staring down her blue-blood nose, haughtily reminding him that she had once tried to have him remove Zenna from the college staff. "Blood will tell!" Zenna could almost hear her sniff.

"It wasn't that I didn't know better," she accused herself unmercifully. "Hadn't Miss Kallie talked to her many times about how easy it was to get involved in such situations? 'Zenna,' she would explain in her kind way, 'it could happen to anyone, if the right situation develops. The safest way to avoid such a tragedy is to never let yourself get into a position where you could lose your self-control.'" And, then there were the Ten Commandments. Remembering the words "Thou shalt not commit adultery" always caused guilt, dark and threatening like an ominous cloud, to flood over her.

Somehow she managed to carry out her job at the college and do it well. Most of it was routine, anyway. But she had difficulty concentrating in class and especially in completing her homework assignments. There was too much time to think when you were alone. Her grades began to drop.

The question, "What on earth will I do," was an ever-present shadow. "I'll have to go away somewhere," she decided, "and change my name. Maybe I'll go to New York City. It's a large place and there are lots of immigrants. I could establish a new identity there." Maybe there would be some benevolent institution that would care for her and the baby. But she would have to come up with some good reason for going. In the dark hours of the night she often considered suicide.

She counted the days off on the calendar over and over. When five weeks had gone by and there was no evidence that she wasn't pregnant, a sense of desperation seemed to be drowning her. There had never been a time when she had felt so utterly alone. "Not even the night my parents died," she confessed miserably.

Elaine Doss, her friend in the office, mentioned how tired Zenna looked one day during lunch. "Zenna, I don't mean to pry, but is anything wrong? You haven't acted like yourself since your trip home."

"No, nothing's wrong," Zenna assured her, avoiding her eyes. "I...I'm just a little homesick, that's all."

Zenna knew Elaine didn't believe her, but her friend was tactful enough not to pursue the matter any further. "Maybe she's in love," Elaine pondered. "I've heard it affects people like that, but with whom? I've never heard her mention anyone that she was particularly interested in romantically." Aloud, Elaine asked, "Have you decided whether or not you're going to the political rally Friday evening with your Aunt Liza?"

"No," Zenna replied, shaking her head. "Oh, I…I suppose I will. I don't want to hurt Aunt Liza and Uncle Keith's feelings."

"Sounds like great fun to me," Elaine responded, feigning enthusiasm.

Zenna's only response was a slight shrug of her shoulders.

The remainder of the lunch period between the two was drenched in silence. Elaine found it extremely difficult to carry on a one-sided conversation. But she felt no offense. She wisely realized that her dear friend was wrestling with some kind of a big problem, and she wasn't going to desert her. One of these days when Zenna decided to talk about it, she'd be there. Until then, she would just stand by.

The rally turned out to be a good diversion for Zenna. There were a few bad moments when Keith and Liza came by for her. Liza had made a big issue about Zenna being so thin and the dark circles under her eyes.

Mr. Davenport stopped by their table, but only stayed for a few minutes. He was on assignment.

Liza had tried to pressure Zenna into coming home with them for the weekend, but Zenna begged off. "I have a lot of studying to do," she explained, hating the lie. The truth was that she was so miserable she just wanted to be alone.

She had trouble going to sleep that night but finally dropped off. But it was a restless sleep. She kept dreaming that she was trying to get somewhere, but every way she turned, there was some overwhelming obstacle. It was so important that she get where she was going, but she just couldn't get there. She awoke exhausted.

At first she thought the dull ache in her abdomen was from anxiety caused by the dream. But as it persisted and didn't get better but only increased in discomfort, she began to wonder. With shaking fingers she lit the lamp on the bedside table, not daring to believe that it was true. But it was. Her perpetual nightmare was over.

A long letter came from Kallie the next week - bringing her up to date on what had happened since she'd left. The children missed her terribly, she wrote, especially her storytelling.

The next paragraph seemed to jump out at her. *Rob has been working terribly hard. I don't know what I'm going to do with that man! It's not as if we are destitute. The children and I hardly see him anymore. I believe we were happier when we were as poor as the proverbial church mouse!*

Zenna sat still for a long time after she finished Kallie's letter just staring into space. She wished with a terrible longing that she could hold Robinson in her arms and comfort him. Just tell him that she loved him and that everything was all right. But her love for him had helped bring about a terrible wrong and a burden the two of them would carry in their hearts for the rest of their lives. "But it will never happen again," she resolved, hot tears running unheeded down her cheeks. "Even if it means staying away and never going home again!" The thought was devastating.

Zenna made a point of stopping by the bookstore the next week. Aunt Liza had told her that Uncle Keith was planning to do some campaigning back home. Zenna could send the children's books by them.

The bookstore didn't offer much of a selection. She thumbed through book after book - thoroughly frustrated by the contents, "I could do better than this," she fumed. Slowly she laid the book in her hand down, lost in deep thought. She was remembering something Byron Davenport had said to her on the train. "One never knows what one can do until one tries!" Her heart began to pound furiously. "Why not," she whispered softly, eyes wide with wonder.

She paid for her selections and hurried back to the college. If the children enjoyed the way she told stories, then why wouldn't they like reading them? Somehow she knew for certain that her course had been set. Not since the day Miss Kallie agreed for her to attend Mr. Reuben's school had she been so excited.

CHAPTER 42

Robinson walked along the busy main street of Savannah. He had never grown accustomed to the hustle and bustle of the city. Where were all the people going? What were their living conditions like in this teeming city? Did they have personal problems to deal with just as he did...some just as bad as his...some worse? However, there was one thing in particular that he liked about the city, he decided grudgingly. There were enough distractions to help keep a man from thinking about his own troubles much of the time.

Robinson was tired mentally and physically. When he had spare time on his hands, his thoughts always turned toward home and his loved ones. But this was no longer totally pleasant. Inevitably his thoughts of Kallie brought with it feelings of guilt. There never seemed to be any lasting relief from the burden that plagued him. It never let up; never let go for any prolonged period of time.

He had no further business obligations to meet in Savannah. The business matters he had come to negotiate had been settled. All he had to do was kill some time before his train left, but that wouldn't be until morning. He turned away from the riverside shopping area and started walking aimlessly through the residential sections of town. He strolled down one street and up another, studying the architecture of some of the older homes, subconsciously comparing them with his own. Lunch had been offered him earlier by some of the businessmen at the meeting. They had

471

their own private club and had invited him to be their guest. Would he care to join them?

No, he "had not cared" to join them, but he had been careful to make his apologies like a well-bred gentleman should. Jim had been his example in times past for handling sticky situations such as this. However, from his personal point of view, business was business. He had no cheek for mixing business with pleasure. He had long since come to the realization that the highest price one can pay for anything is nothing.

His wandering carried him into a residential section where the houses were rather close together. Children were playing on the sidewalks and in the streets. His thoughts turned toward home again and his own family. But there wasn't the same joy in remembering as there once had been.

He had thought about confessing all to Kallie time and time again. Came real close more than once but never could bring himself to tell her. He didn't know what had stopped him exactly. Maybe it was dreading the pain he would see in her eyes. Or was it that he couldn't bear to think of her finding out that he wasn't the strong, faithful, loving giant that she idolized; that he had feet of clay. He had finally come to the conclusion that confession would not accomplish anything except maybe relieve his conscience somewhat and just cause her a lot of grief. No, he decided his penance was to forever walk in the nighttime of the soul.

Zenna hadn't been home since she had returned to college. She had been faithful about writing, however, and Liza was always bringing them bits of news. He knew that Zenna had been able to find a publisher for her book of children's stories. She had even sent an autographed copy home to the kids. She had never married and for this he was secretly grateful. Even though he knew their short moment had come and gone - to be never again - he didn't like to think of her belonging to anyone else. And these thoughts only intensified his feelings of guilt. "I must not dwell on such thoughts," he groaned. He knew that the Bible teaches that lust is sin and for him to have thoughts of another woman was adulterous. But why should he be concerned about that? God probably gave up on him a long time ago! This thought only added to his despondency.

It never was clear to him how he happened to wind up at a chapel. For one thing, it was at the end of a dead end street. He had failed to read the sign.

The door of the chapel was open. There seemed to be no activity inside or out. The peacefulness of the setting was what attracted him. He would just go inside and look around and maybe be alone for a while.

The chapel was empty, as he had hoped. He walked over and sat down on the back pew just inside the door. It had been a long time since he had been inside of a church; not since his ma's funeral, he reckoned.

"I wonder why some people put so much emphasis on religion," he pondered. It had never worked for him that he could tell. His ma had put great store in it. She had loved God with a devotion that had seemed fanatical to him at times. She really believed along with the Apostle Paul, "that all things happen for good to them that love the Lord; to them who are called according to His purpose."

473

"However," he admitted grudgingly, "it had seemed to give her strength through the tough times." He recalled the mantle and the Bible that had its special place there. How his ma read it faithfully every day.

"Ma," he whispered brokenly, "what would you tell me now?" The longing to sit down and talk with her was so intense that it made his chest ache. What was it about her that made you feel that all you had to do was hang on and have faith and everything would work out? When she prayed, you felt as if she was actually talking to God - on a one-to-one basis. "Ma, if only you were here to pray for me now," he whispered into the silence. "What would you tell me?" Then, from somewhere far back in the recess of his memory, he recalled her saying, "Son, read the Word. It is God speaking to you."

He looked up and down the pew. On the back of the pew in front of him was a wooden pocket. In it was a Bible with a hymnal placed on each side. Hesitantly, almost awkwardly, he reached and picked up the Bible. A red bookmark with the words "The Roman Road to Salvation" had been placed in the Bible. Questionably, he opened the Bible at the bookmark and it was the third chapter of Romans. At the bottom of the page, someone had made the following entry: 1. Romans 3:23, which states, F*or all have sinned, and come short of the glory of God.*

He turned the page, looking for entry Number 2. It was Romans 6:23. *For the wages of sin is death; but the gift of God is eternal life through Jesus Christ our Lord.* On the opposite side, Number 3. Romans 5:8. *But God commendeth his love toward us, in that, while we were yet sinners, Christ died for us.* Number 4. Romans 10:13: *For whosoever shall call upon the name of the Lord shall be saved.* Number 5. Romans 10:9: *For if thou shalt confess with thy mouth the Lord Jesus, and shalt believe in thine heart that God hath raised him from the dead, thou shalt be saved.* Number 6. Romans 12:1-2: *I beseech you therefore, brethren, by the mercies of God, that ye present your bodies a living sacrifice, holy, acceptable unto God, which is your reasonable service. And be not conformed to this world; but be ye transformed by the renewing of your mind, that ye may prove what is that good, and acceptable, and perfect, will of God.*

He sat for a long moment, thinking about what he had read, then he turned back and read Number 1, again: *"For all have sinned, and come short of the glory of God."* He had heard that in church many times - but it had never meant anything to him especially. Now, it was like a reprieve. He laid the Bible aside and leaned forward to rest his head on his folded arms on the pew in front of him. He tried to pray - but there seemed to be some kind of barrier between Him and God. He was totally unaware of the passing of time.

Someone started playing the pump organ up front and Robinson's head came up with a jerk. Why, it was dark already! Someone had lit the lamps and he realized with a feeling of panic that they were preparing for church. It must be a revival meeting. If he ducked out now, it wouldn't look so bad. He never did know exactly why he didn't.

The kindly preacher talked that night about being born again. He read the Scripture about Nicodemus coming to Jesus by night and wanting to know how to be saved. "Was that for real?" Robinson asked silently. "Could a person really be born again spiritually? Be as clean as a newborn babe? His sins buried at the bottom of the sea -, never to be remembered by God anymore?"

"Oh, God," he moaned within him. He wanted to feel clean like that. He was tired of running. It seemed like he had been running from God all of his life. Like a thirsty man stumbling toward an oasis in a hot dry desert, he moved down the aisle. The preacher came to meet him; their hands met.

"I have sinned," he told the preacher quietly. "I want to be born again," his eyes, dark with misery, never leaving the preacher's face.

"And you can be, right here and now, if you just believe that Christ is Lord, ask him to forgive your sins, and commit your life to Him."

"I do," he said shakily, "and I will," he finished, triumph in his tone, tears running unashamedly down his face. He turned and knelt on his knees at the altar. "Thank you Jesus," he whispered, "for giving me back my life." The peace that came over him was such that he felt like shouting. But instead, he just knelt there for quite a while, just talking to God; really talking to God for the first time in his life.

The minister, realizing that this was a man with a great need invited him back to his office after the close of the service. They didn't talk long for the hour was late, but the minister said one thing that Robinson would never forget and that would sustain him in the weeks and months ahead when the doubts returned to plague him: "There's something very important that you must always remember, as you start out on this journey with the Lord, you have asked for forgiveness, and that was granted immediately. God does not lie, your sins have been covered by the blood of Christ to be remembered by God no more. If old sins start coming back to haunt you and make you feel guilty, that's not the convicting power of the Holy Spirit, that's Satan trying to rob you of the joy of your salvation. Resist him, defy him, and remind him who you are; a sinner saved by the blood of Jesus Christ." He then stood and walked over to a nearby shelf where he picked up a New Testament from the top of a stack. "Take this with you. Start with the Book of John."

Robinson had a lot of time to explore the New Testament during the train ride home. It wasn't a random casual searching, but an eager expectancy like a hungry man urgently searching for food. "I can see it, now, why I couldn't find peace, Lord," he confessed, his thoughts in the form of a prayer. "It takes total commitment, complete surrender. No bitter demands for explanations and answers; total trusting faith like that of a small child. Ma trusted you that way, Lord, no matter what! It gave her strength strong enough to overcome tragedy and to defeat the pain of heartbreak; even death."

From the minute Robinson arrived back home and stepped down from the buggy, Kallie could tell that something was different about him. He walked with a spring in his step, and when the kids ran out to meet him, he grabbed them and hugged them with tears of joy in his eyes. When he turned to embrace Kallie, there was a fierceness about his caress as if he couldn't hold her close enough. Joyously he picked her up and swung her around.

"What in the world has happened," she wondered apprehensively, while at the same time, enjoying every moment.

Later on, when they were alone, he didn't make a big thing out of it. "Kallie," he said quietly, "I've been born again, and I want to be baptized again."

She stared at him for a long moment. Of all the possibilities that she might have thought of that could have brought about this change in him, a spiritual experience was the last she would have considered. Then, her face crumpled and she began to cry. He gathered her in his arms. "I…I wish Ma Stuart could have heard you say that," she whispered through her tears.

"She knew," he said hoarsely, fighting hard to control his emotions. "I…I think she always had faith that sooner or later I'd come to know Him as my Lord and Savior." He was quiet for such a long moment that she moved away from him far enough to look into his eyes. The peacefulness she saw there brought more tears to her own. "There were so many things I didn't understand, until now," he continued haltingly. "I look back and remember all those bitter years. How I questioned God and demanded answers."

"You mustn't look back, darling," Kallie answered, gently caressing his face with her hand. "If you tried to explain to God all over again about the things you regret, He'd just say, 'What things?' The Bible tells us that forgiven sin is buried in the bottom of the sea, never to be remembered by God any more."

"I know," he whispered brokenly, hugging her close. "It's that peace that passes all understanding. You know, Preacher White had that kind of peace. And

Reuben tried to tell me about it but I didn't want to hear. It...It didn't make sense, back then."

Kallie wondered secretly what had happened to bring Robinson to this new spiritual understanding, but she would never ask. He was her husband, but at the same time, this relationship between Robinson and God was their business and theirs alone.

CHAPTER 43

Byron Davenport told the driver to wait as he turned to hurry up the steps to the front door of the large three-story house built from large stone blocks. The house had once belonged to a wealthy family, but like so many of the homes in the heart of the city, it had relinquished its prestige to even finer ones in the suburbs. Now, its purpose was to house several tenants under its once proud roof. Zenna was waiting for Byron in the front parlor where tenants were permitted to receive guests at certain hours.

"Well," he exclaimed, his face lighting with pleasure as he walked into the room where the light was brighter and he could get a good look at her, "aren't you something to behold!"

Zenna blushed. She had spent a great deal of time preparing for this date with Byron. She was an avid reader of his newspaper articles and had come to admire him for his straightforward approach and fighting spirit. Too, he would always hold a special place in her heart. That night on the train, in just trying to be kind, he had been the buoy that had kept her afloat when she needed help so desperately. Besides, hadn't it been his suggestion that had set her on the course that had given her life purpose and fulfillment? She was becoming well known in the literary world, and his influence to see that she got recognition in his newspaper had also been a large factor in the progress of her career.

Sitting across from her in the restaurant later, the flickering soft lights seemed to make everything about her come alive. Eyes that were calm now replaced the pale drawn expression he remembered from their first meeting. Still guarded, somewhat, but the pain was no longer evident. After all this time, he still did not know what the problem had been, and he had never asked. It didn't matter, really, as long as it didn't seem to hurt her, that way, anymore.

They talked about so many things that night. How the sales of her book were coming along. The new one she was working on. But, strangely enough, as he was to recall later, most of the conversation had been about him. She seemed to have an insatiable appetite concerning his work, and that always pleased him tremendously. Not many people were interested in what it took to get a story in print.

Zenna had come to learn a lot about this man who had become such a vital part of her life. He had been married once, happily, but his wife had died from a massive stroke only weeks before their first child's birth. The baby had died with her. Since that time he had made his work his family and primarily his life.

"Have you ever been in love, Zenna?" he had asked once, realizing immediately that the question had been a mistake. For a brief moment he had caught a glimpse of the old hurt again.

"Yes," she had answered softly, eyes downcast. When she didn't offer any further information, he had quickly changed the subject.

After dinner they had attended the theater. The play was a comedy, and the humor had been good for both of them. Riding back in the coach from the theater, they had several more good laughs just recalling parts of the show. But even though Byron kept the conversation light, which was a special talent of his when the occasion required, he was experiencing strange emotions toward this beautiful lady sitting beside him. It was becoming extremely difficult for him to recall the image of the hurt young girl on the train in the company of this beautifully poised young woman who was a delightful conversationalist. The effect was strangely exhilarating and most pleasant. But he dared not make any romantic approaches. He couldn't risk the possibly of losing her entirely.

At the door he took her hand and making a great show of gallantry kissed it lightly. "Goodnight, dear Zenna. Thank you for a most delightful evening."

"Oh, I thank you, Byron," she objected, smiling her gratitude. Then, on impulse, she did something that might have been considered extremely bold and unacceptable conduct for "nice" girls. She reached up and placing her hand on one of his cheeks softly kissed him on the other. Without a word, she turned quickly to disappear into the house.

Byron stood for a long moment not moving, his emotions fluctuating between joy and a touch of sadness. He had loved her caress, but at the same time, he knew full well that it was not romantically motivated. It was the kind of kiss a sister would lay on her brother.

CHAPTER 44

Zenna tipped the messenger boy and closed the door to her apartment. Telegrams always made her uneasy. Usually they were bad news and this one was no exception:

"KALLIE GRAVELY ILL STOP ASKING FOR YOU STOP CAN YOU COME?"

Zenna stood staring at the yellow piece of paper in her hand, her heart beating so rapidly it seemed to hamper her breathing. Kallie had written several months back that she had not been feeling well. Zenna had sensed between the lines that Kallie was somewhat apprehensive about her condition; however, she had not gone into any lengthy detail about what could be wrong.

When Zenna stepped off the train, Keith was waiting at the station. One look at his anxious expression confirmed the worst of her fears. Keith wasn't wearing his perpetual smile, or joking, this time.

"Is…is she…?" Zenna tried to make the words come, but couldn't make another sound.

"Kallie's still alive," he answered gravely, "or she was when I left for town. Everyone, well… they seem to think she's waiting for you. She keeps whispering your name."

"What do you mean she keeps 'whispering' my name?"

"Well, she's awfully weak."

A sob caught in Zenna's throat.

As Zenna stepped down from the coach and made her way toward the front entrance, Janie Elvina, Robin, and Rosalin came down the steps to greet her. There were no jubilant smiles this time. Without a word, they hugged each other and as Zenna kissed each of them on the cheek, she noted how swollen their faces were from crying.

Liza came hurrying out the front door to greet her. "Thank God! You're here! Kallie's been asking for you." Zenna hurried up the stairs on feet that felt like lead; her heart racing.

She opened the bedroom door and eased into the room. Robinson was sitting beside the bed holding one of Kallie's hands. Doc Evans, sitting on the other side and holding Kallie's other hand, got to his feet without a word and moved away, making room for Zenna.

Zenna's eyes, dark with pain, never leaving Kallie's pale face, slipped to her knees beside the bed. She reached out and covered Kallie's hand with her own. "Miss Kallie?" Zenna said softly, struggling to hold back her tears, "it's...it's Zenna." Gently she leaned forward and kissed Kallie on the forehead.

When there was no response, Zenna looked at Robinson in alarm.

"I...I don't think she can hear me," Zenna whispered brokenly with tears running unheeded down her cheeks.

Kallie's eyelids moved slightly then opened slowly. No longer were her eyes a sparkling blue, but dull and cloudy from fever and pain. Zenna moved closer, unmindful of her tears.

"Miss Kallie? It's me...Zenna," she said lovingly. The cold hand beneath Zenna's moved ever so slightly. Zenna responded by holding Kallie's hand tighter. "I love you, Miss Kallie."

Kallie's fingers inside Robinson's hand seemed to pull on his. With what looked like superhuman effort in slow motion Kallie brought her hand, still inside Robinson's, to rest on top of Zenna's.

"She's trying to say something," Robinson whispered brokenly, speaking for the first time since Zenna had entered the room.

They leaned forward, both straining to hear. And there it was, just one word, only a whisper: "Love."

Suddenly, the milky film that had darkened Kallie's eyes was gone, and her eyes were as blue as they had been when she was a girl; blue as clear deep water. A soft smile touched her lips. She took one shallow breath, and the lids of her eyes closed halfway, almost covering her eyes. Doc Evans, recognizing the signs, moved forward and laid his fingers against the side of her neck. "She's gone," he said gently in a voice that quivered, but not from age.

* * * * *

Robinson and Zenna would discuss it over and over again in the years to come just what Kallie had meant by that one word "love?" And they could discuss it freely because there had never been anything but love shared between the three of them. They finally concluded that they would never really know for sure just what Kallie had meant. Was she only telling them one last time that she loved them? or, that she had

485

suspected something had happened between them and she wanted them to know that all was forgiven; or, was she simply relinquishing the love and care of her family into their hands? Whatever the answer, they would never really know for sure except that Kallie had set them free. The past would no longer haunt either of them.

However, Robinson had his own private conclusion. He believed his ma had the right answer long years ago when Garrett Anderson, Lieutenant Anderson then, had saved Melinda from being assaulted by the Yankee soldier. His ma had said that it was the love in the heart of the Lieutenant for his sisters that had caused him to show mercy.

Now, if his ma were alive, she would understand the pain of human weakness and the tragic results from yielding to temptation. How God loves us and is always ready to forgive the truly repentant heart; the redeeming love and mercy that God provided through Jesus, His son. Jesus' own words made it so plain when He said: "And ye shall know the truth, and the truth shall make you free."

ABOUT THE AUTHOR

At age fifteen Afton wrote her first short story that received recognition and her dream since then has been to write a novel. *Raindrops and Sawdust* is her first. She has a collection of poetry that she has written, and she occasionally enters a short story in the local newspaper. Recently, Afton was awarded first place for a short story she entered in a writing contest sponsored by the Northeast Writer's Forum, Booneville, MS. Judges for the contest were members of the English Department, Northeast Community College, Booneville, MS.